MOVEMENT OF THE PEOPLE

NEW ANTHROPOLOGIES OF EUROPE

Michael Herzfeld, Melissa L. Caldwell,
and Deborah Reed-Danahay, editors

MOVEMENT OF THE PEOPLE
Hungarian Folk Dance, Populism, and Citizenship

Mary N. Taylor

INDIANA UNIVERSITY PRESS

This book is a publication of

Indiana University Press
Office of Scholarly Publishing
Herman B Wells Library 350
1320 East 10th Street
Bloomington, Indiana 47405 USA

iupress.org

© 2021 by Mary N. Taylor

All rights reserved

No part of this book may be reproduced or utilized in any form or by any means, electronic or mechanical, including photocopying and recording, or by any information storage and retrieval system, without permission in writing from the publisher. The paper used in this publication meets the minimum requirements of the American National Standard for Information Sciences—Permanence of Paper for Printed Library Materials, ANSI Z39.48-1992.

Manufactured in the United States of America

First printing 2021

Cataloging information is available from the Library of Congress.

ISBN 978-0-253-05781-5 (hard cover)
ISBN 978-0-253-05783-9 (paperback)
ISBN 978-0-253-05782-2 (web PDF)

To Bill Roseberry, who first got me thinking about hegemony.

CONTENTS

Preface ix

Introduction: The Aesthetic Nation 1
one Making the Nation-State in Nineteenth- and Twentieth-Century Hungary 23
two What Kind of Nation? Folk National Cultivation in the Interwar Period 51
three Socialist Cultural Management, Civic Cultivation, and Associational Life in Late Socialism 84
four The *Táncház* Revolution: Reviving Folk Dance as Social Dance 111
five Folk Dance as Mother Tongue: National Conduct and the Production of Collective Memory 147
six Socialist State Formation, *Táncház* Frameworks of Sense, and the Origins of the Postsocialist Cultural Turn 181
seven The Place of Heritagization: Culture Talk amid Shifting Property and Citizenship Regimes 214
Conclusion 247

Bibliography 261
Index 291

PREFACE

I WRITE THESE WORDS AS a powerful movement for Black lives manifests itself on streets across the United States and parts of Europe, a movement that is pushing to change policies in New York City, where I live, sparked by the callous murder of a Black man by police in a country spottily locked down due to the COVID-19 pandemic. This movement honors Black lives and emphasizes the racist structures and (un)consciousness that have been normalized in my country of citizenship since its foundation. The child of an interracially adoptive family, a social experiment of sorts, I have always had difficulty fitting within the absolute boundaries that define identity at home. I thank my parents, Bincy and Snowden Taylor, for starting me on this journey of exploring how racialized and ethnonational affects are crafted and how citizens are cultivated, a journey from which this book has emerged.

A long time coming, this book has only materialized due to the encouragement of friends and comrades in Eastern Europe and the Balkans, many of whom I met through my work with *LeftEast* and its summer schools, who convinced me of the value of the content of my 2008 dissertation. This was despite my status in the academy as one of the many PhD holders who have not found secure work as a professor. Along with these supporters, I am committed to understanding the world toward the end of changing it. I hope this book contributes to the struggle to understand and undermine the workings of ethnonationalism and racial capitalism. While I am indebted to many people for their help in making this book come to life, any mistakes and weaknesses are mine alone. Among the weaknesses are a few incomplete references. My eagerness to take notes from sources in archives and libraries when in Hungary sometimes got in the way of noting complete reference information. I have tried to fix this the best I can.

I am indebted to so many people, alive and passed on, whose knowledge has informed this book. First and foremost, I must thank the countless *táncház*-goers, musicians, dancers, and organizers who welcomed me into their world, shared food and drink with me, talked and argued with me, drove me around Transylvania, and taught me to dance. Thank you, most especially, Ágnes Bély and Zoli Légradi. I am also deeply grateful to the many Transylvanian villagers who hosted me and shared their thoughts and feelings and homes. I owe thanks to the late Béla Halmos, and to Sebő Ferenc, Lászlo Kelemen, and the many others at Hagyományok Háza who helped me with my research in various ways. Kristina Nagy and Tibor Vasváry-Toth, librarians at the Martin Médiatár, as well as the librarians at Magyar Művelődési Intézet and the Selyemgombolyító library deserve special mention. Thank you to the ethnographers at the Ethnographic Research Institute of the Hungarian Academy of Sciences who engaged me when I was a guest there, and since then, foremost among them Ágnes Fülemile, my teacher, advisor, and critic since 2000, and Mihály Sárkány, who pushed me in front of a podium at the Institute. Iván Vitányi and Lászlo Borsányi also contributed to my research process in invaluable ways. I owe a great debt to the good friends and family in Hungary who hosted and fed me, laughed with and at me, and commented on my impressions in 2004–5, most notably Gábor Valcz, Csaba Lódi, Edit Garai, Ábel Köves, Zsuzsa Fehér, Sándor Striker, and Bea Vidacs.

As this project began during my PhD studies, I want to acknowledge my committee members, Gerald Creed, David Harvey, and Jane Schneider, who offered valuable comments that shaped the research from which this book is crafted. I also wish to thank Ellen DeRiso, Michael Blim, Vincent Crapanzano, Katherine Verdery, Donald Robotham, Talal Asad, Chris Hann, and Shirley Lindenbaum and students in the writing group she facilitated. I am grateful to the Fulbright Program and the Hungarian-American Commission for Educational Exchange in Budapest for funding my 2004–5 research and to the Anthropology Department at the City University of New York for a travel grant.

As I wrestled with the text that you have before you now, I had the enduring support of my colleagues at the Center for Place Culture and Politics (CPCP): Ruthie Gilmore, David Harvey, and Peter Hitchcock. The annual CPCP seminars and conferences have been spaces of rich knowledge production, rigorous analysis, and experiments with solidarity, and I can only hope that this book reflects a small part of what I have learned there. Thanks to Ágnes Gagyi, my dissertation was read by with many young Hungarian scholars and scholar activists. Among them are Gergő Pulay, Eszter György, Csaba Tibor-Tóth, and Marton Szarvas, who met to give me valuable feedback in Budapest just days after Indiana University Press offered me a contract. I wish to thank Johanna Bockman and Gerald Creed for their careful comments and for pushing me toward submission and the two anonymous reviewers of my manuscript for their extensive comments. I am indebted to Piroska Nagy and Matt Frost, who generously shared their photographs, to all the photographers whose work I accessed through open source means, and to Barbara Szecsődi, who helped me locate images at the Folklore Documentation Library and Archive at the Hungarian Heritage House. Thanks to Zoárd Heuzé for digitizing my Hi8 footage. I am eternally grateful to the entire team at IUP that saw me through all of the stages of bringing this book to light. Special thanks to Jennika Baines, to the scrupulous copyediting team who worked behind the scenes and to Jeremy Rayner for making the index.

Countless friends and colleagues have supported me in various ways as I was researching and writing. Thank-yous go most fiercely to Moira Tierney, Nathan D. Woods, Mariya Ivancheva, Saygun Gökariksel, Mamyrah Dougé Prosper, Malav Kanuga, Banu Karaca, Saneta DeVuono Powell, and Rodrigo Carrasco, and Teresa Warren for their deep and multifaceted support. I have surely failed to name all of those who have influenced me and some of those people who have aided me in completing this book. I hope you will forgive me if you are among them. Last and not least, thank you to Bob Marley, whose words I have borrowed for the title of this book.

MOVEMENT OF THE PEOPLE

Introduction
The Aesthetic Nation

EVERY YEAR, THOUSANDS OF MOSTLY urban Hungarians spend their valued summer vacation time at camps devoted to Hungarian folk dance. Most of these camps are not in Hungary but rather are located across the border in neighboring Romania, in the region of Transylvania where upward of one million ethnic Hungarians reside. Learning dances and music specific to remote villages and socializing with ethnic Hungarians who live in them, visitors invest in (re)producing "Hungarian" landscapes, sensibilities, and bodily practices. The visions of Hungarianness that frame them are conditioned by the folk revival movement known as dancehouse (*táncház*), which arose in the 1970s, as well as by local and global political and economic circumstances.

During the 1980s, dancehouses organized through this movement were frequented by a broad range of Hungarians dissatisfied with the Communist Party state. Today, many Hungarians associate the revival with right-wing nationalism. *Táncház* continues to ground itself institutionally and organizationally, tying tens of thousands of people together through practices of and venues for folk dance and music. What does it mean to call *táncház* nationalist? How is it connected with other movements that valorize folk practices, nationalist, populist, or other? And why, if the movement is tied to the exclusionary nationalism or "populism" that Hungary has become famous for in the last few years, has it been lauded by UNESCO as a best practice of safeguarding heritage and for serving to promote respect for diversity? What can examining this social movement aimed at promoting folk dance in the everyday life of Hungarians tell us about citizenship in the state socialist period and what appears to be a rising tide of ethnonationalist politics since 1989? What can this local movement dedicated to Hungarian culture tell us about global relationships of governance, in a postsocialist and neoliberal age in which the nation-state has been purportedly losing significance?

Accordingly, the book examines the long history of Hungarian folk movements and the most recent folk revival wave(s), the *táncház* movement, through the lens of the aesthetic cultivation of citizens and the formation of the state. Having arisen in the 1970s, and drawing on traditions of folk dance and music revival and populism, the *táncház* movement has spanned the socialist and postsocialist periods. In 2011, the *táncház* method was named to UNESCO's list of best practices for safeguarding intangible heritage, and in 2013, *táncház* actors and processes figured centrally in the Smithsonian Folklife Festival in Washington, DC, as part of the *Hungarian Heritage* exhibit. Providing a historical picture of how the idea of the folk, folk movements, and folk practices are intimately tied with the ethical politics of citizenship (*Bildung*, civic cultivation), this book examines what kind of citizens are cultivated in folk movements *and how*. Drawing on the *táncház* folk dance revival movement and its practices as its ethnographic core, the book aims to tell a deeper history of Hungarian folk movement and critique. This story is ultimately one about hegemony, the processes by which the ruling classes construct popular authority. By examining these processes, informed by struggle at any historical conjuncture, I seek to shine light on how the dominant classes succeed in turning alternatives into (a never complete) consent (Gramsci 1971; Hall 1988).

In Budapest today, one can find a packed dancehouse with dancers ages seventeen to sixty, accompanied by a live folk band, on almost any night of the week.[1] There, dancing bodies display nuances of dances from villages in the Hungarian culture area, a geographical space twice the size of the contemporary nation-state. Revivalists borrowed the term and meaning of *dancehouse* from one region that lies outside of today's Hungary where ethnic Hungarians make up a sizeable minority. A familiar feature in Hungarian national mythology, Transylvania has been part of Romania since 1920.[2] There, in some villages in what Hungarians call "the heath" (a *mezőség*), the word *táncház* means both "the house that hosts the dance" and the event itself, "the ball."

With dances often lasting into wee hours of the morning and the atmosphere intoxicated by the exhilaration of live fiddling, dancing, sweat, and alcohol, dancehouses are sites of intense social interaction, at once quotidian and ritual, in which, at least traditionally, villagers come together to enact and cultivate social norms. Temporally bound events, dancehouses *are* associative space. This form of associative life, in the context of the revival, is a cultivating and constituting practice of an "alternative framework of sense" (Melucci 1988, 247). Among its effects are the production and reproduction of particular constellations of collective memory about Hungarianness that cultivate the senses and inform the political personhood of *táncház* participants.

Táncház is among many movements that have defined citizenship by emphasizing the folk over the last century. Yet the meaning of this term is slippery. In Hungarian, as in many languages, "the folk" (*a nép*) can point to the ethnic nation, a people defined by common oppression, and/or the inheritors of and potential wielders of popular power/sovereignty. These meanings often overlap. Interpretations of the term are sensitive to political and economic conditions and are tied to state formation processes. In contrast to the focus on folk revivals and folk dance performance as *expressions* or *symbols* of nationalist sentiment, national culture, or national pride, I investigate how folk movements are *constitutive of political personhood*. And rather than accepting the tired argument that state socialism suppressed age-old ethnic hatreds that sprang to life after its collapse, I examine the role of folk dance and its revival in processes of national *Bildung* over time. While I show the role of *táncház* in the cultivation of nationalist sentiment and national boundaries, especially in the postsocialist period, I also reveal how its participants enacted citizenship in important ways and that the movement was both a product of and a challenge to a system designed to encourage socialist enlightenment. Examining the refractions of folk revival, folk movements, and constitutive folk-related practices over the *longue durée*, I illuminate how folk dance–centered practices aimed at the cultivation of citizens are related to state formation and how they assume an ethnonational character. As such, this book contributes to a history of the present, when Hungary is seen on the world stage as ethnonationalist and its leader, "populist."

The meaning of *the folk* shifts across its spectrum of possible definitions in relation to processes of state formation and, in particular, the formation of the nation-state. As with all identities, the folk appears to us through contrast with its other, and folk movements and critiques in Hungary over the last century have given more or less weight to the ethnic or class content of the term in the context of a world increasingly made up of nation-states. As Slavoj Žižek (1993) points out, the broad opposition against Communist rule before 1989 conflated and combined *Gemeinschaft* (essentialized community) and *Gesellschaft* (constructed society), contributing to the salience of *Gemeinschaft* in the postsocialist period. Yet the local environment is far from the only source of essentialized notions about the folk, nation, and culture. Other sources of this "cultural turn" are experienced as part of a "'postsocialist' condition" (Fraser 1997) that is not confined to Eastern Europe.

The study of folk dance in the context of folk movements offers glimpses into national affect in the making. If concrete material practices, rather than some kind of essence, lie behind the consensus that people claiming to be, or to champion, the folk or nation *feel*, and even act on in the political sphere, it is essential that we give attention to the body and to the question of how intersubjectivity is formed in associative environments. To see how the broad network of *táncház* institutions and practices is linked to struggles over the meanings of the people, folk, nation, and citizenship, I approach it through the ethico-aesthetics of political personhood.

The Dance Event: Embodiment, Association, and the Cultivation of Personhood

Táncház emerged rebelliously from the rich soil of Hungarian folk practices and their revival. In this aesthetic revolution, folk dancers stepped off the stage and onto the dance floor. By the 1970s, the genre of staged folk dance had become a niche for performing folk dancers and musicians in professional and amateur performing troupes that had proliferated under socialist cultural management. Reintroducing qualities of social dance, and drawing on features of socialist cultural management, the revival sparked a new kind of participatory public. In the dancehouses from which the movement takes its name, distinctions among performer, spectator, artist, and audience are relative and porous. In this social space, folk dance (the dance of the folk) is really the provenance of the people. While stage dancers do take part, there is great effort made to teach regular people. In this environment, it is believed that with a little discipline, anyone can learn to folk dance.

The way we think about the relation of folk dance revival to political personhood is enhanced if we note how ethics and aesthetics meet in the space of the associative sphere. For early modern thinkers of the aesthetic—from Anthony Ashley Cooper, third Earl of Shaftsbury; David Hume; and Immanuel Kant to G. W. F. Hegel and Friedrich Schiller—moral and aesthetic value were not easily distinguished. Discussions of taste were, in fact, the basis for "investigating ... a broader range of issues concerning intersubjectivity" (Gracyk 2004 [2002], 3). These were pressing concerns relevant to the emergence of a bourgeois social order under which, in contrast to absolutist coercion, "power would become *aestheticized*" (Eagleton 1990, 20). Questions about the aesthetic, then, are tied to questions of hegemony and to how social order is constructed on the basis of virtue, custom, and opinion (ibid., 26).

As aesthetics emerged as a discipline, thinkers grouped certain practices into the category of fine arts (Gracyk 2004 [2002], 2). Kant, for example, took pains to differentiate them from the practical arts (craft) and entertainment, arguing that fine arts were defined by their disinterest (ibid.). Distinctions drawn between fine and performing arts also reflected "emphasis on art as individual expression and as private property" (Firth 1996, 116). Banned from art proper, folk arts were often relegated to the category of amateur art, to be drawn on for purposes of civic cultivation. But as it showed up on the stage, quite often enacted by professional dancers, folk dance was also treated as a performing art. Revered for its role of representing the nation and cultivating national pride and sentiment, the role of folk dance in socialization (beyond a message to an audience) seemed to disappear. Its associative qualities obscured, the question of disinterest fell into the background.

Whether described as art, ritual, text, symbol, or propaganda, dance has been a socializing practice as far back as we can trace. Dancing and dance events have been sites of contention in Europe since at least the Middle Ages, when the church banned "pagan dances" (Pesovár 1982).[3] Whether we note the role of European courts and ballrooms in teaching manners and etiquette, the banning of jazz in Nazi Germany, or the politics of the Ghost Dance, Vodun, and Rumba farther abroad in the colonial and postcolonial Americas, it becomes difficult to ignore the powerful role of dance as a contested medium of socialization. While many studies point to dance's socializing power (Mooney 1991 Deren 1953; Cowan 1990; Langman 2003; Nemes 2001; Daniel 1995), the role it plays in its associative form tends to be upstaged by modern ideas about the dancer and about dance as art.

Jane Cowan (1990, 232) highlights the associative aspects of dance by writing of the dance event: "symbolically resonant and sometimes politically valorized, dance events are . . . intense sociable sensual and aesthetic experiences . . . configured by power relations." Edicts against dance and dance events, the integration of dance into regimes of national cultivation, and dance's role as a symbol of national or ethnic identity, a form of heritage, and even of cultural property compel us to consider the work it does.

As the *táncház* revival was blossoming, cultural manager and theorist Iván Vitányi (1974) defended it against the charges of nationalism. Drawing on the ideas of utopian socialists Pierre-Joseph Proudhon, Robert Owen, François Marie Charles Fourier, and Saint Simon, he had earlier (1971) argued that the value of folk art lies in its power to create and maintain community. Once we approach dance's function as a social activity, we can ask about the power relations in which its practice is implicated and about how folk dance is related to notions of identity and community and to the cultivation of particular kinds of subjects and citizens.

I follow a long line of researchers who have provided insight into how expressive cultural practices (which are also associative) are implicated in the construction and maintenance of identity, values, sentiment, and personhood in an array of contexts (Caton 1990; Cowan 1990; Feld 1990 [1982]; Stokes 1992; Silverman 1983; Laušević 1996). Steven Feld (1990 [1982], 14) shows "how expressive modalities are culturally constituted by performance codes that both actively communicate deeply felt sentiments and reconfirm mythic principles." Steve Caton (1990) reveals how poetry is a constitutive practice, demonstrating that the media and contexts of production and reception of different genres ensure that they address and constitute different kinds of publics. Examining a dance milieu not unlike that of *táncház* (although not the result of a revival movement) in Greece, Jane Cowan illuminates how dance events and everyday sociability combine with discourses about dance to perpetuate ideas about and practices of gender roles. Mirjana Laušević explains how Muslim songs sung at home by Bosnians came to be symbols of a national Bosnian Muslim identity on a much greater scale as Yugoslavia burst into ethnonational war. José Muñoz (2000) points to the affective and performative (re)production of the ethnonation and its others in the United States by showing how the performance of racialized affect is performed in relationship to a dominant (ethno)national affect that limits access to normative identity politics for minoritarian subjects.

While products of the *táncház* movement do reach a wide and diverse audience, my ethnographic focus is primarily the public made up of regular participants in *táncház* events. *Táncház*-goers have intersubjective experiences as participants in a sensed activity, as practitioners of the collective and disciplined bodily practices of a particular tradition of dance/music. They make up an associative public for whom the material forms of dance and its related etiquettes are connected, however contradictorily, with values. My concern is how participation in these events (re)produces a public that shares material practices, values, sentiments, and political views or acts. I am concerned with how participants engage in collective action, sometimes in the political sphere, and how participants take part in making place, territory, and scale.

Social movements are productive of knowledge practices, and *táncház* can be regarded as productive of collective memory and of sensibility.

While Maurice Halbwachs argues that collective memory emerges from shared material practices and objects, and the (changing) beliefs held about them, Alberto Melucci (1988) proposes that the production of alternative frameworks (and communities) of sense are a significant part of the work of social movements.[4] Charles Hirschkind (2001, 623–24) enhances this approach with his attention to the role of disciplined practices in cultivating an ethically responsive sensorium through which the world is made perceptible.[5] He presents the practice of listening to cassette tape sermons among mosque-going Muslim men in Egypt as a "practice of ethical self-discipline" that aids in honing "requisite sensibilities that they see as enabling them to live as devout Muslims in a world increasingly ordered by secular rationalities" (624).

The linkage between listening and sense is not simply "established metaphorically," Hirschkind (2001, 628) argues, "but also through discipline, the training and inculcation of sensory habits," including bodily dispositions. Just as Hirschkind's listeners learn more than the moral lessons of the sermons as they cultivate in themselves "the ethical habits and the organization of sensory and motor skills necessary for inhabiting the world in a manner considered to be appropriate for Muslims," so do *táncház*-goers cultivate in themselves those habits appropriate for the practice of a certain kind of historically located *Hungarianness* through the practice of "folk dance as mother tongue," naturalizing the dance language as if it were the first language they spoke—their mother tongue, so to speak. While such practices could conceivably work to *preserve* a communal ethic, they are more likely to be *transformative*, like the social movements that cultivate alternative frameworks of sense that, in turn, may promote collective action (Melucci 1988).

This cultivation of the self is an associative practice and practices we see in *táncház* were developed in relation to various twentieth-century projects to cultivate certain kinds of Hungarians. The effects of these projects—and how they relate to the idea of the folk, to practices and policies of citizenship, and to cultural distinction—rely on selective memory and interpretation. What is cultivated through associative folk dance revival emerges through the dialectic of form and meaning that produces collective memory.

CIVIL SOCIETY AND CIVIC CULTIVATION: CULTIVATING
CITIZENS OF THE NATIONAL STATE

I learned to view folk dance through the lens of cultivation from *táncház*-goers and organizers and cultural managers close to the revival in its early days, who used this term (*művelődés, művelés*) to talk about what the revival does. I use the term here to indicate that process resulting from struggles within the space of "civil society" concerning the education and conduct of the people. This process is recognizable in (but not limited to) activities we label adult education, moral education, public education, public cultivation, extracurricular education, cultural (or aesthetic) enlightenment, and consciousness-raising—all of which can be related to the European tradition of *Bildung*. I place the term *civic* before the term cultivation to highlight the historical processes out of which the modern tradition of *Bildung* arose—the radically transforming political contexts in which citizenship was coming to be defined as something attainable by "the people," as subjects were becoming citizens.

Both the meaning of the term *civil society* and whether it existed in socialist and postsocialist Eastern Europe have been topics of debate. My use of the term here is tied to the historical perspective central to this book. I draw on the broad definition of civil society as a space of association between the family and state while also using the term as a heuristic for the "decisive locus of operation of modern power" (Scott 1999). Both uses require attention to state formation as a process in which two seemingly distinct entities, civil society and state, mutually inform one other. With Antonio Gramsci (1971), I regard civil society as the educational arm of the bourgeois state, and alternatively, the space in which the foundation of a communist society might be built (via a "war of position"). To point to the space of civil society is to point to the practices and struggles that produce the dynamic formation of the state (Abrams 1988).

The emergence of the associative space of civil society in "Hungary" was intimately tied to the making of nation-states out of feudal kingdoms enveloped in the Habsburg Empire, as the nation-state was emerging as the dominant form of polity in Europe. So-called associational life blossomed during Hungary's nineteenth-century period of reform and national awakening or romanticism (Trencsényi and Kopeček 2007). Formal and temporal associations aimed to articulate the nation through promoting economic and political independence and the firming of a national culture. Such efforts were made sometimes in opposition to, and sometimes in cooperation with, governments as coalitions formed around specific interests. Debates over who should be included in the political nation and its relationship with the ethnic nation were intimately tied to questions concerning the privileges and requirements of citizenship. Questions of culture, or *cultivation*, were key. To flourish, the state would have to "inculcate in its citizens the proper sorts of spiritual disposition" (Eagleton

2000, 6–7). Culture, "a kind of ethical pedagogy aimed at producing citizens" (*Bildung*), rather than a thing already possessed, would be central to this project (ibid.).

The development of the nation-state system and associated social transformations were connected with revolutionary demands for civil rights and liberties. The idea that the nation was to be made up of a body of citizens "in contract" with the state required a transformation of the nature of sovereignty. While much time would pass before the population as a whole would enjoy political rights (if this has ever been fully achieved), "nationalism stimulated the move from the status of private subjects to citizenship" (Habermas 1996, 285).[6] This process required a transformation of subjectivities, and efforts were directed at making citizens out of the agrarian classes, often referred to as "savages" (Weber 1976). The production of civil society, then, is inextricably tied to the production of national selves.

Terry Eagleton (1990, 24) notes that the "early bourgeoisie was preoccupied with *virtue*, the lived habit of moral propriety, rather than laborious adherence to some external norm." To cultivate virtue, an "ambitious programme of moral education and reconstruction" was required as there was no guarantee that subjects emerging from feudalism would "prove refined and enlightened enough for power to found itself on their sensibilities" (ibid.). What was at stake in this social and cultural revolution was "the production of an entirely new kind of human subject," one who would, "like the work of art itself, discover(s) the law in the depths of its own free identity" rather than in "some oppressive external power" (ibid., 19).

Although capitalism and the nation-state were "joined at birth" (Meiksins Wood 1999), it is important to attend to the particularities of processes of nation-state formation and incorporation that took different forms in different places, according to positions vis-à-vis empires, colonialism, and the emerging capitalist world system (Wallerstein 1974; Wolf 1969, 1982; Weber 1976; Anderson 1984; Gellner 1983; Joseph and Nugent 1994; Chakrabarty 2000; Corrigan and Sayer 1985). The opposition between civilization and culture, or outer and inner spheres, would be important here.

In his study of the emergence of the "civilized personality" in the sociogenesis of the state, Norbert Elias (1978, 50) proposed the moment of colonial conquest as the point when "nations consider the process of civilization as completed within their own societies." Comparing France and Germany, he showed that, as the French empire reached its height, civilization was asserted as universal and as a justification for rule. For the besieged German nation, however, "constantly [seeking] out and constitut[ing] its boundaries anew," the term *Kultur*, stressing the particular identity of groups, would come to have more salience (5–6). In both cases, however, there was movement toward the control of impulses, for in this "civilizing process," "prohibitions supported as social sanctions are reproduced in the individual as self-control" (186–90).

Eagleton (1990, 27) argues that where "political dominance assumes... more openly coercive forms," the response might appear as "aesthetic counter strategy—a cultivation of instincts and pieties over which such power rides roughshod." Thus, the ethic of *Bildung*, in which personal cultivation was detached from political expression, arose in eighteenth-century Germany. The concept of *Kultur* developed among the German bourgeoisie to distinguish the deep and spiritual against the formulaic and ceremonial of the court, or "civilization." As social conditions changed, and the hexis of the bourgeoisie expanded to become characteristics of the nation, what began as a class distinction became a national one (Elias 1978, 31). The equation of one language, one people, and one territory became a guiding principle in the making of the system of nation-states (Errington 2001; Irvine and Gal 2000; Taylor 2016).

Among the territories that composed the Habsburg and Ottoman Empires, Hungary, in its various historical forms, offers an interesting case for probing the tensions between *Kultur* and civilization that Elias identified in "the civilizing process" in the context of modern power. We can identify coercive forms of dominance and uneven geopolitical relationships similar to those in reaction to which the ideology of *Kultur* and the practice of *Bildung* arose in Germany.[7] Further, while imperial rule of these lands differed in significant ways from that of the overseas colonies of European states, Hungarians engaged in struggles for nation-statehood in conditions that some saw as colonial at a time when European colonial powers relied on discourses of backwardness and civilization, conceptions of the prepolitical, and the pseudoscience of race to establish colonized peoples as outside modernity and unprepared for self-rule or citizenship (Chakrabarty 2000, 43).[8] The technologies and discourses that emerged to "know" and "govern" these European populations (Foucault 1991), and the uses of the concepts of *Kultur* and civilization, coexisted and coevolved with those applied by Western European powers in the colonies.

The becomings of the future nation-states in this region occurred as modern techniques of government came into fruition in colonies and within European states.[9] The census, a technique of modern governmentality, was applied by the Habsburg bureaucracy to "know" its "peoples" or "tribes" (*Volkstäemme*). Peoples of peripheral East Central Europe were both subject to and subjects in a discursive process of Orientalism based on East-West dichotomy, and "nesting Orientalisms" would play a central role in nation-making projects (Bakić-Hayden 1995; Wolff 1994; Kideckel 1996).[10]

Partha Chatterjee (1993) identifies "the rule of colonial difference" as being central to anticolonial nation-state formation. David Scott (1999, 37), urges us, however, to "impose historicity on our understanding of the rationalities that organized the forms of the colonial state," by taking a closer look at particularities in Europe. While modern power may indeed have operated by "rules of difference" in its colonial career, in ways that differ from its operation in Europe (ibid., 32), Eastern Europe was hardly metropole Europe. And further, attacking the conditions that produce behavior is central to modern power. Its "distinctive strategic end" is the government of conduct or habits, and its "decisive locus of operation" is "the new domain of 'civil society'" (ibid., 33–34).[11] In this new political rationality, "power works . . . through the construction of a space of free social exchange and through the construction of a subjectivity normatively experienced as the source of free will and rational, autonomous agency" (ibid., 37). To be counted as political, the colonized would have to play this new game of politics (ibid., 45). In peripheral Europe, under conditions not quite captured by a colonizer-colonized binary, the people, the so-called folk, with its dialectic of class and nation, would also have to play this game.

Although Chatterjee (1993) might not agree that the rule of colonial difference has operated in Hungary, he nevertheless gives us important insights into this context. Arguing that we have failed to recognize a vital historical development present in anticolonial nationalism, he writes, "We have all taken the claims of nationalism to be a political movement much too literally and . . . seriously" (1993, 5). This is because anticolonial nationalism "creates its own domain of sovereignty within colonial society well before it begins its political battle with the imperial power" (6). To do this, it divides the world of social institutions and practices into two domains: the outside, material, domain of economy and statecraft, science, and technology and the inner, spiritual, domain bearing the "essential" marks of cultural identity. From the view of anticolonial nationalism, the greater one's success in imitating Western skills in the material domain, the greater will be the need to preserve the distinctness of one's spiritual culture (ibid.).

This insight into how an inner sphere of sovereignty is constructed in contrast with an outer sphere shines a light on the binaries of spiritual and material (sometimes political) and national and civil that show up in the *táncház* context. We might argue that this has to do with Hungary's late formation as a nation-state emerging from an imperial context, and its semiperipheral status in the capitalist world system. We can also note that in the German context to which Elias and Eagleton point, the idea of *Kultur* took its place in response to that of civilization. Terms such as *Bildung* and *Kultur*, expressing the self-image of the German intellectual class and contrasted with watchwords of the rising bourgeoisie in France and England, tended to draw a sharp distinction between a pure spiritual sphere of genuine value and a political, economic, and social sphere (Elias 1978, 27).

Táncház participants tend to understand the movement's work to be on the terrain of the spiritual, which they contrast with the material. This contrast can be found in ideas about the folk (*nép*) as Hungarians asserted nation-state ambitions within the Habsburg Empire and, after its dissolution, in the neofeudal conditions of interwar Hungary. In Hungarian folk critiques, we see emphasis on the inner, or spiritual, sphere as a domain of sovereignty. Where whole populations were barred from citizenship, preoccupation with the people and things related to the folk were central facets of the nation-building problematic and intimately connected with the assertion of modern citizenship rights.

Rights to citizenship, in Hungary as elsewhere, were often circumscribed for many classes of people via land ownership and literacy requirements that limited the franchise. In the age of European colonialism, citizenship was denied or greatly circumscribed for colonial subjects and metropolitan working classes and peasantries alike, consigned as they were to the "waiting room" of self-government (Chakrabarty 2000). The premodern status assigned to these groups implied that they were not prepared to take part in political citizenship, to act as citizens (8).

Civil society, a site of modern power, and civic cultivation, a technique of modern power, are tied to the dialectic of civilization and *Kultur* as it relates to citizenship and to the mandate for and assertion of unique difference in the form of *national* cultures. To *táncház* and the interwar populist movement that preceded it, the ethnic nation and the folk are elements in the process of the ethico-aesthetic cultivation of certain kinds of citizens. Examining cultivation in relation to specific historical struggles over citizenship allows us to more deeply probe the relation of nation and civil society and the subtle process that produces self-evident oppositions between inner and outer and spiritual and material spheres and their mobilization in the process of state formation today.

Socialist Civil Society and Postsocialist/ Neoliberal Ethnonationalism

If we define it as the space of association between the family and state, there is no doubt that civil society existed in socialist Hungary when *táncház* emerged (see Hann 1996, 6). There is also no question that the socialist state apparatus, using techniques of modern power, worked to cultivate members of society as certain kinds of citizens. Scholars and socialist postsocialist citizens alike have critiqued civil society–building projects originating in, or ideologically linked to, the West that appeared in Hungary in the 1980s and that continue today (see, for examples, Staddon and Cellarius 2002; Creed and Wedel 1997; Ivancheva 2011; Mandel 1993). Recent political trends associated with postsocialism, "postsocialism" (see below), and neoliberalism stress the political and civic aspects of citizenship, delinking the idea of democracy from the value of social citizenship, fought for and achieved in this region in specific ways. The notion of civil society and its role in postsocialist Europe is not unrelated to this devaluation of social citizenship in the neoliberal era. Civil society is indeed an arena of civic cultivation.

The view that there was no civil society under conditions of actually existing socialism was widely held by Western scholars. This view justified an influx of civil society–building NGOs to the region after 1989 and encouraged anthropologists to approach the concept critically (Hann 1996; Verdery 1996; Gal 1996). Exploring the historically specific ways that notions of nation, Europe, and civil society have interacted in this region, Katherine Verdery (1996) showed how the notion of civil society, "revived" by dissidents in the late 1980s as a term for a "sphere free of politics," competed with the term *nation*.

In the postsocialist era, civil society, held together by impersonal bonds of interest, signifies a return to Europe for some. Yet for others, it signifies a neoimperialist encroachment of Western European or cosmopolitan values (see Verdery 1996; Gagyi 2014). To many postsocialist subjects for whom social citizenship had been the primary form of citizenship, civil society appears as the unwelcome bed partner of the inequalities and dispossessions that have beset their lives following shock therapy and the emergence of (neo)liberal state and social formations. For some, the nation, informed by traditional bonds such as kinship, religion, and ethnicity, represents a sphere free of both socialist and liberal influences, both understood as foreign.

Challenging the idea that there was no space between the state and family in socialist Eastern Europe in which individuals could engage in autonomous association, scholars presented evidence of the existence of civil society–like spaces (for example, Buchowski 1996; Hann 1996). They also urged others to enlarge the concept to encompass "alternative forms of social relationship to those assumed by liberal-individualism" (Hann 1996, 5). If "the main distinguishing feature of the opposition to communism in Eastern Europe was its anti-political character" (ibid., 8), and if politics has been a "dirty word" in the region (Gal 1996), we would have to look for politically meaningful associations in places not explicitly political or confined to registered associations (Hann 2006).

An emphasis on association allows us to "recognize the way in which older local institutions and values—including perhaps those associated with Socialism—may be adapted to meet contemporary conditions" (Hann 2006, 162). Recently, for example, Gerald Creed (2011) brought attention to a civic dimension in Bulgarian folk practices reinvigorated in postsocialist years that has been overlooked by Western scholars who name the lack of civil society "as the cause for democratic difficulties in postsocialist contexts." Yet he argues that a critique of democracy that can diminish civic engagement as understood by these scholars is also present in this context (ibid., 24).

The political significance of the *tánchaz* movement is ambiguous and complex. While it arose within state socialist institutions, it served as a critique of socialist governance. Participants generally agree that this dance movement stood in spiritual (rather than political), opposition to the Communist regime, making it part, perhaps, of the "ethical civil society" identified in the socialist polities in this region (Renwick 2006). But the institutional and organizational support it received and its emergence in state cultural facilities, complicates any simple image of two discreet sides in this struggle. Indeed, much struggle to change socialism occurred in spaces "*within* the state" (Hann 1996, 9).

Tánchaz was among the forms of associational life that flourished in the state-funded yet semi-entrepreneurial culture houses and clubs in the last few decades of "Gulash Communism" (Striker 1989b). This liberalizing cultural sphere and *tánchaz*'s folk critique of state products and initiatives and the meaning of Hungarianness, along with its practices of citizenship, provided the cultivating terrain behind some of the most significant political protests of the late 1980s, centering on the demand for a public burial of 1956 reform/revolutionary hero Imre Nagy and the opposition to the village destruction initiatives in Romania, which were viewed as an attack on ethnic Hungarians.

To claim one's Hungarianness through participating in *tánchaz* was a way to subtly oppose what was seen as foreign rule and an engineered socialist culture. *Tánchaz*-going was a manner of exercising citizenship in a situation where action in the political sphere was circumscribed and simultaneously everything was potentially political. In a flawed yet nominally centralized political system, popular and populist *táncház* practices helped delegitimize the regime while legitimizing a sphere of sovereignty not unlike the *Kultur* and *Bildung* over which coercive power "rides roughshod" (Eagleton 1990, 27).

Local forms of association must be regarded in relationship to governance and political and economic shifts at multiple scales. Rather than comparing local forms of association to standards of civil society now in vogue, my interest lies in civil society as the associative space between family and state, and in civil society as the decisive locus of operation for modern power (Scott 1999). How do folk movements take part in the dynamic of governance and social movement and in the processes that produce hegemony? In what ways does *táncház* as a form of association play a part in cultivation of citizens? How does it produce and reproduce a framework of sense (Melucci 1988) and to what effects?

These questions about political personhood can be answered only with attention to political economy. The emergence of the concept of civil society was inextricably tied to the development of capitalism (Meiksins Wood 1990). In contrast to other conceptions of society, it is associated with specifically capitalist property relations. Only after the distinction between the private home and the public state had emerged, and only after "the economy" had been abstracted from a "political economic unity," could civil society emerge as a "network of distinctively *economic* relations, the sphere of the market-place, the arena of production, distribution and exchange" (ibid., 61). While Hungary was not outside the dynamics of the capitalist world system in either its early twentieth-century neofeudal moment or its state socialist one, the demise of the Soviet bloc marked a new conjuncture of incorporation. Today, the kind of cultivation folk dance revival will do is wrestled over on the supranational terrain of heritage under conditions of neoliberal globalization.

RESEARCH CONTEXT

Although many studies of *táncház* have referred to it as a movement, few have approached it as an element in a process of state formation spanning distinguishable political economic regimes. My analysis here is based on several forays into the *táncház* revival in Budapest and to camps in Transylvania from 2000 on, one year spent conducting participant observation among revivalists in 2004 and 2005, and several returns through 2007. I emerged with a clear picture of folk revival as a historical process and offer a historical perspective that allows insight into the context in which the revival arose and into how and in which ways elements of *tánchaz* have changed over time.

This historical approach requires attention to the social changes in Hungarian society over the last century, in relation to which practices of folk critique, movement, and revival, as well as the authority of particular practices and places, have developed. As such, in addition to interviews with participants and participant observation, I have relied on literature and archival materials to elucidate earlier moments and iterations and their relationship to *tánchaz* as well as earlier periods of and transformations within *tánchaz* itself.

I entered into everyday practices and venues of the *tánchaz* movement in a similar manner to how any newcomer would: by regularly attending dancehouses and learning dance motives and etiquette over time. Beyond attendance, conversation, and interviews, my methods of participant observation included my exposure to tacit knowledge through participation in bodily and spatial practices engaged in by revivalists. "Dance ethnography" (Sklar 1991; Cruz Banks 2010), the sensual, bodily participation in dance and dance events was essential for investigating the ways in which a framework of sense is produced through *tánchaz* practices.

Participation in *tánchaz* and my status of guest at Heritage House (Hagyományok Háza) and the Ethnographic Research Institute of the Hungarian Academy of Sciences immersed me in a network of individuals with various connections to and knowledges of and about the *tánchaz*, including those who had ceased to participate for one reason or another. Beyond those connections, my research benefited from hours of discussion with Hungarian friends and acquaintances not involved in *tánchaz*. I am grateful to all who were willing to engage me. Convinced that what they are doing is good and believing, despite my stated intentions, that my study was motivated primarily by my recognition of the beauty of folk dance and music, and the efforts to keep them living traditions, *tánchaz*-goers reluctantly accepted, if they ever did, that this would be a critical study. I could not have gained the knowledge I share here without their gracious acceptance of and faith in me. From among them I have gained dear friends and respected colleagues, I have learned to hear "Hungarian" music and to dance to its lead, and I have learned a history of struggle.

THE CHOREOGRAPHY OF THIS BOOK

In this introduction, I have aimed to give analytical and historical context that invites the reader to approach folk movements and the associative environment of the dance event as interwoven with struggles over hegemony and the cultivation of political personhood across shifting terrains. This approach requires careful attention to history while also recognizing the emergence of new conjunctures (Hall 1988) as the logics and sites of power change.

The following chapters are organized chronologically to illuminate historical dynamics. Although *táncház* forms the ethnographic core of the study, the book is equally about the history of the folk and folk movements as elements in nation-state formation. A few notes on temporality are due here. I employ the terms *postsocialism* and *postsocialist* to refer to the conditions in those countries in Central and Eastern Europe and the Balkans once governed by Communist Party states roughly between the end of World War II and 1989. I use quotation marks, as in "postsocialism" and "postsocialist," to refer to a near global condition that has also emerged since the demise of state socialism: the "'postsocialist' condition" that is related to the delegitimization of socialism and communism as viable alternatives to capitalism (Fraser 1997). I use *socialist*, and its counterposition, *postsocialist*, as conventional markers of a broadly acknowledged period roughly before and after 1989 in the region, and I think it important to note continuities across these periods and change within the socialist period itself. Thus, I write of the "late socialist" period in Hungary. Good arguments have been made for why we should give up the language of transition (Chelcea and Druţă 2016) so often used in studies of this region. Understanding the processes at work in this story, however, requires that we examine local specificities within longer temporalities and other scales of the "postsocialist" condition. Local and regional shifts summed up in "the transition" from state socialism or to capitalism articulate in particular ways with broader global shifts regarding financialization and the assembly of new kinds of property rights in which various kinds of investment have become more lucrative than production. These processes have been crucial to continued primitive accumulation or "accumulation by dispossession" (Harvey 2003; see also Caffentzis 1995; Federici 2004).

A final temporal concern emerges from the fact that I have not conducted participant observation with the *táncház* environment since 2006. While I address some developments related to *táncház* in the years since, I cannot discuss the opinions and political views of *táncház* participants after this date. References made in chapter 7 and the conclusion to later events are not drawn from my own fieldwork, and I do not try to comprehensively cover all things that have happened in *táncház* or that have been connected with it since then.

Chapter 1 gives an overview of the dynamic relationship of nation and state formation in Hungary until the 1930s, showing how linguistic nationalism in the nineteenth-century Age of National Awakening and independence struggles served to delineate peoples, cultivating them as such, and tying them to national territories. The territorial and demographic shifts brought about by the end of World War I, through which the Hungarian nation-state would come to comprise one-third of the territory of the Hungary that existed before 1920, had strong effects on the emerging traditions of ethnography and folk music collection. Hungary's first folk dance revival and the multifaceted youth folk arts movement that emerged in the context of interwar truncated Hungary are introduced.

Chapter 2 focuses on the interwar populist movement that emerged to champion the agrarian working classes, its ethico-politics of folk national cultivation, and the practices and institutions developed to pursue that cultivation in the context of the political and spiritual parties that stood in opposition to the authoritarian interwar government(s) in a climate leading toward World War II and the Shoah. This ethic and its related practices, suspicion of the political sphere, and the opposition between "folk" (populist) and "urbanite" (*urbánus*) intellectuals that emerged in this period would have lasting influences.

Chapter 3 presents institutional sites of civic cultivation in the state socialist period in which *táncház* emerged. It focuses on the Institute for People's Culture, home to the Hungarian State Folk Ensemble, and the system of houses of culture, which were envisioned as primary sites for socialist cultivation and were also the hearth (Siegelbaum 1999) of *táncház* activities. Approaching houses of culture as sites of social and political activity and attending to continuities and discontinuities between socialist and folk national cultivation, this chapter uncovers the conditions that led to the emergence of new forms of association, including *táncház*, in the 1970s.

Chapter 4 describes the *táncház* folk revival's emergence in the 1970s and institutionalization through the 2000s in weekly dance events, tourism to Transylvania, dance camps, and various organizations. It shows how *táncház* constituted an aesthetic revolution by reviving folk dance as a widespread associative activity in contrast to staged performance. While socialist institutions and civic initiative combined to support it, this revival movement, preoccupied with the cultural practices of ethnic brethren over the border in Romania, defined itself in opposition to (or at least autonomous from) the socialist state. In tune with international patterns of participation-based arts movements and folk revival, *táncház* also reflected the particularities of Hungarian and socialist cultural management and the geopolitics distinct to the region.

Chapter 5 explores how *táncház* practices (dance, etiquette and sociable conversation, and tourism) contribute to the cultivation of an embodied collective memory of the territorialized ethnonation. It shows how this collective memory emerges from the relationship of concrete bodily practices and landscapes and broader conditions of state formation (property and citizenship regimes, reflected in shifts in the meaning and usage of the term *folk*). Addressing many participants' insistence on *táncház*'s apolitical character, and the slippage between ethics and politics in Hungarian folk movements, this chapter illustrates how this *táncház* framework of sense is implicated in collective action and, therefore, in state formation.

Like the populist movements from which it borrowed methods and techniques, *táncház* has engaged a transforming political sphere since the time it emerged and throughout the transition to capitalism. Chapter 6 illustrates what I term (after Walter Benjamin [1969]) a "moment of danger," when *táncház* interaction with the political sphere became visible and this "community of sense" (Melucci 1988) engaged in collective action, in protests urging the Hungarian government to intervene in the Romanian government's destruction of ethnic Hungarian villages in 1988. I set this against a backdrop of changes from the time of the 1956 revolution until the regime change of 1989, tracking state transformation and uncovering the seeds of the "culture talk" (Mamdani 2005) that would come to characterize the postsocialist period.

Chapter 7 argues that culture talk has become a central way of describing the world and that culture has become central to the assembly of new forms of property rights under postsocialist, "postsocialist," and neoliberalizing conditions. After examining another moment of danger, a referendum on granting citizenship to Hungarians over the border that was mutually reinforcing with political polarization in Hungary, I zoom out and "jump scales" (Smith 1996) to explore the production of place in Transylvania. Noting how different interests converge around culture's expediency at the current conjuncture, I discuss how *táncház* tourism to ethnic Hungarian villages in Romania takes part in the reorganization of everyday life in the context of the emergence of heritagization as an organizing logic and the legislation of dual citizenship for Hungarians over the border.

The conclusion describes shifts that have occurred in Hungarian society and politics more recently and discusses how, under conditions of (neo)liberal hegemony and a supranational heritage regime that functions to impart national *Bildung*, the current liberal-illiberal divide masks

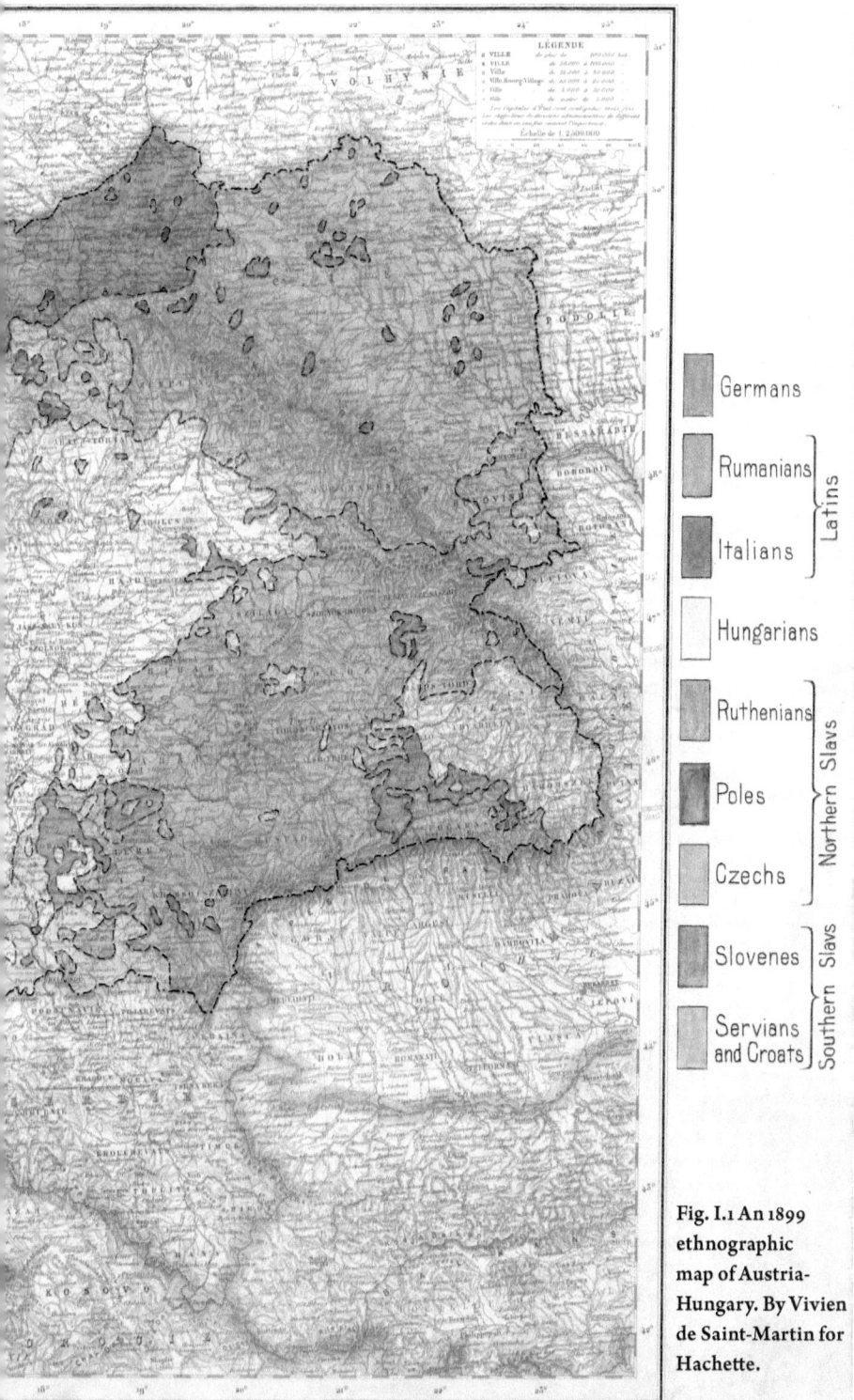

Fig. I.1 An 1899 ethnographic map of Austria-Hungary. By Vivien de Saint-Martin for Hachette.

convergences with regard to approaches to culture and cultural diversity. I point to Hungarian and regional scholarship that draws on critical analysis of the capitalist world system and decolonial approaches and touch on a call for a revival of the interwar *népi* movement. I ask how aspects of historical folk critiques are taken up through these lenses and question their limitations and possibilities, given the ethnic pull on the term *nép*, and the complex relationships the *táncház* folk movement has with the ethnonationalist and authoritarian trends widely associated with populism in Hungary today.

NOTES

1. This line was written before the lockdowns that have been put in place due to the Covid-19 pandemic, which prohibit such gatherings.

2. Hungary occupied parts of Transylvania during World War II.

3. Andrej Tarkovskij artfully captures the church's disdain for pagan dance in his 1969 film *Andrej Rublev*.

4. Halbwachs was interested in intersubjectivity in the Durkheimian tradition, particularly the ideas of the collective conscience (*l'âme collective*), which appears outside the body in practice, and collective effervescence, which speaks to sensually experienced and collective emotional states. Halbwachs was interested in understanding how collective conscience is maintained between moments of effervescence.

5. Borrowing the term *habitus* from Marcel Mauss, and heeding his call for attention to body hexis and its production, Bourdieu (1977) stressed a systematic and class-related cultivation of the body and of sensibilities, but neglected the question of self-cultivation (see also Mauss 1973). Hirschkind addresses these lacuna by drawing on the work of Michel Foucault and Talal Asad.

6. Habermas (1996, 284) also asserts that democracies have proven less stable "wherever national movements and wars of liberation against a foreign enemy had first to create borders for nascent national states."

7. The eastern lands of the Habsburg Empire and western lands of the Ottoman Empire were not modern colonies of Western metropolises in the sense usually captured when we say "colonial" (perhaps only Bosnia under Austrian rule might be described this way). Nevertheless, anticolonial arguments were made by those pursuing Hungary's independence (Nemes 2001, 808) in the context of the geographical specialization of economic activities as Habsburg rulers attempted to pursue self-efficiency and lift the empire out of its semiperipheral status in the world economy (Verdery 1983, 128–33). Today, there are diverse uses of the language of coloniality and empire to talk about the historical and contemporary conditions of the region. See, for example, Chirot (1976), Böröcz (2001), Chari and Verdery (2009), Todorova (2009), Tlostanova (2014), and Gagyi (2016).

8. See Janos (1982) on how these discourses were used in Hungary, before and after the 1867 Compromise.

9. Governmentality, as Foucault (1991) conceived it, involved the emergence of population as the object of political rationality. The focus on the "right disposition of things" supersedes the sovereign focus on territory and relies on multiform tactics and techniques/technologies.

10. See J. Schneider (1998) for another example of the refraction of Orientalist discourses in peripheral Europe.

11. Chatterjee (2008) has more recently developed a distinction between civil and political society that I do not draw on here.

Chapter One

Making the Nation-State in Nineteenth- and Twentieth-Century Hungary

IT WAS ONLY ABOUT A hundred years ago that Hungary can be said to have taken the form of a modern nation-state. At the end of World War I, powerless to change the new borders imposed by a coalition of forces, a short-lived government declared an end to the union with Austria and established the Hungarian Republic. Although Hungarian citizens delineated by this new territory had diverse "ethnic" identities, a polity called Hungary had never been as ethnically homogenous as this new nation-state.[1] Approaching the formation of the state and the formation of the nation as separate processes that are conjoined due to the predominance of the nation-state idea, this chapter addresses Hungarian state formation in the nineteenth and early twentieth centuries.

Intended to give the reader a taste of the history and breadth of the preoccupation among Hungarians with the nation and the so-called folk, this chapter surveys different approaches to the definition, practice, and invention of national and folk traditions informed by varying political and aesthetic ideologies and political economic conditions in nineteenth- and early twentieth-century Hungary. As I hope to make clear, not only is nation-making always connected to state formation, but the ways in which citizens engage with representations of the nation are determined in part by state forms with which they interact. Various representations of the nation and the people also point to competing ideologies and forms of citizenship. There is nothing natural about the nation-state, and no story about a nationalism seen as "bad" can be thorough without attending to the naturalization of the nation-state form and its relationship to subjectivation via popular culture.

As Stuart Hall (1981) stressed, popular culture is a dynamic terrain of hegemonic struggle taking place under shifting arrangements of power and institutional formations. It is therefore closely connected to the question of how people are cultivated as citizens (or subjects) of a state or as members of a nation. As "an issue of power" and a "problem of politics," popular culture can thus only be understood in relationship to state formation (Joseph and Nugent 1994, 15). Scholars have long revealed the role of state formation processes in ordering societies and making a capitalist economy possible through the regulation of social forms of life (Corrigan and Sayer 1985; Joseph and Nugent 1994). To "bring the state in without leaving people out" requires "a concept of popular culture that can be analyzed in relation to a notion of state formation that equally recognizes the importance of the cultural dimension of historical process and social experience" (Joseph and Nugent 1994, 12). Any "revolution in the way the world is made sense of" occurs in the way both subjects and the state elaborate their experience and in the manner in which "state activities, forms, routines, and rituals" for "the constitution and regulation of social identities are elaborated" (Corrigan and Sayer 1985, 2; see also Joseph and Nugent 1994, 14). Gilbert Joseph and Daniel Nugent's (1994, 15) observations about popular culture, often framed "within the terms of an older tradition of studies of folklore," in another peripheral region, Latin America, are insightful for East Central Europe. While their definition of popular culture as "the symbols and meanings embedded in the day-to-day practices of subordinated groups" highlights meaning rather than material practices, their emphasis on the quotidian and on processes of struggle is key (17).

The invention of national tradition by the Hungarian elite was an element in nineteenth- and twentieth-century nation-state-making. This includes "both 'traditions' actually invented, constructed and formally instituted, and those emerging in a less easily traceable manner within a brief and dateable period . . . and establishing themselves with great rapidity" (Hobsbawm and Ranger 1984, 1). Although I write this chapter in a time when the concept of the nation-state has "so thoroughly conjoin[ed] the state with the nation that it is almost impossible to think of one without the other" (Sharma and Gupta 2006, 7), the events I account in the rest of this chapter occurred in a period when the national state was only just coming into its dominance in Europe and had yet to be solidified in Eastern Europe.

Beginning with an overview of institutions and practices connected with peasant romanticism and the invention of a Hungarian national culture, I contextualize these in relation to reforms in the late nineteenth century, when Hungary was a political entity subsumed within the Habsburg Empire, through the early twentieth century, when a "sovereign nation-state" was declared.[2] I then examine the sudden political territorial and population shifts resulting from the breakup of the empire after World War I and the consequent mismatch with a legacy of ethnographic and folkloristic material, ideals, and practices attending to a territory much larger than the truncated Hungarian nation-state that emerged at that time. Finally, I discuss practices and institutions dedicated to folk music collection that provided the conditions for the revival and staged performance of folk dance in the first half of the twentieth century.

NATIONAL AWAKENING AND STRUGGLES FOR INDEPENDENCE

In the first half of the nineteenth century, struggling to retain its fading power in the emerging system of European nation-states, the Habsburg Empire witnessed the "national awakening" of a number of peoples, or nations, within its borders. What is referred to as the age of national awakening was the East Central European response to the historical processes bringing about the dominance of the nation-state system and the capitalist mode of production in Western Europe. Hungarian elites embraced the language and goals of the nation-state, formulating resistance to the empire to which the Hungarian kingdom was subordinated by stressing distinctive national characteristics and traditions that they invented in this process. This new formulation of the nation-state required a shift in the meaning of the Latin word *natio* from its earlier usage as a narrow category of those with political rights within a feudal polity to one that included the people of Hungary in a republican sense.[3] Institutions of national culture played an essential role in this task of national awakening, and the study of peasant culture developed in Eastern Europe precisely to serve this project of national cultural history (Hofer 1989).[4]

While the polity of Hungary was subsumed within the empire for nearly four hundred years, it would be a mistake to think that Hungary had never existed as some form of political entity. Habsburg dominance emerged from a disputed claim to the throne of Hungary's monarchy beginning in 1526; however, the Hungarian feudal diet continued to function, and it was there that attempts were made to assert independence in the face of an absolutist state. Habsburg attempts to centralize the state were always partially foiled by the insistence of Hungarian nobles on their constitutional privileges. Because of their need for revenue, Habsburg rulers did not dare neglect the constitution (Verdery 1983, 116, 182). By the early nineteenth century, reform movements aimed at economic independence and national development arose around the notion that Hungary was the victim of colonial exploitation. This belief was justified in part by the uneven development connected with the productive division of labor in the regions of the empire. Eastern parts, Hungary included, remained largely agricultural, while western parts became more industrially developed (Verdery 1983, 129–30).

In 1848, revolutions exploded across Europe, spurred on by radical political and economic changes and inspired in part by aspirations focused on the nation-state form. Within the Habsburg Empire, increasingly burdened by stagnant economic and military performance, revolution broke out in Vienna and quickly spread (Verdery 1983, 182). In Hungary, revolutionary activities were sustained by an uneasy alliance of factions seeking national independence, some of which sought broader social reforms or even radical changes in the social structure, while others defended a feudal social order. The goals of these factions were only partly compatible, and the failure of the revolution may be attributed in part to the contradictions between them. At the root of this tension was the reformulation of the meaning of the nation to cover all those "legally empowered citizens" of a nation-state (Habermas 1996, 282; see also Sugár 1969).[5] The switch to the meaning of nation as "a body of associates living under common laws and represented by the same legislative assembly" (Sieyes 1964, 58) was connected to the broader social revolution involving the transition from feudalism to capitalism and the adoption of Enlightenment ideas about citizenship in the relatively homogenous polities of Western Europe. In this process, the language of representation and the rights of man and citizen became coupled with the language of the nation.

Even in the West, "'the people' identified with 'the nation' was a quite revolutionary concept, more revolutionary than the bourgeois–liberal programme which purported to express it" (Hobsbawm 1962, 81, 82n). However, as Katherine Verdery (1983, 115) asserts, this mutual reinforcement between economic transformation and state centralization on the one hand and the development of nationalism on the other resulted in different phenomena in Western nation-states than in the Habsburg Empire: "While these processes interacted in Western European nation-states to transform class systems within unified nation-states, they gave rise in the Empire to the emergence of 'nations.'"

During the revolutionary period and afterward, while advocating independence for the kingdom vis-à-vis the Habsburg Empire, many among the Hungarian nobility remained reluctant to give up their feudal privileges. While the revolutionary legislation of April 1848 abolished serfdom, tithes, forced labor, and capital punishment, many found the granting of these basic rights to be scandalous (Frigyesi 1994, 258). Differences over the meaning of "the nation" were thus implicitly tied to stances on citizenship. Who should belong to the political nation and what kind of citizenship a member of the nation would be entitled to were critical questions.

The decades leading up to 1848 were marked by movements of national reform and by peasant romanticism in Hungary, and "Institutions of National Culture" were key to the creation of an image of a "National past" (Hofer 1980). These years witnessed the establishment of the National Museum, the National Theater, and the Hungarian Academy of Science, while Hungarian (Magyar) was made the official language of the state (1843–44) (Hanák 1991, 97). "By 1848, 'associational fever' had taken hold, with more than 500 associations in Hungary" (Nemes 2001, 806), united by a "rejection of the status-quo cosmopolitan culture, a corporate social hierarchy, and an economic policy perceived as damaging to Hungary" (810).

Among these were economic associations aiming at national reform, including the Protection Association, founded in 1844 by the National Diet to "prevent Hungary's impoverishment by promoting domestic industry and commerce" (Nemes 2001, 808). Members of the association pledged to buy only domestic goods and employ only domestic craftsmen for six years (808). Although the campaign itself lasted for only two years, "it was on the dance floor and in social life, as much as in meeting halls and merchants' warehouses, that the Protection Association had its greatest and most lasting impact" (809).

It was in this context that the Hungarian nobility embarked on inventing a national dance from motifs borrowed from "the folk" resulting in the introduction of the newly invented dance, the *csárdás*, as a ballroom dance.[6] While its name, meaning "of the pub or inn," indicates that it is derived from popular sources, no single dance with this name appears to have existed before.[7] By the mid-1840s, the *csárdás* had become de rigueur at many balls, including those organized by the Protection Association.[8] At these dances expressing and promoting Hungarian patriotism, the use of the Hungarian language and the sporting of "national dress" were highly encouraged, while the German language and dances such as the waltz were frowned on (Nemes 2001, 813). And although patriotic associations were able to nurture a "virtual consensus" that social life should be more

Hungarian (809) through their interaction with the press and its public, what "Hungarian" meant continued to be broadly interpreted.

HUNGARIANNESS: THE LINGUISTIC NATION
AND THE HISTORICAL NATION-STATE

The association of nation with language was coming to be central during this time. The developments in philosophical thought that produced the construct of a *Sprachnation* had a destructive effect on the old multinational empires, including the Habsburg (Burger 2003, 2). While for many Enlightenment thinkers language was understood as a means to an end—mainly toward the acquisition of education and science—the so-called first linguistic turn philosophers, Johann George Hamann, Johann Gottfried Herder, and Wilhelm von Humboldt, placed emphasis on the diversity of languages, each connected with a particular worldview (2). Herder famously asserted that language could not be reduced to a tool, for a national language was a historically produced treasury of thoughts specific to any given nation. As such, language was both representative of and constitutive of the *Volksgeist* (Herder 1968, 143; Burger 2003). In this paradigm, nations, in theory at least, should be distinguishable from one another by the languages spoken by their members. As Hannalore Burger (2003) writes, "After the term *nation*, in the sense of *Sprachnation* (language nation)—a concept which was constructed by Fichte, Herder and others—became very popular, diglossie and even more polyglossie come under strong suspicion. Multilingualism suddenly appeared as an indication of *decadence* and a danger for the still rather delicate construct of *national identity*. Unlike former conceptions of *nation* which were mainly based on territory, religion or forms of government, with the beginning of the 19th century language became the only criterion for the term *nation*" (1–2, italics in original). The new republican understanding of nation conflicted not only with the feudal use of the Latin word *natio* but also with the contemporary use of the term *nationality*—*Volksstamm*—within the Habsburg Empire. The latter, associated with language groups and determined according to mother tongue, was used in the census to map nationalities within the empire.[9]

Hungarian thinkers were deeply affected by Herder's prophecy that as it existed as an island in a sea of Slavic and Germanic languages and peoples, the Hungarian language (and accordingly, the Hungarian nationality itself) was destined to disappear. According to Loránt Czigány, this reference in his *Ideen zur Philosophie der Geschichte der Menschheit* made

Herder a household name among Hungarians, encouraging the development of the discourse about the death of the nation (*nemzethalál*), popularized by leading poets of the period (Czigány 1984, 103). Nation-state aspirations had encouraged a revival of the use of the Hungarian language by the nobility, many of whom until then had spoken German more comfortably. By the first quarter of the nineteenth century, the language reform movement initiated at the end of the eighteenth century had already supplemented the Hungarian language with tens of thousands of new words (Haselsteiner 1990, 161; Hanák 1991, 99). Involving standardization of spelling, grammatical restructuring, the adoption of foreign terms, and the coining of new Hungarian words, this reform aimed at adapting the language to express modern thought, with an emphasis on scientific and literary expression. Nevertheless, reflecting the tension between this Enlightenment approach and first linguistic turn romanticism, language was also understood as the bearer of national values. Accordingly, the Hungarian Academy of Science supported the collection of folk songs and regional vocabularies (Kósa 1998, 27, 29).

The language of the folk had also become an important resource for poetry and national songs, resulting in an increasing interest in the collection of folk verse and folk songs in the first half of the nineteenth century. Believing folk poetry to be the "real poetry," poets, including hero of the 1848 revolution Sándor Petőfi (born Petrovics), committed themselves to writing poems based on folk songs (Kósa 1998, 27).[10] János Arany, an esteemed poet of the period, worked at the Academy of Sciences, collected folk songs, and wrote scholarly works formulating how to base poetry on them (Hooker 2013, 172–73; see also Czigány 1984). By the 1840s, this romantic literary style, often taking the peasantry as its theme, was at its height. Literary historian Czigány (1984) writes that this *népies* style came to be identified as *népnemzeti* (which he translates as "national classicism") "because it was thought that slowly and gradually the best features of *népies* literature were coming to assume wider implications: their validity was extended to national traditions (hence: *nemzeti*)—or rather, to use political terminology, 'the people' and 'the nation' were successfully amalgamated in a unity of national literature which was supposed to express the cultural aspirations of *all* Hungarians."

Language reform and the collection of folk language reflected and provided a basis for the conviction that language was both the bearer and signifier of nation.[11] In the *Sprachnation* paradigm, a Hungarian speaker was a Hungarian; language signified nationhood. As the empire charted *Volksstämme* according to language use, Hungarian aspirations for nation-statehood required evidence of a Hungarian majority. The subsequent ethnolinguistic assimilation that took place in the form of Magyarization was part of a political project—a project of reform connected to independence from the empire and the establishment of an independent nation-state. Accordingly, in the 1870s, after the Compromise that established the Austro-Hungarian Empire, there appears to have been a decrease in tolerance toward minorities reflected not least in the closing of many "minority language" gymnasia (Kann and David 1984, 380). With the 1869 law on education the Hungarian government supported Hungarian language education, to the outrage of ethnic Romanian leaders (Kürti 2001). Such acts reflected, on the one hand, an offensive action on the part of Hungarian nation-state makers and, on the other, a defensive reaction to claims to autonomy by minorities, or "nationalities," argued along the same lines as Hungary's claims of independence vis-à-vis the empire (Kann and David 1984, 380).[12]

The notion of what we might call an ethnically Magyar, Hungarian language–speaking nation-state did not easily allow for multiethnic or multilingual (much less polyethnic or polylingual) notions of the polity.[13] Rather, the establishment of official status for the Hungarian language and related policies combined with age-old social relations hindering ethnic equality to cause tension with the non-Magyar populations that made up approximately half of the population of Hungary (including Transylvania), sparking their opposition and intensifying their own national movements (Verdery 1983, 188).[14] Although the failure of the revolution hinged largely on the nobility and aristocracy's jealous defense of privilege, the tension between nationalities over their relationship to states and citizenship helped seal Habsburg victory. Fearing oppression under an independent Hungarian state, and seeking nation-state status for themselves, minority nationalities entered into alliances with the empire (189). Jews and Roma, having no nation-state to join, were exceptions.

While the meaning of the Hungarian nation was coming to be defined with language as its primary marker, the argument for an independent Hungarian state stressed historical precedent: the crown lands of Saint Stephen, Hungary's first Christian monarch. By the time of the 1848 revolution, Hungary had existed as a polity for over eight hundred years. In 1001, the tribal leader Vajk had embraced Christianity, accepting a crown from the order of Pope Sylvester II; changed his pagan name to István (Stephen); and established a feudal state (Kontler 2002, 52).[15] In subsequent centuries, rulers encouraged the development of a multiethnic kingdom. Not only were there societies already dwelling in the Carpathian basin at the time of the Magyar conquest in 896, but successive Magyar kings also actively promoted colonization of the region, inviting foreign experts for development and offering special status to groups settling in border areas along the Carpathian Mountains (Szűcs 1990, 13).[16] The 1526 victory of forces representing the Ottoman Empire at the battle of Mohács marked the beginning of a three-hundred-year period in which the territorial integrity of Hungarian (Magyar) sovereignty over the crown lands of Saint Stephen was to remain constantly under threat.

With disputes over the Hungarian throne that left a portion of Hungary in Habsburg hands in 1526, and Ottoman occupation of the central part of the kingdom in 1541, a period began in which the territory of the historic kingdom of Hungary would come under the spheres of influence of the two empires and be divided in various politico-bureaucratic configurations. A century and a half later, the Ottomans were expelled from Hungary, but the price paid was Habsburg domination over the entirety of historic Hungary, with Transylvania administered separately from the other lands. Not until the Compromise of 1867, over three hundred years later, when Hungary became a partner in what was then renamed the Austro-Hungarian Empire, or the dual monarchy, would a Hungarian state again govern the territory of historic Hungary (Verdery 1983, 182; Hanák 1991).[17]

The Development of Ethnography and Folk Music Collection under Changing Territorial and Demographic Conditions

It was in such a context of constant threat and oppositional status that a national culture was being invented in the process of nation-state-making. The cultural politics of national reform and romanticism continued after the failed 1848 revolution, the following period of repression, and the subsequent partnership in the dual monarchy, evidenced by the opening of the Liszt Academy of Music, the Hungarian Opera House, the National Ballet, and the Great Market Hall. Increasingly, especially from the 1880s on, national reform was expressed in Hungary's participation in international industrial fairs entailing the display of items considered uniquely Hungarian and the production of these items for the market. The 1885 national cottage industry exhibition featured lifelike peasant rooms, while at the 1896 celebration of the millennium of the Hungarian conquest of the Carpathian basin, ethnic villages were displayed together with their inhabitants in City Park. "The metamorphosis of Matyó embroidery into merchandise," described by Marta Függedi (2000), is illustrative of the processes involved.

From the turn of the century onward, the National Cottage Industry Association (Országos Háziipari Szövetség) worked to propagate and popularize the embroidery of the Matyó, featured among Hungarian items at the world's fair of 1911 in Turin (14).[18] That same year, during carnival season, Archduchess Isabella, the "chief patroness of cottage industrial art," organized a Matyó wedding, at the Isabella ball, which aristocrats attended in "Matyó peasant wear" in order "to popularize handicrafts" (15). Local intelligentsia, soon to be followed by merchants, placed orders with peasant women, providing lucrative income (13). Such engagement with folk forms spanned interests as broad as nation-building, economic development, and entrepreneurialism. The discipline of ethnography was emerging from this process as well.

Tamás Hófer (1980) argues that the role of the ethnographic sciences in Eastern Europe was to produce the material on which national symbols would be based. In Hungary, as elsewhere, ethnographic collection preceded the emergence of a distinct academic field of ethnography.[19] The Hungarian Academy of Sciences was founded in 1830 "to serve national development and the interests of economic reform" (*Pallás Lexikon* 1893, 233). Beginning in 1832, the academy undertook the collection and publication of folk songs for the purpose of scientific research and preservation, and to "serve the formation of a national taste" (Sárosi 1993, 188). The Ethnographic Department of the National Museum (later to become the Ethnographic Museum) was founded in 1872, followed in 1889 by the inauguration of the Hungarian Ethnographic Society, whose journal, *Ethnographia*, would appear a year later (Kósa 1998, 33). The first academic department of ethnography in Hungary, however, would not be formed until 1934 at Budapest University (Györffy 2000).

The Hungarian term *néprajz*, "ethnography," is today often used interchangeably with the terms *ethnology* and *social anthropology*. However, the specificity of the term attests to a particular Central European tradition in the development of this field. A brief examination of this history will help elucidate assumptions about these terms and about their objects of study and aims. According to Mihály Sárkány, the term *ethnography* resulted from "an emerging interest in ethnic and cultural differences in Germany in the middle of the 18th century" (Sárkány 2002, 559; see also Stagl 1998). The term Herder used in the 1770s—*Völkerkunde*, in reference to the study of "peoples"—was later used interchangeably with the Latin-based term *ethnologie*, "the study of peoples," in keeping with French usage.[20] In imperial Austria, whence Hungarians inherited the term, *ethnography* was used to refer to data or the *writing* about the peoples (*Volksstämme*) of the empire. In the empire, the legal definition of a *Volksstamm* was based on language (Arens 1996, 19) and was sometimes contrasted with, and sometimes used interchangeably with *nationalität*, or nationality.[21]

Today, the term *ethnography* that developed out of the German and Austrian traditions has become assimilated to the dominant international idioms of ethnology and anthropology. Retaining the word *ethnography* (*néprajz*), however, allows us important insights into this discipline's relationship to nation-building and perhaps into certain popularly held notions about the peoples of Hungary as well. Written into the history of Hungarian ethnography—into the term itself—are the tensions inherent among the Hungarian meanings of nation, nationality, and people.

The establishment of the Hungarian Ethnographic Society (Kósa n.d.) in the late nineteenth century by a professor of Germanistics was linked to three aims, the most far reaching of which was "to strengthen 'imperial patriotism' of the multilingual Austro-Hungarian Empire by helping its peoples (*népeit*) to learn about each other and so promote closer cultural and emotional ties among them." For this reason, the society enjoyed the support of court circles in Vienna and of the crown prince himself. The second aim was "the comparative study within the Empire of the peoples of the Hungarian state who also spoke many languages" (ibid.).[22] The third "was for the operation of the Society to strengthen the position of Hungarian national identity, of the Hungarian language and culture which were isolated and without relations in their environment" (ibid.). The potential for contradiction among the three aims is glaring, for what they amount to is a project of mapping difference within the empire meant to simultaneously enforce imperial patriotism *and* Hungarian national identity. There is a tension here between linguistic nationalism, with language understood as the basis of *Volksgeist* (the spirit of the people, presumably of the *nation*), and the arrangement of peoples within the empire, a nonnational state. Whereas empires had contained multiple languages (and peoples), nation-states were to have one people speaking one national language.[23] As peoples or nationalities—or their elites, at least—embraced Herderian ideas, the emphasis fell on proving their nation-ness.[24]

In this same period, the definition of a "people" in terms of language/ ethnicity was gradually being adapted to the "scientific" notion of race, espoused by theorists in colonizing states (and the basis of the French field of anthropology), which was clearly present in Central Europe by the interwar period. Hungarian ethnography, while developing out of a nation-making exercise, approached its peoples in the manner that the empire had: it studied each group as if distinct; each people—*Volk*—had its own language, its own spirit, its own customs. While the state engaged in active attempts at assimilation, ethnographic collection attended to supposedly distinct groups. The tensions in the three goals of the Ethnographic Society mentioned previously can also be seen among the terms *Magyar nép* (the Hungarian people), *Magyar nemzet* (the Hungarian nation), and *Magyarország nemzetiségei* (the nationalities of Hungary).

By the early twentieth century, new technologies offered opportunities for documenting and collecting folk culture. "Folk music science," or the study of peasant music, was an important tool in establishing the existence of a "folk soul," or *Volksgeist*, that was "authentic, coherent, and persistent" (Hirsch 1997, 201–2). Béla Vikár, general secretary of the Hungarian Ethnographic Society and the first in Europe to make use of the phonograph to record folk music, began recording Hungarian music in 1895. Not long afterward, with the support of the society, composers Béla Bartók and Zoltán Kodály began collecting—in 1905 and 1906, respectively. With funding provided by Ministry of Culture on the condition that it be made accessible to public, Vikár established a phonogram collection at the Department of Ethnography of the National Museum (Sebő 2001, 111). The Hungary that they documented using new technologies was historic Hungary, the roughly thousand-year-old politico-territorial entity that would be dismantled again a few decades later. As such, the wealth of material left to academic, ethnographic, and folkloristic posterity—the ethnographic record, so to speak—would come to contradict the new territorial definition of Hungary from 1920 onward.

Hungary had entered World War I as part of the dual monarchy and exited it as a nominally sovereign state but without any power to defend its borders. Designed and enforced by the Allied powers and happily accepted by neighboring states, the 1920 Treaty of Trianon placed two-thirds of the territory of what had been Hungary since the 1867 Compromise outside the borders of the polity. While this resulted in a political body that more closely resembled a monoethnic nation-state, it left sizeable Hungarian ethnic minorities in neighboring states and resulted in a massive influx of refugees from these regions to the now truncated Hungary. "Between 1918 and 1924, an estimated 426,000 Hungarians left territories ceded to Czechoslovakia, Romania, Yugoslavia and Austria" (Mócsy 1983, 10). The National Refugee office, established in 1920, had three goals: (1) to unify and centralize aid to all refugees and distribute the available funds fairly; (2) to ensure the collection of accurate data on the magnitude of the refugee problem; and (3) *to organize refugees into regional cultural and political associations to preserve group cohesion and cultivate loyalty to lost homelands* (Mócsy 1983, 10; emphasis mine).

It should come as no surprise that many Hungarians found the breakup of the crown lands of Saint Stephen unjust or that they continued to think of the severed territories as part of Hungary. Trianon was to them the latest in a three-hundred-year series of threats to territorial integrity. Moreover, well before the (more or less) current borders of Hungary were set, folklorists and ethnographers had amassed a collection of artifacts, musical recordings, and studies reflecting the folk cultures of historic Hungary. It is thus that living and yet-to-be-born Hungarians, inside and outside the new borders, were left with a national identity and territorial relations that did not correspond with these revised boundaries. The ethnographic scientists—the suppliers of national symbols—had documented a Hungary quite different in territory and population than what now existed.[25]

In the 1930s, the phonographic collection of folk music accelerated.[26] From 1936 to 1944, under the auspices of the Academy of Sciences and, later, the Museum of Ethnography, a large number of folk music recordings were made in the studios of Hungarian Radio under the direction of Béla Bartók, Oszkár Dincsér, Zoltán Kodály, and Gyula Ortutay (Kelemen 2000, 51).[27] In 1936, 4 experimental records were produced under Bartók's direction. Each record (of the 50 produced) was accompanied by transcriptions of the music, lyrics, and background information on collectors and performers as well as photographs (Sebő 2001, 112).[28] The transcriptions were made by playing records slowly enough to reveal information not discernable at the normal speed. In later decades, these materials would "provide listeners with an important guide, one that would enable them both to understand an all but forgotten world of music and make it a part of themselves" (Sebő 2001, 112). In 1941, under Ortutay's direction, and with the guidance of Bartók, Kodály, and ethnomusicologist László Lajtha, the Pátria record company released 107 records as the Pátria series (Martin 1982, 242; Sebő 2001).[29] Technical instructions for the reconstruction and performance of these vanishing forms were included. The emergence of later revivals and the forms they would take, then, must be understood in relation to not only the living practices of certain isolated peasant communities but also the materials—stored according to a rigorous methodology for salvaging disappearing forms and ensuring their playback in the future. Finally, all this was paired with a commitment to public availability.

The fact that the music of historic Hungary was recorded using powerful new devices, techniques, and methodological rigor aimed at its reproduction in the future would be a determining factor in the content of the folk revivals to come. These recordings not only would help make it possible to revive the customs recorded but would also become a basis of authenticity. Notably, many of the sources of these "authentic" recordings were made in locations outside of truncated Hungary—especially in Transylvania. The commitment to public availability was especially important, as these collections were made in the context of efforts to revive peasant practices and integrate them into the everyday life of all Hungarians in the decades after Trianon. This happened against the backdrop of the government's efforts to revise the borders imposed at Trianon and its annexation of parts of Czechoslovakia and Carpathian Ruthenia in 1938 and of northern Transylvania in 1940.[30]

Reviving Folk Dance in Truncated Hungary

World War I was a cataclysmic event in the region. The sudden collapse of the Habsburg Empire and the decisions supported by the victorious Allied powers and their local allies to carve its territories into independent (and supposedly homogenous) nation-states left contentious results. A partner in the empire, Hungary was treated as an aggressor in the war. The subsequent awarding of two-thirds of Hungary to neighboring countries had deep and lasting political and economic effects (Kürti 2002, 69). As the war neared its end, the short-lived liberal government that had declared the First Hungarian Republic gave way to a Republic of Councils that declared a dictatorship of the proletariat in 1919. Neither had been able to stop the occupation of territory by Hungary's neighbors, each attempting to carve its own nation-state from the corpse of the dead empire.[31] Although Communist rule lasted only about six months, it was characterized by red terror, giving justification to the counterrevolutionary measures of the next short-lived government. Into the widening vacuum of legitimacy, and with parts of the truncated country occupied by Romanian forces backed by the French, marched the National Army of Admiral Miklós Horthy, marking the beginning of the counterrevolutionary Christian National regime, which enacted its own much further reaching white terror throughout Hungary. Despite concerns about the Horthy faction, it received international support, partly due to fear of the spread of communism and partly because it claimed to represent a broader social spectrum (Mócsy 1983).[32]

By 1920, Horthy had ascended to the position of regent and would remain in it for twenty-five years. The new governing coalition, with nobles displaced from the neighboring lands represented in far higher proportions than their percentage in society, based its politics on exclusive rule by the historical classes—the aristocracy, middle nobility, and landholding gentry as well as the bureaucratic, military, and intellectual layers that

Fig. 1.1 A map of the breakup of the Austro-Hungarian Empire. Made by Moira Tierney in consultation with the author, drawing on map by P. S. Burton: https://commons.wikimedia.org/wiki/File:Dissolution_of_Austria-Hungary.png.

had developed from within them—and the cry "Justice for Hungary." Opposed to any far-reaching social reform, the governments of the Horthy era could conveniently point to the unjust peace settlement as the source of the country's social and economic problems. They further pointed to the failure of the liberal and communist efforts that preceded them as proof that social revolution could not solve the problems the country faced. These governments ruled with the conviction that only the historical classes should participate in the political sphere. It was these groups that would ensure that the country remained Christian and national (Borbándi 1989, 37).[33]

This conviction that the historical classes alone should participate in politics was justified by the idea that the country had not yet reached the point of development at which peasants and workers could take part in affairs of the state and that the bourgeoisie (*polgárság*) should only be allowed to do so within limits (Borbándi 1989, 37). Accordingly, the franchise was rolled back from the breadth legislated by the short-lived first republic (and applied in the 1920 elections) to well below 50 percent of the country's adult population (i.e., "between 26.6 percent and 33.8 percent of the total population") and further inhibited by open voting in the countryside (Vardy 1983, 10). Nevertheless, capital and the urban bourgeoisie were "organically built into the counterrevolutionary system and satisfied with the political roles that reached them" (Borbándi 1989, 37).

It should be noted that in this period the terms *bourgeois* and *middle class* were not interchangeable. The *polgárság* was urban and included merchants, tradesmen, self-employed businessmen, and intellectuals; however, in the antisemitic circles of the bureaucratic/officer class, the so-called *középosztály* (middle class), *polgár* was also used as a gloss for Jew. Jews and those of Jewish descent were indeed represented in Budapest (but not in the countryside) at much higher numbers than the general population in the bourgeois professions (Karády 2008: Borbándi 1989; Mócsy 1983).[34] In this moment when truncated Hungary was faced with absorbing massive numbers of ethnic Hungarian immigrants from the territories, the tension between social revolution and the defense of near-feudal relations was often expressed in terms of a tension between Hungarians and foreigners. Despite the fact that the territory of the country had been reduced to one-third of its former size, the state apparatus remained undiminished thanks to its having absorbed the bureaucratic middle class that had fled the neighboring territories (Mócsy 1983, 185–86). Not coincidentally, a numerus clausus bill for Hungarians of the Israelite faith was established in 1920, limiting the percentage of Jewish students permitted to study in the universities (Braham 1981, 30).[35]

At the base of the distinction between the so-called bourgeoisie and middle class was profession.[36] Because of persisting feudal relations, the nobility had resisted education needed for bourgeois professions/occupations, preferring instead to work in the traditional noble provinces: the military and the state bureaucracy. While the state apparatus retained its massive size, the goal of the numerus clausus law was to nurture an ethnically Hungarian Christian bourgeoisie to replace the bourgeoisie perceived as Jewish. Even when cooperating with capital, the ruling classes continued to define themselves in opposition to the bourgeoisie. At the same time, their power rested on the oppression of the majority of the agrarian population, excluded from the political process and experiencing rapid changes brought about by the tensions between feudal relations and the processes of capitalization and urbanization.

The New York Stock Exchange crash of 1929 led to a sudden drop in the price of grain and precipitated the collapse of the framework that supported Hungary's economy. As prices and volume dropped, tax revenues fell, foreign credit sources diminished, short-term loans were called in, and earnings from grain exports declined. The League of Nations, from whom Hungary sought financial relief, insisted on a rigid austerity program. Unemployment grew rapidly. Even government workers lost their jobs or suffered severe pay cuts, and peasants were forced to revert to subsistence farming. As foreign demand diminished, industrial production dropped, and businesses were bankrupted; the standard of living became unbearable for many. Rightist politics gained increasing legitimacy.

It was in this environment of recent and extensive territorial losses, a firm hold on power by the historical classes, economic depression, and irredentism that Hungary's first folk dance revival arose. While the *csárdás* and *verbunkos* had been invented by nation makers who freely borrowed from peasant motifs, their creation was not indicative of revival, for revivals aim to restore a "system believed to be disappearing or completely relegated to the past for the benefit of contemporary society" (Livingston 1999, 66). The invention of the *csárdás* and *verbunkos* as society dances reflected new techniques of nation-making but were also examples of a centuries-old process of mutual influence between social spheres, as the dances of the folk and those of society in Hungary had always shown strong reciprocal borrowing tendencies (F. Pesovár 1978; Kaposi 1991; Vitányi 1964). Indeed, up until the twentieth century, the folk adopted new dances (including the *csárdás* and the *verbunkos*) from the court and assimilated them to local paradigms (Vitányi 1964).[37] Yet by the twentieth century, the new dances had begun to replace the older ones due, in part, to the emergence of dance masters (Vitányi 1964, 11), often called "dance and courtesy instructors" (*tánc és illem tanárok*). In addition to their contribution to society dances, folk dance and folk music served in this period as inspiration for several forms of "high art," including ballet and opera. But these were connected more closely to practices of invention than to revival as understood here.

The desire to promote tourism and benefit from it economically seems to have played a key part in the shift to revival. Zoltán Szabó points out that in Hungary, the first ethnographic journal and the first journal on tourism appeared in the same year: 1889. It was not until the interwar period, however, that significant tourism developed, although it had begun much earlier in parts of Europe—Scandinavia (Löfgren 1999) and Switzerland (Bendix 1989), for example. This tourism, centered on ideas about fitness and health and nature and the outdoors, was at first the pastime of an elite avant-garde (Löfgren 1999; Z. Szabó 1998; Bendix 1989). Gradually, these rural trips began to include interest in folklore as well (Z. Szabó 1998, 170). This convergence offered new opportunities for the performance of folk dance and folk music and connected with regionalism (Bolle-Zemp 1990) and the assertion of local identity (Bendix 1989). In England, folk dance revival took off at the turn of the twentieth century with the reemergence of Morris dancing, led by folklorist Cecil Sharp (Vitányi 1964, 13). Iván Vitányi (2003) points out that this movement was stronger in the peripheries—in Scotland, Ireland, and Wales—than it was on "English soil."

Village tourism was developing rapidly in Hungary in the early 1930s, inspired, in part, by the success of tourism in Italy, Switzerland, and Austria (Pálfi 1970, 119). Based on the unique qualities of Hungarian culture, such tourism was intimately tied to the development of cottage industries—notably the production of embroidered fabrics that, when displayed at world fairs and expos, made specific regions and villages known throughout Europe. With the development of photography and film, certain locations, such as the village of Boldog, became known for their folk art and charming village life, making them tourist destinations with regularly planned sights, such as women fetching water or elaborate wedding celebrations; some even became sets for films.[38] All this was facilitated by the construction of transportation and communication networks, notably the train system and bus services. As villages became known for their folk art, associations built guesthouses and houses of folk art to accommodate tourists. In a Hungary with a ruling class that supported an expansive territorial vision, tourism was also a way to encourage *honismeret* (knowledge of the homeland), which was thought to be lacking in the population and potentially the reason for Hungary's losses (Behrendt 2014).[39]

Hungary's first folk dance revival, the Bouquet of Pearls (Gyöngyös Bokréta) movement, emerged in 1931 in the context of these trends. Journalist Béla Paulini, the key catalyst behind the emergence of the movement, had written the text for *Háry János*, Zoltán Kodály's 1926 opera, based on Hungarian folk tunes. He subsequently taught the piece to an "art loving" (*műkedvelő*) peasant association in the village of Csákvár, which performed it in 1929 and later in 1930 under the name of the Hungarian Cultivators' Theater (Magyar Földműves Játékszín) (Vitányi 1964, 15; Pálfi 1970, 118, 118n). These earlier efforts were dwarfed by the successes of the Bouquet of Pearls. Paulini assembled resources from diverse parties to establish the Association of Bouquets (Bokrétás Szövetség) and bring groups of provincial folk dancers from villages from different parts of Greater Hungary to the Budapest stage each year on Saint Stephen's Day from 1931 to 1944 (Pálfi 1970, 120). Close to a quarter of the approximately one hundred villages registered with the association were located in territory outside of truncated Hungary (Pálfi 1970, 147–50).

The success enjoyed by the Bouquet of Pearls can be attributed to a confluence of forces. The promise of expanded tourism had won support from the Budapest City Council along with a plan for annual celebrations in Budapest on the recently designated national holiday Saint Stephen's Day.[40] The formation of Bouquet of Pearl groups served the village tourism industry as much as it did Budapest's, as groups would perform in Budapest or other places at festivals and locally, for tourists. Middle-class proponents of these activities, such as Paulini, argued that they would be the answer to the economic woes of the rural poor while reinforcing and encouraging pride in their own traditional provincial culture. The popularizing of local folk art and cottage production through fairs and expos, journalism, and the new amateur activity of photography was key to promoting village tourism. Let us look at two tourist towns of this period, Mezőkövesd and Boldog, both of which had Bouquet of Pearls groups.

Photographs taken by Archduchess Isabella of the wedding performed on the occasion of her visit to the Matyó town of Mezőkövesd were published in the *Sunday News* (Fügedi 2000, 318). This attention to the Matyós as the typical Magyars sparked regular visits by tourists to Mezőkövesd (319), and in 1926, Matyós performed for an audience of four thousand at the International Exposition for the Defense of Man (Embervédelmi Kiállítás) in Budapest (319). These events too were covered in the press (321). As the depression took its toll, a council was formed to promote tourism to Mezőkövesd. In 1932, various celebrities and government officials promoted a big event there, drawing three thousand visitors in one day (323). By the 1940s, visitors were being hosted in country houses (*tájházak*) where they were provided with meals and treated to performances, while Matyó women also traveled to spas and seaside resorts to sell their embroidery (325–26).

The story was similar in the town of Boldog, to which a group of fifty tourists was brought in 1931; later that year, the Capital City People's

Cultivation Council (Székesfővárosi Népművelési Bizottság) brought groups of English and American tourists who were provided entertainment, food, and handicrafts for sale (Újváry 1982, 67).[41] In 1932, Boldog was visited by Hungarian Radio and reported on in the press, and filmmakers visited in search of locations (67). A number of films were subsequently shot there, employing locals as extras. Boldog used funds from the National Tourism Council to build a tourist guesthouse (*idegenforgalmi vendégház*) in 1935, and the IBUSZ travel bureau, the sleeper car bureau (*hálokocsi íroda*), and the booking office (*menetjegy íroda*) each brought groups there. In 1937, the Ministry of Foreign Trade sponsored a film made in Boldog, entitled *Cottage Industry and Folk Art* (85).

It is perhaps not surprising that both Boldog and Mezőkövesd featured Bouquet of Pearls folk dance ensembles. Beyond membership fees, the Bouquet of Pearls financed itself with support of the Budapest City Council, the Municipal Tourism Bureau, and the Ministry of Culture. In addition, Bouquet of Pearls groups in Transylvania and the regions north and south of truncated Hungary where ethnic Hungarians lived, and where territory was being annexed, received support from the Ministry of Defense. This allowed Paulini to pay performers and produce the *Bokrétások Lapja* (Bouquet Journal), which featured debates over the proper direction of the movement. By 1934, the association had won "the exclusive rights to organize a folk group" by the Ministry of Religion and Public Education (Pálfi 1970, 122).[42] According to Imre Romsics (2001, 24), "a meeting was held at the Ministry of Culture in June, 1934, in which it was agreed to prevent by law any activities of folk art outside the Association."

The fact that in 1935 alone, members of the Association of Bouquets attended the annual congress of Cecil Sharp's International Folk Song and Dance Society in London and Bouquet groups also toured in Western Europe (Romsics 2001, 22–23) should remind us that this phenomenon was tied to broader trends in folk dance revival (Vitányi 1964, 14).

The Bouquet of Pearls had a mutually informing relationship with ethnography, being both championed and policed by ethnographers. István Györffy, the first to teach the discipline on the university level, claimed to have suggested the idea to Paulini (Pálfi 1970, 120). While Paulini argues that "we should leave the village art for the village, on the one hand to be sensible, and on the other hand for reasons of integrity" (Paulini, cited in Palfi 1970, 131), the truth was that dance material and costumes were often embellished by leaders of Bouquet groups while adapting them for the stage according to their tastes and worldviews (Romsics 2001, 24). By 1936, this fact had come to the attention of the Ministry of Religion and

Public Cultivation, which placed the movement under the supervision of the Hungarian Ethnographic Society (Pálfi 1970, 125; Romsics 2001, 24). Assigned to oversee the "authenticity of dances and costumes," ethnographers checked them against the ethnographic record, often conducting new research to this end. Yet without any real authority of enforcement, their conclusions had little to no effect on performances (Pálfi 1970, 126).

According to György Martin, "the Pearly Bouquet Association was an extremely solid, strictly closed peasant movement averse to any kind of urban or intellectual initiative intent on reviving folk tradition. The community of participants of different ages, of different property status and of different social position who met on the stage annually on St. Steven's Day for fourteen years, made the peasantry conscious of their own cultural values" (Martin 1988 [1974], 8; see also Cardaro 1998, 107).[43] Yet Pálfi (1970, 135) argues that Paulini promoted the movement by personally seeking support from the "the leading social powers of the village." While this may not have always meant the intellectual or landowning class, Pálfi does indicate that teachers, notaries, and priests, especially Protestant ones, were typical local Bouquet organizers (135). It appears that this "peasant movement," the Bouquet of Pearls (Gyöngyös Bokréta), was centrally organized by the urban elite and locally organized by village intellectuals, usually teachers or clergy members, likely all part of the middle class (Romsics 2001, 21; Pálfi 1970, 135). The examples of the founding of ensembles in two villages, Kalocsa and Boldog, will help flesh out this picture.

In Kalocsa, the Bouquet of Pearls group was "founded and operated under the auspices of the Young Farmers' Association" (Romsics 2001, 22), which selected dancers to be members of the group.[44] Romsics (2001, 25) writes, "Because of the high price of folk costumes, only young people from well to do families could afford to dance in the Gyöngyös Bokréta groups." The formation of the Bouquet of Pearls group in Boldog is described in detail by Újváry (1982, 59): "In the community of Boldog, near Hatvan, the folk art movement started in the 1920s. Amidst the oppressive economic situation and unemployment which was crushing the villages too, the chief notary, Jenő Bruckner, wished to bring attention to his village by publicizing folk art-precipitating folk costume, embroidery and folk customs—and in this way boosting tourism and wages and at the same time strengthening and protecting local traditions." Bruckner was also responsible for organizing the participation of Boldog residents dressed in folk costume in parades and helping to promote the village. By 1930, he had managed to acquire the status of "place of folk costume" (*népvíseleti hely*) for the village from the government (Újváry 1982, 59).[45]

Bruckner's bureaucratic position as a notary suggests that he was quite probably of the gentry class. This does not mean, however, that he did not engage in agricultural production or that he was wealthy. That is, he might have identified or have been identified as a peasant or as a member of the folk. Indeed, we know that the poorest peasants were landless and that large proportions of the gentry had become smallholding peasants who differed from nonnobility only through distinctive consumption habits, the exercise and flaunting of citizenship rights, and positions in the state bureaucracy. The use of the word *peasant* often obscures class relations and can become a tool in constructing a rural-urban opposition.

While technically the Bouquet of Pearls existed until 1947, it floundered after Paulini's suicide upon Soviet occupation of the country. Yet the movement would have lasting effects on both folk culture and folklorism in a number of important ways. First, dance researchers assert that the Bouquet of Pearls had a strong influence on the preservation of folk dance. György Martin (1980c, 108) writes, "Wherever the Gyöngyös Bokréta planted its feet, the interest in tradition remained alive for a good period of time." Second, a complex relationship between revival practices and the ethnographic record was established in the Bouquet of Pearls. Struggling with the authenticity of the Bouquet groups, ethnographers focused heavily on Bouquet villages. It is no coincidence that a number of these villages are the sites of classic studies and ongoing visitation by ethnographers. Bouquet villages are likely to have a living dance tradition *and* to be visited and documented by ethnographers, the suppliers of national symbols.[46] Finally, the Bouquet of Pearls "awakened the different youth organizations (especially the scouts), and contributed to the complex practices of the staged performance of Hungarian dances and customs found today" (E. Pesovár 2003, 3).

These conditions in which the Bouquet of Pearls emerged were also giving rise to what Vitányi calls the "folk art movement of the youth." Developing in a milieu strongly influenced by the *népi* movement, discussed in the next chapter, and made up primarily of students, it "differed fundamentally from the Bouquet of Pearls" (Vitányi 1969, 26). While peasants were the dancers in the Bouquet of Pearls, the youth movement was made up mostly of urban students who had not been raised with folk songs and folk dance (ibid.). While "the Bouquet of Pearls wanted to preserve the folk tradition within peasant circles... the youth movement wanted to transform it into the common treasury of the nation" (ibid.).

Like the inventors of the *csárdás*, the folk art movement of the youth did not seek to conserve folk art in an unchanged form. They utilized folk art as the basis for their creative activity, making stage dances, as well as social dances, and renewing them with folk sources (Vitányi 1964, 26). Whereas Paulini felt that peasants should preserve folk culture and artists should produce new art influenced by it (ibid., 25), "authenticity was not especially important" for these populist-influenced youth, who thought of themselves as the "people" (*nép*) (26). Vitányi argues that while the Gyöngyös Bokréta fit into the dominant structure, this youth movement, with its goal to build a new society, existed in opposition to it (ibid.). Rather than to conserve relations of the past, Vitányi argues, this youth movement sought progress (27). But what kind of progress was this?

CONCLUSION

The invention of national tradition in late nineteenth- and early twentieth-century Hungary was part of the nation-state-making process. While a nation-state form was not inevitable, these struggles over culture and cultivation took place en route to Hungary's current form and helped to shape it under the pressure of global transformations with regional characteristics.

By ending this chapter with the Bouquet of Pearls movement of the interwar period, I have illustrated the shift toward revival practices integrating tourism, economic development, and questions of culture. Conditions in Hungary in the 1930s gave rise to the essentially conservative Bouquet of Pearls movement in which urban and rural elites encouraged villagers to perform and preserve their own culture, considered distinct from that of the urban elite.

As we move forward, we will have to keep in mind the problems inherent in our use of the words *peasant* and *folk*. Uniting rural against urban, the (re)production of the urban-rural distinction often functions to obscure the oppressive nature of feudal relations that served the interests of the nobility cum middle class. Nostalgia for an agrarian society from within the conditions of rapid urbanization, and the related romanticization of the peasant and village life, can function to gloss over the oppressive social relations and real class differences that existed in rural Hungary. While developing in a milieu in which the backward rural was contrasted with urban progress (Creed and Ching 1997), such romanticism ascribes order to a past from the perspective of a disordered present (Roseberry 1989, 59). Indeed, "*perceived* in the past" from this perspective, the agrarian "moral economy" becomes a resource for "protest and accommodation, despair and hope" (ibid.).

The Bouquet of Pearls movement emphasized the staged performance of folk dance and folk customs for tourists. It sought to bring revenue to the country and countryside and better the economic conditions not by changing the social system but by encouraging peasants to take pride in an authentic tradition that was theirs alone. As one goal of the Bouquet of Pearls movement was the preservation of folk dance, it became involved with issues of ethnographic authenticity. The same conditions in which the Bouquet of Pearls emerged also gave rise to other formations, providing inspiration for the folk art movement of the youth and the many organizations that enlivened it (including the scouts). This youth movement is best understood in the context of the *népi* movement that sought to improve the social conditions of poor peasants or, the folk, through dramatic political and social changes. In addition, this movement, to which we turn now, pursued the project of people's/*Volk* national cultivation, seeking to integrate folk culture into the everyday lives of citizens writ large—to make it "national." What Vitányi considered progressive was full of contradictions, as we shall see.

NOTES

1. See Thomas Hylland Eriksen (2003) on the emergence of ethnicity.

2. I put "sovereign" in quotes here because Hungary was not in a geopolitical position to choose the borders and (many of the) policies of the new polity after World War I. From a world system point of view, like all semiperipheral and peripheral states, Hungary's possibilities were, after World War I and today, quite limited.

3. For discussions on the historical complexities of the term *natio*, see Sugár (1969), Verdery (1983, 116), and Habermas (1996).

4. Anthropologists have examined the role of the peasantry in national consolidation in Latin America (Roseberry 1994) and Israel (Lees 1997) and to ethnonationalist movements in Brittany (Maynard 1997), to name only a few examples.

5. The term *nationality—nemzetiség, Volksstämm*—was employed within the empire, in East Central Europe, the way that many today would use *ethnicity*. This is not insignificant—it reflects both the identification of groups within the empire and the adaptation of the Western idea of the nation to conditions of the empire. There is a tension between nationality, seen as primordial, and the nation as constructed (Sugár 1969).

6. In the second half of the nineteenth century, the chasm between the aristocracy and the (often impoverished) gentry was vast, even while they together had defined "the nation" (Frigyesi 1994). Under the influences of French revolutionary thought, the gentry came to envision itself as the people, *populus*, and the "vehicle of the constitution" (261). The loss of feudal privileges sent many in this group into further impoverishment. While it could no longer cling to the phrase that the nation is made only of nobles, the gentry continued to define itself as "the core of the Hungarians" (263). The claim that traditions were adopted from "the *Volk*" or "peasantry" may obscure the origins of the practices. In the early years, what came to be known as the *csárdás* was often called the "magyar." This was the name by which István Széchenyi apparently requested it in the late 1830s (see Hooker 2013, 41–42). Another contender for the status of national dance, the *verbunk* or *verbunkos*, a men's solo dance, derived its name from Werbung Kommando, the recruitment arm of the Habsburg standing army, instituted in the first half of the eighteenth century. Developed as a coercive technique for recruiting soldiers, the dance was

another site of contact between old and new and local and regional dance styles. While late in the century the practice was replaced by regular conscription in the other areas of the empire, it continued in Hungary and Transylvania (Lányi, György, and Jenő 1983).

7. For centuries, there was diffusion between the cultural practices of nobles and nonnobles. The noble classes, especially the aristocracy, of Hungary were incorporated into a cosmopolitan world of European nobility, and it was the social dances of this group with which they were familiar. Nevertheless, examination of popular dances has revealed historical patterns in dance styles that indicate waves of diffusion and borrowing (Vargyas 1980; E. Pesovár 1980).

8. Márk Rozsavölgyi, the famous composer and violin virtuoso of Jewish descent (who Magyarized his name from Rosenthal) who played for the national theater, and Béla Wenkheim, a Hungarian baron of Frankish descent who belonged to the Reform Party in Parliament and would later become interior minister in the post-Compromise government, were typical of those popularizing the *csárdás* (*Pallás Lexikon* 1893).

9. Similarities with Western Europe are apparent in that language was seen as a unifying nation-making force (Weber 1976; Anderson 1984) and language standardization used as a nation-making technology (Bourdieu 1991), yet the dynamics of nation-state-making were different here, as *state* and *nation* were arguably less coterminous.

10. Czigány (1984) also writes: "Of course, the *népnemzeti* trend inevitably led to academicism, the essential feature of which was a rigorous conservatism." This is important to note regarding the use of the terms *népnemzeti* and *népi-nemzeti* in the interwar period.

11. See Silverman (1983, 55) for the Bulgarian parallel.

12. The language of minorities can obscure the dynamics a bit. Jewish "emancipation" (i.e., civil and political equality), put on the table in 1848, was legislated at the time of the Compromise with the empire in 1867. The willingness of Jews to identify as Hungarian and to adopt the language as a mother tongue was key to this support. Here we can see a tension between the treatment of "nationalities" (which threatened to claim territory) versus other kinds of "minorities." In 1895, the Jewish religion would be officially recognized as one of the accepted religions and was accorded rights enjoyed by the Catholic and Protestant religions.

13. The term *ethnicity* did not become common until the 1970s (Hylland-Eriksen 2003), yet the tensions reflected in the uses of *nation* and *nationality* in the case of Central Europe—associated with language use and religious denomination—point to the way in which *ethnicity* would be taken up as a term. Here I use *ethnicity* and *minority* as ways to point to diversity and its treatment in the construction of the nation-state. See Sugár (1969) on ideas about nationalities and nations in the region operational at least until the early twentieth century.

14. In this system, ethnicity and class quite often combined in a single social taxonomy. For discussions of why and how, see Verdery (1983) and Szűcs (1990).

15. By "feudal state," I mean a Christian kingdom in which control is somewhat territorialized and centralized and primogeniture is established (Hanák 1991, 28). It was characterized by a Christian king, a constitution of sorts (the Golden Bull), and a feudal diet.

16. There is much contention among Hungarian and Romanian scholars over the extent of the Romanian (Dacian) presence in the Carpathian basin at the time of the conquest. See Verdery (1983, 1991) and László Kürti (2001) for details of these debates. The granting of nobility to Szeklers and Saxons in exchange for their performance as border guards led to a tight relationship between *class* and *ethnicity* in feudal Transylvania.

17. I adopt the commonly used descriptor "historic Hungary" to refer to the crown lands of Saint Stephen, covering the territories considered to be under the sovereignty of the Hungarian crown in the year 1000 with the foundation of the feudal Hungarian state. I occasionally use the designation Greater Hungary to refer to this territorial aim, which justified the annexation or occupation of regions by the Hungarian state in the period of World War II.

18. The Catholic population of the region around the town of Mezőkövesd—130 kilometers northeast of Budapest. In 1860, a train line linking Mezőkövesd to Budapest was built, making it easily accessible.

19. While the French would use the term *ethnology*, the Germans used the tern *ethnography*. It is likely that because the Austrians were engaged in the census taking of their population, the statistics—which, indeed, were ethno-*graphies* of different "ethnic groups"—came to be known as ethnography.

20. The term *ethnology* was coined by the French philosopher Alexandre Chavannes in 1786 (Bitterli 1982, 399; Sárkány 2002). Explaining the contemporary disjunction among the term *ethnography* and its relatives *ethnologie* and *anthropology*, Sárkány (2002, 2) explains that while in "the English-speaking countries, ethnography has taken the meaning of descriptive undertaking ... in the Marxist classification of science in the Soviet Union and in the German Democratic Republic, it covered the whole research procedure of description, analysis, and comparison of ethnic, cultural, and social differences."

21. While the "nationalities" of Austria were surveyed as early as 1850, it appears that it was not until 1880 that a regular census using language as a parameter of nationality began (Arens 1996).

22. The website states, "Around 50% of the population of Hungary at that time belonged to the Hungarian ethnic group while the other 50% was spread among a few larger and a dozen smaller ethnic groups" (L. Kósa n.d.). Scholars are quick to point to the relationship of religion to ethnic identity in Hungary and the Habsburg Empire. While they did not form very neat boundaries, religious differences were related to national consciousness and nation-building projects. In Hungary, 80 percent of the population was said to have become Protestant during the Reformation, coinciding with Ottoman and Habsburg occupation. Yet by the turn of the twentieth century, the majority was Catholic. In Transylvania, Calvinist (and some Catholic) Hungarians and Lutheran Saxons are distinguished from Orthodox Romanians. See Verdery (1983) for a nuanced discussion of religious groups in the Habsburg Empire.

23. See Errington (2001), Irvine and Gal (2000), Burger (2003), Taylor (2016).

24. Anderson (1984) points to the development of print capitalism and publication in the vernacular as being an important factor in popular imaginings of national community. He also points out that "official nationalisms" involved the naturalization of Europe's dynasties as national (82). He and other scholars of nationalism also point to military conscription as a mechanism in the creation of national consciousness. The complicated military system of the Habsburg Empire makes this argument problematic for Hungary. In his rich discussion of the officer corps, Deák (1990) argues that an imperial identity was enriched there. For other classes, however, there might be some argument to be made about the sense of serving in a foreign army. Folk songs about the "poor Hungarian lads" going off to serve in the Austrian army stand as one indication of this.

25. Hungary would later annex some of this territory beginning in 1938 by entering into an alliance with the Germans. Annexation of northern Transylvania was completed by 1940. These territorial gains were lost with the Allied victory. The monoethnicity of the citizenry was further honed after World War II when, under the direction of the Allied Powers, population transfers took place between the states of the region (see S. Balogh 1990).

26. There was a slowing of collection in the 1920s, during which time Bartók and Kodály were mainly concerned with processing earlier collections and engaged in vigorous debates about them: for example, Bartók's conflicts with Hubay in the 1920s and later conflicts with Romanian scholars regarding how he represented his Romanian material (Hooker 2002; see also D. Schneider 2006).

27. Bartók and Kodály are internationally recognized composers. Dincsér was an ethnographer. Ortutay, an ethnographer and populist, would later be minister of culture from 1947 to 1950. In

1957, he would become the head secretary of the Hazafias Népfront and in 1967 the director of the Ethnographic Research Group (Néprajzi Kutató Csoport) at the Academy of Science.

28. The timing of these endeavors suggests that they might have benefited from the New Spiritual Front (Új Szellemi Front) policy announced by the government in 1934, discussed in chapter 2.

29. Others were later produced in this manner by the Folk Music Research group of the Academy of Sciences formed under Kodály in 1953 but were not accompanied by the same degree of documentation.

30. Hungary's friendly relationship with Germany included trade agreements that eased the conditions of Hungary's economic depression but also made economic recovery dependent on Germany. This close alliance also resulted in adjustments to Trianon borders (later rolled back at the end of World War II) in the form of the First and Second Vienna Awards. The First Vienna Award gave territories in southern Czechoslovakia and southern Carpathian Rus (present-day Slovakia and Ukraine) to Hungary in November 1938. The Second Vienna Award reassigned the territory of northern Transylvania from Romania to Hungary in August 1940.

31. The infrastructure of industrializing Hungary had been built to fit the territory associated with historic Hungary. Thus, in addition to losing population and territory considered Hungarian by the grace of God, Hungary lost natural resources, major cities, and the functionality of the road and rail systems connecting them.

32. The white terror, although explicitly targeting communists and their supporters, had an antisemitic character, enforcing and enforced by a discourse conflating Jews and communists.

33. According to Gyula Borbándi, the Horthy era use of *national* contrasted it with *international*, and, in this way, with movements such as communism, liberalism, and Freemasonry. These movements were also associated with "foreigners" in Hungary—Germans and Jews, especially.

34. *Polgár*, like *bourgeois*, is derived from the German *burgher*.

35. This was "the first major anti-Jewish law in post World War 1 Europe" (Braham 1981, 30). Jews were not considered to be a nationality and thus, at this time, were identifiable bureaucratically if they practiced Judaism and therefore identified as Israelites.

36. Writing about contemporary Hungary, Chris Hann (2006, 48) points out that the term *polgár* means both "bourgeois" and "citizen," another sign of the tensions between feudal and capitalist relations. He also notes that Ferenc Erdei, who we will later encounter as a populist writer and activist, was concerned with the "stymied" bourgeoisification of the rural peasantry (ibid.).

37. I mean by this the social dances of the court.

38. See the archive on the website of the Hungarian Ethnographic Museum referencing the exhibit entitled *Pictures of Boldog*. Boldog served as a set for several films, including a French production in the 1930s.

39. See Behrendt (2014) on the connection between projects to encourage *honismeret* to the discipline of geography in Hungary.

40. Recall that the territorial dimensions of historic Hungary are associated with Saint Stephen.

41. Boldog is located nine kilometers south of Hatvan and approximately sixty kilometers (north)east of Budapest, at the foot of the Mátra Mountains.

42. It is perhaps not a coincidence that in the same year, Prime Minister Gyula Gömbös launched the New Spiritual Front, discussed later.

43. Folk dancer and folk dance researcher/ethnochoreologist György Martin worked at the Institute for People's Culture and was an important influencer of the *táncház* movement, as will be seen in chapter 4.

44. Eighty-eight miles south of Budapest, near the contemporary border with Serbia.

45. Újváry (1982) uses this term. I do not know what it entailed. Given what Romsics and Pálfi state about the legal monopoly the Bouquet of Pearls established, we might assume it was connected with the association, but 1930 seems early for that.

46. Bouquet of Pearl villages in Transylvania also central to the *táncház* movement include Szék (Sic), Gyimesközéplok (Lunca de Jos), and Kalotaszentkirály (Sâncraiu). Each of these is the location of long-standing dance camps, due to the living traditions in the 1970s, and the dances of each village are broadly known in *táncház* circles.

Chapter Two

What Kind of Nation?
Folk National Cultivation in the Interwar Period

THIS CHAPTER EXPLORES THE CONTEXT in which Iván Vitányi's (1964) "folk dance movement of the youth" took shape within a set of projects pursued by the *népi* movement in the context of struggles over *művelődés*, in interwar Hungary. Viewing culture, along with Terry Eagleton (2000, 7), as "a kind of ethical pedagogy which will fit us for political citizenship," I translate *művelődés* as "civic cultivation," and define it as a process resulting from struggles within civil society concerning the education of the masses toward the practice of citizenship. I place the term *civic* before the term *cultivation* (*művelődés*) to highlight the historical contexts of the emergence of political ideologies and conditions in which citizenship has been seen as something attainable by all people. Projects of civic cultivation encompass those activities referred to as adult education, moral education, public education, extracurricular education, cultural enlightenment (White 1990), socialization (White 1990; Gellner 1983), aesthetic enlightenment, aesthetic education, and militant education. This field is much broader and diverse than what Gellner (1983) writes about as the "educational machine."[1] The interwar *népi* movement pursued *népi-nemzeti művelődés* folk/people's national cultivation in a context of deep societal transformation in which the questions of who was a citizen and what citizenship meant were key.

In the age of European colonialism, citizenship was denied or greatly circumscribed for colonial subjects and for domestic working classes, each consigned to the "waiting room" of self-government (Chakrabarty 2000). The premodern status assigned to these groups according to "historicist thinking" implied that they were not prepared to act as citizens and thus to take part in political citizenship (ibid., 8). Given the exclusion of significant proportions of the population from citizenship at a moment in which the idea of the republic had become a political ideal for many, preoccupation with the people/folk, a central facet of the nation-building problematic, was intimately connected with the assertion of citizenship rights. It is at the juncture of civilization and *Kultur*—as they relate to questions of citizenship but also to the mandate for and the assertion of unique difference in the form of so-called national cultures—that I propose we view civic cultivation. It is here, too, that we can observe the development of a discourse of the inner, spiritual, sphere as a domain of sovereignty in a shifting entity called Hungary.

I thus approach interwar civic cultivation as a contradictory process emerging from struggle, which would produce new kinds of citizen/subjects and a distinction between inner/spiritual and outer/material spheres. The *népi* movement emerged as a collective actor pursuing particular ethical and aesthetic ideas of enlightenment, cultivation, and education in this struggle over the production of certain kinds of (national) citizens.

I begin with a brief history of late nineteenth- and early twentieth-century politics of cultivation in Hungary. I then turn to the politics of cultivation in the interwar period, focusing specifically on the *népi* movement, conventionally translated into English as the "populist movement," and the associated project(s) of folk national cultivation (*népi-nemzeti művelődés*). I then elaborate on specific strands of the movement and the practices and techniques participants employed in pursuing their particular ethico-aesthetic and political platforms of *művelődés*. I close with a discussion of the *népi-urbánus*, or populist-urbanist, antinomy central to the way interwar *népi* politics are usually narrated today. The legacies of these practices and discourses, as well as changes in the contexts in which they have been activated, are essential for understanding the more recent *táncház* movement.

THE POLITICS OF CULTIVATION

Exposing its Latin heritage, the root of the English noun *culture* can be seen in the verb *cultivate*, derived from the agricultural usage. In Hungarian, too, a farmer cultivates the land (*földet művel*). In contemporary English, we tend to leave the verb to the laboratory, using the verbs *civilize*, *educate*, *socialize*, or *enlighten* when referring to the act of imparting culture. In Hungarian, the verb *cultivation* carries through, resonating with the German *Bildung*, and with the meanings of both civilization and *Kultur*.[2] An erudite person is said to be *művelt*—cultivated or cultured. The state of cultivation, "culture," is *művelődés*, while the act of cultivating is *művelés*. The root *művel* informs such words as *művelődéspolitika* (cultural politics/politics of cultivation), *Művelődési Minisztérium* (Ministry of Culture), and *nemzeti művelődés* (national culture). Equipped with this etymology, we can now focus on the struggles over *művelődés* as a kind of ethical pedagogy.

In the first half of the twentieth century, access to formal education remained a major distinction between classes in Hungary, aiding the upper classes in maintaining political exclusivity while justifying their beliefs about the inferiority of the illiterate and "uncultivated" lower classes. While reading circles emerged as early as the eighteenth century, it was in the nineteenth century, especially after 1867, that casinos and new associational groups for peasants and bourgeoisie began to multiply (Kovalcsik 2003, 16). The half century of the dual monarchy has been termed the Golden Age in history books because of the rapid urbanization and rich associational and artistic life that accompanied it in Pest, Europe's fastest-growing city in the 1890s (Vörös 1998, 1). In the absence of deeply embedded political party activities in the countryside, myriad associations (*egyesületek*) were central in organizing political life and expressed "the societal closedness and the opposition of individual strata" (Kovalcsik 2003, 366). These new associations functioned among older associative forms, from religious gatherings to agricultural rituals and market gatherings, which continued to have a significant place in social life (ibid., 369). While much extracurricular educational activity took place in the context of religious institutions, we can note that the Agrarian Socialist Union had more than seventy thousand members in the first decade of the twentieth century (Romsics 2015, 175).

Groups struggled over education/cultivation in accord with the political and social ideals they espoused, with different ideals of citizenship and ideas of what it meant to be cultivated. While some fought for social reform, others sought to maintain the status quo. Among the flourish of new workers' homes, reading circles, casinos, and clubs, many expressed that the cultivation of the people (*népművelés*) was the goal. Although primary education (*népoktatás*) had become compulsory after the 1867 Compromise, pressure grew for the development of *népművelés* outside of the schools (Kovalcsik 2003, 404). The pressure resulted in increased government support for libraries, museums, and institutions of "free education" (*szabadoktatási intézmények*), many aimed at providing secondary school education for adults (550), inspired by approaches toward adult education in France and England (405).[3]

While most members of the upper classes did not support education of the lower classes, fearing their political organization (Kovalcsik 2003,

405), many of the pedagogical societies (*nevelési egyletek*) formed in the decades after the Compromise focused on the assimilation of minorities (405–9). In this period characterized by linguistic nationalism, the upper classes embraced language assimilation as important to both nation-making and national sovereignty. Language assimilation was also intertwined with the campaign to Magyarize surnames. Jews, some of whom also converted to Christianity in this period, were especially responsive to these campaigns supported by the government in the last decades of the nineteenth century (Fujimovics 2003 1). Civil associations such as the Uplands Hungarian Cultural Association (Felvidéki Magyar Közművelődési Egyesület) were "dedicated to the spread of the Magyar tongue" among minorities, in this case, ethnic Slovaks (Kann and David 1984, 382).[4] The success of the Magyarization campaign coincided with a decrease in minority schools in the first decade of the twentieth century (ibid., 418).

The short-lived revolution of the 1919 Republic of Councils (Soviets) saw a shift from cultural enlightenment as the concern of individuals and nonstate organizations to being that of the state (White 1990, 58).[5] After the first republic rose and fell, the Republic of Councils pursued its visions of education and cultivation with vigor (ibid.). Communist *művelődéspolitika* aimed at free schooling for all to "eliminate the difference between the learned and unlearned worker" and overturn "the situation in which '*műveltség*' is a privilege" (Kovalcsik 2003, 443–44). The Communists also attempted to eliminate counterrevolutionary activities by controlling and eliminating independent associations. In 1919, all parties and associations were dismantled (*feloszlott*) "whether by their own accord or due to a law," and nonstate and state institutions for socialization and education (*nevelési* and *oktatási intézetek*) were nationalized (ibid., 435–44).

In its turn, the counterrevolutionary Horthy regime restricted many institutions and associations, especially leftist ones, and state *művelődes* aimed at blocking the spread of revolutionary ideas were initiated (Kovalcsik 2003, 462–556). Efforts were made to coerce liberal (understood as Jewish) and petit bourgeois institutions into inactivity while also curbing the power of ultra-right university movements (Kovalcsik 2003, 462). Conservatives and refugees from the recently lost territories formed many organizations, both open and clandestine, with the goal of preserving a sense of national crisis and feeding irredentism through the "ultra-nationalistic reeducation of the country, and especially of the youth" (Mócsy 1983, 165).

OPPOSITIONAL POLITICS IN THE HORTHY ERA:
POLITICAL AND SPIRITUAL PARTIES

In the years after World War I, with Hungary now a small relatively (ethnically) homogenous nation-state, the attitude of the ruling classes toward minority groups was shifting. In the place of assimilation came a nationalist policy of ethnic exclusion (Fujimovics 2003, 2).[6] Jews, who not long before had been encouraged to adopt Hungarian as their mother tongue and Magyarize their names, were subjected to a numerus clausus law in 1920 restricting their access to universities.[7] Antagonisms were exacerbated by the effects of the 1929 stock market crash. As the depression deepened, the agrarian birth rate declined, precipitating a panicked discourse about the demographic decline of Magyars, or "death of the nation" (*nemzethalál*), and prompting researchers to investigate the *egyke* (one child) pattern, considered a chief reason for the demographic vulnerability of ethnic Magyars, in contrast to prolific "foreigners" or minorities (Borbándi 1989, 64, 68; see also Vasáry 1989).[8]

The meaning of the nation had begun to take on republican connotations during the reforms in the nineteenth century. This shift had been continuously hindered, however, by entrenched feudal relations jealously guarded by members of the nobility, who touted a "national culture" (*nemzeti művelődés*) invented through borrowing cultural elements from peasants while they continued to limit political citizenship to their own classes. The dualist era was also characterized by rapid urbanization, with Budapest among the fastest-growing cities on the continent from 1873 to 1896, its population doubling between 1869 and 1896 (Vörös 1998, 1). By 1910, Budapest was the eighth-largest city in Europe (Vörös 1998, 1). The saying "Hungarians founded the state and the Germans our cities" reflected the role of ethnic Germans in the urbanization process (Kürti 2002, 41). After legal changes in the 1840s that allowed Jews to settle anywhere but in mining towns, the proportion of Jews in cities, especially Budapest, saw robust growth (Karády 2008). The liberal policies that emerged after the Compromise, including the so-called emancipation law of 1867 that changed the status of Jews in Hungary, attracted Jews from other parts of the empire. Jews came to make up a significant proportion of the urban bourgeoisie and urban proletariat (but not household servants) (Jászi 1929; Karády 2008).[9] The latter was joined by members of the landless and land-poor agricultural classes, who migrated to the city to find work, often as domestic laborers or in construction.

What Kind of Nation? 55

Fig. 2.1 The synagogue on Kazinczy Street, Budapest. Designed by Sándor and Béla Löffner in the secession/art nouveau style, displaying Hungarian national style and motifs (built in 1912–13). Photo by the author, 2019.

By 1928, Hungary had been dubbed "the land of three million beggars" in reference to the impoverished and proletarianizing stratum of manorial servants and their families, agrarian workers, dwarf-holders, renters, and sharecroppers who made up a third of the population of Hungary and 67 percent of the peasant population (Borbándi 1989, 58).[10] Secondary education was a rare achievement for this group. Large landholders did not encourage the schooling of servants, expecting that, rather than striving for knowledge, peasants should be "respectful" and "work righteously and diligently" (63). Unrepresented in the political sphere, the landless and land-poor agrarian laborers carried the more privileged classes on their shoulders.

Via the anticommunist white terror, which had a clear antisemitic character; the banning of the Communist Party; and ongoing oppression of leftist organizations and associational forms, the Horthy regime succeeded in suppressing Communist activity.[11] Despite the authoritarian nature of the regime, and the political nation remaining highly circumscribed, opposition parties did exist, with most of the urban bourgeoisie (*polgárság*) represented by a spectrum of small liberal parties. After a period of repression in which the Social Democratic Party boycotted the elections, it resumed activities, agreeing to restrictions that compelled the party to refrain from political strikes and engage in union activities only outside the political sphere (Borbándi 1989, 41). Constraining the party's ability to represent the interests of urban workers in political life, this pact also put limits on the possibilities for rural agitation (ibid.). The party thus turned its focus to broadening the franchise, land reform, and achieving the secret ballot (ibid.; see also Kovalcsik 2003, 361). These conditions ensured that in a largely agrarian country, rural workers remained unrepresented in political life and that what was now a de facto urban party had little ability to appeal to agrarian and industrial workers together as the oppressed working class.

In an interview, Iván Vitányi made a point of stressing that while in the West, the left was the significant force of opposition, in the agrarian countries of East Central Europe, it was peasant-based oppositions that filled this role.[12] The strongest among the opposition parties in the interwar period was the Smallholders' Party, whose base was comprised of rural landowners—peasants with small and middle-sized parcels—later joined by elements of the rural and Budapest bourgeoisie.[13] Although technically a peasant party, the Smallholders represented a small fraction of the peasantry: those who owned land, but not the large estates. While it was a key advocate of land reform, the party's particular appeal was somewhat undermined with the 1920 land reform (much less far-reaching than those planned by the first republic and pursued by the Republic of Councils but overturned under Horthy), and it was absorbed into the government's Party of Unity by the time of the 1922 elections (Romsics 2015, 194; Lorman 2002). Founded anew in 1930, the party purported to represent the peasantry, yet its efforts did not address the plight of the majority of the agrarian population, which remained politically unrepresented throughout the Horthy period.

While the governments of the Horthy era were authoritarian and antisemitic to varying degrees, and the prime ministers took different positions; they held distance from the parties of the far right, which most of the Horthy governments sought to keep in the margins.[14] The goal envisioned by this far right influenced by national socialism was not the defense of the "aristocracy-gentry-bureaucratic triad" but rather a national socialist "party of the masses," in which the triad would have to share power with the bourgeoisie, peasants, and workers (Borbándi 1989, 26). This far-right opposition which loudly embraced ideas about reconquering the nation and about race (*fáj*) appeared to many to be more democratic than the government parties, because they promised shared power and "to end social immobility and attend to the problems of the workers and the peasantry," who were left out of the political process (Borbándi 1989, 39). By the 1939 elections, the far-right Arrow Cross Party (Nyilaskeresztes Párt) had entered parliament and was most popular among the lowest strata of the working classes (Lackó 1998).[15] Antisemitism and ideas about racial hierarchy had been present in government circles long before 1939. A significant shift came about, however, when Gyula Gömbös, who would later claim to be a fascist, was appointed prime minister in 1932. While he formally agreed to recant his antisemitic and authoritarian positions (Sakmyster 2006, 154), Gömbös's appointment illustrated the state of the struggle between conservative Christian Nationalism and "new" far-right ideologies.[16]

While ideologies, groups, and individuals interwove across this period, reducing differently positioned sets of actors to the same label can make it hard to apprehend the particularities of the power struggles taking place. I focus on aspects of the *népi* movement often less noted than the antisemitism that makes it easy to equate *népi* with the Horthyist Christian National governments (which enacted the 1920 numerus clausus law and several other antisemitic laws later, allied with Germany, and deported Jews to death camps) and with the explicitly national socialist parties (including the Arrow Cross government placed in power under German occupation, which enacted the last stages of the final solution).

My attention to these nuances is not to deny the presence of antisemitism in *népi* circles nor to suggest that the Christian National government was guiltless regarding the Shoah. Rather, by approaching particularities, contradictions, and struggles, and examining the conditions of this historical conjuncture, I attempt to develop a greater understanding of the waves of folk movement in Hungary, and the construction of the people and its others.

While the fairly successful yet incomplete delegitimization of Communists and Social Democrats can be attributed to a number of factors alongside oppression of the Horthy governments, there is no doubt that "the government . . . saw opposition, agitation and illegal deeds in peasant demands" (Borbándi 1989, 62). "A sign of the social backwardness of the country," Gyula Borbándi writes, "is that unlike urban workers, agrarian laborers did not have representation for their interests . . . organizations could not even exist . . . it was not even possible to think of founding unions" (ibid.).[17]

It was into this void that the *népi* movement stepped. The broad set of practices that made up this movement aimed at addressing the woes of the *nép*. The movement focused on the urgency of land reform and bringing legitimacy to the cultural knowledges and practices of the folk via the project of *népi-nemzeti művelődés* (folk national cultivation). Wary of formal politics in an authoritarian regime, this group mainly acted in the sphere of cultivation. Yet by demanding the franchise, redistribution of land, cultural validation, and access to formal education for landless and land-poor peasants, these populists advocated citizenship for the lowest strata of society.

NÉPI POLITICS, NÉPI ETHICO-AESTHETICS

While limits on expression varied across the different governments of the twenty-five-year regime, the press was subject to censorship throughout. In a manner similar to the form that bourgeois struggles had taken in late eighteenth-century Germany, matters of politics were debated in a lively literary scene embodied in journals, coffeehouse gatherings, and salons—in the sphere of spiritual (*szellemi*) or intellectual production rather than in a show of political power.

The interwar *népi* movement is remembered in Hungarian consciousness foremost for the (increasingly bitter) debates between *népi* and *urbánus* (urbanist/urbanite) writers. The significance of the *népi-urbánus* opposition is often reduced to one between antisemitic (*népi*) and Jewish (*urbánus*) writers, but this packaging may be too neat and serve to obscure the particularities and messiness of the struggles over identity and the meaning of progress in Hungary under the conditions of the Christian National regime, with German national socialism on the rise.

Fig. 2.2 Heroes Gate in Szeged, erected in 1936 to commemorate those who fell in World War I, victims of the 1919 Soviet, and the loss of territory at Trianon. Vilmos Aba-Novák's fresco shows Horthy on his white horse. Photo by Mister No, CC BY 3.0, https://creativecommons.org/licenses/by/3.0, via Wikimedia Commons.

Fig. 2.3 Heroes Gate in Szeged. Vilmos Aba-Novák's fresco shows King Steven with the borders of his kingdom. Photo by Matt Frost, 2004.

The movement was far wider than the circle of famous writers, and was made up of groups and institutional forms all pursuing the somewhat elusive *népi-nemzeti művelődés*. By accounting thus the array of sites and practices of *népi-nemzeti művelődés*, I do not mean to deny or diminish the significance of the antisemitism that appeared in the texts of at least some *népi* writers or to ignore the fact that other *népi* actors and writers tolerated such positions. Rather, I seek to paint a picture of aspects of the *népi* movement that disappear when *népi*, Christian National, fascist, and national socialist are used interchangeably to refer to rather different power configurations, visions of society, and associational formations under specific and unfolding historical conditions. The left and democratic strands of the *népi* movement have often been ignored because of the charge of antisemitism or otherwise treated as having cynically partnered with Communists. Recognizing the contradictory character of *népi* positions in the interwar period in the context of class relations will help our understanding of the folk movements that followed.

Népi cultural politics were pursued in the realms of literary and associational life in a sea of competing and overlapping projects of cultivation. The breadth of associational life served the pursuit of a spectrum—from the left (radical to bourgeois democratic) to the right (conservative and fascist)—of political interests. Among the organizations that *népi* projects could be found in were those "faithful to the regime," such as many youth groups, patriotic groups, and religious groups, including the Scouts, the KIE (Catholic Youth Association), the Turul Association, and the protestant Solo Deo Gloria. Other *népi* projects took place in institutions seeking radical change, including left-leaning populist-influenced groups, such as the March Front and the Györffy Kollégium (Kovalcsik 2003, 488). The unity of the populists, whose individual political allegiances could vary widely, was based on their demand for land reform and their focus on folk cultivation, pursued through and embodied in the practices of numerous and fractured *népi* groups.[18] In what follows, I introduce the populist writers, their debate with urbanists, and some methods of popularizing their program. I then describe a few examples of *népi* formations relevant to the institutional history of *tánchaz*, specifically regarding practices of folk song, folk dance, and amateur ethnography.

FOLK WRITERS OR PEOPLE'S WRITERS? FOLK CULTIVATION OR PEOPLE'S CULTIVATION?

The *népi* writers belonged to a generation born around the turn of the twentieth century who made the peasantry the central theme of their work in the interwar period. Producing poetry and prose, many also wrote what came to be called sociographies of the people that earned their place in Hungarian sociology, ethnography, and literature, with international acclaim in regard to literature.[19] In a chapter of his 1984 book *The History of Hungarian Literature: From the Earliest Times to the 1980s*, Loránt Czigány (1984, 381) writes: "Their ideological heritage is still active in the capillary system of Hungarian public thinking, their ideas form a part of the Hungarian national consciousness as an alternative to present day 'official' ideology—for *népi* writers were primarily a political movement, although their literary output is voluminous, and significant on its own. Yet *népi* writers have never presented a united ideological platform, or held identical political views, and were only a loosely connected group."

These writers also occupy a central place in Gyula Borbándi's 1989 book *A Magyar Népi Mozgalom* (The Hungarian populist movement), which places them in a broader *népi* movement. In the face of diverse political views and party affiliations, what bound the writers together most was their attention to the social conditions of the *nép* and insistent demand for land reform. Although most known for writing about the peasantry, some also wrote about the urban poor, composed largely of agrarian workers forced by their conditions to seek wages in the city. Most of them identified as being of peasant origin (Borbándi 1989, 132).[20] Borbándi argues that those who labeled these writers *népi* originally sought to distinguish them from those they considered *népies* (folksy) writers (133). While the use of folkloristic elements might have qualified a writer's style as *népies*, this writer "still could not be considered *népi*, because he did not tie his representations and images of the village to a demand for the transformation of society and held themselves distant from 'radical political movements'" (ibid.).

Today, it is not the distinction between *népi* and *népies* that is widespread and salient but rather the opposition, which returned with renewed intensity in the late 1980s, between *népi* and *urbánus*. While today many reduce the difference between the *urbánus* and *népi* worldviews to one between "Jewish" and "Hungarian"—that is, between a universalizing European-centered liberal leftism and a tradition-based right-wing populism—the diversity within the *népi* camp seems to have been much broader than this implies (Lackó 1998, 25).

While some date the *népi-urbánus* debates to the publication of Gyula Illyés's *Pusztulás* (Ruin) in 1933, individuals later associated with the urbanist camp had already pointed to assertions made by those later labeled *népi* as nationalist and excessive (Borbándi 1989, 191).[21] *Népi* writers asserted that large landowners and capitalists, sometimes glossed as Jewish, were responsible for the "commercialization of the spirit of urban cultivation" (192). It was common for urbanists to be of Swabian or Jewish descent, and *népi* writers were mostly ethnic Hungarians, yet the divide between the two groups was not always so clear (Borbándi 1989).[22] Some writers started as *népi* and ended up in the *urbánus* camp and vice versa (Kolozsi 2016), and there seem to have even been lasting associations, if not friendships, across this boundary.[23] Borbándi notes that left-leaning *népi* writers tended to have closer associations with urbanists. He claims that the antinomy only became apparent between those who were involved in debates organized around the opposition between Western urban progress and progress defined around a Hungarian third way, or between capitalism and a kind of socialism that would take Hungary's agrarian conditions into account (Borbándi 1989, 196).[24]

An important thing to note about the *népi-urbánus* divide is that both of its poles occupied an oppositional stance to the Horthy regime. They offered their competing models for progress as alternatives to the conservative Christian National and neofeudal approach of the government. Both believed in progress, including land redistribution and expansion of the franchise, but the former wanted to build on an agrarian path, while the latter favored urbanization that was also associated with the West.

Employing different literary styles, these populist writers were united by their focus on the *nép*, articulated as the lowest and largely rural stratum of society, yet disagreed over whether the movement should remain in the spiritual/intellectual sphere or enter politics proper. Those arguing against forming a political party did not want to steal support from the existing oppositional parties and asserted that it was their responsibility to bring the spirit of the movement to "every social and political frame" (Borbándi 1989, 255–56). Populist writer Géza Féja (in Borbándi 1989, 257) concludes in his article "The March Front": "the movement should remain an intellectual movement—a sociological and literary movement guiding the world view—because in today's politics things would only become stagnant."[25] There is an implicit argument here that entering into the formal politics of the day meant compromise. As the conundrum of the Social Democratic Party found itself in suggests, suspicion of formal politics was grounded in real concerns.

Opposition was not simply a political matter; on the contrary, *népi* writers opposed engaging in the formal field of politics of a corrupt regime, working in the spiritual, or inner, sphere, and producing this sphere in the act. This resembles the ethical civil society that would be identified in the dissident movements in the late 1980s. Whether for practical or ideological reasons, the attention of *népi* actors to the spiritual sphere set a precedent for a particular type of cultural politics, seen sometimes as oppositional to, but frequently as outside of, the political sphere.[26] It also meant that the common platform of the *népi* writers, land reform and suffrage, remained distant from its implementation in formal politics.

While Vitányi asserted to me that most *népi* writers were connected with either the Social Democratic or the underground Communist Party, at least some of them sympathized with the far right. Given the political breadth of the writers, an overarching populist political party appeared impossible. A political party would eventually emerge from this group in 1939, guided by its left-leaning wing.[27]

In 1935, Gyula Gömbös initiated the New Spiritual Front (Új Szellemi Front), which attempted to enlist intellectuals—especially the influential *népi* writers and well-known artists associated with folk music, such as Béla Bartók and Zoltán Kodály—to its cause by "uniting nationalist efforts." Gömbös had formally renounced his antisemitism upon his appointment as prime minister (Társoly et al. 1996). His promise of widespread (and contradictory) reforms and his assertion that his reform-minded government needed to adopt the values of the intelligentsia intrigued some of the *népi* writers, drawing a number of them to attend a meeting with Gömbös. Although accounts suggest that no agreement to work together was achieved at the meeting, and that the writers passionately demanded land reforms, allegations that they had sold out to the government filled the newspapers in the following weeks (Borbándi 1989, 172).

The writers nevertheless continued to face persecution, suggesting that "the government's stance toward them did not change" (Borbándi 1989, 174). By 1937, the writers were more consistently persecuted by the authorities, and a number of them were brought to trial in attempts to censor their work (294–96). The idea that the *népi* writers took central part in the New Spiritual Front remains widespread, but it is not clear just what this entailed. First, some *népi* writers were open to the idea of working with the Gömbös government, especially if it supported land reform. Second the antisemitic expressions of some writers would certainly have contributed to a "spiritual front" that legitimized antisemitism both in everyday life and in the policies of the Christian National (cum fascist) government(s) (and later, the Arrow Cross). As Jewish urbanists, along with other Jews and their converted descendants, would face a series of laws restricting their citizenship, and the increasing chance of death as the antisemitic policies and practices that made up the Holocaust/Shoah were enacted, the expressions of at least some *népi* actors could legitimate antisemitic violence, whether or not they admitted it.[28]

Népi and *urbánus* writers both stood in opposition to the neofeudal Christian Nationalist politics of the Horthy regime, and they shared similar agendas regarding the franchise, land reform, and democratic freedoms. Their differing visions of progress for this agrarian country were tied to the questions of culture and cultivation. This was of course not a minor difference. *Népi* writers promoted agrarian visions of the future that were neither feudal nor urban and that built, at least at times, on cultural essentialisms. Even writers not widely known for their antisemitic views tended to refer to Jews as a foreign influence (Tóth 2012) and seem to have tolerated the presence in their circles of those who did. It is easy to see how this could have contributed to the climate that permitted the Shoah to take place.

While some of this small yet influential group of writers did limit their project(s) to their literary works, their influence lay in the way they were able move other people to act on *népi* ideals, particularly around the idea of *népi-nemzeti művelődés*, a term that, in the absence of nuances, including attention to the class conditions of the peasantry, might converge with the government's Christian National project or with the far-right elements it sought to keep in check. But this does not mean the *népi* movement can be reduced to them. Beyond the writers, what, then, was the *népi* movement? Which ideals were acted on and how? And how did they work to achieve their goals?

Népi-Nemzeti Művelődés

The term *népi-nemzeti művelődés* (sometimes *nép-nemzeti művelődés* or *népi művelődés*) stresses the role of the *nép* in national (civic) cultivation.[29] In contrast to a national culture derived from the Christian National middle-class or imported Western (or, for that matter, Soviet) models, folk national cultivation stressed the development of a national culture drawing on agrarian cultural traditions—"folk knowledges," you could say. This cultivation, along with the distribution of rural land into socially reproductive plots and the right to vote, was seen as an essential element for the poor agrarian classes to achieve full citizenship. To get at what the term *népi-nemzeti művelődés* means, it is useful to explore the etymologies of the words *nép* and *nemzet* and the work these words do.

The term *nemzeti művelődés* is translated most often as "national culture." The peculiar history of Hungarian nation-state-making has served to make it a term with contradictory meanings. While *nemzet* points to nation in the modern republican sense, a tension remains in this word between ethnic nation and civic nation. In the Horthy period (at least until Gömbös came to power), the Christian National government wanted to reproduce a more or less feudal distribution of power (i.e., the *natio*) while establishing a state that would rule the territories of historic Hungary. *Nation*, in their sense, meant the *natio* ruling over a "national" state justified by historical precedent, not by ethnic and territorial homogeneity. *Nép* translates into Slavic languages as *narod*, into German as *Volk*, and, from there, into English as *people* or *folk*. The ways in which the term and its cognates can be employed within and between different languages reflect the breadth with which *nép* is employed in Hungarian. As such, what one understands as the *nép* can vary from meaning an "ethnic folk" to meaning "the people," as in popular or nonelite social classes. Similarly, in its adjectival form, *népi*, "of or like the *nép*," can vary from meaning "folk," as in "folk costume" or "folk art," to meaning "populist" or "popular," as in the common translation of the interwar *népi mozgalom* as the "populist movement." While the term was used to mean "the people," during the state socialist period, Communist usage never wrested it fully from its ethnic or agrarian connotations.[30] It continues to bear these contradictions. For this reason, I will often use the terms *nép* and *népi* and translate them at times as "people" or "folk" to allow the reader to experience the constant challenges produced by this tension firsthand.

Népi-nemzeti művelődés was employed as a critique of both the content and domain of *nemzeti művelődés*. This critique suggested that Hungarian national culture should be informed by the traditions and practices of the *nép* rather than those of the Christian National class derived from the feudal *natio*, or those espoused by the urbanites. In his 1939 pamphlet *A Néphagyomány és a Nemzeti Művelődés* (Folk tradition and national cultivation) the "father of Hungarian ethnography," István Györffy, defines *nép* as "the nation's lower social stratum."[31] He continues: "In a wider sense, however, *nép* is every 'herd' that has not turned into a nation.... Nevertheless, in a rarer sense, we understand nation in it" (Györffy 1992, 8). Györffy's definitions illustrate quite clearly that the word *nép* can be understood, and employed, in contradictory ways.[32]

While he insisted on overlaps with the *népi* movement, Vitányi told me that the Social Democrats had espoused a *nép-nemzeti* approach and that to them *nép* meant the lowest stratum of society.[33] But for many populists, for whom the plight of the three million beggars was the central concern, *nép* was often a gloss for the ethnic sense of "the people," which to some meant rural Hungarians subjected to an urbanizing process that benefitted Jews and foreigners. This was at root the distinction between the *népi* and *urbánus* understandings of progress. While according to Vitányi, Social Democrats did use the term *nép*, their idea of *nép-nemzet* meant a modern citizenship-based nation in which the *nép*, the people of multiple ethnicities, would be protected by the achievements of labor agitation and protection. For many populists, the *népi-nemzeti* idea hinged on the notion of a third way, a "Garden Hungary" that could be achieved through land reform and through which the *nép*, the *Volk*, would be protected from capitalist (and communist) urbanization and the decay of rural values (Szelényi 1988). Through this they hoped to preserve the agrarian base of Hungarian culture and economy. This was tied also to the idea of cultural validation for agrarian workers—that is, peasants or "the people."

Pursuing Népi Művelődés

If the goal of the *népi* movement was to popularize a particular kind of *népi* cultivation, in what ways was it pursued in practice? While the writers are known for their medium, and their individual positions, the movement itself developed in the associative sphere. Below I follow a few organizational threads as they intertwine yet remain distinct enough to name. While the movement lacked a clear ideological or political unity, the main glue that held *népi* actors together was the plight of the three million beggars; the impoverished landless and land poor peasantry. While the terms *populist writer, sociographer,* and *village researcher* have been used interchangeably in reference to the movement's emphasis on knowing these conditions, the movement would have remained quite small and insignificant had it been limited to those people now identified as such, especially if it had not involved the youth.

As László Kürti (2002, 113) points out, in the "modernist" period, regimes on the right and the left worked to "control and monitor young people." The youth promised a hopeful future, while at the same time looming as an unruly threat. These controlling regimes held "the belief that the youth had been corrupted by the previous regime." Vitányi's folk art movement of the youth took form in a broader field of youth-oriented activities and associations, among them, the Levente paramilitary training group and a number of Boy Scout organizations.

Népi activities were thus often pursued within organizations, nearly all of them "counterrevolutionary" (Bimbó 2013), that were in no formal way *népi* oriented. To reduce the entire village research movement to the positions held by the government or the extra government far-right would give this array of activities too much unity and obscure *népi* emphasis on the contrast between large landowners (whether the Catholic church, the aristocracy, or "Jews") and landless and land-poor peasants. Not only did disparate groups engage in village research, but the character of these groups and their participants also changed over time. In some cases, *népi* politics were adopted by individuals and small groups within these larger organizations in a clandestine or open manner, and in other cases, *népi* techniques/technologies were adapted toward Christian National ends. In many cases, government and populist interests seem to have converged, especially by the late 1930s and during the war (Hirsch 1997, 207), reflecting, on the one hand, a lack of ideological coherence and *népi* commitment to affect the entire political spectrum and, on the other hand, the government's efforts to harness *népi* influence. In the following, I describe the field of activities that took place in the village research movement, the "caroling" (*regös*) Boy Scouts, the movement to found people's colleges, and the March Front.

According to Borbándi (1989, 203), writer Dezső Szabó "first spurred the youth to become familiar with the life relations of the peasantry" in 1923. Szabó was right-leaning and antisemitic, and related both capitalism and socialism to "the Israelites." Born in 1879, he was a generation older than the *népi* writers but modeled a kind of "deep Hungarianness" that the latter would become known for (Borbándi 1989, 203; Czigány 1984, 2). *Népi* writer Gyula Illyés, at the time considered a leftist, proposed that the youth should go among the people and record sociological data from what they saw, like German wandering youth (Wandervogel) (205).[34]

The Míklos Bartha Association took inspiration from the activities of the Sarló Scout movement in Czechoslovakia, whose ethnic Hungarian participants engaged in activities between 1928 and 1933 that would later become institutionalized in the *regös* Scouts (Borbándi 1989, 112). In 1930, the association published a pamphlet entitled "Out to the Village," in which it stated, "Hungarian culture could only become real culture if it rejects its foreign bases" (113, 204). While by 1931 the Sarló had become overtly leftist, the Míklos Bartha Association would take on a national socialist character by 1932. Poet József Attila, who is known for his connections with the Social Democratic Party, experienced village research in this association and argued that rather than teaching the *nép*, youth must learn from it (204).

Zoltán Kodály, the internationally acclaimed composer and folk music researcher, bemoaning that members of the Hungarian intelligentsia were more likely to visit Paris than a village, encouraged youth in the Scouts and other associations to organize smaller groups and begin village research activities in select villages (205). He recommended that collection should be approached from the perspective of the racial and national question:

that of ethnographic collection (*néptani, néprajzi gyüjtes*) and that of cultural (*művelődési*) and social studies.

Youth also conducted village research under the auspices of István Györffy's Institute of Hungarian Studies (Magyarságtudományi Intézet) and the Young Hungarian Sociographical Workgroup (Fiatal Magyarság Szociográfiai Munkaközösség) founded by *népi* writer Zoltán Szabó, who is known as an antifascist.[35] Still other research groups developed in the Pro Christo Student House, built in 1934 with help from the YMCA for Protestant youth.[36] Members of the sociography group of the Eötvös Kollégium also pursued collective research (Borbándi 1989, 207). By 1938, the government had founded the National Regional and Folk Research Center (Országos Táj es Népkutató Központ).[37] The youth who participated in such activities, mainly students, were primarily of the middle classes, many from rural backgrounds. Their motivations, like those of their sponsors, were diverse, yet they were unified by similar activities and practices and by the belief that familiarity with the cultural practices and dire conditions of the *nép* was important for Hungarian cultivation.

The Boy Scouts emerged in Hungary in the first decade of the twentieth century, with the translation of parts of Baden Powell's *Scouting for Boys* (Vitányi 1964, 29; Gergély 1989, 20), and also provided a home for *népi* activity.[38] The Hungarian Scouts Association took many forms, and its member groups encompassed many tendencies. By the early 1920s, the Hungarian National Defense League (MOVE) had made inroads into the Scouts for the purposes of cultivating nationalist youth. In 1922, Count Pál Teleki would be appointed chief Boy Scout and would press for the importance of the Scouts in building a new national society, like that of the United States or England (Gergély 1989, 53). Vitányi (1964, 29) writes that the interwar Scouts movement generally served reactionary goals: "to raise youth in every layer of society susceptible to serving the goals of the ruling classes."[39] According to Eric Hirsch (1997, 207), the Scouts were comprised mainly of "Christian urban middle class boys." Power struggles were persistent in this decentralized association of groups, around whether the Scouts would take part in military training, over whether there would be any association with the Hitler Youth, and over the participation of Jews (Gergély 1989). Certainly, the Scouts were seen as a technology for cultivating national, or Magyar, youth, even while the meanings of these terms were contested.[40]

The wandering, or caroling, Scouts (*regös cserkészet*) was made up of a number of groups that developed in the early 1930s within the Boy Scouts, mainly among the Protestant members of the KIE/YMCA (Vitányi 1964,

31). Vitányi claims that working-class youth were represented in higher numbers in this group. Taking its name from the word *regölés*, "wandering/caroling," this movement within the Scouts adopted many practices familiar to, and intertwined with, the village research movement. But more so than the college-aged youths embodying the latter, school-aged *regös* Scouts focused on collecting folk songs and dances.[41] Visiting villages and learning material from villagers, they then performed this material for various audiences. They also taught folk songs and dances to villagers "who no longer possessed them" (Vitányi 1964, 30). The tasks of the *regös* Scouts thus included collecting folk practices, learning them, incorporating them into their own lives, and popularizing them among both rural and urban populations (Vitányi 1964, 31; Hirsch 1997, 208). *Regös* Scouts also emphasized collective activities, such as singing together, through which "the experience of recognition and sense of commonality" (Hirsch 1997, 209) was honed. Vitányi (1964, 32) writes that with these Scouts the "daily good deed" of the Boy Scout became a "socialization (*nevelési*) program to know the Hungarian *nép*, Hungarian society, and together with it universal culture and art too. . . . At its center was the question of who is Magyar, what is Magyar."

These goals were embedded in *regös* practices themselves. To earn rank, *regös* Scouts needed to learn fifty required and fifty chosen folk songs, three folk tales, two folk ballads, and five poems for performance in villages; five campfire games; five open-space games; and a *regös* performance piece. In addition, they had to have taken part in five village ethnographic collections. If a youth was from the city, he also had to have spent at least one day participating in the work of a peasant family (Vitányi 1964, 32). The list of guest speakers at *regös* camps includes such *népi* luminaries as Ferenc Erdei, Péter Veres, Imre Somogyi, "father of ethnography" István Györffy, and *népi* pedagogue and publisher of folk songs Sándor Karácsony (29).[42]

By the 1940s, many of these youths had become incorporated into the *népi* movement, and no longer needed the Scouts. Yet it was their experience in the *regös* Scouts that guided many (the young Vitányi included) down the *népi* path. In other words, the *regös* Scouts produced a generation of youths who practiced folk dance and folk songs not simply as staged performance but as a performance meant to cultivate community via singing and dancing together collectively. Vitányi refers to this group as the "folk art movement of the youth," and argues that *regös* Scouts "were the first to create a movement out of folk dance, which then outgrew them" (1964, 33). Most members of the first generation of nonpeasant performing folk dancers before World War II began to dance in the *regös* Scouts, and many dancers and choreographers in later performing folk dance groups came from the *regös* generation (ibid.).[43]

By 1939, Pál Teleki had become prime minister, and *regölés* practices received his "support to mount an aggressive campaign for ethnography related activities" (Hirsch 1997, 208; Gergély 1989, 220).[44] As it was "intended to foster territorial identification . . . after 1940, major excursions were organized into territories recently occupied by the Hungarian military" (Hirsch 1997, 200, 208). Collection activities were by that time overseen by the Museum of Ethnography and the National Regional and Folk Research Center, with the government deciding the "where and when of *regölés* undertakings" (Hirsch 1997, 208). While Vitányi argues that the *regös* Scouts were a kind of counter movement within the Scouts, by the early 1940s, they clearly enjoyed the support of and, presumably also some direction from, the government. By 1941, folk singing had come to dominate over the urban popular songs at Scout campfires (Hirsch 1997, 208).[45]

The most overtly political of *népi* efforts before the Peasant Party was founded in 1939, the March Front resulted from the broad popularity that the work of the *népi* writers had achieved among college students and young intellectuals (Borbándi 1989, 247). According to *népi* writer Imre Kovács, it was an attempt to give a name to the movement emerging from their influence (Borbándi 1989, 247). On March 15, 1936, the anniversary of the eruption of the 1848 revolution in Hungary, a group representing the March Front presented a list of demands authored by *népi* writers on the steps of the National Museum in Budapest. By choosing this date, and this place—the very steps where poet Sándor Petőfi had stood to announce the revolution and call the people to arms—the March Front shrouded itself in symbolic significance. On that day, Kovács read aloud a list of twelve points emphasizing the franchise (*szabadságjogok*), land reform, people's colleges, village seminars (*faluszemináriumok*), the brotherhood of the peoples of the Danube basin, and cooperation among workers, peasants, and intellectuals (Borbándi 248, 250).[46]

That year, both *népi* and communist students planned to use the celebration of the March 15 national holiday to their ends, and the March Front emerged from an alliance between these (not mutually exclusive) groups, bringing progressive youth together to agitate toward democratic ends (Borbándi 1989, 249). Until the spring of 1938, several thousand youths inspired by the March Front organized and participated in literary evenings, lectures, and conferences, especially during months when university classes were in session. While the Front was supported by the National Association of Hungarian University and College Students

(MEFHOSZ), events were attended by peasants in addition to students (257–58). Although the government made efforts to discourage the movement, just as it attempted to suppress the far right, student groups in other college towns connected with the Budapest March youth and the illegal Communist Party continued to meet and organize events. Elements of these groups would continue to be united in the underground antifascist and anti-German resistance movement.[47] Government persecution of the *népi* writers in this period was related to their connections with and obvious influence on the front. While a number of journals openly supported the front's goals, government- and Catholic Church–sponsored publications vigorously attacked them, and one member of parliament countered the claims of the front, saying: "It is not true that three million peasants have no possibilities in life." Horthy himself announced that they had not forgotten how to "clean our home and nation" of "anarchic elements" (254).

The March Front lost its momentum, partly, it seems, because of the dominant *népi* view that it was in the spiritual sphere, not the political sphere, that their activities should take place (Borbándi 1989, 256). Kovács himself claimed that rather than an organized movement or political party, the March Front was a "community of feeling" made up of those who "read the populist writers, ran journals, appeared at lectures and took part in some functions" (257). Facing increasing difficulties getting permits for their activities, and increasing censorship, the movement was faced with the choice of becoming a political party or fading away. In 1939, with Germany now Hungary's next-door neighbor, far-right parties fared well in local elections (321), and a circle of *népi* writers and their agrarian supporters formed the National Peasant Party, which remained, like the Communist Party, illegal until 1945 (326).[48] Not all *népi* writers agreed with forming a party. Some argued that there was no way that a single party could represent the movement, which they claimed was spiritual, not political (325). In 1944, the party joined the Magyar Front, which unified the parties of the resistance (326). This would soon open the way for the party's shift from oppositional status to that of member in the ruling coalition of the interwar period from which one-party Communist rule would emerge (344).

The youths who created and sustained NÉKOSZ (Association of *Népi* Colleges) are called the Bright Winds generation.[49] The first *népi* college (*népi kollégium*) was founded in 1940 with the sponsorship of the Turul Association, a nationalist student association that developed a left strand from 1938 to 1941.[50] This first college, Bolyai Kollégium, provided student housing for secondary and university students of peasant/rural origin; it was a dormitory (Kardos 1977, 25).[51] According to László Kardos (492), when this left strand lost power, the association withdrew its support from Bolyai. After parting with the Turul Association in 1942, the Bolyai Kollégium took the name of István Györffy, who was an inspiration for the project (Borbándi 1989, 315). As with this first *kollégium*, the broader movement was aimed at founding these colleges as residences for students of peasant/rural origin who came to the city to study.

Characterized by peasant romanticism, the movement shared many convictions with the *népi* writers. "Collegers," alongside peasants and working-class youths, participated in protests focused on the agrarian question and democracy. Rather than simply places where students went to sleep at night, the colleges were active sites of socialization and politicization. Among other activities, residents engaged in village research and organized lectures, inviting *népi* writers, and luminaries, from the local environment and from abroad (Kardos 1977, 44).[52] It was not until after the war that the movement reached its full force and NÉKOSZ was founded.

Collegers were key actors in the broader "folk art movement of the youth" and participated in folk dance groups inside and outside the framework of NÉKOSZ. Having learned to folk dance and to sing folk songs in the *regös* Scouts, many continued their activities in this new environment. While also performing at events, each of these groups also functioned as clubs, as spaces of association, for their members. A telling example is the group that formed around Elemér Muharay. While Muharay's NÉKOSZ ensemble only came into being in 1946, Vitányi (1993, 32) begins the history of the "Muharay ensemble" in 1940. In 1939, Muharay was running the Fóti Faluszinpad (Village Theater of Fót), but after it was shut down by the government, he turned his attention to the youth. In 1942, he became director of the Levente's art ensemble (Levente Központi Művészegyüttes). The Levente organizations (1921 through 1944) were tasked with socializing boys ages thirteen to twenty-one according to the counterrevolutionary values of Horthyism while (not so) discreetly preparing them for military service (Kardos 1977, 490; Vitányi 1993, 33). While the Levente initially aimed to recruit boys not attending school, and therefore attracted mainly working-class and peasant youth (Hirsch 1997, 207), attendance become compulsory after 1939.[53] Vitányi (1993, 35) writes that Muharay was willing to take his chances at the Levente, despite his political positions. For various reasons, the ensemble basically disappeared in 1944, but the leftist circle that had formed around Muharay continued to work together in the interest of the resistance (Vitányi 1964, 62). Despite its host organization, this tight circle of folk dancing youths (former Levente ensemble dancers) engaged in debates over the meaning of democracy and the role of folk art in society and acted as a cell in the underground anti-Nazi resistance movement. Muharay's circle included individuals who would become well-known public figures, such as filmmaker Míklos Jancsó, aesthete and cultural manager Iván Vitányi, and painter and pedagogue Pál Jonás. Another of Muharay's students organized the dance group of the Györffy Kollégium (Vitányi 1964, 70). When the NÉKOSZ ensemble was founded in 1946 with Muharay at the helm, it drew the top figures of the folk dance movement (ibid., 70; Vitányi, personal communication).

By 1946, over fifty *népi* colleges were functioning, responsible for "rais[ing] 10,000 democratically minded and self-sufficient residents" (Kardos 1977, 18).[54] While the first colleges in the interwar period were associated with the National Peasant Party, other parties in the governing coalition, as well as right-leaning factions within the party, attempted to steer the movement in other directions (Aczél 1977, 8). After attempting to influence NÉKOSZ from within, some parties founded their own colleges (9). Although students in the movement had played an important role in the opposition to the Germans and the local Arrow Cross Party, and despite the fact that it was a stronghold of local communists, NÉKOSZ and all the colleges were disbanded along with other organizations in 1949, as the Communist Party coercively took control from within the coalition. The decision to put an end to the colleges was justified by the political council of the Hungarian Workers' Party because of NÉKOSZ's association with Lászlo Rajk, an important local communist figure who had just then been arrested, tried, and hanged as a "Trotskyite pest" (Kardos 1977, 456).

The National Peasant Party was formed in 1939 and joined the resistance (the Hungarian Front) during the war. It later entered into the coalition, the Hungarian National Independence Front (1944), with the Communist Party, the Social Democratic Party, the Civic Democratic Party, and the Smallholders Party. While the overwhelming majority of votes in the 1945 elections were for the Smallholder's Party, the Communist Party was able play "a decisive role" through this coalition (Hanák 1991, 214). The Communist Party engaged in a series of purges and delegitimizations, aided by merging the party with the Social Democratic Party in 1948 (216). Despite having received only a small proportion of the votes, the National Peasant Party secured positions as minister of public works (Péter Veres, later József Darvas), the minister of defense (Péter Veres), and the minister of agriculture (Ferenc Erdei) (Borbándi 1989, 445–47). While it too would soon be dissolved along with other parties, and

Fig. 2.4 NÉKOSZ members in May Day procession, May 1, 1947. Photo by Pál Berkó, courtesy of Fortepan.

NÉKOSZ as well, the fact that many populists had been left leaning meant that a number of them continued to occupy positions of influence during the Stalinist era; others suffered various levels of persecution.

CONCLUSION: THE LEGACY OF THE NÉPI MOVEMENT

This chapter has introduced the *népi* movement and contextualized its ethico-aesthetic and political project(s) of *népi-nemzeti művelődés* in the broader context of civic cultivation. I have shown how the interaction of competing and overlapping feudal, ethnic, and civic visions of the people and nation under the very specific historical and geopolitical conditions of interwar Hungary resulted in particular constellations of cultivating projects. I hope to have added a nuanced understanding of these struggles and formations. While I show that leftist positions that attended to the dire conditions of the agrarian working classes were significant, this does not mean that these positions were devoid of prejudice, particularly with regard to Jews. The question of the three million beggars was central to these populists in what was largely an agrarian country. While neither the nation-state form nor ethnonationalism were inevitable, and neither was the Shoah, certain processes allowed for the consolidation of positions that appear to us today as a historical block. To reduce the *népi* movement to Christian National, fascist, or national socialist positions, however, is to ignore important aspects of the struggles over what Hungary would be and who could qualify as a citizen.

I have also hoped to show how the tension between the spiritual and political/material spheres led to *népi* projects being conceptualized and pursued in different manners thus refracting differently in different moments in the making of the Hungarian nation-state. The geopolitical conditions that threatened the long awaited and only briefly gained territorial integrity and political independence of the crown lands of Saint Stephen had strong effects on the way that the nation would be conceived and on the goals and activities of institutions of national culture. The repression of socialists, and especially communists, the denial of citizenship to the majority of the agrarian population in a largely agrarian country and the nationalist rhetoric of the ruling classes combined to encourage the particular populist and nationalist tendencies found in a newly truncated Hungary as national socialism and fascism were on the rise in Europe. The project of *népi-nemzeti* cultivation helped produce a generation of Hungarians with particular attitudes toward the *nép* and its role in the formation of a peculiarly Hungarian cultivation. As will be shown in later chapters, the institutions and practices that emerged from these project(s) of *népi-nemzeti* cultivation had important effects on the so-called *népi* movement, *táncház*, that would develop in the late socialist context.

The interwar *népi* movement did not see folk dance as something that should belong to the peasantry only but rather as something that all members of Hungarian society should enjoy, and from which they could derive cultivation. Vitányi pressed his opinion (in an interview) that this *népi* movement should be seen as progressive rather than conservative: its participants sought to change society for the better rather than to preserve it in unchanged form. However, as we have seen, *népi* thought and action seem to have bled together with Christian National, far right, and leftist initiatives of this period. The interwar *népi* movement left a complex legacy, shaping later practices of folk dance and folk song revival, village visiting, amateur and professional ethnography, and the validation of folk practices as well as ideas about how these practices are related to cultivation. They shaped the use of the terms *nép* and *népi* as well as notions of the purity of the inner sphere and its oppositional value.

Liberal, socialist, and communist urbanists shared ideas and platforms with *népi* actors at times, but it is generally forgotten that they advocated any overlapping projects. Without nuance, it becomes easy to accept the neat populist-urbanist opposition that has reappeared to haunt contemporary Hungarian political rhetoric and everyday speech as a repeat of the interwar period. While the *népi* movement advocated land reform and rights for land-poor and landless peasants and a vision of progress building on Hungary's agrarian character and economy, it is for its peasant romanticism, if not ethnonationalism and antisemitism that it is most often remembered today. The dominance of national thinking and the association of Jews with urbanization and Westernization left the movement vulnerable to essentialism. With the particularities of the oppression of the Christian National regime well forgotten, upstaged by the more recent and acute memories of communist cum state socialist oppression, urbanists and populists appear as the primary opposition.

As the words *peasant* and *villager* may function as glosses for *rural* without differentiating among middle landowner, impoverished nobility, landless peasant, or uprooted urban domestic servant, their use may serve to romanticize an agrarian past without attending to the extreme class differences prevalent in the countryside. The governments of the Horthy regime consistently ignored the plight of the three million beggars, while catering to the enormous bureaucratic military class, the majority of whom were nobility. However, because anxieties about urbanization were often felt as nostalgia for a lost rural society, for which the territorial losses of World War I and the rise of capitalist relations could be blamed, the irredentist rhetoric of the Christian National Horthy regime was powerful and uniting. The term *nemzeti*, national, came to be associated with this rhetoric (Borbándi 1989, 34).

Contemporary views often conflate the *népi* movement with the Christian National position(s) of the Horthy governments to which it was oppositional, due to their shared antiurbanist positions. It is often difficult to ascertain what kinds of peasant origin most *népi* writers and activists and residents of the people's colleges might have had. While Eric Hirsch's assumption that they represented the same interests as the government is problematic, the bulk of *népi* activists and writers appear to have derived from ethnically Magyar and Christian backgrounds. Given the difficulty poor peasants would have had achieving higher education, we can assume that most of the intellectuals did not come from the lowest strata (at least until the *népi* colleges were formed). However, to assert that they represented the same interests as the government obscures the fact that regardless of their own class background, they were concerned with the conditions of agrarian poor oppressed by the government and advocated citizenship rights on their behalf.

While the distinction between *népi* and *népies* has fallen by the wayside, the *népi-urbánus* distinction is alive and well, having been revived in the 1980s. Because populists worked to reveal the desperate conditions of the agrarian classes, nostalgia for peasant traditions was in many cases tempered by an understanding of the role neofeudal relations had on peasant misery. As we will see, the late Socialist and contemporary understanding of *népi* have tended to be divorced from the social politics of land reform and is indeed often ethnicized and romanticized. Hungarian populists across time have often derived legitimacy from being outside politics, despite the fact that the National Peasant Party developed from their ranks in 1939 and was even a member of the coalition understood to have facilitated the Communist rise to power. Thus, while the populist writers and the movement inspired by them embodied a spectrum of political stances their legacy is mainly remembered through the contemporary content of the *népi-urbánus* opposition. The range of positions encompassed in the *népi* movement is occluded by this distinction.

Ferenc Fejtő (2001, 7), an *urbánus* writer of the period, writes, "The point was that the populists wanted to stick to their strategy of agrarian reform through thick and thin, while we Westernizers were convinced that what Hungary first needed was democracy, and that the land issue could only be solved when the Hungarian people were mature enough for democracy. We laid emphasis on liberties, democracy and the fullness of human rights. But ideological differences meant little to the Populists; what counted were successful tactics." For Fejtő, it was this indifference to ideology that allowed some populist writers to find their way into the National Socialist Arrow Cross Party while others collaborated with the Communists. Borbándi (1989, 179), too, writes: "Indeed ideology is missing, but the writers did not produce ideologies. Rather, they projected the (*vetették fel*) burning social questions, throwing them into the public consciousness in a really pragmatic mode."

After the war, not only were *népi* practices diffused throughout much of society, but *népi* efforts were also institutionalized in NÉKOSZ, the Peasant Party, and the Institute of Népi Cultivation (Népi Művelődési Intézet). Challenging the commonly held view that the populist writers were oppressed by the Communists, István Deák (1999, 56) argues that they were actually favored by the party leadership. It was precisely because they were not Jews, he claims, that they were seen as "likely to serve as a bridge between the Party leadership and the people" (ibid.). While formal populist institutions were dispersed in 1948, populist influence lived on. We find it in the persistence of certain institutional forms, practices, techniques, and ideological content (or the lack thereof), as well as in the *népi-urbánus* opposition.

Notes

1. This term, *aesthetic enlightenment*, used by Freidrich Schiller in his book *On the Aesthetic Enlightenment of Man*, nicely sums up "the relation of the turn to the aesthetic and problems of absolutist power" (Eagleton 1990, 5). White (1990, 75) uses the terms *aesthetic education* and *cultural enlightenment* when referring to Soviet-influenced projects, presumably after Russian-language Soviet usages.

2. *Acculturate* could also go on this list but differs in the sense that it assumes the existence of discreet cultures.

3. This combination is often grouped in later endeavors at "adult education" as well.

4. *Felvidék* (uplands, upcountry or "upper Hungary") is a term used to refer to a region of historic Hungary, most of which lies in present-day Slovakia.

5. White (1990, 6) translates the terms *nevelés* and *művelődés* as "cultural enlightenment," as she does the Russian *vospitanie* and Polish *wychowanie*. She translates *népművelés* as "cultural work for and among the people," paralleling it with the Russian *kul'turnomassovaia rabota* (26). Following its Hungarian etymology, I translate *művelődés* as "cultivation."

6. Braham (1981, 28) points out that "while the total number of Jews declined to about half its pre-war size," their percentage remained about the same in the total population. With the nation now resembling a much more "homogenous and ethnically integrated state," he notes, "the Jews lost their importance as statistical recruits to the cause of Magyardom" and became scapegoats.

7. Act 25 of 1920 did not introduce any legal definition of Jewishness (unlike the second anti-Jewish law, Act 4 of 1939), leaving it to local academic authorities to apply these restrictions to "converts" or not. While legally Jews were defined by religious belonging only, cases are known in which the numerus clausus law was applied to people baptized in Christian churches because of their Jewish origins (Karády and Nagy 2012, 14).

8. *Egyke* is the diminutive of the word *one (egy)*.

9. Jews made up 20.3 percent of Budapest's population in 1910. Up until 1918, Budapest Jews made up more than a quarter of Hungarian Jewry, and after Trianon they would make up half of it. Even conservative estimates show that Budapest Jews were represented in the bourgeoisie at much higher rates than gentiles and members of the provincial Jewry (Karády 2008).

10. Journalist György Oláh published the book *Hárommíllio Koldus* in 1928. The term was adopted in public debate and literature to refer to the poorest strata of peasant society (Borbándi 1989, 58; Vitányi, personal communication, 2004). In 1935, 30 percent of agricultural land consisted of large estates of more than 1,000 cadastral yokes (575 hectares), and 48 percent was held in other estates larger than 100 cadastral yokes (57.5 hectares). More than 45 percent of the peasant population belonged to the agrarian proletariat, and "if we include owners of less than 5 cadastral yokes (2.88 hectares) of land" in that category, 70 percent of peasant population "lived entirely or largely from wage labor." Only 30 percent of the entire peasant population could make a living from their land without undertaking wage labor. This structure of land distribution remained unchanged until 1945 (Varga 2009, 24n3).

11. I follow Jewish Voice for Peace (2017) in my spelling of antisemitism.

12. Vitányi, personal communication, 2004. For more on the agrarian movements and parties in the region in the first half of the twentieth century, see Eellend (2008).

13. Endre Bajcsy-Zsilinsky founded the National Radical Party to address land reform, which bourgeois radicals believed would both boost industrialization and help the peasantry. While critiquing the antisemitism of the far right, it pressed for monopoly capitalism reform with the intention of redistributing privilege from the hands of Jews into those of Christians. The party eventually merged with the Smallholders (Borbándi 1989, 58).

14. The far right was embodied, for example, in the Nemzeti Front (National Front), the Hungarista Párt, and the Nyilaskeresztes Párt (Arrow Cross party).

15. The party had garnered over 20 percent of votes in the 1939 elections and had thirty seats in parliament. When the Germans occupied Hungary, they installed the Arrow Cross as the governing party.

16. Gömbös was a founder of MOVE and was a key actor in the army that facilitated Horthy's rise to the regency, including the white terror. He founded the Hungarian National (racial protection) Party and became one of the primary leaders of the opposition to prime minister István Bethlen. By 1928, he had returned to Bethlen's Party of National Unity and was appointed major general and minister of defense by Horthy in 1929. In 1932, Horthy appointed him prime minister and Gömbös publicly recanted his previous antipathy to Jews and promised not to enact any racially motivated laws or cause economic harm to the Jews through his general policies. While Gömbös appeared more or less to honor this promise, he catered to antisemitic demands (Klein 1982). He identified as a fascist and was particularly interested in Mussolini's model, but he also pursued close relationships with Hitler's Germany.

17. Consider the contrast with the first decade of the century, when the Agrarian Socialist Union (connected to the Social Democratic Party) boasted nearly seven hundred branches with more than seventy thousand members between 1905 and 1908 (Romsics 2015, 175).

18. Recent publications flesh this space out (Bimbó 2013 and Bartha 2013).

19. The historical record that I was able to access told a nearly exclusively male story. There were certainly women involved in many of the activities covered in this chapter, but I am not able to speak to them in any meaningful way.

20. Use of the word *peasant* makes it difficult to know which strata they came from; certainly many were born in the rural provinces. Gyula Illyés accounts his experience as a child of (not the worst off) farm servants in his 1933 book *Pusztulás*. Given the class relations of the time, it might be reasonable to assume that many *népi* activists came from the layer of the lower and sometimes impoverished gentry who were, indeed, peasants yet who also enjoyed certain privileges of citizenship and status.

21. József Erdély was explicitly antisemitic, published in far-right newspapers, and was active in the Arrow Cross. The very popular Lászlo Németh made many statements that are easily read as antisemitic. Ferenc Erdei, cofounder of the Peasant Party along with Németh and others, is generally not spoken of as antisemitic. See, however, Csaba Tibor Tóth's (2012) discussion of how Erdei's sociological work relies on what can be seen as antisemitic tropes. Zoltán Szabo was known as an antifascist and publicly opposed the anti-Jewish laws when many other public intellectuals did not (Noszkai 2009). In this period, Jewish writers struggled with defining a Jewish Hungarian literature, some espousing essentializing attitudes toward converted Jews and their offspring (Réthelyi 2018). See Kann (1945) for a nuanced vision on the "nationality problem" that structured the "Jewish question." Kann argues that Jászi's (1929) work on the former issue is brilliant yet critiques his position on the Hungarian Jews. Jászi took this position (which fits into tropes considered antisemitic) as a person whose parents changed the family name from Jacobuvits and converted to Calvinism when he was a young child.

22. Swabian is sometimes used as a blanket term to indicate German speakers but specifically means those who immigrated to Hungary in the eighteenth century, often in connection to the demographic repopulation and Catholicization projects of the Habsburgs, led by economists and statisticians. The urban bourgeoisie tended to be German speaking (Kürti 2002).

23. Vitányi told me he was a rare *népi* student in *urbánus* (and Marxist) philosopher György Lukács's circle. Attila József and Gyula Illyés both frequented the liberal salon of Karl, Laura, and Mihály Polányi's mother, Cecila Pollacsek. This was early on, however, and does not necessarily reflect ongoing association across this boundary as it solidified.

24. While one cannot help but see parallels with the Russian *narodnyik* movement, the Bulgarian agrarian populist movement and others in the region, and the German revolutionary nationalists, their own accounts appear to play down this influence, aligning themselves with Scandinavian movements instead (see, for example, Borbándi 1989, 194).

25. Féja was an organizer of the March Front and a NÉKOSZ activist.

26. Renwick (2006) examines practices of "ethical civil society" engaged in by the opposition during the socialist period. He considers its conception as a practical or absolute stance in relation to the development of "political society" in the postsocialist period.

27. The National Peasant Party will be discussed later.

28. In conversations with me, some Hungarian ethnographers and *táncház* participants expressed a distinction between *zsidózás* (calling someone a Jew or complaining about Jews), a verbal act, and *antiszemitizmus*, which they identified as actual discrimination.

29. There are differences between the terms *népi-nemzeti művelődés, nép-nemzeti művelődés*, and *népi művelődés* but I have not been able to tell if the different terms were used interchangeably by some, or, on the other hand, consistently by discreet groups. In an interview Vitanyi told me the Social Democrats used *nép-nemzeti*, but populists seem to have preferred *népi-nemzeti*. *Népi* can mean of the people of folk, but *nép* used, for example, as in the name of the polity during the socialist period, the Hungarian People's Republic (Magyar Népköztársaság) has an explicit socialist or communist character. The Social Democratic usage is likely tied with this usage and might be spelled with no hyphen. Today it is more likely to hear people say *népi művelődés*. I try to be faithful to the variants I know people used, but generally I address them as part of the *népi-nemzeti művelődés* family.

30. In the 1950s, ethnographer Gyula Ortutay, minister of education and religion, "redefined" *nép*, which had both the German meaning of *Volk* and the French meaning of "people," asking "anthropologists to restrict its usage to the working people"(Sárkány 2005, 89). While this may have "extend[ed] the scope of anthropology to include the working class" (ibid.), it did little to diminish the salience of the other meanings. Indeed, other trends continued to "give succour to those who were determined to explain cultural differences in terms of ethnic differences" (90). The leftist tradition of referring to the working class as the *nép* in the region dates to long before the 1950s.

31. Györffy was the first to teach ethnography at the university level in 1926 (in the Faculty of Geography, thanks to his friend Pál Teleki) and would head the first Department of Ethnography at Pázmány University in 1934 (Györffy 2000). He was a pioneer and supporter of the village research and *Népi Kollégium* movements. His name does not usually come up when naming *népi* writers, yet he represents the kind of figure who might be associated with the *népi* position while also somewhat aligned with Christian National positions. His take on *népi-nemzeti művelődés*, as well as the very purpose of the pamphlet itself, indicating his willingness to provide advice to the government, shows the blurriness of the *népi* category. One might regard Györffy's pamphlet as evidence of the existence of the New Spiritual Front and as a potential suturing of positions into a hegemonic bloc of sorts. See Taylor (2008) for an earlier attempt at placing Györffy's role.

32. While it is true that most people in the lower stratum of society were agricultural workers (although many were working as servants and construction workers in the cities by this time), it is rare that we find the word *nép* or *népi* referring to the urban working classes and much rarer to "Gypsies." On the other hand, the *népek* of the Carpathan basin would usually mean the "peoples," as in nations or proto nations, rather than "the working classes" of this region. This is because *nép* retains a meaning of "people" as in "the nation" in an ethnic sense. Ethnic minorities in Hungary were not usually called *népek* (peoples) but rather *nemzetiségek* (nationalities, used the way ethnicity would be used by many). In the early twentieth century, *népfáj* (race) was also in use. While I found that in common parlance *nép* was always used to speak of the folk (with ethnic meaning built in), the socialists and communists adopted *nép* as "the people," those oppressed by the class structure (perhaps capitalizing on its resonance). The newspaper of the Social Democratic party—founded in the 1870s—for example, was called *Népszava* (Voice of the people).

33. Vitányi pointed out to me that it was the Social Democratic Party of Hungary (Magyarországi) rather than the National Social Democratic Party (Nemzet).

34. Illyés had volunteered in the Red Army of the 1919 Hungarian Soviet Republic and afterward emigrated to Paris, where he befriended a number of surrealist writers. He returned to Hungary in 1926 after an amnesty. In 1934, he visited the Soviet Union for two months, financed by the Soviet Union (Pastor 2018). The term *Wandervogel* covered an array of romantic youth-oriented activities and groups that focused on hiking, camping, and independence from the late nineteenth century onward. While the organizations were banned under Hitler, some of their techniques were incorporated into the Hitler Youth and most consider the Wandervogel its precursor.

35. Zoltán Szabo was not of peasant descent and showed no inclination toward the right or antisemitism. He insisted on democratic freedoms under the Horthy regime and the Communists afterwards.

36. According to Bimbó (2013), Bartha Miklós actually functioned from here.

37. Count Pál Teleki founded the National Regional and Folk Research Center in 1938 (Borbándi 1989, 238), putting it under the direction of his good friend Györffy, under whom the center produced an exhibition on landownership showing the absolute need for land reform. Teleki had the exhibit closed down as a political embarrassment for the government (238). Prime minister from 1920 to 1922 and again from 1939 to 1941, Teleki taught political geography at the Economics University (207). Having adopted some of the ideas of racial hygiene and Turanism, he devised an "ethnographic map" to refute the borders of truncated Hungary (Ablonczy 2006; Jobbitt 2011).

38. While Baden Powell is associated most strongly with the Boy Scouts he founded in Britain, it is quite telling that he based the organization on the paramilitary boy's group that he created in Southern Africa while a British officer during the Boer War (Tyle 2003).

39. For a general history of the Scouting movement in Hungary, see Gergély (1989).

40. See Gergély (1989) for a detailed account of these currents and struggles in the Hungarian Scouts movement(s).

41. Hirsch (1997) uses the word *ethnography* to represent what he calls the "*regölés* program" within the Scouts. Because it has no etymological connection to the Hungarian word *ethnography* but is derived from the word for a folk practice akin to caroling, I choose to use the terms caroling or wandering.

42. Lawyer, agrarian economist, and *népi* sociographer Ferenc Erdei was a leader of the March Front and later a Peasant Party politician and NÉKOSZ activist (Kardos 1977, 494). *Népi* writer Péter Veres was a Peasant Party politician. Sculptor, agrarian expert, and pedagogue, Imre Somogyi had an important role in organizing of the Györffy Kollégium and was later a Peasant Party politician, serving on the National Council (504). Sándor Karácsony was active in the NÉKOSZ movement (499).

43. These include Elemér Muharay, István Molnár, Miklos Rábai, Iván Vitányi, Sándor Timár, György Martin, and the Pesovár brothers (Vitányi 1964, 33; Timár, personal communication).

44. Geographer Teleki, who was responsible for ethnography being taught in the university, was prime minister in 1921 and again from 1939 to 1941. He was a consistent sponsor of the Scouts.

45. Scouts organizations were banned under state socialism, and while some central figures in the Scouts ended up doing similar work in the Pioneer organizations, Hungarian Scout groups in exile became an important site for folk dance and the reproduction of Hungarian national identity in the émigré community in the United States.

46. Imre Kovács, one of the younger writers, author of *The Silent Revolution*, began his village research career at the Village Research Workgroup of the Pro Christo Student House. He was later a Peasant Party politician and editor of its journal, *Szabad Szó* (Free word), to which many *népi* writers contributed.

47. Terminology is a problem here as the term *antifascist* is often used in the Hungarian context to describe both/either anti-German and anti–national socialist positions and

groupings. Being anti-German, however, did not necessarily mean one was not antisemitic or against positions more generally associated with fascism today.

48. Imre Kovács, Pál Szabó, Ferenc Erdei, Ferenc Farkás, and Péter Veres (Borbándi 1989, 323–26).

49. Referencing a folk tune to which words were set and was sung by népi college activists, *Fényes Szelek* (Bright winds; titled in English *The Confrontation*) is the title of a film by internationally acclaimed filmmaker and one-time NÉKOSZ activist Míklós Jancsó. The film critiques authoritarian practices of the Communist Party on its rise to power via the story of NÉKOSZ activists, depicting NEKOSZ's struggle to defend its version of leftism in the face of a Soviet-imposed regime. The use of folk dance as a protest technique is central to the choreography in the film. On Jancsó's relationship with Muharay, see Bacsó.

50. The *Turul*, a bird of prey, is an oft-used symbol in Hungarian nation-making projects.

51. *Kollégium* is the commonly used word for dormitory in Hungarian, but it can also mean a group or institution. Here I translate *kollégium* as college and the activists as collegers.

52. Such institutions may be important sites of citizen making. Dipesh Chakrabarty (2000) and Partha Chatterjee (1993) have pointed to similar "dormitories" and formations within them as important sites of socialization.

53. Kürti (2002, 84, 84n) notes the proliferation of political youth organizations in Hungary from 1945 to 1949.

54. The term László Kardos uses is *nevel*, or raise, as in raising or socializing a child. In 1947 alone, the one hundred colleges hosted six thousand students (Kardos 1977, 451).

Chapter Three

Socialist Cultural Management, Civic Cultivation, and Associational Life in Late Socialism

IN HER BOOK ON URBAN change in postsocialist Budapest, Judit Bodnár (2001, 92) writes: "Every epoch has its own type of building that indicates the symbolic and financial preferences of their age. The preindustrial epoch found its form of expression in the temple, the church, the palace, the agora, or the city hall; hotels and restaurants are the incarnations of symbolic power today."[1] Expanding on this list, she notes: "*the characteristic contribution of state socialism came in the form of party headquarters, prefab housing estates and 'houses of culture'*" (ibid., emphasis added).[2] In this penetrating study of the transformations in relations between public and private, Bodnár finds houses of culture important enough to mention as symbols of power. Focusing on the postsocialist period, however, she does not analyze their significance as public places, as she does with what she sees as their postsocialist correlate, the shopping mall. Houses of culture were indeed widespread in the state socialist countries of Eastern Europe and in Hungary as well, where many continue to function with the combination of state-mandated municipal/local funding and other resources.[3] Numbers alone attest to their significance (the Council of Europe listed 3,661 in Hungary in 2004) yet scant attention has been turned to their role in cultural life and their relationships to specific activities. This chapter examines houses of culture not as *symbols* of power but as significant sites of associational activity— *táncház* among them—in the everyday lives of Hungarians in the socialist period.

Houses of culture were the products of a communist "reimagining of sociability" (Siegelbaum 1999, 78). Despite the popular vision of state socialism as a totalitarian system, far from all of the activities taking place inside Hungarian houses of culture were designed by the centralized bureaucracy or party. Given the position of houses of culture as sites of cultural events and activities, an assessment of them and how they functioned is perhaps crucial to understanding the politics of cultivation in all Eastern European countries (and parts of the Soviet Union) during the socialist period. By examining the network of culture houses and a series of related institutions that can be called the Institute for Culture, this chapter gives insight into the world of cultural management and its dynamic relationship to associational life in socialist Hungary, providing crucial background for understanding the emergence and development of *táncház*.[4] Examining the interaction of houses of culture with forms of association gets us closer to questions of intersubjectivity, a key element in how *táncház* does its work. Considering the voluntary activities characteristic of socialist Hungary, the ideologies informing them, the spaces designed to promote them, and the people who embodied them will help us see how *táncház* emerged. As Margaret Kohn (2003, 156) writes in her book about Houses of the People in Italy, "physical spaces mark off a context in which certain attributes are intensified and others are diminished." Among these attributes is the experience of association.

I begin with a brief overview of the historical precursors to the socialist-era houses of culture, including the workers' homes of the labor movement, the folk high schools founded by church organizations, and the people's colleges designed as dormitories for rural university students. I orient the houses of culture within a tradition of related activities and associational spaces and institutions within local and European practices of civic cultivation, dispelling the idea that there was no continuity between the presocialist and socialist periods. I then describe the development of the socialist system of culture houses and the Institute for Culture, examining their roles, the contexts in which they functioned, and their changing relationships with the state and market across the socialist period. I touch on the privileged place of amateur art in Hungarian ideas about voluntarism, which had important effects on policy and the development of certain kinds of associational activities, before exploring the relationship of the houses of culture to various cultural initiatives, focusing on the baby boom youth culture of the 1960s and 1970s. I elucidate the role of socialist cultural management in creating and structuring spaces for association that gave rise in often unexpected ways to cultural activities, including *táncház*, which in turn, affected this management.

INSTITUTIONS OF CIVIC CULTIVATION AND
HOUSES OF CULTURE BEFORE 1948

Emerging from the struggles over citizenship in the nineteenth-century civil sphere, houses of culture appeared in myriad forms. The last decades of the century, Hungary's Golden Age, was a time of rapid industrialization and urban growth. With urban living quarters appallingly cramped, social life took place in an array of public places, such as casinos, coffeehouses, pubs, and inns, and was organized roughly along class lines. Houses of culture appeared in this broader context of associative life in the city and were influenced by observations Hungarian reformers had made during their travels to Western Europe, where struggles over citizenship and the education, or cultivation, of the people had resulted in the proliferation of adult education and university extension programs, public museums and libraries, and Houses of the People.[5]

Tied closely to the labor movement and Social Democratic Party, Hungary's first workers' homes (*munkásotthonok*) were founded in 1907. In addition to serving as union headquarters, workers' homes housed libraries and hosted continuing education courses, "art-loving activities," social dances, and other activities (Kovalcsik 2003, 507–14).[6] Soon after, resulting from "the compromise between the reform goals of the Social Democrats and capital," factory management also began to support the establishment of workers' homes (510). By 1911, a workers' home cooperative (*szövetkezet*) was established, which defined the legal status of these institutions and ensured the social and material bases for their perpetuation (ibid.). Soon thereafter, in the context of "the struggle over the free time of workers" (531), other political parties, religious organizations, and the government itself founded similar institutions. In 1908, the Ministry of Religion and Public Education (Vallás and Közoktatásügyi) offered support for the initiation of houses of public education/cultivation (*közművelődési házak*) in a number of cities across Hungary to "elevate the individual into a higher polity" and "initiate their participation in the nation" (*nemzeti gondolkodás részeseive avatják*) (551).

Beyond the sprinkling of workers' homes, reading circles and clubs were becoming common (Kovalcsik 2003, 366). Surveys conducted in 1921 and 1937 indicate that there were reading or farmers' clubs in half of the existing communities, although not distributed evenly across the country (White 1990, 58). While it is difficult to assert how many houses of culture existed in dualist-era Hungary, it is quite clear that they were becoming a significant feature of struggles over civic cultivation and associative life in the first decades of the twentieth century.

In the early years of the Horthy regime, minister of culture Kuno Klebelsberg (a count from Transylvania) oversaw educational reforms toward the goal of counterrevolutionary socialization, including the expansion of houses of culture (Kovalcsik 2003, 462, 556). In the Klebelsberg era, schoolchildren began the day with irredentist slogans, such as "No, No, Never!"(Kürti 2002, 70). Most *művelődés* experts I interviewed pointed to Klebelsberg when I asked about the origins of the Hungarian houses of culture, presumably because Klebelsberg's ministry was the first to implement an extensive government project to proliferate houses of culture. Establishing such institutions was championed equally by state *népművelés* and the political opposition, although each had different goals (Kovalcsik 2003, 557).

Demonstrating the spectrum of interests behind the construction of houses of culture in the 1920s, Kürti (2002, 74) writes:

> For radical workers, the Worker's Home—originally built in 1920, although for some time even earlier workers and union organizers had been actively engaged in building a cultural centre—was a site of political and cultural activities. It was an important centre of grassroots activity organized and conducted by the workers themselves.... Exhibits, workers' choir and brass bands, nature rambles, readers' and writers' clubs, theaters, youth clubs and anti-alcohol campaigns counted among its many activities, while other, more political efforts included organizing strikes and enabling the local cell of the illegal Communist Party to operate within its confines.

He compares the workers' home with the cultural center in the same town: "Whereas the Worker's Home was a cultural and political institution uniting progressive youth of the left, the Cultural Centre was created to unite Christian, fascist and conservative groups of the right, signaling the division of youth along political lines. And there were signs on the horizon that neofascist and extreme right religious circles were slowly gaining the upper hand" (ibid.).

The clandestine Association of the Etelköz (Etelközi Szövetség) took over the lodges of the outlawed Freemasons, along with the legal Hungarian National Defense League (MOVE) that Prime Minister Gömbös would later boast had been the "first fascist organization in Europe" (Mócsy 1983, 162). Individuals connected to MOVE, "the principal political organization of military officers, which was originally brought to life to aid the refugee officers," also organized secretarial schools for wives and daughters of the intelligentsia (181).

Népfőiskolák—folk high schools—were established in the 1930s. Inspired by the Danish folk school movement, English and Swiss settlement movements, and German ideas about the *Volk*, their founders wished to provide education to the agrarian population that still lacked practical access to education (Kovalcsik 2003, 558).[7] In a country with a Catholic majority, it was Calvinists who initiated the folk high school movement and founded the majority of the schools in church buildings (Tóth 1983 220). Because the Catholic Church, among the largest landholders in Hungary, benefited from the status quo, and therefore tended to support it, Calvinists tended to be more closely associated with popular radicalism (ibid.).[8] In his study of the folk school movement, János Tóth (221) writes: "Contemporary cultural policy, pursuing the educational ideals of conservative Christian nationalism, lay great emphasis on making its influence felt in the most populous section, i.e. the village population. The most serious challenge and thus potential alternative to the monopoly of this nation-centred conservative ideology was due to the fact that the progressive popular trend of their age treated national problems most radically as social issues." He admits, however, that a spectrum of ideologies could be found among their management. While the need for land reform was a shared sentiment, only the more radical schools taught modern agricultural methods and exposed students to banned texts (ibid.). The schools formed a coalition that sought government financial support, yet demanded a "full degree of internal freedom" (223). The government was able to secure a supervisory role, however, by making curriculum approval a requirement for licensing of such schools (ibid.).

Dissolving Bourgeois and Feudal Institutions, Building Socialist Culture: The Institute for People's Culture

The brief period after World War II known as the Coalition period, lasting from 1945 until 1948, witnessed a robust associative life focused on civic cultivation and extracurricular education. Associational life was in full swing, with new organizations springing up out of the ruins and losses of the war and hopes for the future. Political parties founded cultural centers (*kulturközpontok*) (Vitányi 1993), and the Association of People's Colleges (NÉKOSZ), which came to manage 160 colleges and socialize ten thousand students, was founded in this period (Aczél 1977, 8; Kardos 1977, 26; Borbándi 1989, 316). As the coalition gave way to Communist Party control, by 1949 most of these cultural institutions had been dissolved by the administration of the Communist Party state.

At this time, in the words of Iván Vitányi (in Striker 1989a), "The term 'people's education' was introduced with all its paternalistic overtones, and the wide spectrum of self-educational programmes which flourished during the brief post-war coalition period was for the most part dissolved and 'limited to the amateur artistic movement and the dissemination of knowledge.'"[9] Sports clubs and folk dance troupes were among the institutions that were not dissolved but placed under the authority of the unions.

Perhaps they were not considered ideological, or perhaps, due to their popularity, they were seen as apt tools for recruitment. The state socialist administration made every effort to consolidate rule by dissolving previously existing bourgeois or feudal institutions and replacing them with socialist venues for adult education. Among the new institutions was the Institute of Folk Art, later called the Institute for Peoples' Culture.

Népi writers Gyula Illyés and László Németh had founded the Institute of Népi Cultivation (Népi Művelődési Intézet) in 1946 with the support of the Council for Free Cultivation (adult education) (Szabadművelődési Tanács).[10] While it was dismantled in 1948 along with most other cultural institutions (Vitányi 1993, 22), "the same institution," supposedly modeled after the Soviet House of Folk Artists (Népi Alkotások Háza), was reopened in 1951 as the Institute of Folk Art (Népművészeti Intézet), under the authority of the newly formed Ministry of People's Culture/Education (Népművelési Minisztérium) (K. Polgár 1994, 7).[11] According to Katalin Polgár, the task of the institute was to provide existing groups of artists a new institutional home, given that they had been formed "within the counter-revolutionary institutions/conditions of the earlier period" (ibid.). Although these groups subsequently found shelter in the trade unions, the need for new institutions remained (ibid.).

The role of the institute would change significantly over the years, but the tasks set out in the founding decree were decisive:

1. To aid in shaping the artistic direction of the movement spreading in the unions, mass institutions, and culture houses.
2. To sponsor activities of cultural production in the unions and mass institutions and publication of a trade journal of the mass movement.
3. To recruit cultural groups into the work of ethnographic collection and making material available to institutions of the ethnographic discipline while also ensuring that reworked material is returned to the cultural mass movement in appropriate form.
4. To catalyze the production of new folk songs and mass dances.
5. To seek and support new artistic talents from among the working people and to further the training of leaders of the cultural mass movement.
6. To aid the participation of official artists in the work of the cultural mass movement. (K. Polgár 1994, 13)

The institute housed the Hungarian State Folk Ensemble (Magyar Állami Népi Együttes) brought into being at this time, supposedly on the model of the Soviet Moisejev Ensemble.[12] Experts working at the institute were to serve the ensemble by gathering ethnographic material from which it could draw for its choreographies, and to serve the folk dance

Fig. 3.1 The Budai Vigadó (Buda Concert Hall built in 1899) in 2018, after renovations. Home of Magyar Népi Művelődési Intézet and its many descendants and, currently, Heritage House. Photo by the author, 2019.

movement in general, which included several hundred amateur folk dance groups "modeled on the highly successful Soviet folk ensembles" (Halmos 2000, 35–36).[13]

By the time of Stalin's death in 1953, orders had come from the party for a more focused fight against counterrevolutionary ideology, help with institutions of *népművelés*, a deepening of the institution's connection with the masses, further training of workers, and help with legitimizing the economy (K. Polgár 1994, 23). In light of these developments, K. Polgár suggests, the emphasis on folk art (*népművészet*) gave way to an emphasis on *népművelés*—people's education/cultivation, which now became the institute's main goal (ibid.). Indeed, by 1955, the role of the institute had expanded to include working with village libraries, building houses of culture, and organizing competitions, yet according to Erika Gyarmati (1993, 12), its main occupation remained folk art.[14] In Hajnalka Polgár's (1994, 10) view, because the groups the institute dealt with were given no voice in its work, employees of the institute were able to develop it along a *népi-nemzeti* path.

Insight into the institute's continued *népi-nemzeti* orientation is significant, as toward the end of the coalition years and during the first few years of Communist rule, noncommunists and many local leftists, including a number of left populists, were purged from positions of influence and replaced by urbanite, or so-called foreign, communists considered to be loyal to the Soviets and to espouse Soviet and urban models of socialist progress rather than locally salient models of communism, socialism, or left populism.[15] The institute remained a populist stronghold. Confused by why the Communists would have supported this populist effort, I inquired about this in interviews. A number of people claimed that populists, other noncommunist leftists, and even communists had been tucked away in marginal cultural jobs such as those at the institute. How marginal the institute was, however, depends on how we view it.

During the 1956 revolution, the revolutionary council formed at the institute released a statement on the party's handling of culture and art, suggesting that research, not party dictates, was required for the creation of a public culture that could be grasped by the people (K. Polgár 1994, 33–35). The council argued that the distinction between artist and cultivator/educator of the people (*népművelő*) needed to be dissolved (ibid.). The institute's director from 1950 to 1956, Jenő Széll, was a significant player in revolutionary minister Imre Nagy's cabinet, and held a directing position at the revolutionary Free Kossuth Radio. In the months and years following the revolution, purges were made within the institute. Some who were purged, including Széll, were sent to prison and replaced with new management (K. Polgár 1994, 42–43; Gyarmati 1994, 16).[16]

In 1957, now under the authority of the new Ministry of Cultural Affairs (Művelődésügyi Minisztérium),[17] the institute's name was changed to the Institute for People's Culture (Népművelési Intézet), and its departments rearranged to meet the requirements of new directives (Gyarmati 1994, 16). Emphasis on folk art was gradually cut back as more attention was directed toward extracurricular *népművelés* and the organization of festivals and anniversaries (18–19). Two major sections were named: the Arts Section included the Theater, Fine Arts, Folk Decorative Arts, Dance, and Music Departments, while the Scientific Section included the Departments of *Népműveléstudomány* (science of people's cultivation), Ethnography, and Methodology (ibid.). By 1958, sponsorship was being further directed away from the Arts Section and into training for nursery school teachers and other teachers. The *Népműveléstudomány* and Methodology Departments were combined to become the Department of Theory and Methodology, while a separate Department of Education was formed, responsible for, among other things, further training of culture house workers. An Occupational Circle (*Szakkör*) Department was also formed to deal with "circles and voluntary movements" (24).

By 1959, all but the Dance and Music Departments had been placed under the Department of Theory and Methodology, and in this period, many people working on folk art were dismissed from their positions.[18] According to György Martin (1981, 42), an employee at the time, "the only department that remained untouched" by the transformations, and the only organization giving direction to the folk art movement in the tradition of the Népművészeti Intézet was the Dance Department. In 1964, this department was also dissolved, forcing the institute's folk art achievements even further into the background. At this time, ethnographic collections and collecting work were transferred to the Hungarian Academy of Sciences (44). Béla Halmos put it this way in an interview: "After the 1956 revolution Széll was imprisoned and they dissolved the group (the folk department, *néposztály*) ... it was then that Kodály invited Martin to do dance research." This move marked the formation of the Folk Dance Research Group (Néptánckutatási Osztály) at the Academy of Sciences, headed by Zoltán Kodály, and an associated shift from a cultivation-focused setting to one emphasizing research (Martin 1981, 43).[19] Before we visit further transformations at the institute, it will be useful to get a picture of the system of culture houses.

CULTURE HOUSES: AMATEUR ART AND LEISURE
TIME ACTIVITIES IN SOCIALIST HUNGARY

From 1948 on, houses of culture were considered important tools for building socialism, although it was not until the 1970s that the subsidized construction of culture houses led to their broad proliferation across the country (Kúti, Marschall, and Nyilas 1986, 182). Until the early 1980s, "the network of culture houses and cultural centers provided cheap or even free cultural services for the general public in Hungary" (Striker 1989a, 6). Functioning on meager budgets, they offered courses and hosted art clubs, film screenings, theater performances, exhibitions, discos, and more. Under the logic of state socialism, houses of culture were not expected to make a profit. Classified as "surplus interested" by the Ministry of Finance, they needed only to submit a yearly report stating the amount of subsidy remaining after their expenses for any fiscal year (ibid.). As we might expect in an economy of shortage, houses of culture spent all the money they received in order to avoid cuts to their budgets in subsequent years.[20]

In her study of houses of culture in the USSR, Poland, and Hungary, Anne White (1990, 102) states: "In the party apparatus, cultural enlightenment, as a component of ideological work, falls within the remit of propaganda or agitprop departments, and, it would seem, to some extent also of culture departments, where these exist." Yet she also observes that party involvement in cultural affairs was often minimal, due in part to the "over-involvement" of party committees "in economic matters at the expense of ideological work" (103). In fact, there appears to have been a "curious lack of coordination between Party and state administrations" (104). The complexity of Hungarian culture house governance appears to have precluded tight coordination. From the start, different houses of culture came varyingly under the authority of the party, the state, enterprises and corresponding trade unions, and the youth league, in many combinations. With the decentralization underway after 1968, local or municipal council governments became responsible for most houses of culture. These local governments were embedded in a tiered hierarchy that built upward from settlement to *járás*, county, and finally central administration, ensuring great variation.[21] The level of communication between houses of culture and local councils also varied greatly across institutions (110).

Beyond the regionally supervised houses of culture, state-owned enterprises also funded culture centers and club spaces, using the cultural fund they were mandated to provide for employees (Kúti, Marschall, and Nyilas 1986, 180). Trade union representatives held full-time positions at the larger enterprises, and the management of cultural activities fell among their duties. Host enterprises funded club activities expressly for employees, very few of them open to the public. With time, however, more would open their doors for specific public events. Run by enterprises and their related unions, these houses of culture did not fall under the supervision of the local councils or under that of the local party branch.[22] Further, as Sándor Striker expressed in an interview, these cultural activities were rather insignificant from the company's point of view: "The party and trade union officials were concerned about the workers' behavior during working hours, not in their leisure time." Enterprises also provided "club spaces" (*klubhelyiségek*) for related club activities, many intended for youth, which came under the management of the Communist Youth League (KISZ, Kommunista Ifjúság Szövetsége). According to Striker, the KISZ committees of the companies tended to be quite weak, and young workers often took a condescending attitude toward them.

Universities also hosted clubs for students, run by their KISZ committees. These, too, suffered problems of legitimacy. However, by the late 1960s, things had taken a turn. The club movement had taken off, and youth clubs were proliferating in these spaces. Under KISZ supervision, these club spaces were less closely monitored than the houses of culture, which were required to file an annual report to the council that held financial authority over them. To understand the club movement, it is useful to look more carefully at the role of amateur art in socialist cultural management.

The role of the houses of culture in socialist-era Hungary can best be understood with attention to the special role that amateur artistic activity was understood to play in extracurricular, or "voluntary," education—civic cultivation. By the time that the Communist Party took power, a strong focus on amateur art had already developed in the sphere of Hungarian civic cultivation. Amateur art, in contrast to "professional art," can be defined as art engaged in for purposes other than earning a living.[23] Amateur art had been considered an important part of associative life and civil society in the civic cultivation and extracurricular education movements that spread across Europe in the nineteenth and twentieth centuries. In Hungary, the broad popularity of choirs and choruses and the fact that the workers' choir (or speaking choir) movement was actively suppressed by the interwar government suggests that the cultivating qualities of amateur art were understood.[24] Amateur art activities were effective means for attracting people to workers' homes and other spaces (Kovalcsik 2003, 510), thus playing an important role in political recruitment and socialization. The testimonies cited by József Kovalcsik suggest that it had often been this kind of cultural activity, rather than libraries or explicitly political activities, that drew young workers toward the workers' movement. They were attracted by the experience of community resulting from these activities (517–19).

Attention to the community-making qualities of amateur art did not disappear during the state socialist years. White (1990, 70) writes that during this period "most cultural enlightenment was heavily oriented towards amateur arts." Communist and socialist theorists stressed the role of art in political socialization, and the role of socialism in broadening the provenance of art. White writes, "Lenin believed that art could and should be used for propaganda, and that cultural enlightenment—primarily the literacy campaign—was a vehicle for political socialization and the extension of Bolshevik power. However, he did not equate art with propaganda" (18). Theorists also stressed the democratization of art, which thus far had been the privilege of the elite. "Through art," White writes, "Lukács believed, the individual could experience unity with the species . . . aesthetic education and access to art must therefore be provided for everyone" (12).[25] "Public access to art" might have been achieved simply through education about high art coupled with access to museums. So why, one wonders, was amateur art promoted? Along with other civic cultivation movements, the socialist project stressed community-making. White lists important characteristics emerging from the emphasis of socialist "cultural enlightenment" on mass socialization: "In addition to accessibility, other special features include: 1) the fact that the activities are usually *collective*; 2) its largely voluntary nature (since Stalin's death); and 3) the emphasis on the desirability of active participation rather than passive spectating" (26). The amateur arts, especially those enacted collectively, such as folk dance and choir singing, meet these all of these criteria.[26] Indeed, this approach to socialization stresses that it is achieved most effectively through participation. Within this paradigm, amateur art is considered a kind of voluntary activity, an important aspect in associative life and citizen-making, or civic cultivation. Illustrative of the Lenin's approach to praxis (the dialectic of theory and practice) is the following passage in Lenin's (1975 [1920], 667) "The Task of the Youth Leagues": "You must train yourselves to be Communists. It is the task of the youth league to organize its practical activities in such a way that by learning, organizing, uniting and fighting, its members shall train both themselves and all those who look to it for leadership; it should train Communists. The entire purpose of training, educating and teaching should be to imbue them with communist ethics." Vitányi (1971, 244) argues that the connection of voluntary activity and art in this kind of socialization can only be understood if we step back from the bourgeois definition of art to examine its role in community cohesiveness, as did the utopian socialists.

In a series of seminars on voluntary organizations in Hungary and the Netherlands held in the mid-1980s, Katalin Fábry and Pal Soós asserted that Hungarian adult educators and sociocultural experts question whether it is feasible to consider amateur artistic activity separately from the "problematique of voluntaryism." To them, the amateur artistic movement, its historical traditions, evolutionary trends, fluctuations, and prevailing forms, are "the par excellence manifestation of voluntaryism" (1986, 67). Moreover, Fábry and Soós proposed, although without any explanation, that it is likely that "amateur artistic activity does not play such a primary, dominant, part in adult education and socio-cultural animation of the Netherlands and of Western Europe in general as it does in the East Central European countries" (ibid.).

The Changing Roles of Amateur Art in the Socialist Period

Concerned with the function of "voluntary education" as public communication, Sándor Striker delineated phases of "art-oriented voluntary activities" during Hungary's state socialist period. I draw on his periodization of the relationship of these art-oriented voluntary activities to state and market in order to examine the dialectical development of amateur art activities and cultural management, associative life, and civic cultivation over the socialist period. The houses of culture are the main context for the activities he discusses.

Striker divides the socialist period into two main phases, each made up of distinguishable periods. The first phase, of centralized initiatives, included both "the period of overwhelmingly central initiatives" lasting from 1948 to approximately 1958 and the period of movements initiated by the television, which lasted from 1958 to 1964. The second phase, of group initiatives, began with a period lasting from 1964 to 1972 in which "the initiative of amateur artistic activities switched to the hands of groups." The next period, beginning around 1980, was characterized at first by the formation of associations. This was followed by a "market-coop" period.

Striker demonstrates that across time, the centralized paradigm, in which groups had communication only with the center, was slowly replaced by one in which groups were able to communicate directly with each other as well as with the center. This process was aided, in part, by personal connections. In the first paradigm, "all cultural ventures within a centrally controlled social arena are fully dependent on state provisions" (Striker 1989b, 4). In such a situation, it should not be surprising, he argues, that people strove to make direct connections through movements and associations (1989b, 4). With no access to centrally controlled resources, and deprived of the opportunities of communal communication, informal person-to-person contacts were the only ways of "attaining changes without the risk of appearing rebellious" (1989b, 4). The way in which associative life expressed itself across these periods is clearly connected with economic conditions. With the decentralizing and marketizing New Economic Mechanism introduced by the government in 1968, the economic crisis beginning in the 1970s, and the "failure of the primary productive sphere of the economy at solving the problems," state subsidies for culture, as well as for medical and social care, were cut (1989b, 6). By the early 1970s, institutions were also faced with the difficulties of absorbing the policy-induced baby boom generation, just then coming of age (1984, 102).[27]

Under these changing conditions, the "relationship between hierarchy and culture" was transforming. Cultural producers, now encouraged to become entrepreneurial and to rely less on state funding, responded by standing up for "more political freedom and for artistic and financial independence" (Striker 1989b, 7). Around 1983, the Ministries of Finance and Culture "'gave the opportunity' to certain cultural institutions to become 'mixed interest' institutions" (ibid.), simultaneously decreasing their funding and encouraging profit-oriented activities. Houses of culture began to take on an entrepreneurial role. "Automatically," writes Striker, "activities requiring financial support [became] of less importance" while institutions became more sensitive to the requests of consumers (ibid.).

One of the important effects of the financial crisis was the grueling thirteen-hour workday of the average Hungarian, which was widely evident by 1987 (Striker 1989b, 7). Voluntary educational and other leisure time activities began at this point to develop along two lines. The first involved the financial needs of participants, with coursework focused on teaching skills needed for the second economy or new entrepreneurial activities, while the second involved political activities formed around contemporary issues: local cable television shows, including news programs, and "town protection" associations which sought control over the built environment (1989b, 7; 1987, 240–41). While during this same period amateur art activity reached a low point, Striker notes that folk dance was an exception, continuing to draw large numbers throughout the 1980s. The fact that *táncház* remained popular at a time when leisure activities were becoming either more income related or more overtly political hints at its special role in society. The next section visits each phase delineated by Striker in more detail.

In the first phase, lasting until around 1964, socialist rule was imposed on society, and initiatives were organized by "the Movement," by the activists acting according to the ideology of the "one and only party" (Striker 1987, 235). Striker writes: "The most expressively supported amateur artistic activities were the movement-and folk choirs and on-stage folkdance. These activities were intended to transmit the message of liberated feelings, freedom and participation, as expressed later by one of the choir-composers at the time: 'the musical task and role of the new generation is to transform musical education—which had been reserved for circles of the privileged before—into public property and to enrich, deepen and wide [*sic*] the great achievements. To create a collective!'" (Bardos 1969, quoted in Striker 1987, 233).[28] At the same time, the system of culture houses was introduced, with their programs designed by the center and "executed by visiting activists" (Striker 1987, 235). The introduction of television broadcasts in the 1950s provided a new medium for the movement. Unavailable in most homes, televisions could be found in the houses of culture, "in well-locked glass-windowed boxes'" (ibid.). From 1958 onward, the public could view programs transmitted by Hungarian television in these locations. In addition to these activities, houses of culture became sites of social gatherings such as weddings and similar festivities in this period.

The second period of this phase of centralized initiatives, lasting until around 1964, was characterized by "amateur art-oriented movements initiated by the Hungarian Television and other institutions" (Striker 1987, 236). Striker points in particular to the *Ki Mit Tud?* (Who can do what?) television program introduced in 1962. Organized in subsequent years as a competition among amateur and semiprofessional performers, the program's message "was to show the talents of the young generation the capability and participation of those brought up by the system" (ibid.). These initiatives would lead into the next period, as they were organized in later years as open competitions. Competitions for *Ki Mit Tud?* and its folk category, *Repülj Páva* (Fly peacock) were held in local culture houses, with finals broadcast on television. Finalists were judged by two juries: the professional jury, which awarded the prize, and the audience, who could vote on its preferences. In an interview, cultural manager Iván Vitányi argued that that the popularity of programs like *Ki Mit Tud?* and *Repülj Páva* derived from the fact that the audience was encouraged to vote for their favorite acts. "The only vote that people were permitted to cast," Vitányi told me, this vote meant that Hungarians were allowed—at least symbolically—to participate in shaping the direction in which cultural life would develop. Beyond representing the glory of socialist culture, television competitions like *Ki Mit Tud?* served to scout new talent, produce famous public figures to feed the rapidly growing entertainment industry, and keep an eye on cultural currents and popular opinions about them. In the socialist parlance of the day, strongly manifested currents were called "movements." Movements would dominate the next phase—that of group initiatives.

Characterizing the beginning of the second phase as a moment in which "the initiative of amateur artistic activities switched into the hands of groups," Striker provides four examples: music, film, theater, and folklore. Among the most significant activities, and certainly an important precursor to *táncház*, were those connected to "Beat music," that is, rock and roll. In 1964 alone, nearly three thousand guitars were sold in Hungary, and by the end of that year, 250 Beat groups were performing in Budapest alone (Striker 1987, 236). Film was significant as well. The works of the French New Wave, Italian neorealists, and Soviet greats were shown along with those of Hungarian filmmakers at the club spaces of the universities and enterprises, and amateur filmmaking clubs formed. While amateur theater, in the form of village "art appreciation" activities, had been quite popular during the first phase (ibid., 238), the spread of full-time employment, the rise of television, and very likely its association with the party had eroded the adult participation on which it had once thrived (ibid.). As

Fig. 3.2 The 1977 Ki Mit Tud? Competition at "Pataky" Művelődési ház, Budapest. Magician Halászlaki György, surrounded by members of the Békésszentandrás Páva (Peacock) circle. Photo by Zsolt Zih, courtesy of Rádió és Televízió Újság/Fortepan.

participation shifted to other social strata and generations, the content and style of the plays changed, influenced by the 1968 political movements in Western Europe (ibid.).

Folklore, prominent in the earlier phase in the form of state-supported professional and amateur folk dance troupes, went through significant transformations. In folk dance, as in contemporary theater, participants came down from the stage and the audience became participants. The Népművészet Ifjú Mestere (Master of Folk Art) award was introduced in 1970, and in 1973, the Young Folk Artists' Studio (Fiatal Népmuvészetek Studiója) was founded to bring together youth interested in renewing folk art on the basis of the traditions of material and spiritual culture (*tárgyi és szellemi kultur*) (Papers of the Katalin Landgraf collection).[29] The three main activities of the studio were collection (*feltáro munka*), creation (*tárgyalkotás*), and public cultivation activities (*közműuvelési akciók*). Members were to take part in ethnographic collection, attend lectures and exhibits, read literature of the field, and engage in reconstruction work, using the techniques learned. The studio's most important goal was to "produce useful and beautiful products: playgrounds, furniture, dishes, tablecloths, clothing and toys, and to show these at national and international exhibitions" (ibid.). Finally, they were to hold demonstrations at exhibitions to give children and adults a chance to learn and try out these simple techniques. Frequent exercises, mostly for children, were also to be held at schools and culture houses. Members also produced publications and records (ibid.).

While the staged folk dance popular in the earlier phase continued, a revolution was taking place in the teaching and choreography of folk dance in these groups. The first *táncház*, held in 1972, reflected these changes, marking an expansion of folk dance from staged performance to social dance. This was quickly followed by events aimed at including not only performing dancers but the general public as well.

While centralized initiatives around the television may have given these movements their start, this period was characterized by strained relations between youth (the baby boom generation coming of age) and the post-Stalinist administration, which attempted to maintain legitimacy by distancing itself from Stalinism, promoting consumerism, and embracing a new cultural policy represented by General Secretary János Kádár's statement: "those who are not against us are with us."[30] Accordingly, a policy referred to as the three Ts (*tűrt* [tolerated], *támogatott* [sponsored], and *tiltott* [forbidden]), associated with cultural czar György Aczél, began to characterize cultural politics, with increasing numbers of activities coming under the first two categories.[31] Once a cultural current was labeled a movement, efforts were made to enlist the movement in the task of socialist cultivation.

The next period arose somewhere around 1980, connected with the price crisis of 1979.[32] In Striker's (1987, 240) words: "The shift had been made from a period of movements to a period of associations." Leisure time diminished as individuals focused on more financially important activities. While voluntary activities decreased as a whole, more official associations, oriented around professions or activities (in contrast with the generational grouping of movements seen in the earlier phase), were formed between 1980 and 1982 than in the preceding two decades (ibid.). In 1981, a new law on associational freedoms (Egyesülési Szabadság Törvény) was passed, making a broader array of associations legal. By 1982, culture houses were expected to produce 10 percent of their annual budget. As centralized state involvement and funding decreased, people stepped in to define, demand and create leisure time activities (ibid., 241).

In the last period, as local elections were established in 1985, communication took the form of direct political expression, focusing on the expression and representation of interests of the community (Striker 1987, 241).[33] The professionalization that began in the previous period was taken further as economic concerns heightened, finding expression in the production of video and community cable television and town protection activities (ibid.). This was reflected as well in the increase in courses for driver's licenses and computer skills in culture houses. In this "market or cooperative oriented period" (during which Striker was writing), amateurs and professionals sought new ways to cooperate/associate in order to professionalize and to ensure a living for themselves. In this phase, writes Striker, "the medium of art becomes yet another means of livelihood" (ibid., 242). In this period, even as folk art activities were becoming professionalized, *táncház* was an exception. *Táncház* activities, which had little economic utility beyond creating a marketable skill set for a small proportion of participants, were not expressly political in the sense of the other politically oriented activities developing at the time. Let's now turn to the rise of spontaneous youth culture in the culture houses in the second period. The Beat movement is a useful example and was an important precedent for *táncház*.

Youth Movements and Changing Relations with Central Authority

It was toward the end of the first period that the conditions needed for *táncház* to arise began to ripen, as centralized initiatives began to be overtaken by group initiatives. By the mid-1960s, the club movements—in particular, the Beat movement and the theater movement—had taken off (Striker 1987, 238). Club spaces for youth had been financed by enterprises and universities since the 1950s, but as they were associated with the party, they had suffered a lack of legitimacy. Inhibited by top-down organizing, club spaces had not been embraced by the workers, leaving them and related cultural initiatives necessarily funded but underutilized, if not empty. In the 1960s, however, youth began to use these spaces to congregate and pursue their interests. On their own initiative, they approached cultural managers, in many cases relying on personal connections, to start clubs, many of them music clubs. While in the beginning of this period, club spaces were well funded, the entrepreneurial phase set off by the New Economic Mechanism was about to restructure the way that cultural institutions functioned. While these clubs served the workers or students, the owners made them public to raise money (ibid., 236). The result was that houses of culture opened their doors to a broader range of activities and new publics.

By this time, in addition to giving direction to the network of culture houses, the Institute for People's Culture was conducting studies of the houses of culture and club spaces and the activities taking place within them. Researchers avidly studied the youth movements, and debates raged in journals and meetings over their significance and quality. Were they socialist? Nationalist? Counterrevolutionary? Should activities be forbidden? How could they be utilized toward socialist cultivation? The goals laid out for the institute in 1966 were to:

1. Fight against counterrevolutionary imperialist and bourgeois currents of thought
2. Deal with questions about the spread of socialist democracy
3. Address questions about the politics of the church and religious criticism
4. Give a face-lift to the values of the youth and questions of extracurricular education (Gyarmati 1993, 54)[34]

Tension was apparent between youths and authorities as long hair and the artistic quality of Beat music became issues of contention; young people were accused of hooliganism. The club movements represented a significant change in the cultural sphere because, even as they occurred in public spaces, the forms and content of events were often more in the control of participating youths than of central authorities. The Beat generation had successfully utilized personal connections, gaps in party control, and contradictory aims and practices in cultural management to create Beat clubs in the club spaces of the enterprises and universities. While the law on gathering (*gyülekezési törvény*) dictated the number of individuals allowed to convene, and technically club members were to be registered, enforcement of the law was inconsistent. Indeed, one club founder told me how easy it had been to start his folk club: "What surprised me most was how open the KISZ people were to such a spontaneous initiative." Many clubs were, de facto, open to the general public.

As the clubs proliferated, and the club movement was identified, efforts were made to manage its direction; *klubvezető* (club leader) courses were introduced at the institute. Clubs fell into a nebulous category of cultural institutions not directly under the party's Central Committee (Központi Bizottság), leading this committee to criticize KISZ, the only "authority" over the clubs, for failing to provide the appropriate goals and ensure the appropriate content and frameworks, without which the "desire for community could bring unsocialist characteristics into being" (minutes of the Central Committee, cited in Fonyódi 2003, 25). From the start, the goal of the government, represented by the Committee on Agitation and Propaganda of the party's Cultural Committee, had been to incorporate youth

Fig. 3.3 Youth, surrounded by paintings of Beat musicians, at the "csövesklub" in the basement of the Ságvári Endre Művelődési Ház, Pécs (today's Pécs Third Theater). Photo by Tamás Urbán, courtesy of Fortepan.

movements into the communist youth movement, represented by KISZ.[35] Through its sponsorship of clubs, KISZ was expected to maintain and strengthen their socialist content and to aid in the formation of a Marxist worldview (Fonyódi 2003, 25). Péter Fonyódi (2003, 25) quotes from the notes of the eighth KISZ congress:

> An important level of active cultivation is also the art-appreciation movement. A characteristic form of the spontaneous initiatives of the youth are beat, *táncház*, and the urban folk music movement. We need to employ these movements that activate the large masses of youth to our ends. We should use the popularity of the beat movement when we organize social and political activities to move the larger masses, and at the same time we must endeavor to activate the crowds of youths who are attracted to these groups toward *művelődés* of more ambitious standards. In this interest we must expand the framework and conditions of training for youths playing in the beat bands.

This quote reveals the complex dynamics of cooperation and opposition in cultural management, civic cultivation, and associative life in the socialist period. Beat bands and fans indeed collaborated with official channels in a number of ways. Beyond performing at culture houses or clubs, bands entered into relationships with a host of institutions, including the Országos Rendező Iroda (ORI, the National Events Office) to perform at festivals and to produce records and the Országos Szórakoztatói Központ

(OSZK, the National Entertainment Center), which qualified people to perform in any public arena but did not arrange shows or tours (Fonyódi 2003, 65, 158). The ORI was concerned with, among other things, ensuring "quality" and "appropriate text." In order to perform in public places, bands had to be in possession of a permit of operation (*működési engedély*). On the same occasion that the permit was granted, the fee that the artist or group was allowed to charge was determined by the granting bureau (OSZK or ORI).

Yet Fonyódi writes that in 1969, only 45 percent of the surveyed bands had such a permit. While he does not explain how bands without permits managed to perform, his data suggests that they played at clubs and culture houses without permits. Indeed, it appears that in the beginning, Beat bands had no relationship with the ORI, precisely because they performed in KISZ clubs. Permits of operation, supposedly required for any band performing in a public place, were not required in these clubs, designed to encourage amateur art activities. This was also true of amateur jazz and dance band festivals organized in culture houses (Fonyódi 2003, 47) as well as the dance song festivals broadcast on television.

Beyond the struggles we see within the space of amateur art activities, the slippage between amateur and "performer" seems to reveal a tension with the developing entertainment industry, likely connected with the baby boom and the rise of the second economy. Yet while the Beat movement seems to correlate with the rise of this industry, the musicians were nevertheless subject to ostracism as hooligans.[36] To be a Beat musician was still to occupy a shady space, and as Fonyódi (2003, 66) points out, the identification cards of Beat musicians listed them without a workplace, a crime in the socialist period. "Thus the representatives of beat, notwithstanding greater and strengthening popularity, got neither self-sufficiency nor independence; the representatives could only reach the public and earning possibilities if they adopted, complied with the rules of the game dictated 'from above', if they 'gave to the collective' the popularity and fans they had earned with their own strength" (ibid., 66, 67). Indeed, in Striker's second phase, as theater came down off the stage and art out of the galleries, youths not only took advantage of existing structures, the club spaces and culture houses, but were also active in creating new ones, often asking for government permission and funds and sometimes taking over spaces and insisting on institutional support.

In the 1970s, the Institute for People's Culture went through further transformations. From 1971 to 1980, its activities were characterized by a turn away from "unambiguous socialization of world view and unidirectional

Fig. 3.4 Youth exit the Fővárosi Művelődési Ház (FMH) after Rubik cube competition, 1981. Photo by Tamás Urbán, courtesy of Fortepan.

public cultivation" (*egyértelmű világnézet neveléssel és egy célirányos közművelődéssel*) and toward solving particular problems regarding the cultivation (*művelődés*) of workers and youth (László Harangi in Gyarmati 1993, 68). By 1970, the institute was increasingly concerned with engaging the mass media, with which *művelődés* could spread more quickly and reach broader circles (ibid., 47). It is not a coincidence that the *Ki Mit Tud?* and *Repülj Páva* television competitions had been introduced just prior to this period or that in 1970 producing a *művelődési* program on television was among the basic goals set by the institute (ibid., 56).[37]

Vitányi, who had been a populist activist in the 1940s, a member of the NÉKOSZ folk dance troupe under Muharay, and later a student of György Lukács, became director of the institute in 1972, strengthening its *népi* emphasis. By 1974, he was writing about the *táncház*, noting its success at doing what his generation had failed at (Vitányi 1974). While *táncház* held special significance for populists in the civic cultivation world, it signaled *narodnyizmus*, and/or nationalism, to many.[38] Vitányi engaged in debates with these skeptics, aligning the *népi* line with Béla Bartók.[39] Vitányi was a key player in transforming the language and approach of cultural policy from *népművelés* to *közművelődés*. White (1990, 27) writes, "Népművelés lives on in popular usage, but in the 1970s it was officially replaced by the word közművelődés, which means public (not popular) participation in culture and is an intransitive and reflexive noun: suggesting that cultural enlightenment is voluntary,

Socialist Cultural Management 105

not imposed, and that the system is a democratic one." The *közművelődési* law was passed in 1976, inspired in part by research revealing widespread disuse of culture houses and an increase in numbers of televisions in private homes. The notion of *közművelődés* underscored the idea that the public must be active in its own cultivation. Reflecting this change, the institute became the National Center for Public Cultivation, or OKK (Országos Közművelődési Központ) in 1986. As Striker related to me, among its key tasks was now advising the houses of culture on how to produce income. Formally, the Népművelési Intézet was now housed inside the OKK, along with a new Institute of Cultural Research, "which would use the tools of sociology to examine the status of national *művelődes*" (H. Polgár 1994, i).

Conclusion

It should be apparent that, especially in later periods, activities taking place in houses of culture and in club spaces cannot simply be viewed as official culture, although they took place within a system of socialist cultivation. Since the establishment of the system of culture houses, the regime had succeeded in naturalizing/legitimizing the culture house and the club as public space. The younger generations, feeling entitled to state support for the activities they deemed important, used these spaces to pursue cultural activities and initiate new ones, making them not only for but also by the people. Because they were the spaces in which most cultural activities were held, they could contribute to the maintenance of a degree of centralization. Indeed, some people told anecdotes about surveillance that took place in culture houses.[40]

Throughout the 1950s, and much of the 1960s, houses of culture and clubs supported by the party suffered from a crisis of legitimacy. Those that attended did so because of ideological conviction, because attendance was compulsory, or because a desired resource was offered: television, soccer, a space for a wedding, and similar. While legitimacy remained a problem, a new trend emerged in the late 1960s, in which youths began using club spaces for their own entertainment. The emergence of such autonomous initiatives was possible partly because of the numerous funded and underused spaces that enterprises and universities were required to fund. However, even when the state cut back on funding, autonomous initiatives spread, as the entrepreneurialism the houses of culture were required to engage in encouraged public input. Thus, we can detect a shift in the late socialist period toward a broadening of cultural content, with activities no longer determined from the top down but emerging from an undulating field of popular initiatives intersecting with state cultural managers.[41] The centering of the term *közművelődés* reflects how this pattern affected the approaches adopted by cultural managers in policy and practice, in relationship with economic crisis and reforms. Amid entertainment activities, and skill improvement projects, the struggle over civic cultivation continued. Further, many cultural managers, *népi* activists included, worked to foil the centralized approach of the Communist Party, some remaining dedicated to socialist or communist ideals of democracy. They worked within the system to bring *művelődés* to the people.

The patterns that emerged in the world of cultivation across the socialist period are helpful in discerning both the precedents for *táncház* and the specificities of *táncház*'s rise and continuing popularity. Among these are the continuities in practices of *népi* cultivation; socialist ideas about cultivation and related patterns of funding for culture; and decentralization, entrepreneurialization, and the rise of a market for entertainment, or leisure activities, entwined with the rise of the second economy. Yet *táncház*'s outlier status is also telling. During the period when group initiatives became biased toward economic necessity and political representation, *táncház* remained popular. Participants in fact point to the 1980s as *táncház*'s heyday. We must see the rise of *táncház* as a peculiarly (Hungarian) socialist phenomenon—the result of a particular kind of Hungarian socialist civil sphere where certain forms of association were encouraged and where other forms were allowed or tolerated in an ongoing struggle. As one interlocutor told me, *táncház* was "a movement that was not a movement because it had no written set of ideas, or, you know, things like that. And, you know, the dancehouse movement was the right answer to a totalitarian system because it was an amorphous and informal activity which could not be caught in the legal terms of that system. So no one actually did anything against the actual law of the '70s and the '80s within the dancehouse movement. They did not form an association." But beyond that, the system of cultural management was adapting to moments such as the Beat movement and *táncház*. This relationship will be further elaborated in the next chapter, which describes *táncház*'s emergence and development in the 1970s and 1980s.

NOTES

1. Bodnár paraphrases Charles Jencks with the first list and then expands on it with state socialist examples.

2. She continues: "Post-socialism's symbolic building, then, could be the office building in the inner city and the multifunctional service center, known as the shopping mall, on the outskirts and in the inner suburbs" (92).

3. In socialist Hungary, *house of culture* was the dominant term for these institutions, but in many other state socialist countries, the terms *workers' home* and *house of the people* were more common.

4. While the literal translation of the Népművelési Intézet is "Institute for Peoples' Cultivation," convention has it that *culture*, rather than *cultivation*, is used in its English translation, while *people's* has been dropped in the postsocialist period, making it the Institute for Culture.

5. What I term houses of culture following Hungarian usage are roughly analogous with what were termed houses of the people in Belgium, Italy, and some other places. See Margaret Kohn (2003) for an in-depth examination of the Italian case.

6. In Italy and Belgium, adult education, university extension programs, and libraries were united within the walls of Houses of the People (Kohn 2003).

7. It is interesting that none of my sources pointed to the Russian *narodnyik* movement. There was instead frequent reference to the Danish folk schools, which, while tied to nation-making, also influenced the Highlander Folk School in the United States.

8. Note the similarity to the Scouts in this sense. The aristocracy and traditionally pro-Habsburg camps were Catholic (less so in Transylvania), while the rest of the middle class tended to be Protestant. The poorest of the poor tended to be Catholic, with many converting to evangelical sects. The Catholic Church stood to lose much of its wealth with any radical land reform.

9. The term *népművelés*—literally "cultivation of the people"—is translated here by Striker as "people's education." He reads it as a top-down enterprise. My use of the terms *civic cultivation* or *extracurricular/adult education* emphasize the historical dimensions of the terms and practices, including connections to Western Europe. White's "Soviet type" "cultural enlightenment" seems also connected to these histories, via the language of enlightenment.

10. Under the authority of the Szabadművelési Osztály (Department of Free Cultivation/Adult Education) of the Ministry of Religion and Public Education.

11. The National House of Folk Arts of the Ministry of Culture of the Russian Federation, founded in 1915, is a cultural institution with its main office in Moscow and eighty-nine branches in all administrative regions. It is a chief methodological institution in the structure of the federal Ministry of Culture, dealing with folklore and amateur activities in arts, and the main coordinator for artistic activities, information, publications, and international exchanges in Russia. Its major goals are:
   1. Support and encouragement of amateur artistic activities, traditional culture, and national folklore
   2. Methodological assistance and organizational and PR support for eighty-nine regional centers of folk and amateur arts in all administrative regions
   3. Collection and registration of traditional and amateur forms and spaces
   4. Foundation and development of traditional festivals, contests and exhibitions.
   5. Organization of international cultural exchanges (WIPO 2002).

Carol Silverman (1983, 57) writes of the Bulgarian Center for Amateur Arts (Centura za Hudozestvana Samodejnost), which directed the activities of amateur groups that performed folk music and dances as well as rituals at festivals. Buchanon (2006, 134) writes of the Central House for Folk Creativity, founded in 1954.

12. Formed in the 1930s by Igor Moiseyev, a principal dancer and choreographer for the Bolshoi Ballet, the ensemble performed balleticized versions of folk and ethnic dances collected in the many regions of the Soviet Union. See Olverholser (2008) for a history of the Magyar Állami Népi Együttes.

13. See Silverman (1983, 57–58) for the Bulgarian parallel. While she writes that the government "created ensembles," at least in the Hungarian case what might have been "new ensembles" were old groups that took on new names. People told me that in some cases dancers/choreographers approached unions (or the firms they were attached to) in pursuit of chances to found dance ensembles.

14. In addition to creating performances, agitation pamphlets and publications (*agitációs műsorfüzeteket, kiadványok*), and exhibitions and giving courses within the institute,

summer arts colonies, and unions and councils, Gyarmati (1993, 15) writes, it also conducted ethnographic collection and produced ethnographic studies. In just five years' time, 12,000 songs, 500 collections of local dance material, 250 films of local dance material, and 4,200 songs and dances based on children's games were produced.

15. See chapter 6.

16. Széll had been imprisoned in the 1930s for his communist activities and was ambassador to Romania from 1948 to 1950 (Hegedűs 1994). After serving a sentence for his part in the 1956 revolution, he was "tucked away" as an archivist/librarian at the National Library. In 1986, a volume he edited on the *táncház* movement was published (Széll 1986).

17. Formed by joining the old Ministry of People's Culture (Népművelési) and the Ministry of Education (Oktatási).

18. Including Elemér Muharay, ethnographer and teacher (and Martin's wife) Jolán Borbély, and ethnographer István Almássy.

19. He names Ervin Pesovár and Muharay specifically. On Kodály and state socialism, see Péteri (2017).

20. On socialist economies of shortage, see Kornai (1992). For its relationship to cultural production, see Verdery (1996).

21. *Járás* is an administrative unit between settlement and county.

22. See Siegelbaum (1999) for a discussion of this type of club in the Soviet Union.

23. White (1990, 70) cites one description of amateur arts: "amateur arts are a mighty instrument for the political socialization of the population.... The force of this type of art lies in its mass scale.

24. Szolláth (2009, 116) notes that after the worker choir movement (associated with the Social Democractic Party) was made illegal in 1933, organizations on the right end of the spectrum established choruses.

25. Marxist philosopher György Lukács was people's commissar for education and culture during the Hungarian Soviet Republic of 1919 and minister of culture under Nagy's evolutionary government in 1956. Vitányi was his student in the years following his return to Hungary in 1945.

26. See also Buchanon (2006, 133). While music scholars Donna Buchanan, Marina Frolova-Walker, and Danielle Foster-Lussier point to Soviet Party leader and cultural ideologist Zhdanov's socialist realist dictum, "national in form, socialist in content," I believe Vitányi: that, at least in the case of the institute, these modalities were drawn on not simply for their "national form" but for their communal and "folk" qualities.

27. The birth rate increased 15 percent in the years between 1953 and 1957 due to pronatalist policies pursued by Minister of Health and Welfare Anna Ratkó. The coming of age of this "Ratkó generation" (Striker 1987, 102) coincides with the growth of the second economy, which might be seen as a kind of escape valve that absorbed what might have otherwise been a disruptive force.

28. While Striker is quoting Bardos here, Bardos stresses creating a collective, while Striker stresses showing a message.

29. This archive was housed in a library located in the Selyemgombolyító Gyár (Silk Filatorium factory) on *Miklós Tér* in Obuda, dedicated to public cultivation activities—particularly the *táncház* and folk art movements in the 1980s (Egykor).

30. See Fonyódi (2003) for a discussion of these clashes.

31. See Fonyódi (2003, 81) for further discussion of member of the party Central Committee and the first vice-minister of *Művelődés*, Aczél.

32. The price crisis was tied to the second of the global oil crises in the 1970s in 1979. The first began in 1973 when the members of the Organization of Arab Petroleum Exporting Countries (OPEC) called an embargo, targeting nations supporting Israel during the Yom Kippur War. The second was due to panic surrounding (the possibility of) decreased oil output due to the Iranian Revolution, which drove prices up.

33. Striker (1989b, 10) points to a telling example: the theater that hosted the first meeting of the oppositional Magyar Democratic Forum (MDF), later to become the political party that won the parliamentary elections in 1990, was threatened by government agencies for having hosted a subversive meeting. It successfully argued that it hosted the event out of financial necessity.

34. If this list seems unclear, it is because I have translated it from its Hungarian articulation, equally unclear.

35. KISZ came into being in 1957. Paralleling the party's name change from Magyar Dolgozók Pártja (MDP) to Magyar Szocialista Munkáspárt (MSzMP), KISZ replaced DISZ (Dolgozó Ifjúsági Szövetsége), which had had the same role. DISZ had earlier replaced MADISZ (Magyar Demokrátikus Ifjúsági Szövetsége, translated as the Association of Hungarian Democratic Youth), formed by the Communist Party in 1945 during the Coalition period.

36. A rich literature exists on the underground cultural and music activities of this period. See, for example, Szemere (2001) and Barna and Tofalvy (2016).

37. Ferenc Sebő was a key personality on a 1970s TV show called *Aprók tánca* (Dance of the little ones) aimed at awakening interest in folk dance in children (Sebő 1981).

38. The *narodnyik* movement, famous for "going to the people," began in late nineteenth-century Russia and advocated land redistribution in favor of the peasantry. Socialist in orientation, its proponents believed that the capitalist phase could be skipped altogether and that socialism could be based on local peasant forms. The Narodna Volya, or "will of the people," organization, made up of revolutionary socialist intellectuals believing in the efficacy of terrorism, emerged from this group.

39. By aligning with Bartók, Vitanyi wanted to show that a *népi* path was not confined to preserving tradition, but also included making newer "modern" works drawing on the essence of folk art. On Bartók's nationalism, see Hooker (2013) and Schneider (2006). On the tradition of combining the unfamiliarly archaic with the avant-garde in Hungary, see Hooker (2013), Lange (2018), and Frigyesi (1996).

40. Both Sebő and Vitányi told me they believed that surveillance in this context was more of a myth than a fact. The example they both gave was that Vitányi was approached by superiors who said there was rumor about people having sex under the piano at the Sebő Club, to which Vitányi responded by pointing out that there was in fact no piano at the Kassák Club, where it was held. However, another youth club leader (not a *táncház* club) in this period shared with me that he had been coerced into reporting on his peers, although he claimed he had deliberately never shared anything of significance.

41. While she focuses on different factors, White (1990, 68) argues that the USSR, Poland, and Hungary each showed a pattern in which houses of culture pulled "increasingly away from Stalinist forms of *political* socialization and highly politicized leisure, towards new forms of cultural enlightenment which use[d] the arts and adult education to attack *social* problems," often by favoring "pure entertainment or non-political hobbies, the revival of national traditions or the adoption of Western fashions" (69).

Chapter Four

The Táncház *Revolution*
Reviving Folk Dance as Social Dance

THE FIRST BUDAPEST *TÁNCHÁZ* WAS held in 1972, hosted by the choreographer of the Bihari ensemble, Ferenc Novák, and attended by dancers and choreographers from four amateur dance troupes (Halmos 2000, 37). Modeled after the dances, or "balls," traditionally organized by adolescents in the Transylvanian village of Szék, this event was the first attempt by the performing folk dancers to engage in Hungarian folk dance as social dance rather than as staged choreography or competition. Sándor Striker (1987a, 112) writes: "Although the location was somehow different from that of the original dancehouses, traditional folk customs were precisely kept, e.g. a bottle of brandy was provided, and even the paraffin fee was collected, guests were welcomed at the entrance." Given the event's great success, participants decided to proceed with subsequent events open to the general public. At these later events, dance lessons were given to encourage newcomers to learn dances and participate (Halmos 2000).

The *táncház* revolution represented a movement away from the "artificial" choreography that had dominated the performing folk dance troupes in the preceding decades. In their search for authentic folk forms, or the "pure source" (*tiszta forrás*), to refresh and replace the dominant choreographed repertoires, these choreographers came to recognize how dances were embedded in the social event.[1] Through their ethnographic research (or village visiting), they were coming to appreciate both the beauty and function of social dance, that is, folk dance in everyday life, a form quite different than that practiced in the performance-oriented environment of the ensembles. In response to the interest of members of the troupes in coming together in a casual social context, Novák and the others organized this first Budapest *táncház*. Folk dance researcher (ethnochoreologist) György

Fig. 4.1 A 1972 *táncház* at Irók Boltja (Writer's store). Photo by Zoltán Szalay, courtesy of the Folklore Documentation Library and Archive, Heritage House.

Martin had in particular encouraged them to organize a social event based on the Transylvanian *táncház*, but their efforts were also enthusiastically supported by ethnographers, writers, actors, performers, and other intellectuals, quite a few of whom were connected with the Institute for Culture (Juhász and Szabó n.d., 11; Halmos 1973, 146).[2] Regarding the role of cultural managers, Katalin Juhász and Zoltán Szabó (n.d., 11) argue that "because the political power needed the representative activities of the folk dance ensembles, it tolerated the 'next to and under' self-organizing and developing activities of the cultural public life of the dancehouses." While cultural managers encouraged such activities (ibid.), there was little that could be co-opted. As Striker recounted in an interview, at *táncház* there was "no program, so to say. How could they launch a political program? How could they influence it? They could sponsor it and that's it.... So the difference between the dancehouse and let's say the Beat bands is that there is an audience rather than an activity that you participate in together.... It had no extra political content that could be controlled... because, you know, if you were a classical dancer to have a show you needed a permit, but this was an amateur thing!" There is no doubt that there were intellectuals and cultural managers, many connected with *népi* activities and ideologies, who genuinely supported *táncház* and struggled for its validation along with those who disapproved of it.

This chapter describes the rise of the *táncház* revival in the 1970s and its development throughout the next decades. Beginning with a description of the first *táncház* event and the conditions that led to it, I examine the movement in its early years, discussing important individuals and activities as well as its relationship with the Institute for Culture and system of culture houses. I draw on studies of *táncház*, including comparisons with other movements and the meager demographic information available to show how the movement was understood and acted on by cultural managers and participants. I describe various forces and actors, important examples of the institutionalization of *táncház* activities and the creation of formal organizations and discuss their effect on the development of the movement.

Reviving Folk Dance as Social Dance

The musicians that accompanied the dance at the first *táncház*, Béla Halmos and Ferenc Sebő, had met in the symphony of the Technical University, where they were both architecture students (Halmos 1973, 145; Sebő 1973, 147). Sebő had already been experimenting with accompanying poems by József Attila and *népi* colleger and poet Lászlo Nagy on guitar, performing them at Pop Island in 1968 and 1969, and also composed music for avant-garde theater.[3] Halmos, whose father was a researcher of folk architecture associated with the village researchers, had grown up singing folk songs with his family. In 1969, he became a household name as "the guitar boy," due to his placing in the top ten in *Repülj Páva* (Fly peacock), the folk music category of the *Ki Mit Tud?* (Who can do what?) television competition (Halmos 1973, 145; Striker 1987a, 107; Frigyesi 1996, 60). The two performed together as a duo in the *Repülj Páva* competition that same year, singing folk songs of the Carpathian basin, accompanied by guitar (Frigyesi 1996, 72; Halmos 1973). Although they did not place in this competition, a chain of events had been set into action nevertheless.

Both musicians had been influenced by the musical environment brought about by the Beat movement and were experimenting with new musical forms. Their interest in folk songs had been peaked when, at an international camp for architecture students, visiting Greek students had sung folk songs together to guitar accompaniment. According to Halmos, the collective singing impressed the duo, inspiring them to set local folk songs to guitar, creating their repertoire for the competition. Meanwhile, having seen Sebő hit his *citera* with a bow while accompanying a theater performance, ethnomusicologist Béla Vikár asked him whether he was familiar with the *ütőgardon*, an instrument used in Gyímes, Transylvania, that is played by hitting the strings with a bow (Sebő 1983, 74; Frigyesi 1996, 61).[4]

The leap to playing Hungarian folk music on such traditional instruments came once Martin and ethnomusicologist Lajos Vargyas offered Sebő and Halmos the opportunity to hear recordings in their collections at the Academy of Sciences (Sebő 1973, 148). Seeking new sources for inspiration, and not wanting "to spend time on reinventing what already has been known and used for hundreds of years," the young musicians gladly accepted access to the recorded legacy of Hungarian folk music (Sebő 1983, 74). Sebő found that the exotic quality of the music was in tune with his avant-garde sensibility. He said of the first time he heard Hungarian folk music: "it was a totally strange situation—as if it were Tahitian folk music. We had never heard anything like it before" (1976, 189).

Martin (1981) also introduced these musicians to the choreographers, resulting in their appointment as accompanists for the rehearsals of the Bartók ensemble. This was an important step toward the development of the social dance trend, because the revival of social dance required musicians familiar with the paradigm of village social dances. Musicians needed to be familiar with dance suites and sensitive to the needs of individual dancers.[5] For the musicians, this did not mean a turn away from the avant-garde, for "it turned out that the most authentic performing style sounded the most modern; it was 'stronger' and more attractive even than modernized versions that included electric instruments"(Frigyesi 1996, 66). Further, this reuniting of dance and music in a social context, so crucial to the *táncház* revolution, was in itself an aesthetic element attractive to the musicians. Judith Frigyesi (1996, 67) writes: "One important consequence of this 'tradition-oriented' attitude was that it regarded instrumental folk music as it really was—that is, as functional music, as entertainment. This was not primarily an ideological decision but something that came from practice; the musicians of the movement learned this style in function and found the best context for it also in its function—that is, as an accompaniment to dance."

The dancers at the first Budapest *táncház* arrived along a very different trajectory than the musicians. The folk dance scene in Hungary had been comprised until then of four official ensembles in Budapest, "modeled on the highly successful Soviet folk ensembles" and many amateur ensembles around the country (Halmos 2000, 35–36). By the 1960s, the festival system that provided the main venues for the performance of folk dance had "stabilized" (Maácz 1981a, 71). Festivals were coordinated with a system of awards that determined the reputation of the ensembles (73). László Maácz argues that on the one hand, this system had become so didactic that competitions were often held before an empty house for the sole purpose of judgments and awards and yet that on the other, by the 1970s, folk dance was also beginning to connect more closely with the expanding tourism industry (73–74). As they were better able to adapt to these circumstances than the official ensembles, the smaller and more cost-efficient amateur ensembles tended to generate the "most exciting innovation" (75–77). Amateur ensembles were compelled to innovate because of the prize-awarding competitions and festivals that had developed in the amateur sphere (Vadási 2001, 89). The revival of instrumental dance music provided new opportunities for innovation, which the Bartók ensemble embraced, leading the way (Martin 1981, 45; Széll 1986).

It was thus that while this kind of folk dance was dying out as a village social event in Hungarian village life, folk dance was a widespread performing art and a thriving amateur pastime, involving both professionals and amateurs. As troupes were funded by the government, performers gained the possibility of traveling within the country as well as abroad, even outside the socialist bloc. Many performers pointed to this highly valued opportunity in interviews, as passports for travel to foreign destinations were hard to come by and few had the means to travel. Not only did folk dance provide an opportunity to see the world, but it was also an opportunity to see other "cultures" performed in a particular context of representation, usually festivals and competitions. A set of social practices emerged, resulting from selective tradition-making that emphasized certain forms and contexts. Much like sports teams, ensembles competed against each other for prizes or reputation, in contexts of friendly internationalism in which they represented Hungary.[6]

Whereas festivals provided opportunities for representation, the *táncház* setting allowed opportunities for participation, related to the context of urban leisure activities on the one hand and amateur ethnography and village visiting on the other. Up to this point, ensembles had performed choreographies based not only on the abstraction of folk dance motifs from the larger dance context and the instrumental music needed for its social practice but also from the practice of singing folk songs. In the interwar period, the chorus and *népi* movements had encouraged collective singing. In this same period, composer, ethnomusicologist, and patron of the chorus movement Zoltán Kodály devised his pedagogical method for teaching folk songs. In this method, the importance of the folk song in modern life "was thought to be embedded in the rules of its form, tonality and rhythm," leading to an emphasis on the "melodic essence" of the song and its isolation from instrumental music (Frigyesi 1996, 65).

With the Kodály method, introduced into the Hungarian school system in the 1950s, folk songs were abstracted from their musical and social contexts for the purposes of pedagogy and socialization. In this act of abstraction, Striker (1987a, 105) argues, Kodály "failed to realize that a collective is more of an indirect result of a regular activity executed by a group of people, than a final goal which determines the activity itself." Folk singing became a compulsory part of the school curriculum rather than a voluntary activity of movement participants. As Halmos (2000, 37) writes, under these circumstances, "a child would either learn the folk songs the same way he learned algebra or would come to hate them as something shoved down his throat."

Ethnomusicologist István Pávai told me that the emphasis on collecting songs inherited from Kodály also resulted in the neglect of instrumental music.[7] Further, due to the technologies and methods of collecting, not to mention such biases, folk dances recorded on silent film had been separated from music and song, and instrumental music was collected without record of its relationship to dances. *Táncház* practices reaggregated these elements of social dance that had been isolated from one other. At *táncház* events, participants had the opportunity to reunite the text and melodies learned in school with dance and instrumental music in a (more holistic) social dance context. With this, the revival shifted toward authenticity Community making qualities are the function on which there was emphasis.

The Spread of Tánchaz: Researching and Managing the Movement

Choreographer Sándor Timár and folk dance researcher György Martin had danced together with the influential choreographer István Molnár, first in the official SZOT ensemble run by the National Council of Trade Unions (Szakszövetségek Országos Tanácsa-SZOT), which was shut down in 1954 because its massive size made it too costly (Paluch 2004, 38), and later in its successor, the Budapest Ensemble. Molnár, a modern dancer by training, had been the first to collect folk dance methodically using film, earning his status as "the first Hungarian folk dance expert" (Vitányi 1964, 48).[8] Molnár's dancers, many of whom had begun their folk dance careers in the Scouts, collected new material, taught folk dance, and even worked as guest choreographers with rural dance ensembles (Paluch 2004, 38). When Timár went on to lead the amateur Bartók ensemble, he began developing a training program specifically for the movements found in folk dance, inspired by what he had observed in the movements of dancers in a tradition-keeping (hagyományőrző) ensemble that had performed alongside his at a festival (Paluch 2004, 40).[9] It was then that he recognized how "distorted" the dances in Molnár's style appeared next to dances of those who "spoke their own dance language" (Paluch 2004, 40).

Martin, in the meantime, found his home in dance research, working as an ethnochoreologist first at the Institute for Culture and later at the Folk Dance Research Group of the Hungarian Academy of Sciences (Magyar Szemle 2003). One of his jobs at the institute had been to teach dance material to choreographers. To his disappointment, most choreographers had only been interested in learning isolated motifs, not entire dances. In an interview, Timár explained to me that he and Martin expected their division of labor to be highly fruitful for the folk dance movement, and that *tánchaz* was its result. Ferenc Novák, who had moved to Budapest after the war from his native Transylvania to finish school, had danced together with Timár and Martin in Molnár's Budapest ensemble. In 1954, he founded the Bihari ensemble and in 1958 became a student of ethnography (Bihari János Táncegyüttes 2006), subsequently producing a study on the role of dance in the social life of Szék (Martin 1982).

In Budapest, what had begun as a closed party for members of dance troupes grew within a short period into a popular pastime, spreading to provincial cities as quickly as new folk bands could become competent (Halmos 2000, 38). Key to its success was the decision by the musicians and the Bartók ensemble to hold more events open to the public and to build dance instruction into the event itself.[10] Sebő (1976, 191) describes his sentiments after the first *táncház*: "Based on the experiences I had already had, I began to recognize that if this form of entertainment was capable of bringing together these otherwise oppositional ensembles, then it couldn't be bad. Quite clearly, the dancers are having a great time, and I felt that we have to give the possibility to the people who came in off the streets to try it out, to feel good." Sebő, who had "never in [his] life seen such 'folksy carrying on' [*népieskedés*]," felt that he would only be interested in being involved with the *táncház* if "it were not merely acting like people from Szék [*Székieskedés*] or a closed club for folk dancers [but] that kind of urban form of entertainment whose doors stood open to everyone" (ibid.). To this end, organizers agreed on opening the doors to the public; developing a "common language," or a uniform dance suite; and institutionalizing musical instruction (ibid.).

Soon thereafter, the Sebő Club began to function in the Lajos Kassák Művelődési Ház (Kassák Klub), and in 1973, a weekly *táncház* also began to function at the Capital City House of Culture (Maácz 1981a, 84).[11] The Sebő Club was not strictly a *táncház* but included *táncház*-style folk dancing on its program alongside poetry readings, screenings of ethnographic films, and occasional demonstrations by villagers (Striker 1987a, 113). When the Halmos-Sebő duo was invited to Japan for half a year, another band, Muzsikás (Musician) was formed to take its place.[12] The Muzsikás *táncház* began functioning in 1974 (Halmos 2000, 58). As bands proliferated, each sought to establish its own *táncház* because, as one *táncház* musician pointed out to me, "playing for dancers is the purpose of such a band; the only way to improve is to play for dancers." Martin (1981, 45) also writes that the musicians "realized quickly that it is not possible to do this well without dance, and that inasmuch as they constantly move together, it develops with the dance."

The proliferation of bands and dancehouses also served to enlarge the repertoire beyond the dances of Szék, as each band sought to explore new territory, and dancers were eager to learn new dances and dance suites (Halmos 2000, 38). The Népművelési Intézet's implementation of a *táncház* leader course for *táncház* bands in 1976 further aided this rapid proliferation of *táncház* clubs (Magyar Népművelési Intézet 1976, 24;

Fig. 4.2 A 1976 *táncház*: the Sebő Club (Kassák Lajos Művelődési Ház). Photo by Zoltán Szalay, courtesy of the Folklore Documentation Library and Archive, Heritage House.

Halmos 2000, 38). By the mid- to late 1980s, my interlocutors recall, it was possible to visit a different *táncház* in Budapest each day of the week.

Why did people go to the *táncház*? In the words of Ferenc Sebő (1998, 36): "The experience of authentic folk music and dance in the city as compared to the hackneyed labour movement songs and the stage repertory was revelatory for musicians and the public alike." Contrasting *táncház* with the "discos" common in the period, another participant told me, "right now there are multiple choices for each individual.... In the 1970s, it was the only opportunity to meet with your contemporaries with the lights switched on.... I was myself. I could sing, I could dance, I could meet people with whom I shared something in common, and that was important. And it was a meeting place that was contrary to the disco.... The discos were dark, and you were dancing with someone you could hardly see ... and couldn't talk to.[13]

Fig. 4.3 A *táncház* at Fővárosi Művelődési Ház (FMH), Sebő ensemble, circa 1976. Photo by Zoltán Szalay, courtesy of the Folklore Documentation Library and Archive, Heritage House.

As seen in chapter 3, studies were conducted at the Institute for Culture both to investigate the characteristics of new movements and to facilitate their development. Under the supervision of Iván Vitányi, himself a former Muharay ensemble dancer, researchers produced a number of studies on the Beat and *táncház* movements. But the role of the institute did not stop there. The institute sponsored *táncház* by offering the *táncház* leader courses mentioned previously; publishing the Sebő Club's journal, *Síppal, Dobbal* (With a whistle, with a drum); and continuing to provide advice and resources to dancers, musicians, and culture house workers.

Studies of the *táncház* compared it with earlier revivals and youth movements. In her 1978 article entitled "The Táncház," Mária Sági asserts that discipline was what distinguished the *táncház* from both the Beat movement and the Coalition period folk art movement of the youth (as represented by the Muharay dancers). The fact that *táncház*-goers were required to learn dances and dance suites in relationship to the music made the environment of a *táncház* quite different than that of discos or Beat gatherings, where individuals danced as they pleased. She argues that the discipline practiced in *táncház* appeared to be a perfect point on the spectrum between community and self-expression.[14] *Tánchăz*-goers expressed this as well, albeit in a less academic way. In the words of one, quoted by Sági (1978, 74): "After having been to *tánchăz* I could not go [to the disco] to dance. It would seem completely ridiculous. In the disco they flop around, if they must. But in *tánchăz* they feel like they are not just standing there and doing it but that they know something, and in this way I appreciate myself."

Vitányi, whose "A Magyar Néptáncmozgalom Története 1948-ig" (The history of the Hungarian folk dance movement until 1948) had been published in 1964, writes that he hadn't seen anything like *tánchăz* since the Coalition period, noting that while Muharay's troupe had wanted both to perform and to bring folk dance into everyday life, they had largely failed at the latter. He argues that conditions necessary for *tánchăz* to emerge had not yet ripened in the Coalition period. While his generation had tried to activate such a movement, the appropriate musical developments had not yet occurred (Vitányi 1972, 15). The collections made in Szék, for example, had not been available to his generation, as they were to this one. Thus, while the Muharay ensemble formed a band and wanted to do what the *tánchăz* bands do, he argues, "it didn't work" (Vitányi 2003).

The state of musical pedagogy in socialist Hungary appears to have contributed to the conditions needed for dancehouse bands to emerge. Sebő and Halmos are examples of this development. Sebő had gone to a music high school, where he played in the symphony. Later, he met Halmos playing in the symphony at the Technical University, where both were students (Siklos 1977, 21). Halmos, too, studied music in his school years (albeit not at a music high school), playing in chamber orchestras and symphonies. The fact that such a musically adept generation was available for such activities resulted partly from the music education policies instituted in the previous two decades under Kodály's influence. In addition to his interest in folk music and composing, Kodály had been an active promoter of the chorus movement in the interwar period. His experiences and aspirations had led him to develop the afore-noted Kodály method, adopted in Hungarian schools during the socialist period. It appears that the *művelődési* program inspired by Kodály left a strong mark on comprehensive music education in Hungary and the musical preparedness of the *tánchăz* generation (Sebő 1993, 57). Even though the Kodály method was mainly aimed at singing, the results of Kodály's efforts explain the preparedness with which *tánchăz* musicians embraced their task, as well as the ease with which young *tánchăz*-goers engaged in singing folk songs.

Indeed, while some interlocutors described their begrudging participation in singing folk songs at school, others suggested that their broad knowledge of folk songs had made it easier for them to engage in collective singing once in the *táncház* context; they knew many of the songs, even if only paired with simplified melodies. This system of musical pedagogy had also produced a generation of well-trained musicians who were not necessarily expecting to become professionals; the aim was "not to train professional musicians, but to give music-loving youngsters a real understanding of music" (Friss 1966, 133). As the official system faced increasing difficulty in absorbing the baby boom generation (Striker 1987, 103), musically trained young people seized unofficial opportunities to engage in semiprofessional musical careers. Many, including Sebő and Halmos, earned a part of their income from playing music and from *táncház*-related activities.

But the developments Vitányi had in mind were not limited to music. Researchers of the *táncház* pointed to the fact that Hungarian society itself had not been in the position for such a revival to emerge in the 1940s and 1950s. Martin notes that by the 1970s, Hungarian society had become more uniform, allowing collectors to meet with an openness and readiness that had not existed in the past (Martin 1988, 109). According to Frigyesi (1996, 70), in contrast with members of earlier generations, *táncház* revivalists developed an intimate relationship with informants: "musicians are not informants whom one may record and then store the material in an archive; rather, they regard them as partners and masters." Martin further points out that the choreographies that developed in the 1940s and the following decades reflected the fact that little was known about the structural qualities of Hungarian folk dance. By the 1970s, the collections necessary for the revival had been amassed in a usable way, and ample material had been collected and analyzed by researchers, a project in which Martin himself was intimately involved (Martin 1974, 64; Budai 1988, 109).

Finally, in 1970s Hungary, youths had ample leisure time to engage in such activities as well as opportunities to travel, if mostly only to neighboring countries. As Sági (1978, 71) writes about the Muharay generation, "who had time in the middle of land reform, rebuilding and organizing People's Colleges to take a month to learn a dance motif or to practice for a year so that a sound similar to that of peasant musicians would strike out from the viola (*brácsa*)?"[15] In the socialist period, because both folk ensembles and researchers received government funding, some of these activities even benefited from government aid. The travel expenses of folk ensembles were usually paid, and the institute funded some collection efforts as well.

Because Hungary's economy was relatively stronger, Transylvania was a cheap (both familiar and exotic) destination for Hungarians and convenient, too, as it did not require knowledge of a foreign language.

In her 1977 study, "Táncház a Kassákban" (Táncház in the Kassák Club), Sági examines the demographic of *táncház*-goers, discovering from this case study of the Sebő Club that participants ranged in age from sixteen to thirty-five, with the majority (58 percent) hovering between nineteen and twenty-four (Sági 1977, 2). While the majority of participants were elites or intellectuals, she found that a significant number of workers, and even more children of workers were participating as well. The average number of attendees on a given night was seventy-four, half of whom reported attending other *táncház*es on other nights of the week. This study conducted in the 1970s informs the assumption held by most *táncház*-goers I met with through 2006: that *táncház* is primarily the activity of intellectuals and youths.[16] Yet as Szabó (1998, 173) writes, by the 1980s, *táncház* could be "considered an avant garde '*közművelési*' activity . . . meeting the demand of larger masses of people." Anecdotes suggest that by the mid-1980s, *táncház*es may have been one of the most actively attended popular culture leisure activities in Budapest, and *táncház*-goers report that by the mid-1980s, it was possible to attend a different *táncház* any night of the week, each with its own crowd of regulars.

In their work on Beat and *táncház*, both Vitányi and Sági point to the important role art played in precapitalist societies in which art was an everyday community form (Vitányi 1974; Sági 1978). Referring to the ideas of (Austrian-born) communist composer Hanns Eisler, Sági distinguishes the enjoyment of music in prebourgeois society from that in bourgeois society by its relationship to discipline.[17] Asserting that music of a socialist society should turn back to discipline, she argues that self-expression without discipline "necessarily becomes merely an object of enjoyment" (Sági 1978, 73). In 1971, in his book *Második Prométheuszi Forradalom* (Second Promethean revolution), Vitányi had already argued that theme, content, form, and material (substance) had not been separate in prebourgeois political economies but, rather, made up an "untroubled naive whole" (251). The societal function of art in "that perfectly different world system had the emotional and meaningful (*érzelmi* and *értelmi*) effect of helping to orient people in that world" (252). In the capitalist system, he argues, art is taken from its community context, and community (*közösség*) is replaced by audiences (*közönségek*). With this process, the two forms of art—the art for art's sake of the initiated and the kitsch of the masses—become more and more differentiated (253).

As is clear, these people were not just studying and theorizing but doing so from the perspective of cultural managers toward the end of building a socialist society. Another writer asserts that only on "the basis of folk art is a radical break from the petite bourgeois (*nyárspolgári*, 'philistine') commercial, capitalist culture of kitsch possible" (Szalay 1974, 54). In 1974, writing in defense of the *táncház*, Vitányi argued, "Socialist cultural politics (*művelődéspolitika*) cannot relax into this kind of separation of the everyday of communities and art. Rather, *művelődés* wishes to provide that kind of structure in which art with an active and creative character gets a place in the life of the everyday" (1974, 11). Two years later, we find Sebő (1976a, 5) expressing a similar position: "At the beginning, we were immediately preoccupied with what folk art is about; that it creates community and spreads the basis of cultured recreation (*szórakozás*) and awakens the demand for more and better too." While critics feared that the movement was inspired by or might encourage nationalism, supporters, agreeing that there had been a relationship between folk art revival and nationalism in the past, claimed that the new trend should be seen in the tradition of Bartók and Kodály. It reflected, they argued, the serious research of folk forms and their integration into modern life, and was protected from straying toward nationalism by its "robust socialist conception" (L. Kósa 1974, 42; see also Vargyas 1974, 47–48). Vitányi argued it was essential to socialist cultivation (*közmvelodés*) that urbanists (*urbánusok*) and populists (*népiek*) learn to hold hands in the manner exemplified by Bartók (Vitányi 1974, 10). This required, in his estimation, "not more and better culture, but different shape and structure" (10).

Articles pointed to the role of members of the Sebő ensemble as cultivators (*népművelők*) in contrast to that of the members of Beat bands as stars (Sebő 1976b, 188). One of Sebő's interviewers described their activities as a "particular apparatus of cultivation" with the goal of "spreading folk music and folk dance not on the stage but in everyday life" (192). "It was clear from the beginning," Striker (1987a, 113) writes, "that this initiative is more than a leisure time activity: it had a cultural-educational mission as well." Arguing that nationalism should not be considered the main content of the "folklore new wave," Vitányi (1972, 15) warns that while they had missed the boat on utilizing the "mobilizing power" of the Beat movement, they still had the opportunity to align this new movement to the developing system of *közművelődés*.

By 1976, the plans had been finalized for the *táncház* leader course offered by the institute's Department of Pedagogy (Oktatási Osztály) to facilitate "strengthening community spirit with the patriotic [*hazai*] and people's [*népi*] character of today's living everyday dance language and music" (Magyar Népművelési Intézet 1976). Timár, Sebő, and Halmos were appointed chief instructors. For those holding a performance permit, the program lasted for two years and for those without, three. Meetings took place every third weekend, with one- and two-week intensive training camps scattered throughout the year. From the late 1970s onward, training for musicians and dance instructors was regular but "only on the peripheries of the official education system" (Halmos 2000, 38), organized usually as summer camps or workshops "primarily under the auspices of cultural centers and dance ensembles" (ibid.). The result of the 1976–78 training course for *táncház* musicians and dance instructors run by the institute "was an upsurge of *táncház* founding in provincial towns, and several more established in Budapest as well" (ibid.).

With this, the repertoire of dances also began to expand. "The dances of Hungary's minority groups—Romanian, South Slav, and 'Gypsy' dances—had been taught from the very first. Before long, independent ethnic dancehouses were being set up, South Slav, Greek, Bulgarian, Romanian" and other dance suites (Halmos 2000, 38). In other words, while "ethnic dances," or the dances of the "nationalities," first appeared as elements within *táncházes,* separate events began to develop around the dances of particular ethnicities, foremost among them Greek and Southern Slav.[18]

As might be expected, *táncház* events were (and are) primarily held in culture houses, "generally managed by the members of the orchestra and dancing instructors," who "sign the written contracts with the state-run cultural centers" (Halmos 2000, 34). The fees, Halmos writes, do not cover the expenses, which means that "the operation of practically every *táncház* depends on state subsidies" (ibid.).

Beyond a few examples, Juhász and Szabó (n.d., 10) note, scientific interest in the *táncház* theme had practically disappeared by the mid-1980s. Today, studies on Hungarian folk dance and folk music abound, aided by the professonalization of the *táncház* generation, and there are many papers published on the *táncház* yearly. Yet Juhász and Szabó are right in the sense that the systematic sociological study of the character of *táncház* as a movement has been replaced by studies focused on more specific elements. These include aesthetic aspects (Frigyesi 1996), *táncház*'s relationship to tourism (Z. Szabó 1998), its status as a phenomenon of folklorism (Juhász and Szabó n.d.; Striker 1987a), its rise and general precursors (Halmos 1994, 2000), the spread of Transylvanian dances and the *táncház* technique to the United States (Cardaro 1998), membership in a dance group as a community of practice (Langman 2003), and issues of gender and ethnic performance and their intertwining (Hooker 2005, 2007). A more comprehensive review of the literature toward the conclusion that *tánchaz* as a movement is a successful model of safeguarding the "core participatory social-aesthetic" can be found in Quigley (2014). The majority of these studies have been produced by participants, whether from Hungary or abroad.[19] Studies based on surveys distributed at the annual Dancehouse Meeting (which I go on to discuss) have also appeared in *FolkMAGazin*, a quarterly published by the Táncház Foundation, yet it is questionable how representative of the population that regularly engages in *táncház* activities those who attend this meeting are.

Village Visiting Revisited: Transylvania and Other "Pure Sources"

While the primary location of *táncház* clubs was and remains in Budapest, with some also in provincial cities, the movement cannot be understood without attention to the rural locations that provided the pure source for dances and dance cycles. As a result of historical conditions and the geography of uneven development, and partly in response to ethnic repression, ethnic Hungarians in Transylvania had preserved folk traditions to a greater degree than had those in "truncated Hungary." As described previously, early *táncház* revivalists found not only musical and dance influences but also culturo-aesthetic influences in the dance culture of Szék, leading them to adopt the social form of the dancehouse. The relatively high living standards in Hungary at the time provided many with the opportunity for Eastern bloc tourism, including the possibility to travel to Transylvania to experience "living folk culture." Following in the researchers' footsteps, musicians and dancers visited villages in the Hungarian countryside and in Transylvania. The desire to learn from living masters in authentic places resulted in patterns of village ethnotourism, most notably to Transylvania, where visitors became acquainted with the Hungarian-speaking minority in what was, of course, another country: neighboring Romania. During this period, the ethnic Hungarians and Hungarian-speaking Roma who hosted participants of the *táncház* risked punishment for their wholehearted welcome of Hungarian nationals in their homes, an act technically illegal under the nationalist policies of the Nicolae Ceausescu regime that ended in 1989 (Ronay 1992; Z. Szabó 1998, 175; Kürti 2001). *Táncház* musicians visiting Transylvania believed that "this music can be learned only in practice and only from the musicians who still play it" (Frigyesi 1996, 70; see also Hooker 2002).[20]

Because of the long-established professional niche of this ethnic group as musicians, the majority of the masters of this musical form in Transylvania were Roma.[21] This placed Roma, a universally oppressed group in the region, in an interesting position vis-á-vis the Hungarian nation, as well as their *táncház* students, as guardians of the national musical tradition (Bartók 1976; Hooker 2005). As understudies to Roma masters, *táncház* musicians became intimate with them in the process. As Sándor Csoóri Jr. related to me, fiddler "Ádám István told his children to treat me as their brother. He adopted me as his own son." Frigyesi notes the novelty of this relationship. Rather than treating the musicians as informants, as had been done in the past, revivalists approached village musicians as masters. She notes that by the 1970s, the urban-rural divide that had plagued Bartók and Kodály in their collection efforts had been diminished to the extent that "the musicians of Szék accepted the long haired hooligan-looking students from Budapest without any problem" (Frigyesi 1996, 70). This novelty reflected not only the relationship between urban and rural people but also that between "Hungarians" and "Roma."[22]

This was by no means the first time Roma and national music had been connected in the Hungarian culture area. Importantly, Roma, or *Cigányok* (Gypsies), as these musicians tend to refer to themselves (as do revivalists), were and are associated with the romantic popular Hungarian "folk music," or *Magyar nóta*, and associated genres that originated in the nation-making projects of the gentry in the nineteenth century and which revivalists consider to be inauthentic.[23] The two are so closely associated that orchestras playing the contemporary music influenced by *Magyar nóta* and the popular dance repertoires of *csárdás* and *verbunkos* are referred to as *Cigányzenekarok* (Gypsy bands) (Frigyesi 1994, 268; 1996, 70).[24] While the large majority of musical masters were Roma, there were ethnic Hungarian musical masters as well.

In contrast with the repertoires of paid musicians, often broad enough to serve three ethnic communities, most of the dancing masters from whom revivalists learned were familiar exclusively with the local dances of their own ethnic group of their respective villages. The exception was generally those who had danced in performing groups or who were taking part in the Transylvanian *táncház* movement.[25] Therefore, Hungarian dances were associated with Hungarian informants; Romanian dances, with Romanians; "Gypsy" dances, with "Gypsies"; and so on.[26] Researchers and revivalists collected music and dances not only of ethnic Hungarians but also of these other ethnic groups, resulting in a body of scholarly literature acknowledging the borrowing and diffusion of forms between groups and aiding the appearance of dances associated with these groups in the regional or place-based dance suites danced by revivalists. Nevertheless, while its participants worked with Roma and collected Slavic, Romanian, and Jewish songs and dances in addition to Hungarian ones, the *táncház* developed and maintained a national(ist) emphasis. Not only has most of its energy focused on ethnic Hungarian music and dance, but its focus on classification has also helped to fix distinctions, boundaries between ethnic versions of dances.[27]

The social form and name of the *táncház* was borrowed in the 1970s from the traditions of the town of Szék (Sic, in Romanian), located in the Transylvanian heath not far from the city of Cluj (in Hungarian, Kolozsvár), the largest Transylvanian city. The prominence of Szék in *táncház* was partly due to the ethnographic record: there was a rich tradition of collection there. Kodály had commented on Szék to ethnomusicologist László Lajtha in the 1940s, saying, "In a place where such beautiful and unique embroidery lives to this day, there must be interesting music too" (Martin 1981, 241). In seeming response, Lajtha's most important and far-reaching work (including the notation and publication of the music) would be on the musical traditions of this town.

The music of Szék had been included in the ambitious Pátria record series, produced in the 1940s (Martin 2001, 32); Szék had also hosted a Bouquet of Pearls dance group, organized by the local pastor, which performed yearly in Budapest from 1941 to 1943. The village research activities of the interwar period and the emigration of students from Cluj to Budapest after the war further resulted in dances from Szék appearing in the repertoires of the NÉKOSZ and Muharay ensembles as well as in the works of the first choreographer of the Hungarian State Folk Ensemble, Míklos Rábai. György Martin, responsible for introducing the *táncház* musicians and dancers and encouraging them to pursue social dance, had also researched the dances of Szék, writing in 1981: "There is no place in the Hungarian culture area where music and dance traditions have been collected in this quantity" (248).

Such ample collection was due to the "living" status of folk dance traditions here. The town of Szék (Székváros, as locals often say) had been a free royal town due to its location near a salt flat. According to Martin (1981, 248), "after it's blossoming as an agrarian town, time stood still." There, "in the middle of the 20th century the old organization of community dance life was thriving" and was only beginning to be replaced by the "new style," making it an important source for historians of dance (248). The town's participation in the Bouquet of Pearls had contributed to the local appreciation of tradition and high regard in which dancers and musicians were held (Martin 2001, 32). It is worth recalling Martin's (1980, 108) statement, quoted in chapter 1, asserting that villages with Bouquet of Pearls groups tended to preserve their folk dance traditions.

Ferenc Novák, the choreographer responsible for organizing the first Budapest *táncház*, produced his thesis, entitled "The Role of Dance in the Social Life of Szék," for a degree in ethnography at Eötvös Loránd University (Martin 1981, 276). As choreographer of the Bihari ensemble, he was in a perfect position to teach the dances to the group.[28] In due course, Sándor Timár, choreographer of the Bartók ensemble, whose knowledge of the dances of Szék had come mostly from silent films, began to invite Szék villagers whom he encountered on the street to dance at rehearsals, in order to develop a better understanding of the dance (Siklos 1977, 15; Paluch 2004, 40).[29] Until the 1970s, many people from Szék continued to wear folk costume in everyday life. On the streets of Budapest, their distinct attire made them recognizable to those in the know not just as peasants or villagers but as people from Szék.

The fact that the dance steps of Szék are "more archaic" and the "form of the dance is simpler, more regulated and communal than elsewhere" (Martin 1981, 249) made them ideal for the spread of folk dance among nondancers in the *táncház*.[30] Easy to learn, these dances made a good starting point for the original generation of *táncház* revivalists. Further, if the youths were to find not just musical but culturo-aesthetic influences in the dance culture of Szék, this meant paying close attention to the function of dance within the social event as well as to the role of the dance event in society. Martin emphasized the community-making aspects of *táncház*, a goal toward which revivalists attempted to preserve as much context as possible. "The principle of the directors of the dance-houses was that there had to be a reason for those dance cycles as they existed in villages and one should at least try out whether they work in the modern context" (Frigyesi 1996, 68). Activities that stressed active participation and cooperation were second only to the tradition-faithful activities characterizing *táncház* (Z. Szabó 1998, 173). One might say that it was the participatory aspect of the social dance tradition that seemed to be the most attractive to the participants.

Thus began the trips by *táncház* participants to the Transylvanian countryside inhabited by ethnic Hungarians, a romantic agrarian environment increasingly endangered not only by urbanization and modernization, but also by the nation-making politics of the Romanian administration. Village visiting was back. As village life was transformed by labor migration, state-imposed demographic policies, secularization, and modernization, the traditional settings and ritual cycles to which folk dance events were central were diminishing (see Kligman 1988). Among the traditions under threat was the institution of the village *táncház* (and dance events similar to it), which, until then, had been widespread throughout the region. What made dancehouses distinct from dance events attached to occasions such as weddings and funerals was their express association with unmarried youths (Halmos 2000, 30).[31] Organized by eligible bachelors (lads), the *táncház* served the purpose of dancing together with eligible girls (lasses), encouraging courtship and locally appropriate sociability with dance at the forefront. "A married man who wanted to dance had to wait for a holiday, a wedding or a ball; for him, *táncház* was off limits" (31). What had been a Transylvanian activity for village youth became the model of sociability for the urban youth revival in Hungary. The *táncház* context was an ideal environment for courtship, and the first generation of *táncház* revivalists was made up of a similar age group.

Perhaps the most important factor for *táncház* tourism was the fact that the popular arts of Transylvanian villages, dance included, had been maintained into the 1970s if not entirely unchanged at least in "living form" (Halmos 2000, 36). Villagers had continued to engage in folk dance in everyday life rather than as a staged event. Beyond villages like Szék, where dance continued to be a vital element in village sociality, dance events had also sprung up in the cities of Romania where migrant ethnic Hungarian villagers could meet and socialize. Martin (1982, 1) tells of the dances held by domestic and agricultural workers from Szék in Cluj, the regional capital. "Dressed in their distinctive folk costume the people from Szék gathered to sing and dance in the main square of Kolozsvár (Cluj)" and in other places as well (2001, 32; see also ibid. 1982, 1). Further, just as in Hungary, Romania had its Soviet-style performing troupes. Beyond the sporadic participation of some ethnic Hungarian groups in nationwide Romanian folk festivals, the ethnic Hungarian autonomous region, which existed until 1968, featured its own dance ensemble.[32]

Ethnic Hungarian musicologists in Romania also engaged in research and collection, some under János Jagamas, a student of Kodály's teaching at Cluj University. While Transylvanian ethnographers worked with those from Hungary even when the Romanian government began to take a more explicitly nationalist stance under Ceaușescu, participants suggested that this collaboration became more difficult beginning in the early 1970s. An important resource for folk songs among *táncház*-goers was a collection by Transylvanian teacher and ethnomusicologist Zoltán Kallos, who, early *tánchác*-goers told me, drew huge crowds during his visits to Hungary in the 1970s.[33] Transylvanian Hungarians point out that they had their own *tánchác* movement, developing in parallel and relation with the Hungarian movement but subject to the specificities of conditions in Romania.[34] Unlike the Hungarian one, they claim, the Transylvanian movement was not "rootless," for the "urban layer in Transylvania was very thin"; just about everyone had relatives in a village. Beyond the migrant workers holding dances, and student intellectuals holding dancehouses in the cities, youth in Transylvanian villages themselves also embraced the trend, donning folk costumes that had been abandoned and turning to their elders for material and inspiration.

In the 1970s and 1980s, most trips by *tánchác* participants were made informally. While the institute provided some support for collection trips, the majority of *tánchác*-goers took advantage of networks of acquaintances and the famous hospitality of Transylvanian villagers. They joined them at weddings, christenings, and dancehouses, bringing them in appreciation gifts of treasured goods, such as coffee, sugar, and clothing, and purchasing folk crafts and folk costumes in a mutually supportive relationship.[35] Some visitors quite consciously purchased goods from Transylvanians in order to help relieve their desperate economic situation; the conspicuous use of such goods simultaneously marked buyers as supporters of this cause. Meanwhile, the questionable legality of visits, combined with their feeling that Hungarians, in particular, faced discrimination, deepened visitors' sense of adventure and pursuit of justice.[36]

INSTITUTIONALIZING TÁNCHÁZ

By the 1980s, *tánchác* was experiencing several important forms of institutionalization, setting important institutional and organizational precedents: the solidification of the folk dance camp form, the establishment of the yearly Táncház Meeting (Tánchácztalálkozó) in 1982, and in 1987 the formation of the Táncház Chamber, as the organizational body behind it. In 2001, Heritage House (Hagyományok Háza) emerged from within the Institute for Culture (by then, the Magyar Művelődési Intézet) to become an independent state-funded institution, under the authority of the Ministry of Cultural Heritage.[37] At the time of my research, it continued to share a building with the institute.[38]

Socialist Hungary had a tradition of training camps to which the international architecture camp that Sebő and Halmos had attended belonged.[39] In the early 1970s, the Young Folk Artists' Studio began to organize camps with the help of the institute. Some camps for young folk artists, including music and dance as branches of folk art, even featured *táncház* bands. In 1975, the first Kassák Club camp was organized by the Sebő ensemble. Participants surveyed folk architecture while staying at a campground in the Tokaj region. The second "Sebő camp," which had about thirty-four participants, was held in 1976 in the Zirc-Bákony region, where they surveyed water mills for the ethnographic museum. The Pioneers (Úttörök), the youngest section of the Young Communists (and based on the Scouts), also organized camps around folk art with the involvement of the Young Folk Artists' Studio, Timár and the Bartók ensemble, the Sebő-Halmos duo, and folk singer Laura Faragó (Trencsényi 1985, 7). The first camp of the *táncház* leader course, organized by the institute from 1976 to 1978, was held in Abaújszántó; the second, in Székesfehérvár. The first camp focused specifically on folk dance took place in 1981, hosted by the Jászberény folk ensemble in Jászberény, where a camp is still held.[40]

In 1983, according to accounts of band members, the Téka ensemble, along with a group of folk artists and *táncház*-goers, decided to go camping together in Zala County, east of Lake Balaton. They explained to me that because there was no place they could play late into the night, they decided "to go to a place where they could play for a week straight without getting kicked out." This "camping trip" is referred to as the first Téka camp; an annual camp that lasted for twenty-one consecutive years. In 1985, the Téka ensemble won the permission and sponsorship of the local council of the village of Nagykálló to have a camp at a site where architecture students would build structures designed by architect Dezső Ekler.[41] While most accounts suggest that the first camp was a casual gathering of friends, according to band members, permissions with the local council had been arranged by one of the artists. Significantly, although no one mentioned it in reference to these camps, members of Téka had been trained at the 1976 *táncház* leader camp in Abaújszántó, thus "qualifying them" to run *táncház* events and as *népművelők*. A program for the first camp that I came across at the Folklore Documentation Archive at Heritage House in 2019 suggests that the gathering was not as spontaneous as accounted, as it lists the Gutenberg Művelődési Ház as a cosponsor.

In the heyday of the Téka camp, band members reported, 1,200 people came for the one-week camp. In the early 1990s, they applied for and received sponsorship for three years from the Soros Foundation, which at that time was funding cultural initiatives (civil society) in the now postsocialist countries. However, according to band members, the money made by the local council of Nagykálló from the annual camps was not reinvested into the campground or into the events, creating problems with the camp

Fig. 4.4 László Porteleki and György Lányi (Téka ensemble) play by campfire. Téka camp, 1985. Photo by György Szeles, courtesy of the Folklore Documentation Library and Archive, Heritage House.

itself. After seventeen years (1985–99), the Téka camp left Nagykálló but continued to host camps elsewhere for another two years, deploying funds from various foundations to buy land for this purpose. By 2004, Téka was no longer hosting a dance and crafts camp but still hosted a music camp for Transylvanian schoolchildren. Meanwhile, at the Nagykálló campsite, the tradition of an annual *táncház* and craft camp continued (still referred to by participants as "the Téka camp"), hosted by other organizers and relying on other bands.

The Téka and Jászberény camps can be seen as precedents for the summer *táncház* camps that began to flourish around 1990, after the "regime change," most in Transylvania. What had been ad hoc tourism to Transylvania in the 1970s and 1980s had become institutionalized in camps by the 1990s, "where those interested can learn from the best informants to sing and dance in an organized environment" (Z. Szabó 1998, 177). Beyond dance instruction, camps often have musical and folk song instruction as well as nightly *mulatság*s (festivities) at which visitors may dance to live accompaniment, often provided by famous Roma fiddlers. Some camps also feature folk craft activities.

Unlike the Téka and Jászberény camps, those in Transylvania are explicitly tied to living culture. The camps focus, more or less, on the authenticity of the places in which they are held, with the music, songs, and dances of that village and region taking precedent. Local informants, often quite elderly, are invited to perform for the visitors and teach dances and songs, while well-known regional fiddlers or entire bands provide musical instruction. These camps will be discussed in much more detail in the next chapter.

The first Táncház Meeting was organized in 1982 as part of the Budapest Spring Festival, which has functioned annually since 1981. By the mid- to late 1990s, the event was drawing twenty-five to thirty thousand people annually (Juhász and Szabó n.d., 174).[42] Different in nature than individual dancehouses, where participatory dance is primary, the Spring Festival is a spectacle where consumption and viewing take precedent (although there are ample opportunities to dance, as well).[43] The event, at which new crafts created by masters are sold alongside vintage folk costume and folk objects, draws a large number of people who are not regular participants at dancehouses. Since its emergence, the Tánczháztalálkozó has been a main source of statistical data on the *táncház* movement.

The Táncház Chamber was founded in 1987. According to István Berán, "the need for joining together emerged chiefly from among musicians, primarily because of the Dancehouse Meeting. There were a few dancers, but only those strictly tied to the *táncház*—dance teachers who effectively teach in the *táncház*." Berán, *táncház* musician, editor of *FolkMAGazin*, and a member of the Táncház Guild's board of directors when I interviewed him in 2004, explained that between 1982 and 1987, the Táncház Meeting had been organized by different institutions. The chamber was founded to fulfill the task of organizing the meeting in a successful and consistent manner. The chamber became the Táncház Guild in 1990, with "the mission . . . to organize events, publications, collection efforts, and educational activities in collaboration with its members and in cooperation with other institutions and organizations" (Bakonyi 2001, 54). Responsible for the annual Tánczháztalálkozó, the guild has also organized the annual fall *táncház* season opening event, "generally attended by 1800–2000 participants" since 1990, and the Budapest Folk Festival, since 1993 (55).[44] In addition, in 1996, the guild released a series of CDs entitled New Living Folk Music (Új elő népzene), mainly featuring revivalist musicians and edited by a member of Téka (ibid.), and has continued to produce a new one annually on the occasion of each Tánczháztalálkozó. The guild also works closely with the *Táncház* Foundation, which, with the sometime sponsorship of the institute, the Association of Folk Art Societies, the Elemér Muharay Folk Art Society (56), and the National Culture Fund and Ministry of Cultural Heritage, has published the (usually) quarterly *FolkMAGazin* since it was established in 1993 (ibid.).

During my fieldwork, I was the guest of Heritage House. Located in the building that still sported the sign "Népművelési Intézet" when I visited frequently in 2004 and 2005, Heritage House was established in 2001 as the National Institution of the Ministry of Heritage.[45] At that time, László Kelemen, ethnomusicologist, musician, and early participant in the Transylvanian *táncház* movement, was director, and Ferenc Sebő was creative director at the Hungarian State Folk Ensemble there. Sebő expressed to me in an interview that the establishment of Heritage House was inspired by the idea of creating a national institution funded by the state that was dedicated to the "mother tongue" of sound and movement. Conceived as a state institution, he explained, Heritage House was modeled after the national institutions established in the nineteenth century, such as the National Theater (which, in the spirit of nation-building, sponsored theater performed in Hungarian). Referring to Kodály, Sebő stressed that communication is more than language. It includes song, dance, movement, and speech. When the national institutions were established, he explained, music and dance were nevertheless left out of the picture.[46] Founders conceived of Heritage House as the remedy for this lacuna.

Heritage House was thus designed to research and provide services involving the "higher levels of language": music and dance. It was important to the founders, Sebő told me, that this be a state-funded institution and that the state consider it important enough to grant it that status. While like the Hungarian Institute for Culture, Heritage House was intended to serve the purpose of Hungarian *művelődés*, Sebő stressed that Heritage House must be separate, for in the past, this kind of project had been subordinated to the approaches embraced by the institute. Hagyományok Háza has three different layers: the state folk dance ensemble, the archives, and the task of *közművelés*, or service to the community and public relations. Heritage House is also home to the Martin Media Library, a constantly enriched collection of folk dance documentation, both written and video based, with (the late) György Martin's own library as its core, and the Táncház Archivum, an archive of materials about the táncház movement, founded and run by Béla Halmos until his death in 2013. Among the many projects of Heritage House was the Új Pátria/ Utolsó Óra series of CDs and related projects. Explicitly referencing the Pátria series mentioned in chapter 1, and supported by EEA and Norway Grants (together, 85 percent of the funding), the Hungarian Ministry of Education and Culture, and the folk music club FONO, the project recorded and released fifty CDs documenting Hungarian folk music (Utolsó Óra, n.d.).[47]

The institutional split that produced Heritage House as distinct from the Hungarian Institute for Culture illustrates the diversion of two different approaches toward culture: one attending to cultivation and the other, to heritage or tradition. The relationship between these two notions of culture is in flux, as periodic changes in the name and tasks of the Ministry of Culture reflects. People at Heritage House were not eager to speak to me frankly about the relationship between Heritage House and the Hungarian Institute for Culture (Magyar Művelődési Intézet, henceforth MMI). It was clear that there was some tension between the institutions, which is not surprising given the meagerness of state support and the inevitable competition for funding and space. But I suspect that the competing approaches toward culture and their associated emphases were also quite important to this tension. Heritage House representatives spoke to me as if the need for its establishment as a separate institution was self-evident. When I suggested that it was a pity to disconnect folk art from other questions of *művelődés*, they argued that they had always been separate and that folk art had always been marginalized in the context of the institute. Yet as we saw in chapter 3, this relationship has been in flux within the institute and outside it. If anything, the separation and ideological alienation of the two institutions points to a new constellation of relationships between cultural elements under current conditions. Examining the missions of the two institutes may shed light on this trend.[48]

As mentioned in chapter 3, the National Center for Public Cultivation (OKK) was formed in 1986, according to the notion that the *művelődési* structure was needed to encourage democratic consensus and mutual tolerance in a state changing from a dictatorial party state to one based on democratic rights (Nemzeti Kulturális Örökség Minisztériuma Közművelődési Főosztálya 2000, 45). Functioning within the OKK were the Népművelési Intézet, along with a new Cultural Research Institute (Művelődéskutató Intézet) that employed the tools of sociology to examine the status of national *művelődés* and the Methodological Institute (Módszertani Intézet), whose main tasks were: (1) community development (*közösségfejlősztés*), toward which the Department of Culture Houses would encourage "citizen activities" (*állampolgári aktivitást*); (2) reform and *művelődés*; and (3) revival of the folk high school movement (*népfőiskolai mozgalom* [see chapter 3]) by establishing the Hungarian Society of Folk High Schools (Magyar Népfőiskolai Társaság) in 1988 (H. Polgár 1994, i).

In 1992, the OKK was replaced by the MMI.[49] The law bringing the MMI into existence states:

The Magyar Művelődési Intézet was founded with the goal that the institute analyze the cultural activities taking place in the community, townships, associations, social establishments, cultural institutions (művelődési intézményekben); to develop programs to spread the conditions for community culture (közösségi művelődés); to sponsor new cultural initiatives (művelődési kezdeményezéseket), such as the folk art which is an organic part of universal art, the creative perpetuation of the living cultural traditions of Hungarians and nationalities living in our land, the transmission of the cultural values of the Hungarians living over the borders and of neighboring countries and cooperation with their cultural institutions and organizations. (Magyar Kulturális Minisztériuma 1992, 225)[50]

In 2006, the MMI's website described its mission in the English language as promoting "the continuous development of the organizational framework and contents of community education and community arts," facilitating the "modernization of community education duties by some peculiar professional instruments," and contributing to the investigation of "characteristics of cultural life and community education, the presentation and publication of different contexts and interconnections, and the promotion of the professionalism of national and local decision-making processes through organizing and performing research" (Magyar Művelődési Intézet n.d.).[51]

Unlike the MMI, Hagyományok Háza had not posted its "mission statement," but its website stressed that it is a service center with three units that employ different tools all dedicated to folk culture (népi kultura) and that it addresses a broad audience interested in tradition as well as professionals. Three units outlined were the state ensemble; the László Lajtha Folklore Documentation Center, which makes text and audiovisual materials available to the public; and the folk art methodology studio [népművészeti módszertani studio], which sponsors civil and professional organizations and the organization of events, engages in outreach to marketing and educational services, and broadens international connections in the folk art professions"(Hagyományok Háza n.d.).

Key terms for the MMI, then, were *community education* and *community arts*, while for Heritage House they were *folk tradition, folk culture*, and *folk art*. While it may be assumed that folk art serves the goals stated by the MMI (and we find it stating such in earlier statements from the organization before the split) *Hagyományok Háza* does not state community building as its goal, and the MMI rarely pointed to folk culture as a source of community building. Indeed, according to their websites in 2006, the approaches of the two institutions seem to completely diverge. I will take up reasons for this in chapter 7 and the conclusion.

Socialist Cultivation or Civil Society?

Many characteristics of the early *tánchaz* discussed previously fit into a larger trend of youth movements connected with folk music and folk dance in Europe and the United States (Slobin 1996, 5). Owe Ronström (1998) writes that European folk revival movements of the late 1960s and early 1970s stemmed from the processes of urbanization, centralization, and modernization. He points to a number of contributing factors, including rapid population growth after World War II and the rapid expansion of the world economy in the 1950s, leading to migration into the cities. The children of this migrant generation had little experience of the countryside, no experience of war, and less insecurity about the future (39). The postwar period was marked by social engineering projects aimed at the creation of the "new man" and the development of new technologies, the experience of which "came to divorce this generation from the preceding ones" (ibid.). Connected to these changes was the possibility to cultivate music in new ways with new recording and playback technologies. The growing gap between old and new, or tradition and modernity, meant that the lives of the generation born in the 1950s were radically different from those of generations past. Being completely "abandoned," the earlier lifestyles had been "well documented and transformed into cultural heritage," preserved by museums and experts (ibid.).

In the 1960s, the economy expanded even further and college students flooded the cities. These youths tended to have both spending power and leisure time, making it harder for the state to retain centralized control. Changes in media policy brought original folk recordings to the air waves, and youths began to use this new resource to distance themselves from their parents' generation. The music scene arising from these conditions was by no means limited to folk, but it pursued interesting new sounds and methods, among them, those of folk music. As Ronström (1997, 40) suggests, with their focus on process, not product, these movements turned away from the big, grand performances, flags, and parades of the earlier generation and toward amateur ethnographic research and the development of "alternative lifestyles" and amateur activities. Such activities led to a different understanding of folk culture and tradition as creative process, requiring participants to "develop a better understanding of how this creative process worked" (ibid.). According to Ronström, revivalists recognized that "music and dance ... [were] only a part of a much larger context" (39). He does not touch on the relationship of such movements to cultural policy or to discussions relating folk art to community building, a central concern in the Hungarian discussion of *tánchaz*.

Although activities were in some respects spontaneous, the role of the Institute for Culture illustrates mutually informing links between state cultural management or cultivation and this youth movement. Initial participants of Beat and *tánchaz* bands had their first taste of publicity in the state run *Who Can Do What?* and *Fly Peacock* competitions, while folk dancers had functioned mainly in the world of festivals and competitions. All derived support from state institutions that provided, among other things, the naturalized spaces of cultural activity and association: culture houses and clubs. Youths responded to the "manufactured" programs of socialist planning, or perhaps simply the discontents of urban life, in creative ways, with the materials and in the contexts available to them, producing the Beat movement and, later, the *tánchaz*, movement while cultural managers tried to steer these initiatives or at least legitimize them. Two things that distinguished the *tánchaz* movement from the Beat movement were that *tánchaz* took participation further, blurring the lines between performer and audience and thus creating a participant base much more involved than Beat "fans," and that it was connected with place; *tánchaz* sought authenticity in locally based practices.[52] While these innovations were reactions to the Beat and to conditions of late socialism, it was not the first time that Transylvania had loomed large in the quest for authenticity. We see important continuities in the focus on Transylvania and in the practices of amateur ethnography and village visiting. As before, this authenticity was combined with an emphasis on justice (this will be taken up later). The nation, of course, loomed over it as well.

The Beat and *tánchaz* movements were studied by the Institute of Culture, which made recommendations for sponsorship based on ideals and realities of socialist socialization. Negotiation was not only made between some abstract state and organized and reified movements, but between actors and factions of actors, many in cultural management. In this way resources and contexts become available to youth movements through the state, just as state approaches were also subject to change in reaction to these movements.

It would not be useful to regard either the Beat or the *tánchaz* movement as top-down state projects or as strongholds of the party. Yet one might ask if the particular characteristics of these movements make them, at least in part, socialist movements. They were the products of the convergence of international trends and the specific conditions and discourses of late Hungarian socialism, notably of community-making and of *művelődés*. Further, while institutions such as the Institute of Culture made it their task to support those movements that could be used or harnessed toward the end of socialist cultivation, this did not necessarily do so "in the interest of the socialist state." As Alexei Yurchak (2005, 8) has pointed out, "for many, 'socialism' as a system of human values and as an everyday reality of 'normal life' . . . was not necessarily equivalent to 'the state' or 'ideology'; indeed, living socialism to them often meant something quite different from the official interpretations provided by state rhetoric." Writing about Soviet cultural managers, Lewis H. Siegelbaum (1999, 79) asserts that "most clubs endeavored to perpetuate the enlightenment functions of the pre-Revolutionary societies; others sought to promote a revolution in daily life . . . and encourage the creative self-expression . . . of workers." Vitányi, a committed socialist, suggested to me that his job had been to nurture civil society. His 1993 book tells of a pact he and some *népi* friends, fresh out of the resistance movement, made during the Coalition period. As they saw the Communist Party slowly wresting control from the coalition, they agreed to engage in the April Front. Harking back to the March Front, they agreed to continue to work toward democracy in Hungary.

When cultural managers professed their interest in building socialist society, and when youths spoke of *művelődés* or community-building, they may have been engaging in what Yurchak has called the "normalization of language." In the case of the Soviet Union, Yurchak (2005, 53) shows how "with increasing emphasis on the replication of form, what meanings or functions concrete texts and slogans had was becoming increasingly unpredictable; meaning was sliding in unprecedented directions." Rather than seeing the experience of socialism in binary terms, Yurchak suggests we consider the reproduction/employment of authoritative discourse as resulting in a growing gap between the performative and constative dimensions of the speech act (93). Yet even this opposition, Yurchak shows, is not a prosocialist/antisocialist one. He accounts the experience of one Komsomol (Soviet Youth League Organization) secretary, who "came to believe that many basic socialist values that he thought were important—education, professional work, social welfare, a collectivist ethic—were enabled by bureaucratic rules and that some forms of the Komsomol work had to be repeated just at the level of the ritual although others had to be performed with a particular focus on meaning" (ibid.).

Conclusion

Táncház practices arose in 1970s Hungary from a convergence of interests in folk music and dance crucial for reviving the social dance event. Further, they connected youth with practices much like the village visiting of the interwar period did, with Transylvania emerging as an important site for a number of reasons. These initiatives were supported by researchers and cultural managers sympathetic with the *táncház* movement, who stressed that its participatory elements were productive of community and in line with socialist consciousness. As spontaneous as the *táncház* appeared, its conditions had been nurtured by these researchers and cultural managers, many of whom had been connected with the populist activities of the interwar and Coalition periods, and by widespread music education in socialist Hungary.

The *táncház* movement thus emerged through the interaction between youth movements and projects concerning the performance and preservation of folk forms as well as projects of cultivation that occupied various positions vis-á-vis the "liberalizing" Hungarian state within international conditions promoting a turn toward folk revival. Youths in Beat bands, "young folk artists," and *táncház* participants interacted with a state-funded yet decentralized system of cultural management that encompassed professional and amateur ensembles; ethnographic, ethnomusicological, and dance research efforts; and television competitions and festivals.

The development of *táncház* reflects the political economic period in which it merged. The state provided a particular environment for associative activities both consistent and inconsistent with the stated ideology of late Hungarian socialism that "all who are not against us are with us." Not only did key movement participants emerge from state-run competitions, but state-run culture houses were key locations for movement activities. In the case of the *táncház*, resources were requested and received from state institutions in the form of courses for folk music and dance instructors and the establishment of summer camps. The flexibility of the system of cultural management also reflects the rise of the idea of *közművelés*, a notion of civic cultivation/civil society based on mutual input by managers and the public, the cultural and economic thrusts of the tourism and entertainment industries, and the decrease in state funding and concurrent emphasis on entrepreneurialism. Even as the state rolled back subsidies for culture and relied on entrepreneurialism in the cultural sphere, this generation continued to develop a strong expectation that state resources should be available for culture. This expectation did not disappear after 1989, even as other sources became available. As Halmos would write in 2000: "Practically every *táncház* depends on state subsidies" (34).

The institutionalization of the *táncház* in the late socialist period, and throughout the transition, happened in an environment of flux with regard to organizations as well as the language and ideologies that explain their existence. The continued functioning of *táncház*es in houses of culture (to which local councils have been required to provide financial support) is one instance of the reliance of state subsidies; the establishment of Heritage House is another. Heritage House's status as an independent institution further reflects the sustained historical development of the institute and its legacies with all of their continuities and discontinuities since 1946. The language employed and the goals set by Heritage House indicated a move away from the formal institutions of *művelődés/közművelődés*/community arts and an explicit move toward heritage and tradition. This is partly the result of a different attitude or approach toward *művelődés* by those involved in *táncház* management. As members of the Téka ensemble told me when I asked if their camp emphasized *népművelés*, "sure, but through example, not by blabbering."

Changes in language and the disaggregation of approaches to culture raise questions about the transition to capitalism and shifting citizenship regimes. Having covered the rise of *táncház* and its institutionalization, I will examine in the next chapter the process of collective memory production through which a *táncház* framework of sense is formed under changing political and economic conditions.

Notes

1. Maácz (1981a, 92) attributes the term *pure source* to Novák, but the term appears in "the libretto of Bartók's Cantata Profana" (1930), based on a Romanian colinda Bartók translated into Hungarian verse. The phrase "Csak tiszta forrásból" (Only from a pure source) is repeated several times at the end of the piece. In a letter to Romanian colleague Octavian Beu, he also wrote, "nem vonom ki magam semmiféle hatás alól, eredjen az szlovák, román, arab vagy bármiféle más forrásból. Csak tiszta, friss és egészséges legyen az a forrás!" (Bartok in Demény 1976, 396–97). Thanks to Lynn Hooker for this reference.

2. Juhász and Szabó (n.d., 11n) mention writer Sándor Csoóri, folk song collector Zoltán Kallós, ethnographer Bertalan Andrásfalvy, folk dance researcher/ethnographer Pesovár Ferenc, and ethnographer Arpád Együd.

3. Attila József was an acclaimed social democratic poet of the interwar years. Having been an avid participant in the Miklós Bartha Society, he took part in various undertakings of the *népi* movement while becoming more and more involved with the communist strand of the worker's movement and the underground Communist Party. Lászlo Nagy attended a Népi Kollégium and some consider him a to be a *népi* poet of the state socialist era.

4. A *citera* (zither) is a category of stringed instrument of which the dulcimer is one type. It has strings the length of its soundboard and is usually plucked or strummed.

5. Dance suites, or cycles, are sets of dances in a particular order. Each of these dances has stylistic features that define it, but in most dances, the successful improvisation within the limits of the stylistic rules is what marks a good dancer. Dance will be discussed more in chapter 5.

6. For an interesting article on the representative work of folk dance internationalism, see Böröcz (2018).

7. Pávai is the director of the Department of Folklore Documentation at Heritage House.

8. Molnár began as a gymnast in his native Transylvania. After pursuing expressionist modern dance in Paris, he adopted the Bartók program, the idea that that further development of folk dance depended on its collection. Upon his return to Hungary in 1939, he began collecting on silent film (Vitányi 1964, 48). A romantic and *melymagyarista* (promoter of deep Hungarianness) like *népi* writer László Németh (ibid., 49), he led the Szent Imre Kollégium *népi együttes* (ibid., 52). In 1940, he worked as teacher at a Catholic and right-leaning Katolikus Agrárifjúsági Legényegyletek Országos Testülete (KALOT) folk high school (*népfőiskola*) (ibid., 51) while also leading the folk dance ensemble of the Györffy Kollégium, which many characterize as left leaning. He was also the dance leader in the Levente Együttes under Muharay (ibid., 61). Some members of this group went to Weimar and toured Scandinavia with Molnár in 1942, and others went with Muharay to Florence (ibid., 51; Paluch 2004, 38).

9. The people I spoke with distinguished tradition-keeping ensembles from amateur ensembles in that the former are made up of local villagers carrying on local traditions.

10. According to some accounts, Novák feared reprisals against what would be conceived as nationalist activities if they opened up to the public.

11. On the Kassák Club during this period, see György (2019). The Municipal (literally translated as Capital City) House of Culture (Fővárosi Művelődési Ház; FMH) was run by SZOT (the National Council of Trade Unions).

12. This band was arguably the best-known Hungarian folk music band on the world music circuit until my fieldwork period. Its singer, Márta Sebestyén, became well known from the soundtrack of the film *The English Patient*.

13. *Disco* here does not refer to the style of music but rather the act of spinning discs—that is, records. Frigyesi (1996, 55) defines it as social event characterized by "light popular music," or dance club.

14. While she does not refer to it, it is probably no coincidence that this view echoes György Martin's views from his copious research on improvisation in Hungarian folk dance.

15. The *brácsa* is a folk contra fiddle, or viola. It is one of the essential instruments for the most popular *táncház* dance music, along with the *hegedű* (violin) and the *bőgő*, a folk version of a stand-up bass, which is a bowed rhythm instrument.

16. In East Central Europe the term *intellectual* is applied to all those who are university educated (Frigyesi 1996).

17. Eisler composed the anthem of the German Democratic Republic and was a longtime friend and collaborator of Berthold Brecht.

18. Hungary has always had a "multiethnic" population, even after the border changes. So-called southern Slavs have traditionally lived within the territory of the contemporary Hungarian state. Many more live in the territory of historic Hungary, which included Croatia and parts of Serbia and Slovenia. Further, some had relocated to the Budapest area during the Turkish occupation between the fifteenth and seventeenth centuries. There has been a small Greek presence in Hungary dating from the sixteenth century. A large population Greeks came to settle in Hungary after the Greek civil war between 1948 and 1950. Some of the first collection trips Halmos and Sebő made were near Halmos's hometown of Gyula, where they collected Romanian tunes and dances along with Hungarian ones.

19. *Táncház* is a well-known revival movement and has been a model for revivalists across the world. As its forms (both Hungarian folk dance and the pedagogical methods) have spread, so has interest in it. Not only do people (ethnic Hungarian and other) in North America, Japan, and Western Europe participate in *táncház* activities at home, but they also travel to participate in *táncház* activities in Hungary and Transylvania in increasing numbers.

20. There was also concern about ethnic Hungarians in Czechoslovakia and Yugoslavia. One Heritage House administrator told me that it is now in Slovakia that one can experience what the *táncház* was like in Transylvania in the 1970s. At the moment of our interview, ethnic tensions were on the rise in Slovakia, with a far-right party part of the ruling coalition and tensions having

arisen from the question of dual citizenship. Tensions also revolved around whether the Bénes decrees, which deported and dispossessed ethnic German and Hungarians from Slovakia after World War II, should be reconsidered.

21. *Roma* is the plural of *Rom*, the word for "man"/"human" in the Romani language. It is considered the politically correct alternative to the word *Gypsy* and its equivalents, which are deemed derogatory. *Táncház*-goers and Roma with whom they work tend to use the Hungarian variant of "Gypsy," *Cigány*, when referring to the ethnic group generally among participants. I use the term *Roma*, but when I am referring to the use of a person or group that uses the term *Cigány* or citing them (even in translation), I use that or its translation "Gypsy."

22. I put both ethnicities in quotation marks here to acknowledge that the boundaries between these groups is socially constructed. These groups have mixed with each other and other ethnic or linguistic groups (nations, nationalities, and minorities) in Hungary and the Carpathian basin for centuries.

23. These songs are generally distinguished by scholars and revivalists, along with "new style" songs, from pentatonic songs that are older in origin. While there is a general attitude in the *táncház* that old-style songs are more authentic, late night (often drunken) collective singing tends to include *Magyar nóta* songs, an indication of their folk song status. Frigyesi (1994, 272) writes: "In the 19th and 20th centuries, there were probably very few Hungarians who did not know dozens of these songs." See Hooker (2007) on a similar divergence from the normalized authenticity in dance camps and dancing.

24. Such orchestras accompanied performing ensembles until the 1970s, when the *táncház* band was added as a supplementary element, first for rehearsal and then for performances.

25. *Táncház*-goers told me that in mixed ethnic villages, people had learned the dances of the other groups in order to celebrate together at events. The ethnographic record shows patterns of cross borrowing. Today, it is claimed that each group tends to be familiar only with their own ethnic dances, unless they are involved in a revival group that teaches them otherwise.

26. I want to highlight the different conditions of music and dance collection here and their relationship to authenticity. I do not want to play down the cultural interaction of ethnic groups in the Carpathian basin. While researchers have done comparative work showing borrowing, *táncház*-goers tend to understand them as different and discrete. The actual conditions in different villages show different patterns of sociality between groups. For example, in Gyímes, Roma are not completely segregated from the social life of Hungarians, while in many places they are. In Szék, for example, Roma told me that of course they do not dance Hungarian dances, as they had their own. Although there is a trend among contemporary revivalists to dance "Gypsy dances," I have not seen an ethnic Hungarian Transylvanian villager dance one.

27. István Pávai has written extensively on ethnic interaction (mainly in musical production) and the need to make ethnic labels more nuanced. Like other comparative musicologists, he uses the kind of categories that sustain the idea of discrete difference while also providing evidence of mixing. Hooker (2007) discusses the ongoing debates around whether "Gypsies" are playing "their own" music.

28. The Bihari ensemble was the ensemble of the VDSZ, the Union of Workers in Mixed Industry, Energy Industry, and Related Professions.

29. The Bartók ensemble was the ensemble of the Ironworkers' Union.

30. Szék's dance cycle features a dance for four (two women, two men) that does not allow for the men to distinguish themselves much and is more similar to women's circle dances and Balkan dances. In addition, the town's "lad's dance" is also done in a coordinated manner, contrasting with many other place-based forms where each man competes with the others with his own unique choreography.

31. In Szék, the word *táncház* referred to the dance event itself as well as the place where it was held.

32. In an interview, István Pávai told me this was to appease the Hungarians in the light of the oppression of political expressions after 1956. Material from Szék did not have a large role in the Romania-wide festivals, although Martin (1982, 76n) cites a few examples.

33. While folk song was widespread in Hungary due to the Kodály method, *táncház*-goers pointed to the appearance of the volume of folk songs edited by Kallos as having an important effect on their exposure to folk songs. His imprisonment by the Romanian government for homosexuality was widely believed to have been in fact due to his ethnomusicological research among ethnic Hungarians (Kürti 2001). Of all the folk dance camps I attended, the one run by Kallos had the deepest and most persistent focus on learning to sing folk songs.

34. This movement deserves a study in itself, and I cannot possibly do justice to it here. I will only refer to it insofar as it helps to elucidate the Hungarian *táncház*. See Pávai (2001) and Kelemen (2008) on this theme.

35. An American researcher told me she had heard of revivalists bringing birth control pills as well. See Kligman (1998) on the severe pronatalist policies in socialist Romania.

36. As conditions worsened in the 1980s in Romania, and the revolution (which, unlike in Hungary, was a bloody one) followed, *táncház*-goers as well as other groups rallied to convoy goods to ethnic Hungarians (Nagy 2011; Kürti 2001)

37. Although the Hungarian name literally means "house of traditions," the institution's name is usually translated to English as Heritage House.

38. Since my fieldwork period, the building has been renovated and the institute moved elsewhere. The entire building is now Heritage House (Hagyományok Háza).

39. The role of camps in socialist cultural politics is yet to be examined from a broad perspective. See Kürti (2002) for a discussion of KISZ camps, and Trencsényi (1984) for one of pioneer camps.

40. According to informants, a camp was also held in Gyímes, Transylvania, in 1980 and again a few years later.

41. Nagykálló is approximately 280 kilometers northwest of Budapest, near the Slovak, Ukranian, and Romanian borders. Ekler was a student of famous *népi* architect Imre Makovecz.

42. Bákonyi (2001) translates this as the National Táncház Festival and Crafts Fair.

43. There are *táncház*-like events, official and unofficial, within the event in addition to the many stage performances. After all, *táncház* musicians and dancers show up in large numbers and can set up just about anywhere that there is enough space to dance.

44. Sponsors change with time. When Bákonyi published her article in 2001, it worked in cooperation with the Örökség Children's Society for Folk Art, the György Martin Folk Dance Association, the Elemér Muharay Folk Art Society, the Hungarian Institute for Culture, the Association of Folk Art Societies, the Folklore Society of Slovakian Hungarians, the Gáspár Heltai Foundation of Kolozsvár (Cluj-Napoca, Romania), and the Vajdaság (Voivodina region, Serbia) Center for Hungarian Culture (54).

45. According to Sándor Striker, Hungary adopted the Ministry of Heritage model from England. In 2006, this ministry was rejoined with the Ministry of Education and again renamed, this time to the Ministry of Education and Culture. What people colloquially call the Ministry of Culture has changed names many times over the years. The first such ministry was the Vallás es Közoktatási Minisztérium (Ministry of Religion and Culture, 1848–49, 1867–1951). In 1974, two separate ministries existed: the Oktatási Minisztérium (Ministry of Education) and the Kulturális Minisztérium (Ministry of Culture). The Művelődési Minisztérium (Ministry of Culture/Cultivation) was founded in 1980. In 1990, it became the Művelődési és Közoktatási Minisztérium (Ministry of Culture/Cultivation and Public Education).

46. This is an interesting view, because the Hungarian Opera and Ballet, occupied with music and dance, respectively, were founded in this period. Their emphasis on Hungarianness reflects a different "civilizational" impetus in nation-making, in which the universal form of ballet or opera was to be produced in Hungarian.

47. EEA and Norway Grants represent contributions of Iceland, Liechtenstein and Norway to reducing economic and social disparities in the European Economic Area (EEA) and strengthening the bilateral relations with 15 EU countries in Central and Southern Europe.

48. Institutions and organizations are in flux under the current circumstances. I cannot account for changes after 2006.

49. This happened during the tenure of the Hungarian Democratic Forum (MDF), whose minister of culture was ethnographer Bertalan Andrásfalvy.

50. Peter Halász, who beceme the director in 1992, had worked as an independent ethnographer and for the Magyar Néprajzi Társaság (Hungarian Ethnographic Society).

51. This discussion of the MMI and Hagyományok Háza websites is based on my reading of them in 2006. While Hagyományok Háza appears to be the main institution in the building now, the MMI seems to be no longer in existence. I believe that it become the Magyar Művelődési Intézet és Képzőművészeti Lektorátus in 2007 and seems to have closed around 2013 (1.kerulet .ittlakunk.hu).

52. Beat musicians also set folk songs to rock music, possibly opening up a pathway for the popularity of *táncház* among Beat fans. Certainly, there was overlap.

Chapter Five

Folk Dance as Mother Tongue
National Conduct and the Production of Collective Memory

IN 1974, WRITING IN DEFENSE of the infant *táncház* movement, cultural manager Iván Vitányi (1974, 11) demonstrated his concern with the movement's community-making qualities: "But from what comes the elevated role of folk art? It would be a misunderstanding to think that it is only because it is Hungarian and to place the important momentum of... national culture at the spine of the whole conception. The significance of folk art is more important and more essential than this. In its original form folk art is a community art; an organic part of the everyday life of one or another community that practices it actively in a creative and transformative way." Vitányi argues that as a form of folk art, *táncház* has the potential for building community and, thus, to contribute to the building of socialist culture. Noting that folk art has become an elemental part of the public cultivation (*közműveltség*) of the Hungarian people's democracy (*népi demokrácia*), he argues that the most ancient function of folk art is that which most elementally connects with the life of communities "in as much as its form is determined by the practice of a long line of generations" (1974, 10).

It is this community-building potential of *táncház* and the contradictory definitions of community that are explored in this chapter. How does a community come to be constructed through *táncház*? How does it come to conceive of itself, and how does it act as a community? I focus on the tensions between the notions of an essentialized ethnic community and of a constructed community created through association within the *táncház* public of practitioners.[1] Approaching *táncház* as a social and sociable activity, I explore the production of collective memory through the relationship between form, or material practices in time and space, and political economic conditions over time.

I begin by introducing my theoretical orientation toward collective memory, discussing the relationship of form and material practices that develop in this associative environment to the production of "alternative frameworks of sense" (Melucci 1988). I then turn to the relationship of specific practices of *táncház*-goers in order to get at their relationship to collective memory. I show how collective memory is made accessible by "attaching it to something concrete, something fixed and permanent" (Basso 1996, 64), through spatial practices and dance.

Although *táncház* has been frequently referred to as a movement since the 1970s, participants express apprehension about the use of this term to describe their activities. Noting the Communist administration's use of the term in reference to political movements instigated and maintained or (ostensibly) harnessed by the party, such as the "workers movement" or the "youth movement," they see the term representing a centralized and political initiative. Further, arguing that it is simply the love of folk dance and folk music that brings them together, participants insist that there is no ideological thread that unifies them. Despite this, I observed that *táncház* participants, united by activities and practices promoting the perpetuation of "folk traditions" in everyday life, shared ideas about the nation and about citizenship, upon which they acted in their private and public lives.

The field of social movement studies is vast, and researchers have defined social movements in myriad ways, some focusing on rational action and the strategic use of mobilization (Tilly 1978; Tarrow 1988); others, on identity formation (Pizzorno 1983 Touraine 1985, 1977; and still others, on the production of alternative sensibilities or knowledges (Melucci 1988; Casas-Cortes, Osterweil, and Powell 2008). While recognizing that táncház has had effects on public policy, I see *táncház*'s status as a movement that is both transformative and transforming in broader processes of state formation (see Tilly 1983). This requires not only looking past communities and movements as mystified things to examining the process of their production but also looking past the notion that the effects of nonutilitarian social movements are reducible to the production of identity alone. Along with scholars who identify knowledge practices as central to what movements do, my approach is influenced by the work of Alberto Melucci. I find it useful to think of knowledge as both *savoir* and *connaître*.[2]

Lamenting the conceptual fragility and overuse of the term *movement* in explaining the "social nature of collective action," Melucci (1988, 247) suggests that what collective actors in many social movements have achieved is to practice "alternative definitions of sense" by creating "meanings and definitions of identity which contrast with the increasing determination of individual and collective life by impersonal technocratic power." He argues that it is the networks made of those who share such "frameworks of sense" that make mobilizations possible, "rendering them visible in a punctual manner at moments when confrontations with public policy emerge" (248). Yet he points out that "within these networks there is an experimentation with and direct practice of alternative frameworks of sense, in consequence of a personal commitment which is submerged and almost invisible" (ibid.).

I suggest that a *táncház* framework of sense is produced in the associative space of *táncház* events and through the practices of dance, etiquette, and sociable conversation and that this framework may congeal into a fragile and contradictory "community of sense" in moments of collective action beyond participation in the social event.[3] I connect this process with what I call the practice of folk dance as mother tongue: the mastering of the paradigm of folk dance as social dance and its use in everyday life. A crucial element of mastering this paradigm is familiarity with dance suites associated with particular places on the map of historic or Greater Hungary.

While contemporary discussions of association tend to stress the formal aspects, such as membership in or goals of such associations, or on access to group resources (Putnam 1993, Portes 1998), I focus on the social aspects of associational life, the gathering of individuals in physical space, as key to the production of alternative frameworks of sense. This aspect of association is noted by Georg Simmel, who asserts that the importance of associational life cannot be reduced to special interests pursued. "Above and beyond their special content," he argues, associations satisfy "an impulse to 'sociability'" (Simmel 1971 127). Simmel suggests that in "society" (*Gesellschaft*), where people associate without an expressed common interest or agenda, but rather for the purposes of sociability, form becomes paramount.[4] It is good form, or tact, he argues, that allows for "meaning and stability" and the "mutual self-definition, interaction of the elements, through which unity is made" (129). For such association to be possible at all, he argues, a sense of tact, an adherence to "good form," must be observed.

If, as Simmel asserts, in the absence of a shared ideology or agenda beyond the social event itself, form is what holds "society" together in an associative environment, the adherence to form appears to be key in the production of frameworks of sense. Believing sociability to be the "play form of association" from which "nothing but the satisfaction of the impulse to sociability—although with a resonance to be left over—is to be gained" (Simmel 1910, 130), Simmel does not explore how adherence to form may contribute to the behavior of the individual once outside the sociable event, that is, its role in socialization. Yet if shared form in associational contexts contributes to the production of a framework of sense, and frameworks of sense "make mobilizations possible" (Melucci 1988, 248), then further consideration of their production allows us to consider just this.

After institutional change and the selection of new elites, Melucci (1988, 249) argues that a third measurable effect of the practice of alternative frameworks of sense is cultural innovation: "the production of models of behavior and social relationships that enter into everyday life and the market, modifying the functioning of the social order by means of changes in language, sexual customs, affective relationships, dress, and eating habits."[5] The practice of folk dance as mother tongue among *táncház*-goers is an innovation of this sort. As we have seen, unlike in earlier revivals that focused on staged performance, *táncház*-goers engage in folk dance as social dance. At *táncház* events, participants adhere to a number of explicit and implicit rules of tact, or good form. While there is no formal institution that controls them, manners governing gender roles, dance forms, and language use are generally agreed on and practiced with tact.

While good form, or good manners, are learned within the context of *táncház*, they cannot be explained without reference to things outside it, for these forms are modeled after those practiced in the village social dance contexts that inspired *táncház* in the 1970s. Rather than in choreographed dances divorced from social context or by "free dancing" without adherence to the appropriate idiom, *táncház*-goers engage in this social activity according to custom. It is from the context of the everyday life of peasant communities from which good manners in *táncház* are thought to be derived, and the form that these individual dances, dance cycles, and events—or material practices—take that gives *táncház* its authenticity. It is because *táncház* practices adhere to such forms that it can claim to be traditional and authentic, the heir to a living tradition.

How do forms of tact within *táncház* interact with things outside of it to play a role in the socialization that lies behind a framework of sense? Here, attention to the dialectical process of collective memory production as theorized by Maurice Halbwachs can be helpful.[6] Distinguishing collective memory from historical memory and history and defining it as "the active past that forms our identities," Halbwachs located its production among groups (Olick and Robbins 1998, 111). Groups maintain memories not by "directly reproducing" the past but rather by producing a picture of it (Halbwachs 1992, 101). Arguing that this picture of the past is produced through the interaction of an institutionally preserved practice and the circumstances of the present, he accounts for continuity and change in collective memory through time. Halbwachs distinguishes between rites, which consist of a body of gestures, words, and liturgical objects established in material form, and the beliefs by which the rites are interpreted (116).[7] He points to the way that the meanings of these "rites" have changed over time: "as meanings of forms and formulas become partially forgotten, they have to be interpreted" (117).[8]

In this view, while the stability of material forms and institutional practices over time gives collective memory an appearance of unbroken continuity, changing interpretations renew their contemporary relevance. The form of material practices within *tánchàz*, of dance, music, and manners, is an important element in the construction of a collective memory shared by participants. Equally important, however, are the political economic contexts in which the forms of *tánchàz* emerge and operate and from which meaning and relevance are derived.

If collective memory is reproduced in part as a response to contemporary conditions, then its analysis requires us to examine the circumstances external to *tánchàz* yet within which the revival movement "remembers." Not only are the forms institutionalized in *tánchàz* based on interpretation informed by particular notions of revival and tradition that foreground particular forms, but the interpretation of these forms and their significance also continues to respond to current circumstances.

Although the associative environment of *tánchàz* is highly dependent on the adherence to good form, it is also the site of conversations informed by the political economic environment.[9] In interviews, many *tánchàz* managers described *tánchàz* as a community: a "virtual community" that comes together at certain moments (like the Dancehouse Meeting) or (as one revivialist told me), a "virtual circle... which is not definable but rather a feeling, if a person says now that 'I am a *tánchàz* goer (*tánchàzas vagyok*)!'" This shared framework of sense, I argue, extends to the ways in which people act outside of the *tánchàz* setting. This is because this associative event is also a socializing event involving concrete material practices. Relying on linguistic theory, Juliet Langman (2003) points to the socializing aspect of the participation in a folk-dancing public, speaking of a folk dance group as a "community of practice."[10] Yet despite contemporary emphasis on constructivism and the learning that goes into constituting "community" in the social sciences, community continues to be understood by many *tánchá*z participants, at least in certain moments, as primordial, as always already there (Creed 2006). That is, while *tánchá*z participants voluntarily participate in *tánchá*z as a leisure activity, and learn the forms by doing so, many find "evidence" of the deep Hungarianness of participants in that act. Much like language in the age of linguistic nationalism, the practice of "folk dance as mother tongue" is seen as a manifestation of Hungarianness at the same time as it is seen as a tool for cultivating it.[11]

In her study of the Houses of the People in interwar Italy, Margaret Kohn (2003, 140) articulates problems with the distinctions made between "communalism" (*Gemeinschaft*), thought to be "based on organic bonds developed gradually over long periods of time in a given locality," and "association" (*Gesellschaft*), thought to be the "product of deliberate choice; an aggregation of autonomous individuals who choose to pursue some joint end." The idea of association, she argues, relies on the centrality of the notion of the self-interested individual, while the communalist subject is "defied to some extent by the community of which they are a part" (141). Seeking to find a better description of the kind of community produced through the activities of "municipalism" that produced the Houses of the People and the activities in them, she contrasts both conceptions with the Greek "*homonoia* . . . unanimity or likemindedness." "Unlike communalism," she argues, "*homonoia* does not assume an organic unity created though a shared history" but rather a unity created "through a political project" (140). The shared world of the municipality is "not passively inherited but actively (re)created through practices of citizenship" (ibid.).

Népi movement(s), including *tánchá*z, can be seen as practicing *homonoia* because they are formed through practices of citizenship. Organized, however, in relation to the notion of the *nép* in its dual sense, they draw on communalist ideas about community and common history. While the *tánchá*z framework of sense may be produced through *homonoia*, through shared practices of citizenship, it embodies the tensions between associational and communitarian conceptualizations of Hungarianness, citizenship, and the people.

Slavoj Žižek points to a similar tension in the oppositional civil society of late socialism and its development in the postsocialist period. He noted that in the former period, the democratic opposition united all "antitotalitarian" elements under the sign of civil society in its fight against the "Communist power." Unity in opposition obscured the fact that the same words were being used to refer to "two fundamentally different languages, to two different worlds," those of *Gemeinschaft* and *Gesellschaft* (Žižek 1993, 211). Žižek argues that the same conceptualization of communism as an element foreign or alien to the organic body of the nation (*Gemeinschaft*) has been applied to capitalism in the postsocialist period, its crucial features seen as foreign. Oppositional attitudes vis-á-vis the state have been formulated according to this opposition, for the view of communism from a perspective of *Gemeinschaft* contributed to a "desire . . . for capitalism without the 'alienated' civil society, without the formal-external relations between individuals" (ibid.). As we have seen, communist ideology and language stressed community too, often converging with historical patterns of speaking about community and cultivation. Cultural managers often justified the value of cultural initiatives by arguing that they contributed to the making of community.

In *táncház*, the community referred to can easily slip from the village community into the revivalist community and into an essentialized ethnic Hungarian community. Even for Vitányi, who looks forward in the piece quoted at the beginning of this chapter to the creation of a socialist community, the model community that informs the shape of folk art appears to already exist. It is the passing down through generations that gives folk art its community quality or, we might say, its authenticity. Whence the authenticity of form is derived has important implications for collective memory. Is it that it derives from a community, from a peasant or village community, or from an ethnic Hungarian community that makes it authentic? Is it because it sustains an already existing community or creates a community that makes it valuable? Looking closer at the idea and practice of folk dance as mother tongue and its relationship to socialization in the revival of Hungarian folk music and dance will help us consider how a community created through practice comes to see itself as a manifestation of a preexisting primordial or ethnic community and to see such activities as evidence of belonging to it.

MAKING FOLK ART PART OF EVERYDAY LIFE:
GENEALOGIES OF FOLK DANCE AS MOTHER TONGUE

It is the name of acclaimed composer and folk music collector Zoltán Kodály that is most widely associated with the notion of "music as mother tongue," due to the international popularity of the Kodály method, a pedagogical tool that uses folk songs reduced to basic tones to teach children familiarity with music.[12] Kodály was central to the developments of the Hungarian choir movement and believed that musical education should inform basic education. His method was applied throughout the school system in the socialist period in Hungary. Kodály appears to have made use of the concept of mother tongue in two ways. First, he "wanted to make the folk song the mother tongue that is the natural musical expression closest to the child" (Dobszay 1972, 24). Second, Kodály asserted that the child should learn the folk songs of his native language first, just as he learns his mother tongue before learning foreign languages (Choksy 1999, 2). Kodály's insistence on folk songs in the mother tongue was because they had "national and aesthetic value" (Dobszay 1972). It is likely that he saw "national value" in Hungarian children learning specifically Hungarian folk songs.[13]

Kodály's contemporary Béla Bartók (1976, 343–44), also an internationally acclaimed composer and folk music collector, used the phrase "peasant music as mother tongue," writing, "In this case, the composer has completely absorbed the idiom of peasant music which has become his mother tongue. He masters it as completely as a poet masters his mother tongue." This statement was in part a challenge to the romantic tradition that tended to adopt elements of folk music in new compositions without an understanding of the paradigm from which they came. His interest in ethnomusicology stemmed from a commitment to absorbing the idiom of peasant music rather than borrowing motifs in what he perceived as a superficial manner. Bartók expressed that he "became possessed of the music language of peasantry as a 'mother' tongue so that it could be used as a natural means of expression" (Bartók, in Suchoff 1961, 4).[14] According to Benjamin Suchoff, this emphasis on making folk music a "natural means of expression" is the basis of the "Bartókian idiom" (*Bartóki mód*). This term is used by people close to *táncház* when referring to the use of the peasant idiom to create new and modern artworks.

These two musician-ethnomusicologists were not the only Hungarians making use of the mother tongue metaphor in the interwar period. In 1939, just as Hungary began to annex, with the help of Germany, a chunk of the neighboring territory forfeited nearly twenty years before at the end of World War I, István Györffy, "the father of Hungarian ethnography" published a pamphlet entitled *A Néphagyomány és a Nemzeti Művelődés* (Folk tradition and national cultivation). Originally written as a memo to the Ministry of Religion and Education, the text prescribes a program for Folk National Cultivation (Népi-Nemzeti Művelődés), suggesting ways in which the cultural patrimony of the rural classes (who, in his understanding, are the most Hungarian strata) can be made that of all Hungarians through the incorporation of forms of *népi* culture into everyday life.[15] In 1940, in praise of the Bouquet of Pearls, Györffy's good friend prime minister (and political geographer) Pál Teleki was quoted by the newspaper *A Hagyomány Szava* [Voice of tradition] as saying, "I have approached my allies... our greatest task is that we keep the Hungarian spirit [*lelki*] in this nation, that we teach it to think in Hungarian. Not to wander the world as a beggar [*koldus*], but rather to go on its own legs, to speak Hungarian, to sing in Hungarian, to dance in Hungarian. Because one who does that also thinks in Hungarian" (Teleki in Pálfi 1970, 124). Each of the aforementioned men, of course, was acting in the context in which the practices of the *népi* movement discussed in chapter 2 had become influential. Abstracted from the (at least partly) class-oriented program of populists who opposed the neofeudal government of the Christian National classes, the message to speak the mother tongue was universalized across (at least some) political, ethical, and aesthetic projects.[16] We can see similarities in the approaches espoused by *népi* activists such as Elemér Muharay, leaders of *regös* Scouts groups, and Györffy, with their emphasis on the cultural validation of the agrarian classes; Count Teleki, the Christian National (and irredentist) prime minister who served as "Chief Scout" (Gergély 1989, 51); and, of course, Gyula Gömbös, the antisemitic and fascist prime minister who initiated the New Spiritual Front.

The idea of mother tongue is active today in *táncház*. Recall that the founders of Heritage House presented their argument for the necessity to establish a state institution in terms of mother tongue. Pointing to the establishment of Hungarian language institutions during the period of nineteenth-century linguistic nationalism, Ferenc Sebő explained to me that the mother tongues of music and dance had been overlooked and Heritage House was conceived to rectify the situation.

I encountered the use of the mother tongue idiom other times, as well. The host of one Transylvanian folk dance camp I traveled to in the summer of 2004 stressed the relationship between folk song and mother tongue. In a singing workshop on the lawn, he presented folk song as one element of the broader mother tongue of Hungarian culture. Addressing the (mostly Hungarian) group gathered before him to learn folk songs, he stressed that it is not enough for us to speak the Hungarian language. We must also learn the mother tongue of Hungarian culture, of which folk song (especially in the old style) is a vital part.[17] Perhaps it is not surprising that this message was shared with us in Transylvania, where linguistic and cultural assimilation has been felt as an onslaught by those interested in the preservation of Hungarianness. Although since 1989 the ethnic Hungarian population has managed to (re)establish Hungarian language schools and has achieved political representation, the decreased number of Hungarian speakers has led to widespread fear of assimilation (Tamás 2004).[18]

The pioneering *táncház* choreographer Sándor Timár also used the mother tongue idiom in an interview. Timár articulates his position in his

1999 book *In the Language of Folk Dance*: "it is a basic human right that every child should learn his mother's spoken tongue. We must make this same right appropriate as it pertains to games and dance for our children" (5). Stating his "confidence that similar to our language, our mother tongue is also found in dance," he goes on to argue that one should learn the dances of his/her own place of birth before learning those of other localities.[19] Stressing the importance of such a mother tongue as (birth) right, he writes: "Surely it would be a surprise if the one year old child of an English speaking mother would learn Chinese first, because it is really interesting, has special music, or because many people speak it" (7). In Timár's expression, an essentialized notion of culture is combined with the idea of the right to culture. Mother tongue is utilized both as a way to speak of familiarity with a paradigm as in language use and to stress an essential relationship of linguistic and dance mother tongues to a particular group.

Still an active choreographer and dance teacher when I saw him last in 2005, Timár is a household name among *táncház* participants due to his important role in the aesthetic revolution that shaped the movement. At a time when staged folk dance was comprised of choreographies composed and performed by artists mostly (and blissfully) ignorant of the complexities of village dance practices, Timár and his contemporaries were instrumental in creating a methodology crucial to *táncház*'s emergence, form, and longevity. Influenced by the ethnographic work of peers and by their own trips to Transylvania, they came to recognize that the dances from which their elders had borrowed specific motifs had a coherence of their own, much like language. Further, they recognized that while this coherence was based on limited sets of motifs, the order and style of these motifs could and should be improvised on by the experienced, or "fluent," dancer.

These discoveries influenced Timár and others of his generation not only in their choreographic style but also in the way in which they taught folk dance. With this new pedagogical method, dancers were expected to build up a vocabulary of basic motifs of particular dances. Once the basic motifs and combinations of a given dance were mastered, dancers were encouraged to improvise within this set, each devising his own unique style in the process.[20] It was only when one had built up such a vocabulary that one was considered capable of applying these motifs to choreography. This approach has obvious parallels with those of Bartók and Kodály, and it is no coincidence that they are often cited as predecessors. In this view, folk dance is not a source of abstractable motifs but an entire idiom that requires familiarity, much in the way that language does. Timár (1999, 17) writes: "The improvised dances should be taught in the manner that spoken language is taught. First we devise words and word combinations, and later sentences, according to the rules of the language learned. At first we say or ask simple sentences, later we compose longer and more complicated sentences in response to our thoughts. This happens in the case of dance as well." This generation sought to adopt folk dance as a social form. Rather than simply competing with other performing groups on stage, these youths wanted to get together and dance as the villagers they were learning from did. This required learning the idiom of social dance; borrowed "words" or abstracted motifs would not suffice to this end. As the pool of *táncház* participants broadened to include the general public, the same method was used to instruct nonperforming dancers too. Accordingly, with few exceptions, the standard revival event, the *táncház* itself, begins with a teaching period, during which instructors, usually working as a male-female pair, teach the basic motifs of dances featured that evening, in preparation for their use in the rule-bound but improvisational context of the social dance.

This emphasis on the publicness of folk art, on the responsibility and passion to make the mother tongue of folk dance available to the wider Hungarian public as a part of everyday life, was not new in the 1970s. Indeed, in his book explicitly intended as a manual for teaching folk dance, Timár quotes directly from Györffy's 1939 text: "If we only teach dance traditions to the *nép* and in villages then we will not get very far with it. In this way we will only get the 'Bokréta' which entertains the middle class. If the *népi* dance tradition is to become an element of our national *művelődés*, then we must make it universal (*általános*). We must teach it in Budapest too from nursery school to the colleges of Acting and Physical Education" (Györffy in Timár 1999, 12).

The mother tongue paradigm can clearly be pursued with different goals in mind and with different attention to the results. Nevertheless, we may say all of its applications are attempts to influence the collective memory of Hungarians through the perpetuation of forms related to the sensorium. In all cases, there is an assumption that participation contributes to Hungarianness yet little examination of what that means beyond "form."[21] The acceptance that the perpetuation and universalization of such forms is beneficial for all regardless of ideological concerns deemphasizes any serious consideration of the results or consequences. To take Halbwachs seriously, we must not limit the investigation of collective memory production to the perpetuation of form. We must examine both its institutional context and the changing ways in which form, in this case, folk dance as mother tongue, is interpreted, for this clearly will have an effect on the character of the related framework of sense. The assumptions and intentions behind, and the results of, such projects at any conjuncture depend greatly on the political and economic arrangements, international trends, and related discourses, even if these influences are often obscured by the insistence on form.

If music revivals are social movements "which strive to 'restore' a musical system believed to be disappearing or completely relegated to the past for the benefit of contemporary society" (Livingston 1999, 66), then *táncház* requires a slight revision. *Táncház* is a social movement seeking to "restore" a system in which music dance are codependent.[22] As Tamara Livingston (1999, 70) writes, while a "core of revivalists feel such a strong connection with the revival tradition that they take it upon themselves to 'rescue' it... what they actually do is create a new ethos, [musical] style and aesthetic in accordance to revivalist ideology and personal preferences" (see also Rosenberg 1993). Indeed, revival involves the distancing of a part of everyday life from the context in which it was developed. It involves the abstraction of "naturalized" everyday practices into those self-consciously designed according to the goals and conceptual framework of revivalists. In earlier stages of Hungarian folk dance revival, this was illustrated in the abstraction of motifs from dances and dances from dance events, as when "folk dances" were choreographed for staged performance. We can see it, too, in the isolation of the dance event from the occasion providing its context, from the festive occasions of weddings, christenings, or village balls.

Anthropologists have approached such events through the framework of ritual, often explained as the manifestation or expression and consolidation or reaffirmation of the unity of a community or society (Gluckman 1965; Turner 1995).[23] Toby Volkman (1990, 92) tracks the objectification of the "indigenous media" of the Toraja in Indonesia, via processes of dislocation, decontextualization, disassembly, replacement, reconstitution, reproduction, and interpretation. Discussing the traditional media of the Toraja "ancestor house," "effigy," and "rituals," Volkman notes that practices that once had communicative functions within a system of integrated religion and custom have become objects that represent "Toraja identity" and can be easily packaged for tourists. The transformation of these "objects" that were once media functioning within a small group with a shared interpretive framework was informed by historical processes, including the colonial delineation of the religious from the customary (and their related valuation), the "nationalization" of Indonesia, and the turn toward tourism as a tool for economic development. With Volkman, we can consider what occurs when these media—with the power to broadcast or communicate, often through bodily practices—are abstracted as objects. If the dance event is or was a medium, what happens when it is abstracted from the community in which it developed and incorporated into different spatio-temporal logics and differently constituted publics (see Caton 1990; Rajagopal 2001)?

Although the goal of some *táncház* supporters may have been to consolidate or create community, revivalists rarely address how their own interpretive framework differs from that of villagers.[24] The broadening of the communicative medium of dance and the dance event from a village to a national *táncház* community has effects on the interpretation of form (and thus on socialization, collective memory, and framework of sense). Arising from within revivalist currents already extant, *táncház* revived the social dance event by modeling dances after those of living villagers, aided by documentation and accounts of the past. While *táncház* restored the dance event as a coherent whole, its regular events were held in the context of urban leisure activities and amateur art rather than the village dance institutions of Transylvanian villagers, past or present. Furthermore, *táncház* adopted certain authentic forms—notably, the internal coherence of distinct dances, the coherence of the dance cycle, and the interdependent relationship of music and dance—but the revivalist context has nevertheless required a transformation of the dance event. Of course, interpretation according to any given revivalist ideology may determine which forms will be adopted or how forms will be arranged. We can see this in the light of what Raymond Williams (1966) termed "selective tradition," which preserves those aspects of tradition that correspond with values of the period while also rejecting much of the living culture of which it was part.

As in any revival, certain forms have been institutionalized in *táncház*, through practice and convention that are based on, but not identical to, those imitated. Nevertheless, this imitation is the source of authenticity. *Táncház*-goers believe themselves to be carrying on an uninterrupted (if threatened) tradition, in contrast to something invented, such as staged folk dances of the 1950s and 1960s or *Magyar nóta*. After all, it is the faithful practice of traditional forms that demarcates *táncház* from earlier revivals. The apparent similarity between how things are done in *táncház* and how they are done in the villages is the source of its authenticity.

As Livingston (1999, 71) points out, "reliance upon informants or historical sources in formulating the revival tradition's repertoire, stylistic features, and history" is a feature of revivals. The changes that have come about through adaptation of the forms to the revivalist context are often obscured, and Livingston notes the "tendency of revivalist discourse to

Fig. 5.1 Revivalists practicing at camp in Szék (Sic), Transylvania, 2004. Hi8 video still by the author.

collapse time and space in service to a 'new authenticity' defined by the belief in the practice's timelessness, unbroken historical continuity and purity of expression" (69; see also Bohlman 1988).

The following section explores the specific practices and forms that make up folk dance as mother tongue and factors contributing to their interpretation. I describe what happens when communicative technologies are abstracted according to revivalist ideologies and institutional arrangements focused on the perpetuation of authentic Hungarian practices. I focus particularly on dance/music forms, etiquette, conversation, and place-based tourism. Drawing on the well-examined example of gender relations in the dance to illustrate the relationship of dance event practices and socialization, I point to what other kinds of socialization may be at hand, particularly as connected to place, territory, and the content and scale of the nation.

SPATIOTEMPORAL FORMS: MATERIAL PRACTICES IN TÁNCHÁZ

Táncház events are structured around dance cycles, or suites: relatively fixed sets of dances in a certain order that coordinate with a musical suite.

Each cycle is adopted from a particular village or region. Once the band begins to play, experienced *táncház* goers are both aware of and authorial of what dance "should" and will follow. Upon hearing the music, we are able to determine the village or region from which it originates and can thus author dances within the genre of that locale. Familiarity with a broad repertoire of regional dance forms has been peculiar to revivalists, as villagers have tended until recently to know only local dances (Halmos 2000, 31).[25] For *táncház* participants, along with a growing proportion of revivalist villagers, a "national" patrimony is available from which specific regional variants of "Hungarian dance" can be identified. Each dance cycle can be placed at a particular place on the map of Greater Hungary. The fact that an overwhelming percentage of the dances/dance cycles encountered in *táncház* today are Transylvanian in origin has important implications for collective memory.[26]

Reflecting the geography of uneven development, the majority of communities practicing Hungarian folk dance as social dance in the 1970s were located in Transylvania. As we have seen, the history of ethnography, and the combination of *népi* and Christian National practices and ideologies in the interwar and World War II periods, made Transylvania the focus of collection and authenticity. This process of nationalization of local traditions, mostly from Transylvania, has a few important effects: it abstracts each "local tradition" into the category "Hungarian" and widens the practice of each to all Hungarians, and it cements the identification of specific dances with specific villages or regions, establishing them as sources of authenticity. Furthermore, it associates Hungarian culture with Transylvanian villages. The revival of village practices in *táncház* also serves to make folk dance static or timeless (see Livingston 1999, 69). Because revival has stopped the clock, it is not the contemporary practices of the folk that are the source of folk culture but rather the practices of the parents and grandparents of rural folk—exhibited by the elderly or captured on film, sound recordings, and photographs—and accounts and practices of ethnographers and revivalists. While studies show that the dances of the villages of the Carpathian basin are the result of the sediment of history, reflecting waves of European dance fashions (Martin 1968; E. Pesovár 1980), authenticity is located in the dancers captured on silent film shot in the 1940s and the contemporary practices that correspond with these. It is the experts who emerged from and the participants in *táncház* who are now the police of authenticity, as village tradition is considered adulterated and fractured. Still identified as the source, villagers are often no longer considered capable of properly guarding this tradition. This process is reflected in the fact that in contrast to urban *táncház* participants who dance the full breadth of Hungarian dances, Transylvanian villagers are encouraged to engage in local dances as tradition keepers (*hagyomáyőrzők*) rather than dancing the broader revivalist repertoire of Hungarian dances.[27] While both researchers and *táncház*-goers will note that historical change and the integration of European dances led to the unique forms revived as Hungarian folk dance, *táncház*-goers nevertheless tend to speak of these dances and music as ancient and immutable and to consider contemporary changes inauthentic.[28]

Here we see the tension between living and static forms, as what is deemed the authentic living form is now in the hands of revivalists, while the daily practices of many villagers may be judged inauthentic.[29] This is found in the attitude toward musicianship as well. While in the first years of the revival, *táncház* musicians relied on village musicians, a majority of whom were Roma, to teach them to play, during fieldwork I heard the sentiment expressed that as the older generation of Roma dies out, it is revivalists, rather than village Roma, who play more authentically. As Lynn Hooker (2005, 56) points out in reference to a camp in Transylvania, "the Romani musicians who were the star attraction were both honored as the 'guardians' of instrumental music traditions, and policed carefully as potential agents of pollution, lest they introduce elements of newer popular styles."

At one weeklong dance camp in Transylvania, the tension between historical process and revivalist notions of authenticity became apparent. One evening, a Wednesday, a band with different instrumentation and style than a traditional folk ensemble was featured in the main dance space at the local house of culture.[30] The instrumentation and playing style of the band that night is associated with what is called *lakodalmas*, "wedding," music. *Lakodalmas* can cover a range of popular music and is far more widespread in rural regions than music adopted by *táncház*, but it is not seen as folk music (*népzene*) (Lang 1996, 78). The dance floor was packed that evening with local villagers. *Táncház* guests from Hungary shared their disgruntlement as they searched for authentic folk ensembles, even if made up of revivalists from Hungary, who played authentic music. These revivalists were disturbed that this wedding music was center stage at the camp dedicated to the folk music and dance (*néptánc*) that they had come to experience. In an interview, the camp's organizer justified his reasons for holding this event. He had decided that, because the camps are meant to expose visitors to the life of the villager (*falusi ember*), there was no need to displace the usual Wednesday night event on account of the camp. If visitors were truly interested in the life of the villagers, he argued, they should be exposed to the current lifestyle of the latter, including their contemporary dance/music culture. He noted, too, that the locals use traditional dance motifs to dance to this *lakodalmas* music.[31]

While many *tánchaz*-goers are of the conviction that neither music nor dances should change, the practice of foregrounding of certain forms and practices over others does have its effects. Revivalists adhere to a mother tongue model that prioritizes improvisation within a genre. Dancers often develop their improvisations through close study of ethnographic footage, on motifs taught to them by instructors who have done so or on primary collection among informants.[32] Responding to my questions about if and how *tánchaz* has changed, some longtime participants volunteered that the dances have become much more sophisticated. This was, they suggested, a function of three decades of the development of *tánchaz*, during which research has been done and data codified and made available, while dancers (and musicians) have become more and more expert. Although some felt the dancing had become too complicated, emphasizing performance at the expense of mutual enjoyment, others opined that the dynamism provided by sophisticated dancers was needed to stir others to action.

Of course, such developments in the sophistication of the dances derives partly from the presence of professional (as well as amateur) folk dancers who have advanced training. It also reflects the proliferation of bands and teachers (usually professional dancers who are in teacher training and need to supplement their income or who teach out of dedication to the movement), *tánchazes*, and camps and the concomitant availability of increasingly specialized instruction in regional suites and motifs. In contrast to this growing expertise of *tánchaz*-goers, there is frequent adulteration present in the repertoires of the "informants" (*adatközlők*). Visiting informants at one Budapest dancehouse I attended in 2004, for example, included the Charleston in their village suite. In addition, fewer and fewer young villagers learn or engage in folk dance in a village social dance context, learning to dance, instead, in performing groups if they have interest (Z. Szabó 1998, 177). While historically, dance motifs in specific villages would have evolved with the gradual introduction of innovations by those who had traveled (serving in the army or laboring elsewhere, for example) and by the activities of dance instructors, increasingly expert revivalists contribute to reinforcing distinctions between specific villages or regions. A similar conflict over repertoire—in this case, the validity or lack thereof of *mahala* music (and dancing to it) in the context of a dancehouse camp—is discussed by Hooker (2006).[33]

It is no coincidence that in the early twentieth century, dance teachers were often called dance and etiquette teachers, as, across Europe, society dances were a key site for learning and performing proper etiquette. This socialization took place in a ballroom society as well as at village balls (*táncház*), although potentially into different ethical and class codes. Ferenc Pesovár (1978, 24) claims that peasants adopted rules of bourgeois etiquette along with the dances, while Vitányi (1964, 11) claims that the twentieth-century spread of dance teachers contributed to the "decay of folk dance," as old dances were replaced with new ones. Yet researchers have shown the mutual influence of court and urban dances with peasant dances over centuries (F. Pesovár 1978; Kaposi 1991). Until the twentieth century, the folk adopted new dances from the court and assimilated them to local paradigms (Vitányi 1964). The fact that dance masters, or dance and courtesy instructors became widespread in this period illustrates the dance's role as a means of socialization. The forms of etiquette enforced in the Hungarian village dance event are the result of this mutual influence over time. *Táncház*-goers and folk culture researchers were fond of telling me that Hungarian folk dance reflects an ideal level of bourgeois development in which the individual is given expression within the confines of community.

Among mannerisms related to etiquette, gendered characteristics of dances and dance event are perhaps the most noticeable. In her study of dance events in a town in northern Greece, Jane Cowan (1990, 4) reveals "how gender ideas and relations of everyday life are actively embodied and explored in festive performance." At *táncház* events, asking a partner to dance is considered a male role, and it was only among groups of good friends that I observed women breaking with this custom and asking male friends to dance. Once on the dance floor, the man is responsible for leading the dance ("dancing" his partner), and it is at his discretion that transitions from one motif to another are made. The male dancer is thus the author of the rule-governed improvisation (that expresses his individuality). The woman must be adept at responding to her partner's lead in order to anticipate and enact the transitions while dancing them.[34]

Along with these gendered roles, *táncház* did not import the local function of the *táncház* in which these gender roles were embedded. As mentioned earlier, in Szék, the word *táncház* once referred to both courtship dance events (balls or dances) for adolescents and to the places in which they were held (Halmos 2000, 30). At these dances organized by and for adolescent youths, typically only unwed youths danced, although often under the gaze of the entire village community.[35] As Cowan (1990, 5) writes, "dancing bodies are at the center of scrutiny and simultaneously are the medium of experience," and indeed, villagers have accounted their experiences of dancing under the watchful eye of various family members, each expecting particular qualities (Magyar Televizio n.d.). Although by virtue of having been a youth movement in the 1970s, the revival initially retained the atmosphere of an environment for youths, the age range at present paints a different picture. As Béla Halmos writes in his 2000 work, "the average age of those frequenting *táncház* in Hungary today happens to be the same as of those attending the traditional Transylvanian *táncház*, but within the movement, there is no age or marital-status restriction on attendance. The *táncház* movement welcomes anyone interested in folk music or folk dancing" (34). During the periods that I attended, I encountered a broad age range of participants (roughly sixteen to sixty). The average age depended on the particular *táncház* (weekly event in a particular location), as each tended to attract its own regular crowd.[36] It would be a problem to describe the contemporary *táncház* as a youth movement or as one for unmarried people. While the function the *táncház* event played in the lives of adolescents has not been reproduced (along with this taboo), this does not mean that *táncház* has lost its socializing qualities.

Táncház events continue to have a sexually charged atmosphere, or a "courtship" environment. I learned this initially through my participation in the dance event. In an upsetting but revealing incident, I learned that there are certain implicit rules about with whom to dance. One evening I had danced with a man to whom I had been introduced in the past by another *táncház*-goer. I enjoyed our dance, as he was very skilled and led me adeptly through a dance with which I was not familiar; I was learning in precisely the way one learns in *táncház*, I thought. A few days later, at another *táncház*, a woman confronted me about having danced with this man, exclaiming that I had been inappropriate by dancing with him when he was fighting with his wife.[37] In another case, when a close female friend of mine, a longtime participant, kindly led me in a dance in order to help me learn, we were told by a number of men to stop.

It is perhaps telling that the only *táncház*-goers who expressed discomfort with the gender relations to me were foreigners.[38] An ethnic Hungarian woman raised in England told me that the gender roles in *táncház* annoyed her, while an American woman was frustrated that men would refuse to be led, even when she knew the footwork better. While perhaps not explicitly intended to, gender roles in *táncház* point to expectations about gender roles outside of *táncház*. Another example may help illustrate this connection. At one camp, I danced late at night with a man who had drunk quite a bit of alcohol. He insisted on talking me through each step of the dance while becoming frustrated that I was not responsive enough to his lead. After the dance was over, he lectured me about how the man is meant to be in control in the dance and that I must do what he says in order to learn this better. He went on to suggest that women like me do not know our place in the gendered order, implying that the gender roles in the dance were a model for how the genders should relate outside of it as well.

Many *táncház*-goers, male and female, stressed to me the complementary gender roles not only in dance but in life. Some women made sure to defend the female dance part against "feminist" allegations, pressing that, despite its limited freedoms and the necessity to be led by the man, it is interesting and fun. Others stressed that both on the dance floor and in life, gender roles should be complementary, not interchangeable. The idea that women should not be careerists was also stressed, and Hungarian women I met in *táncház* shied away from describing themselves as independent or strong, not wanting to be confused with "feminists" or "careerists." Cowan (1990) argues that in the context of the dance event, gender roles are not just enacted but also contested, revealing that there is not a simple unidirectional influence. Nevertheless, recognizing the relationship between the associative dance event and gender socialization opens up a space to consider in what other ways the dance event and the practice of folk dance as mother tongue may be connected with socialization.

Táncház events are characterized by heightened physical and emotive states. Dancing involves acceleration of heartbeat, increased perspiration, and, for the "danced" woman, varying degrees of dizziness. Alcohol features prominently at *táncház* events, especially among men, many performing the traditional (male) village practice of brandy drinking.[39] This was not always the case in the revival context. As many longtime participants pointed out, during the socialist period alcohol had not been permitted in the houses of culture, where most events took place. Nevertheless, the role of brandy drinking was considered a ritual related to village sociality, as illustrated in its use in greeting guests at the first Budapest *táncház* (Striker 1987, 112). Even without alcohol the dances themselves are conducive to "emotive states." Cycles are also punctuated with dances of different tempos and different kinds of gendered participant bases: men's solo dances, many others for couples, and (rarer) group dances.[40] Some dances are slow, while others are marked by their fast tempo.

The main body of dances, couple dances, involves intimate contact between partners. Skilled dancing requires rhythmic coordination with one another and with the music.[41] The musicians are watching the dancers,

Fig. 5.2 Revivalists and villagers dance together at camp in Szék (Sic), Transylvania, 2004. Hi8 video still by the author.

quickening, slowing down, or ornamenting the music in order to facilitate the dance. In the case of solo dances, men show their prowess to spectators; in couple dances, much of their skill is focused on "dancing" (*táncoltat*) their partners. A good male dancer entertains the woman by leading her with precision and providing her with the opportunity to engage in interesting steps, notably the turn (*forgatás*). Often done several times in succession, turns can be a somewhat dizzying experience. An element of the man's skill is located in his ability to determine how much of this is enjoyable for the woman and when enough is enough in order create a balance between comfort and excitement in the dance. Women complain to each other that rather than entertaining their dance partner, many men focus more on fancy footwork (usually requiring their partners to stand aside, in a resting dance mode, or sometimes literally supporting him). Men can also build rest periods into the dance, during which footwork is simpler and heartbeat may slow. These rest periods are also opportunities for conversation. Slow dances, which may be accompanied with song, also provide a prolonged opportunity for conversation. One camp-goer reported that she had been told that a particular slow dance is colloquially called "the baby maker" because of the intimacy promoted.[42]

The relative straightforwardness of the relationship between good form within the dance and gendered etiquette and socialization allows us to imagine that good form in the dance event may be connected to other kinds of socialization, particularly relating to place. Despite the contradictory and varied views expressed within *táncház* (discussed later), *táncház* practices involve relationships with specific places, mostly in Transylvania. I have emphasized the physicality of the dance for important reasons. Heightened physical states have been shown to be tied to emotions. Studies show the human tendency to relate heightened physical states with emotions, such as love (Schachter and Singer 1962; Dutton and Aron 1974). By pointing to the relationship of heightened physical states and emotions in *táncház,* insights into the "misattribution of arousal" (Schachter and Singer 1962), can help us consider how visceral experience is connected to belief. These heightened physical states in the dance can re(produce) emotional attachments to Hungarianness and the territory being danced. Like the residents of an East German border town, who Daphne Berdahl (1999, 82) argues reinforced a sense of *heimat* through singing "Eichsfeld" songs and pilgrimage practices, *táncház* practices contribute to the "construction of a meaningful landscape" and the construction and maintenance of local identities.

On the village scale the communicative system of the dance event may have coordinated with appropriate village sociality perhaps primarily with regard to gender roles (and being a local). In the revival setting, practices connect etiquette and Hungarianness, or the scale of the ethnonation, while dancers and musicians perform particular places (in the Hungarian "culture area"). In the context of the revival, such community-making technologies originating in local places are nationalized as Hungarian at the same time that the music and dances performed at each event summon places and territory to the dance event, no matter where it is held. All dances are connected explicitly with place. Each is associated with a particular village (or region) on a map of Greater Hungary and danced in a suite named after it. Because a high percentage of the *táncház* repertoire is Transylvanian and most *táncház* tourism is focused there, these practices are foremost connected with Transylvania. Through participation in the music/dance, one learns the geography of historic (or Greater) Hungary, with special emphasis on Transylvania. Even if one does not visit Transylvania, he/she learns a geography of Transylvania through a repertoire of folk dances.[43] This is no neutral geography.

Tourism practices, which are also similar to pilgrimage, reinforce these relationships.[44] While the revival transplanted the *táncház* form to the youth club environment, it emulated the village form. Many participants have visited villages, especially in Transylvania, conducting "ethnographic research" and seeing for themselves "how it is done" firsthand. Village visiting is therefore a central practice. Longtime *táncház*-goers accounted to me their sense of adventure highlighted by the semiforbidden status of such trips: the experience of arriving in a village with only the name of an acquaintance of a friend of a friend and of benefitting from the famous hospitality of Transylvanian villagers. They also spoke of how they helped these "oppressed" people by sharing in their pride (Ronay 1992). Contemporary revivalists encounter an infrastructure that has evolved across forty years of *táncház* tourism. These practices related to place are important in the production of particular notions of Hungarianness and authenticity related to territory.

Transylvanian villages and the traditional practices of their inhabitants stand as icons of moral order. Yet *táncház*-goers interpret the moral order of the Transylvanian village in a variety of ways. Transylvanian villages, like the dances themselves, can represent small-scale agrarian bourgeois life (a perfect balance between the collective and the individual, as the dances themselves are understood), an idealized and unproblematized precapitalist rural economy, or a time when Hungary was a much larger territorial entity or even a powerful kingdom. Transylvania can represent the unity of the crown lands of St. Stephen and thus the heroic past of the Hungarians as rulers rather than the losers of history. Many I spoke with, seeing folk art as a kind of vessel of ancient practices, consider Transylvanian villagers to have preserved the knowledges, the wisdom, of the Hungarian horsemen who arrived in the Carpathian basin in the ninth century. The presence of ethnic Hungarians in Transylvania, the largest minority of its sort in Europe, also signifies the unfinished work of the nation-state project. Contemporary interpretations meet with *táncház* via the conversations and language use of participants. Just as collective dancing and singing in the village or in *táncház* may be said to produce a "conscience collective," so verbal practices amongst *táncház*-goers represent a form of "collective representation" (Durkheim 1976 [1912]).

SONG AND CONVERSATION: LANGUAGE IN TÁNCHÁZ

Beyond songs sung during slow dances and the late-night (drunken) collective (male) singing, song breaks out, for example, on birthdays when *táncház*-goers sing "Zsuzsa's greeting," exhibiting their shared repertoire, reinforced and broadened relative to the amount of time an individual spends in *táncház* environments.[45] "Old-style" songs introduce the themes of love, loss, agrarian hardship, and sometimes specifically Hungarian hardship.[46] Conversations introduce contemporary themes and interpretations and play an important role in relating past and present in the construction of collective memory. At dancehouses, during breaks between dance lessons or dance suites, some people, often mostly women, partake in folk song instruction on the dance floor, while others form small groups around tables, talking. Some talk throughout the night, and never get around to dancing. While the forms of dance and music offer what appear to be an unadulterated past, conversations reflect the present through the dominant issues that arise, their urgency, and their discursive features. Often revealing quite different views than those expressed in interviews, such spontaneous conversations in *táncház* provided an important ethnographic source for this study. These observations were made during my fieldwork 2004 and 2005 and reflect a particular moment, a conjuncture on which I will elaborate in later chapters.

Participants were fond of telling me that *táncház* provides a neutral environment in which people do not engage in "talking about politics" (*nem politizálnak*). They stressed that *táncház* is a cultural pastime, free of politics. Like Simmel, they believe that in sociable environments conversation is not subordinate to its content. Yet if collective memory is produced through the interaction of institutionalized practices and historical context, then we must see conversation as an important conduit for the way contemporary conditions inform meaning in the *táncház*. During my time in *táncház* environments, I found that certain "political" themes came up quite consistently. Casual talk often included critical comments about "liberals," "communists," and Jews, usually in binary opposition to Hungarians and implicitly, *táncház*-goers. Perhaps the most revealing discussion I had was in an interview with a student of anthropology. She described the difference between her own reaction to antisemitic expression (*zsidózás*) in *táncház* and that of her friend, a French woman of Hungarian Jewish origin who had come to Hungary to discover her roots. While the student told me that she did not consider herself a typical *táncház*-goer—i.e., "a good Christian *táncház*-goer who wants Transylvania back"—she was nevertheless shocked at the discomfort her French friend experienced "when the boys started singing 'Stinky Jewish Trader' or one of those songs." Her testimony pointed to a difference she perceived in the worldviews of liberal leftists and *táncház*-goers. While she herself did not have negative things to say about liberals, her description of her friend was telling: "Well she's

French [laughs], this person who belongs on the social-left who is researching her Jewish identity. She was terribly sensitive to these things."

Another telling example was a conversation with some middle-aged men about Hungarian literature. When one suggested that the writer János Kodolányi was representative of great Hungarian literature, another insisted that he couldn't be "because he was a Jew."[47] I asked whether someone being Jewish would disqualify them from representing Hungarian culture. "Yes," he told me, "because they have different values." Another added that Jews represent a more liberal strand than Hungarians in general. One more "reminded" me that the Communist Party had been made up of Jews.[48] I also encountered conflation of Israelis and Jews. For example, when one dancer told me that the "Jews are buying up Budapest," I asked if they were Hungarian or foreign Jews; he responded that there was no difference between the two.[49] Conflation of liberalism with Jews was also quite common, as when on numerous occasions people suggested that voting for the "liberal" party (Alliance of Free Democrats) or protesting nationalist comments were indications of a person's Jewishness.[50] Others made reference to the "misuse" of city finances by the "liberal" mayor of Budapest and his censure of national symbols and simultaneous protection of Jewish ones by his party. In this way, "liberals," "Jews," and "communists" (and through both continuity and association, we will see, socialists too) came to be conflated, while they all stood in opposition to Hungarian.

The content of Hungarianness was another topic frequently discussed in *táncház*. One issue that arose frequently was the question of granting citizenship to ethnic Hungarians "across the borders," an issue on which citizens voted in a referendum just months before I finished fieldwork. While some participants told me that opponents of dual citizenship did exist within *táncház* circles, I did not meet anyone who admitted to voting no. In fact, unlike many people I knew outside of *táncház*, who chose to not vote at all in hopes that the results would be nullified by reducing the number of voters below the threshold required, *táncház*-goers insisted that this was an issue that could not be ignored. Some argued that not voting was the equivalent to voting no.

Also frequent were conversations about "ancient Hungarians" (*ősmagyarság*). A few *táncház*-goers are self-termed "ethnographers" (*néprajzosok*) or "researchers of Hungarianness" (*magyarságkutatók*), terms they used to refer to both amateurs and professionals. In conversations with these, I frequently encountered alternative histories of and essentializing expressions about Hungarians and other ethnic groups. At one camp in Transylvania, a man who referred to himself as an independent researcher of Hungarianness explained to me that "Hungarian culture is the oldest culture in Europe" and that the wisdom of the Hungarians is that of Jesus, because the Hungarians are descended from the Sumerians. Another suggested that I read a certain part of the Bible, where the correspondence with Hungarian folk culture is so obvious that it is impossible to overlook. Assertions about the Christian provenance of Hungarian folk culture were often tied with ideas about Jews. One musician suggested to me "if the Jews had not nailed Jesus to the cross, there would not have been a Holocaust." Another man told me "history shows that the Jews were punished. Thus, they must have done something to deserve it." Such critiques extended to the so-called Latin, or Roman Catholic, culture and church as well. One man referred to mainstream Hungarians as the Romanized Hungarians (Latin Magyarság), asserting that Hungary has been subject to the corrupting cultural current of Roman/Jewish (read: urbanist) imperialism since the reign of King Matthias in the fifteenth century. Others argued that the Magyar pagans oppressed by Christian rulers in the eleventh century were in fact the true Christians.[51]

Many people shared with me the opinion that what makes someone Magyar is the practice of Hungarianness, encapsulated first and foremost in language.[52] Some even suggested that my mastery of the language was evidence that I had Hungarian roots, while others suggested it meant I could hope to grasp what being Magyar is. The view that the specificities of Hungarian language embody a superior spirituality was popular. A self-proclaimed shaman who began attending *tánchaz* in order to familiarize himself with Hungarian culture after he had been "enlightened by God," explained the importance of language in the preservation of a uniquely Hungarian Christianity. He explained that Hungarian is the most sacred language spoken by an ethnic group since the fall of Babel. He and others argued that the grammatical structure of Hungarian proved its sacredness.[53]

Tánchaz-goers referred to the work of art historian Gábor Pap as a source of many of these ideas. One told me he was pursuing a PhD in Magyarság at the private University of the Philosophical Society of Miskolc, where Pap was a faculty member. Others expressed a desire to study with Pap, and I noticed flyers for the Magyarság courses at *tánchaz* events. Some stressed to me that this department was more legitimate than the "official" departments of ethnography, which they considered compromised by their continued functioning under the Communists as well as by their foreign worldview.

Pap's (1999, 554) work is concerned with the ancient sources of Hungarian folk art. He argues that the Hungarians, whom he believes brought the crown (with which St. Stephen was crowned as King) with them to the Carpathian basin at the time of the conquest, are descended from the Scythians and that the symbols on the crown can be understood only according to the Manichean Christian point of view, not that of the "big church," whether Byzantine or Roman.[54] Pap's account supports the view that Hungarian culture has been colonized by Latin culture via these institutionalized forms of Christianity. In this understanding of Hungarian pagan practices, the folk arts, dance and music included, preserve a particular form of Christianity to which only Hungarians have access. In this view of Hungarian folk culture, form, whether found in embroidery motifs, music, dance, or language, is understood to preserve something not only ancient but ethical. It preserves, codified in folk art, a way of life that is the key to full spirituality and goodness.

Connected to such arguments about the Hungarian language is the belief that the widely supported (until recently) current academic categorization of Hungarian as a Finno-Ugric language was invented and perpetuated by "foreigners" (first German speakers and later communists) in whose interest it was to break down Hungarian national identity and claim their territory by "proving" that the Hungarians who conquered the Carpathian basin were primitive tribal latecomers rather than descendants of the Sumerians or, as Pap (1999, 557) claims, "the group which in practice held all of Europe under the grip of military control": the Huns.

A formally trained ethnographer who attends *táncház* (and there are many of these, too) told me that none of these views were representative of *táncház*-goers and that such extremists were harmless and needed to be gracefully tolerated. These views are indeed not representative of all *táncház*-goers. They are, however, voiced often by many *táncház*-goers, and I rarely heard anyone challenge them in the *táncház* setting. The ideas thus circulate in *táncház* environments with only occasional challenge. When, based on the fact that I rarely heard anyone contest them, I concluded that such opinions were common to most *táncház* participants, I was told that to offer one's disagreement would be *politizálás*, "talking about politics" or "politicizing," an activity that they felt was inappropriate in social environments like *táncház*. While *politizálás* was deemed inappropriate, the themes discussed previously were not. Rather, it was challenges to these views that were identified as *politizálás*, as if the challenge itself made the issue political.[55]

While most participants I interviewed do not agree with my interpretation, on the basis of my participant observation in *táncház* settings,

I view *tánchāz* as a space of tolerance toward such expression on the basis that it went uncontested most of the time. These tropes all work toward defining Hungarianness either by associating Hungarians with something or distinguishing them from others through binary opposition. They connect the Transylvanian village with Hungarianness, locating it as a treasury of ancient practices and a site of an idealized moral economy of the past. They oppose Hungarians with liberals, communists, and Jews (and through association, socialists). Adherence to good form keeps argument about the details to a minimum, allowing a certain kind of consensus to emerge, aided, perhaps, by emotive states.

Conclusion: The Spectrum of Community-Produced or Expressed?

I have stressed here the relationship of good form, conversation, and emotive states in the (re)production of collective memory. While the next two chapters will elucidate the broader context for the conversations described herein, in this chapter I have suggested that there is a link between form and material practices and the internalization or practice of particular values, which reinforces a framework of sense and "mutual definition" among practitioners. My own experiences within the *tánchāz* setting are crucial to this argument. From the time I began as a novice *tánchāz*-goer, I have undergone a transformation. While at first the music meant nothing to me except for Hungarian music, now, my body responds upon hearing music with visceral knowledge of the corresponding dance. I respond by summoning up not simply the appropriate dance but also the name of a region or village from which it originates. I associate these dances with my trips to Transylvania and with particular villages on the map of Greater Hungary.

Through this process of self-cultivation, of learning folk dance as mother tongue, I also came to experience rural Transylvania as source of Hungarianness and of Hungarian folk culture. Through the practice of folk dance as mother tongue, *tánchāz*-goers conjure up an idyllic past, an image of an idealized Hungarian agrarian community located in Transylvania. As Keith Basso (1996, 66) writes of Apache stories about geographical places, "narratives transformed its referent from a geographical site into something resembling a theater, a natural stage upon the land . . . where significant moral dramas unfolded in the past." Transylvania is not simply the site of historical events but a geographical placeholder for an imagined past. While each *tánchāz*-goer may interpret the connections differently, drawing on the multiple and often contradictory elements available, it does not require a great leap to feel that there is something special or peculiar about Hungarians, Transylvania, or their connection. Given the conversations I have encountered in *tánchaz* and the visceral experiences I have had with Hungarian dance and music and Transylvanian villages, it is not difficult to emote a sympathy for things Hungarian; for a simple peasant life; for lost glory; for oppressed minorities or exploited peasants; for a rich expressive culture; for a way of life that is disappearing through urbanization, modernization, globalization, and ethnic assimilation; or for a glorious imperial past. It is hard, sometimes, for me not to think of ethnic Hungarian Transylvanians as Hungarians. I was not alone when lapsing from time to time in saying "here in Hungary" while standing in a Transylvanian village.

As Livingston (1999, 68) writes, the purpose of a (music) revival movement "is twofold: 1) to serve as a cultural opposition and as an alternative to mainstream culture, and 2) to improve existing culture through values based on historical value and authenticity expressed by revivalists." This is consistent with the statements of *tánchaz*-goers, for while they insist that *tánchaz* is simply a pastime, they also assert that it will contribute to the well-being of Hungarians, that it is a resource for community-making, and that it is an important tool of *művelődés*, one to be used against an impending globalization. That is, while claiming that *tánchaz* is not a movement, but rather a leisure time activity, participants also see it as an ethical practice connected to Hungarianness. As Livingston points out, "networks of individuals that form social movements are distinguished from other groups commonly studied by anthropologists" due to their fluidity of membership, ideological focus, and impermanence, and revivals are further characterized by their nonterritoriality and bringing together of people who might not have met except for their revivalist activities (Livingston 1999, 72). To "create a sense of community," she tells us, revivalists produce magazines, journals, recordings, and radio stations to tie people dispersed in space, "while festivals and competitions bring people closer together" (73). It is there that revivalists "actively learn and experience the revivalist ethos and aesthetic code at work and socialize among other 'insiders'" (ibid.).

Engaging with Bordieu's notion of habitus, Charles Hirschkind (2001 623, 624) attends to "the relation between sensory experiences and traditional practices ... from the perspective of a cultural practice through which the perceptual capacities of the subject are honed and, thus, through which the world these capacities inhabit is brought into being, rendered perceptible." Recognizing the practice of listening to sermons on cassette tapes among Muslims in Egypt as a "practice of ethical self-discipline,"

Hirschkind shows how practitioners "hone an ethically responsive sensorium; the requisite sensibilities that they see as enabling them to live as devout Muslims in a world increasingly ordered by secular rationalities" (624). Hirschkind is emphatic that this linkage between listening and sense is not simply "established metaphorically, but also through discipline, the training and inculcation of sensory habits," including bodily dispositions (628). This intervention allows us to connect folk dance as mother tongue to frameworks of sense and sensibility, by examining how disciplinary practices may inform emotions and judgments.

Just as Hirschkind's (2001, 628) listeners may learn, beyond the moral lessons of the sermons, "the ethical habits and the organization of sensory and motor skills necessary for inhabiting the world" in a manner considered appropriate for Muslims, so *táncház*-goers learn those appropriate for a certain kind of Hungarianness through the practice of a place-based folk dance as mother tongue. Transylvanian villages and Hungarianness are tied together by disciplined practices of folk dance as mother tongue, including dance event etiquette and place-based tourism. Yet how these connections are understood and what they mean, vary historically in relationship to the political economic context. With Halbwachs's attention to the dialectic of form and meaning in mind, I now turn to examine the broader political economic processes that have contributed to the emphasis on the essentialized ethnonational "community" I witnessed in *táncház* circles in 2004 and 2005.

Notes

1. While *táncház* continues to be closely connected to the staged performance of folk dance by troupes both professional and amateur, my focus here is on the public of *táncház* event-goers.

2. On social movements and knowledge practices, see Casas-Cortes, Osterweil, and Powell (2008). While I am very sympathetic to this line of thinking about social movement, these authors see themselves as producing knowledge "with or alongside" movements they sympathize with politically. Approaching the *táncház* as a movement that produces knowledges and political analysis is important, but I am not interested in abandoning my critical position as an outsider, as much as I strive to remain in productive conversation with participants and supporters.

3. Melucci (1988) used the phrases *framework of sense* and *community of sense* interchangeably. In this work, I use *framework of sense* to represent the common set of senses and sensibilities discussed in this chapter, while I reserve *community of sense* for those moments in which this network of *táncház*-goers can be seen to congeal into a community in relation to the formal political process. These moments will come into focus more clearly in the following two chapters.

4. The German word he uses here—*Gesellschaft*—has the meaning of both society and party; they are associations of a voluntary nature. It is used in the sociological tradition in contrast with *Gemeinschaft*, usually translated as community.

5. While Melucci does not expand on his use of the word *sense* this example allows us to see a relationship between what Hirschkind (2001, 624) calls senses, or "capacities of aesthetic appreciation," and sensibility, "states of moral attunement, or being," which may structure such sensory experiences. I take the term sense to bear a tension, thus, between aesthetic, or direct sensory experience, and the "sense" one makes of it. This (and Hirschkind's contribution) will be discussed further at the end of this chapter.

6. The (re)production of collective memory can be considered a kind of knowledge practice.

7. After Halbwachs, I take collective memory to be the result of the relationship of "sets of mnemonic practices" (Olick and Robbins 1998, 112) institutionalized within groups and the broader political and economic context that affects their interpretation over time. Interpretations are contested, and emerge from a "field of cultural negotiation through which different stories vie for a place in history" (Olik and Robbins 1998, 126).

8. This is similar in some ways to Hobsbawm and Ranger's "invention of tradition" but focuses less so on the nation-state. It is better seen in light of Alistair McIntyre's (2007) understanding of tradition (see also Asad 1993).

9. As such, *táncház* is the site of production of knowledge practices that relate to, comment on, and are influenced by the broader conditions in which they (re)produce themselves.

10. Langman examines a sole Hungarian folk dance troupe in Slovakia as a space of sociality and socialization and not simply of performance. See Pulay (2014) on how Roma dancehouses in the first decade of the 2000s were a "space where kinds of togetherness could be tried out between Roma and non Roma participants."

11. For an interesting critique of the use of the term *ethnic community*, see Glick-Schiller, Caglar, and Gulbrandsen (2006), who are concerned with developing a "conceptual framework for the study of migration, settlement, and transborder connection that is not dependent on the ethnic group as either the unit of analysis or sole object of study"(613). See Taylor (2016) for an elaboration of this comparison with linguistic nationalism.

12. Leading to the use of Hungarian folk songs in music pedagogy across the world.

13. Kodály was a key actor in chorus movements of the interwar period, which had separate roots from choruses of the labor movement but had overlaps with the regös Scouts in the 1930s (Pethő 2009). See also Kodály (1974).

14. The original Bartók quote can be found in his lecture notes at the Béla Bartók archives, 30 East 72nd St., New York, NY.

15. This connection of the agrarian classes with national essence was shared with the influential Herder and Rousseau.

16. While Györffy had been responsible for a controversial 1938 exhibit entitled *The Situation of Landownership in Hungary*, Teleki, then minister of culture, shut it down after complaints, claiming that the organizers had reached the limits of scientific fact and mixed it with politics (Borbándi 1989, 239).

17. See Schneider (2006) for explanation of "old" and "new" styles.

18. See Brubaker et al. (2006) for a nuanced view on the assimilation of Hungarian language users.

19. Timár told me that ideally Hungarians should not be learning Transylvanian dances, but those of the region each is born in. His statements assumed that a person is "from" the place in which he/she is born, as well as that a person has only one mother tongue.

20. I have written "his" here quite purposefully. In Hungarian folkdance, improvisation is almost completely in the realm of those dancing the male parts. There are few social dance events in which it is acceptable for a woman to dance these parts.

21. Something like a "national" habitus (Bourdieu 1977), a Magyar affect (Muñoz 2000). We see through *táncház* that it is learned in the revival context and can be legitimated as such in a number of manners.

22. This is significant in that it is the dance event that serves to broaden the participatory public.

23. But unlike the majority of cases studied by those focusing on ritual, that take the community as given, or the villages from which *táncház* adopted its practices, in the case of the *táncház* revival, there was no preexisting community. The urban folk dance scene is comprised of a voluntary association of individuals. It is only over the last three decades that any *táncház* community can be said to have developed. Because of this history, the need to examine the content of community becomes even more apparent.

24. Kligman (1988, 260) discusses the difference in meaning of folk traditions for the state and for villagers in Socialist Romania.

25. Villagers are more and more involved as revivalists themselves and may know the larger repertoire. Those involved in reviving folk dance in villages also stress knowing local dances, however.

26. Here, I mean among dancehouses dedicated to primarily Magyar content, which make up the majority in Hungary.

27. They nevertheless learn other suites via the *táncház* environments they share.

28. Another variation I encountered says that Hungarian folk dance reflects the ideal small-scale bourgeois society in which a balance was maintained between individual expression and group belonging.

29. This marks, perhaps, one divergence in the frameworks of sense of villagers and revivalists.

30. Romania had a similar system of houses of culture in the socialist period. Many of these remain central sites today for events from weddings to local dances and community events. They are frequently used for dance camps as well.

31. I did not encounter this attitude in other camp organizers I spoke with, nor did I witness such a blatant divergence from the accepted "authentic" elsewhere.

32. Some dancers told me that original ethnographic research is prerequisite for selection to dance with the Hungarian State Folk ensemble (MANE).

33. *Mahala*, also known as *manele*, is a popular music form drawing on Ottoman influences and utilizing electronic technologies, associated with popular neighborhoods called Mahala, usually performed by Roma bands.

34. There are men's solo dances and women's chain dances, but the repertoire in *táncház* is comprised mostly of couple dances (Hooker 2005).

35. Indeed, until the advent of staged dance in the mid-twentieth century, it appears that it was quite uncommon, and likely inappropriate, for married adults to dance with anyone except his/her spouse (and remained so except among performers). This is illustrated well by the *csujogatás*, a verse sung by women as men dance the *legényes*—lads' dance—sometimes while dancing a circle dance: "Ez a táncház legényeké / nem a házas embereké" (This dancehouse is for lads, not for married people). It both states this rule and suggests that it was/is broken often enough for it to be addressed formulaically. Thanks to Lynn Hooker, personal communication, for this point. On *csujogatás*, see Zilahi (1981) and Kürti (2010).

36. Because of the decentralized nature of *táncház* and the specificities of each weekly event, and taking into account festivals and camps as well, it is difficult to represent participants statistically. The participant base is constantly in flux. We find people who have been actively involved in *táncház* since the start, those of that generation who have only recently become involved, and many who have returned after years of absence. There is a constant influx of young people as well, some children of the first generation who grew up in *táncház* circles and others who were inspired by other means. Many youths who dance in ensembles attend camps although they may not frequent dancehouses.

37. Interviews revealed similar views about the sexual nature of the dance: A Transylvanian Hungarian currently living in Australia who had taken up folk dancing in the few years before

we met told me that she had been confronted a number of times with the assumption that as a woman traveling alone to folk dance camps, she was looking for sexual adventure. The fact that she was married did not discourage this view. Responding to my question about why he no longer frequents *táncház*, a former participant told me: "I don't want to dance with just anyone anymore; I mean it's practically having sex."

38. There, of course, may be Hungarian participants who are uncomfortable with these gendered arrangements, but no Hungarian who attended *táncház* expressed discomfort to me. Because non-ethnic Hungarians are often introduced to the dances abroad and are frequently ignorant of the local political discourses (most don't speak Hungarian), they are less likely to reflect the divide I describe in chapter 6. In fact, I often encountered liberal and left-leaning foreigners in *táncház*. I was once being taught a dance by a woman who danced the male part to lead me, and we were quickly told by men seeking partners to dance with men. I have joined other women in learning the lads' dances before the *táncház* began, but with the exception of my friend mentioned previously, none of them chose to dance these parts once the event began. A colleague told me that she has occasionally "witnessed Hungarian women perform gestural commentary for humorous effect, especially about men who dominate the stage with 'figures' during a couple's dance and leave their dance partners to the side to get bored." No Hungarian *táncház*-goer shared discomfort with these roles when I asked. Some (including the one who taught me during the event) even took my question as an opportunity to talk about how important traditional gender roles are.

39. See Fél and Hófer (1969) on brandy drinking among men and *áldomás* in Hungarian villages. For a more recent discussion of Hungarian wine drinking practices and gender, see Darvas (2003). See also Cowan (1990) on commensality and gender socialization.

40. Szék has a dance for four (two couples), and the "chain dances" of some non-Magyar groups can be mixed gender. Women's circle dances also exist. In contrast to the Magyar *táncház*, Csángó and Balkan dancehouses feature mostly chain or circle dances. While many women are familiar with these dances, I rarely saw them practiced in *táncház* events, in contrast with the ubiquitous presence of male solo dances. Women have taken to learning the men's solo dances in the instructional period, but I never saw a woman perform these dances in front of the band once the *táncház* (as opposed to teaching period) begins. This would violate the "traditional" gendered etiquette of the event. See Hooker (2005) for a similar account.

41. As a New Yorker much more familiar with afro-Caribbean dances and negative claims about its gestures being sexual, the intimate and hands-on features of Hungarian dance (which appears to many as stiff and prudish) were obscured to me as a spectator. I only came to understand the intensity of the contact and coordination by learning the dances.

42. This camp-goer was from the United States and not of Hungarian origin. She did not speak Hungarian.

43. Debates continue between various factions over whether individual *táncház*es should only focus on one village or region or whether the music and dances of other regions should be engaged in at village camps.

44. See Crain (1992) for a discussion of pilgrimage and its relationship to place, Dubisch (1990) for the relationship of pilgrimage and national symbols, and Bohlman (1996) on the role of music in pilgrimage in the claiming of borderland territory.

45. Singing lessons are often part of *táncház*es, usually occurring in the break between dance suites. Camps usually feature singing as well.

46. These songs are often about the "poor Hungarian lads" taken away to serve in the Austrian army. A standing army was instituted in the early eighteenth century and the *verbunk*, a male solo dance, takes its name from the Habsburg state's Werbung Kommando and its coercive recruitment practices—often involving dance and alcohol (Lányi, György, and Jenő 1983).

47. Among other themes, the leftist *népi* writer Kodolányi, who was nevertheless close with those right-leaning writers associated with antisemitism, wrote on the one-child system (*egyke*),

discussed previously. Lukacs called him a "romantic anticapitalist." I have not seen anything suggesting he was of Jewish descent. I sometimes wonder if I mistakenly noted his name in my field notes, instead of "Kosztolányi." Dezső Kosztolányi, who was not associated with the *népi* writers, was a well-known writer and far better known today in Hungary, partly due to films based on his novels. Kosztolányi's wife was of Jewish descent, but he has also been associated with antisemitism. The fact that the statements do not seem to map onto the facts speaks to the ongoing construction of these oppositions.

48. In another situation, one musician asked me why at age thirty-five I had no children. He warned me that if "the whites" continued to act the way I did in the United States, "the blacks" would overtake us. "Don't listen to the Jews when they say you don't need children," he said.

49. Another person suggested to me that one of the founders of Heritage House is a Jew and that he secured his job through Jewish connections. He implied that the person's liberal leanings were evidence of this, but that I could also look up his family history. Another told me that this person's socialist-era connections in KISZ (Communist Youth League) indicated his Jewishness as well.

50. Of course, the equation of liberals with Jews is not new or limited to Hungary.

51. This does not mean that there were not Catholic participants. Although many were not churchgoers, many participants considered themselves Christian, sometimes specifically Catholic. This critique cannot be seen so much as a Protestant critique as a subaltern one, the notion being that Hungarians were already Christian before contact with the Church and that the Roman church brought with it colonizing ideologies and practices. There is in fact a history of violent struggle between pagans and the Church in Hungary.

52. This, of course, contradicts the idea of an absolute distinction between Hungarians and their others. In fact, when claiming that the Hungarian grammatical structure allows for advanced thought, many participants noted Jews among the famous Hungarian intellectuals they gave as examples. Some people contradicted themselves, arguing at one moment that anyone can be Hungarian (and thus have access to this spirituality) because of language use and at another that Jews, by embracing Jewishness, were rejecting their Hungarianness.

53. The Magyar language, classified as part of the Uralic group, and until recently thought to be related to Altaic languages, is indeed very different from the languages that surround it regionally. Most of its words are unrelated to those of Indo-European languages that have shared roots, and its agglutinative structure and vowel harmony are quite different from even the other languages spoken within and nearby Hungary.

54. He actually argues that Manichean ideas are a distorted form of the teachings of the apostles Andrew and Philip, who spread "Scythian wisdom" (Pap 1999, 554).

55. Some people told me that this was the problem with the Jews: instead of pursuing consensus, they pursued difference.

Chapter Six

Socialist State Formation, Táncház Frameworks of Sense, and the Origins of the Postsocialist Cultural Turn

FRAMEWORKS OF SENSE ARE NOT limited to the sociable moments in which they are produced, nor can they be reduced to expressions of alternative identities. A *táncház* framework of sense can be rendered visible in moments of collective public or political action. The broader reach of this framework of sense is revealed at moments in which collective memory appears to have relevance to the political context in such a way that a "community of sense" appears in action.

Stressing the contested aspect of collective memory, Walter Benjamin (1969, 255) writes: "To articulate the past historically does not mean to recognize it 'the way it really was.' It means to seize hold of a memory as it flashes up at a moment of danger."[1] For Benjamin, the danger, which affects both the content of the tradition and its receivers, lay in historical memory becoming a tool of the ruling classes. We might also say that such moments are often responses to what are perceived as dangers. If collective memory is reproduced or altered in part as a response to such contemporary dangers, then it is important to pay attention to conditions in which *táncház* "remembers." While "moments of danger" may represent the "shock experience" that Benjamin believed was required to reawaken critical memory, I use this phrase to point to moments in which *tanchaz*'s actions burst into the political sphere, making explicit the relationship between the framework of sense, collective memory, and politics. While we may not see the revolutionary enlightenment Benjamin hoped for, we do get insight into the (re)production of hegemony.

In this chapter, I present the shifting political and economic context from 1956 until the early years of regime change to examine the mutual influence between the folk movement and the political and economic spheres and to inquire why ethnonationalist sentiment had become so palpable in *tánchaz* settings by the time of my fieldwork. I show the changing conditions and sites of cultural politics and *népi* action that would allow, encourage, and discourage certain formations of collective memory. I begin by discussing what has been identified as a cultural turn associated with the "'postsocialist' condition" (Fraser 1997) and some of the processes that have contributed to its local articulation. Next, we will journey back in time to 1956 to explore transformations in socialist cultural politics and the shifting relationship between *népi* movements and the political sphere in the socialist era. In contrast to the interwar *népi* movement, *tánchaz* did not engage in politics proper, concentrating its activities in the cultural sphere. Under the conditions of late socialism, including the liberalization of cultural production, culture would become an important sphere of action. By "liberalization" here, I mean both the tolerance toward and even sponsorship of previously forbidden or suppressed art and cultural production and the political and economic conditions in which this emerged, as seen in chapter 4. By the late 1980s, *tánchaz*'s complex relationship with the political sphere could be seen in a first moment of danger: manifestations addressing the plight of ethnic Hungarian minorities in Transylvania. After 1989, new conditions would emerge, under which we could observe a process of political polarization, which I discuss as a second moment of danger. This polarization now plays a central role in Hungarian society and is materialized in *tánchaz*.

Culture Talk and the Cultural Turn: Obscuring the Social

Where the focus of many rightist parties in Europe had shifted to fear of immigrants, especially of Muslims (Bunzl 2005), at the time of my 2004–5 fieldwork (long before the "migrant crisis" of 2015) the Hungarian right remained focused on "internal" others: Jews and "Gypsies," ethnic Hungarians in neighboring states, and international investors—the EU, IMF, and NGOs, representing neo-imperialist globalization, and often conflated with Jews and cosmopolitans. Despite this apparent difference, signs of a "cultural fundamentalism" emphasizing "differences of cultural heritage and their incommensurability" were surfacing in both Western and Eastern Europe (Stolke 1995, 4). In her 1995 work, Verena Stolke points out that this "heightened sense of primordial identity, cultural difference and exclusiveness" (a "racism without race"), which takes xenophobia to be part of human nature, serves to make immigrants scapegoats for socioeconomic problems. Stolke (1995) argued that conditions brought about by neoliberal economic policies are implicated in the spread of communitarian logics, among them "populist ethnonationalism," worldwide. As waves of privatization and the rollback of social citizenship were being realized around the globe, recourse to ethnonationalist thinking indeed appeared to be on the rise.

In the process of "transition," the achievement of political and civic citizenship in the postsocialist period came at the price of social citizenship. Rejecting materialist explanations, many Hungarians articulated growing differentiation between social strata not as a function of the economic system but as evidence of conflict between incommensurable cultures. In 2004, a number of *táncház*-goers (and one Heritage House employee) recommended I read Samuel Huntington's book *The Clash of Civilizations*, available in Hungarian translation at vendors' booths at some *táncház* events. In his 1993 *Foreign Affairs* article with the same title, Huntington (1993, 1) asserts that while "nation states will remain the most powerful actors in world affairs ... the principal conflicts will occur between nations and groups of different civilizations. The clash of civilizations will be the battle lines of the future."

Huntington's essentializing and dehistoricized proscription phrased as a prediction appears self-evident to many, not least to many Hungarian folk revivalists. While fluxing generations of *táncház*-goers have participated in the revival for many different reasons since its inception in the 1970s, ethnonationalist sentiment was palpable and widespread at *táncház* gatherings in 2004 and 2005. Yet most participants were not radical rightists, tending to vote for Fidesz, which was at that time a center right party, instead. But many shared essentializing views about culture and ethnicity, expressed not least in disparaging views toward "liberals," an epithet they often used to gloss Jewishness. Most revivalists I met were quite vocal about their support for citizenship for Hungarians over the borders and voted accordingly in a 2004 referendum on the issue (discussed in detail in chapter 7). How can we track this turn toward cultural fundamentalism?

Ethnonationalism has been a much-noted force in the region since the fall of socialism, illustrated most famously in the violent breakup of the former Yugoslavia and, more recently, in popular accounts of the unrest in Ukraine since the Euromaidan and the antimigrant politics pursued by Hungary's current government.[2] While popular journalism has tended to explain the rise of ethnonationalism as an atavistic return to antagonisms stemming from the disappearance of the totalitarian state, it has generally ignored the question of how political and economic processes have helped enforce, if not produce, the (idea of the) ethnonation (Hayden 1992 Kürti

Socialist State Formation 183

2001; Kalb and Halmai 2011).[3] Anthropologists have pointed to the social processes that construct national ethnicity and their relationship to ideas of national self-determination (Hayden 1996; Kaneff and King 2004). Dissent during the late socialist years was often formulated around the logic of the nation. State socialism had cultivated national consciousness in various ways. Official efforts involving folk culture followed Soviet cultural theorist Andrej Zhdanov's "national in form, socialist in content," and participants could in many cases ignore the socialist content. Yet the transition to democratic politics and adaptation to a capitalist economy offered new conditions for national consciousness.

In 1996, Katherine Verdery argued that "overwhelming presence of the master-symbol 'nation' in Romania's political space limits what opposition intellectuals and politicians can do with symbols like 'civil society,' 'democracy' and 'Europe'" (Verdery 1996, 84, 105). She concluded that the monopolization of institutional forces and the symbol of the nation "compels all other political actors in Romania to 'nationalize' their political instruments—and in doing so, to strengthen 'nation' as a political symbol even further" (1996, 129). Also writing in 1996, philosopher Slavoj Žižek suggests that "the more that the logic of Capital becomes universal, the more its opposite will assume features of 'irrational fundamentalism.'" This is because the "supposedly neutral liberal-democratic framework produces nationalist 'closure' as its inherent opposite" (220). At the same time, he argues, liberal democracy cannot be universalized. Because it produces "haves and have-nots," it opens up a space for negative judgment of itself in the form of fundamentalism (ibid.).

In the postsocialist environment in which the dominance of a market economy and the rapid breakdown of the welfare state under the sign of liberal democracy have been accompanied by deepening inequality, Hungarian rightists often point to liberals as the source of contemporary problems.[4] To many I spoke with during my fieldwork period, liberals demonstrate *un-Hungarianness* through their successful adaptation to the market, advocacy for minority rights and suppression of nationalistic expression, alliance with socialists (read: communists), and their supposed Jewishness.[5]

This rise of ethnonationalism is not unconnected to what others had begun to label an "advancing tide of populism" in the region (Krastev 2006; see also Kalb and Halmai 2011).[6] Noting a rise of populism in Europe (for example the popularity of Le Pen in France and Haider in Austria), including attempts by establishment parties to recapture certain themes and messages, Ivan Krastev (2006) points to Central Europe as "the capital of the new populism" in 2006. This term has since come to be used regularly to refer to Fidesz and Viktor Orbán, among other political leaders and their parties. Back then, Krastev argued that populists were rising to power connected with the framing of corruption as a main challenge facing society. Krastev presented populism as a worldview that sees society as separated into two antagonistic groups, "the people" and "the corrupt elite."[7] He argues that while liberals were key architects of anticorruption discourse in many parts of postsocialist society, relying on it as a "populist strategy," they failed to see how popular understanding of corruption diverged from their own.

First, Krastev (2006) argues, while liberals perceive corruption as an institutional issue requiring more transparency and institutional reforms, the public views corruption as a moral issue requiring honest politicians. Second, he argues, liberals regard anticorruption discourse as being about fairness, while the public sees it as about growing social inequality. Third, while liberals tend to believe that corruption derives from a too powerful and large state, and accordingly advocated rapid privatization and state downscaling, a majority of people believe that the power of the market is to blame and thus favor "revision of the most scandalous privatization deals" (ibid.). Finally, he argues, while liberals use anticorruption discourse to legitimize capitalism, the "conspiracy-minded majority" see in it the opportunity to delegitimize capitalism "without the risk of being accused of communism" (ibid.).

While Krastev's 2006 thoughts are useful for thinking about the emergence of antiliberal populisms in the region, he does not present liberalism (or neoliberalism) as problematic in any way, nor does he explore why said populism would take an ethnonational or cultural fundamentalist form. Ágnes Gagyi (2016) argues that "liberal antipopulism" in Hungary has worked to silence and demean opinions of much of the public while calling on formal mechanisms of "democracy." This has enhanced a situation in which these "democracy"-enforcing elites come to be seen in opposition to nationalist elites, who claim to defend national interests in the face of the liberal left.

Although characteristics specific to postsocialist Europe are helpful in explaining the rise of ethnonationalism there, along with Stolke, many other scholars (Jameson 1991; Fraser 1997; Mamdani 2005) have brought our attention to a much more geographically diffuse "cultural turn" paralleling the fall of state socialism and the rise of neoliberalism, defining elements of our "post-socialist condition" (Fraser 1997). Mahmood Mamdani (2005) points to the "rapid politicizing" of the term *culture* arising from the discursive vacuum left at the end of the Cold War. In the place of materialist explanations that examine the role of the economy or the state, the use of culture to explain political events such as 9/11 has become ubiquitous. A now dominant framework for "thinking and speaking—or not—about politics . . . culture talk assumes that every culture has a tangible essence that defines it, and it then explains politics as a consequence of that essence" (17). Not surprisingly, Mamdani notes the popularity of Huntington's clash of civilizations narrative.

Perhaps we should not be surprised that culture talk has gained strength as the socialist paradigm loses its hold, as "the melting away of opposing global forces and hard territorial boundaries after the Cold War has fostered a triumphant neoliberalism as the single source of any agenda for social change and development" (Kalb 2002, 321). Indeed, the rise of culture talk has paralleled the fall of state socialism, the diminishment of the social state, a concomitant chiseling away of social citizenship, and the weakening of Socialist Party agendas across Europe (see Dale and Fabry 2018). Arguments about the end of history (Fukayama 1989, 1992) that delegitimate communism and socialism as viable political paths have had consequences for the ways in which political issues are articulated.

The *népi* movements discussed in this book have always put attention on the cultural sphere. Yet the concept of a sovereign space of the people, the nation, or *Gemeinschaft* as outside of communism (and later capitalism) and the more geographically diffuse "postsocialist" cultural turn interact to produce particular kinds of cultural politics as well as the heritagization that we see in *táncház*.

While *táncház* too is referred to as a *népi* movement, translating it into English as populist, as we would its interwar predecessor(s), is difficult. To equate *táncház* with the political platforms of agrarian populists of the interwar period or with the politicians and parties being called populist today is to lose sight of important details.[8] This does not mean that there are no affinities or overlaps. One thing at stake here are the gaps and overlaps between *nép* and nation. While *táncház* participants made social space for themselves as citizens of the socialist state, they also advocated for ethnic brethren over the borders. Their practice, evidence of a civil society in the socialist period, aligns with the ethical civil society identified in the region as an explicitly nonpolitical sphere of authenticity.

The following discussion of the 1956 revolution helps us spy how the domain of cultural politics developed in particular ways in the late socialist period and gives context for the *népi* cultural politics of *táncház*, its distance from the issues of peasant workers, and an almost exclusive emphasis on ethnic brethren over the borders.

THE 1956 REVOLUTION

The 1956 revolution plays an important role in Hungarian collective memory. While the story is multifaceted and contested to this day, it is safe to say that this brief period of intense unrest was spurred by the forced retirement of Prime Minister Imre Nagy and his expulsion from the party due to his reformist policies. In the days of the revolution, when Nagy reassumed the position of prime minister, symbols of Hungarianness, especially those referencing the 1848 revolution, appeared in abundance. Demands were made for democracy, national sovereignty, the establishment of workers councils, and a cessation of the collectivization of agricultural production (Hanák 1991, 217). Workers councils, young intellectuals, and students played important roles in the revolutionary events (Krausz 2006).

Nagy is often problematically presented as an anticommunist. He is perhaps better understood as a reformist of the post-Stalinist era, and his policies presaged and shaped those made under his successor János Kádár, placed in power once Soviet tanks and troops had crushed the revolution with military might. Many demands of the various factions supporting Nagy adhered to communist ideals, including giving more direct power to the workers, but there was also an emphasis on justice for the agrarian population. To many, the uprising was about national sovereignty in the face of the USSR (whose troops remained stationed in Hungary until 1991); indeed, an important demand was that Soviet troops take leave. The revolution can thus be interpreted by some as having pitted true Hungarians against foreigners. While the Soviets were the most obvious foreigners, oppositions could be put into play to construct others as foreign as well.

Many local leftists had been purged from spheres of influence in the late 1940s and early 1950s in favor of those Hungarians who supported a Soviet urbanist line. Some of the latter had been living in the USSR and returned to Hungary only after Communist power had been secured.[9] Nagy himself had converted to Bolshevism as a prisoner of war in Russia. After fighting in the Red Army, he returned to Hungary to serve the Soviet Republic. He differed however, from the stereotype of the Muscovites, as they were called, in some ways. Unlike many urbanist Muscovites, Nagy came from a rural background, sympathized with agricultural workers, and "gravitated towards those who held nationalist and pro-peasant views" (Granville 2001, 11). As minister of agriculture in the mid-1940s, Nagy had instituted land reforms, breaking up large estates and redistributing the land. His concerns for peasant demands led to this cautious approach to collectivization. While this put him out of favor with the party status quo, it foreshadowed the propeasant policies he introduced as prime minister after 1953 (Rainer 2009; Essig 2007) in response to the demands of agrarian workers, not least in the 1952 uprisings (Rainer 2002).

Nagy was also a gentile, although many other Muscovites were of Jewish descent (Granville 2001, 11). While this group is often constructed as foreign, some of the same people assign Nagy, despite his being a Muscovite and dedicated to Marxism-Leninism, the role of "real Hungarian" because of his resistance to foreign and urban impositions. Interpretations of the revolution can thus be made amenable to the *népi*/Hungarian versus *urbánus*/foreigner opposition, and Nagy can be cast in the role of former. But whether it is his attention to peasants or association with national sovereignty that is important depends on emphasis.

The revolution was aided by a flourishing of civil and political activities. Interwar *népi* activists resurfaced in the political sphere by Nagy's side as the main force behind the Petőfi Circle (named after 1848 revolutionary poet Sándor Petőfi). The circle had hosted debates criticizing the regime in the lead-up to the revolution and organized demonstrations, expressing solidarity with Polish workers on trial after the revolt in Poznan, Poland. The Peasant Party was also reestablished as the Petőfi Party.[10] *Népi* writers articulated demands corresponding with those of the French Revolution, "without equating liberty with big capital or equality with centralized state power" (Borbándi 1989, 471). These ideas were circulated in the journal *Szabad Szó* (Free word), also reestablished at that time. István Deák (1999, 56) writes: "The populists were enthusiastic about the Revolution but because they were generally more interested in public welfare than in the elusive concept of freedom, they were among the first to warn, during the Revolution, against dismantling the welfare state created by the Communist system." Rather than being against socialism, the writers debated "whether our socialism should be the faithful copy of our patrons or the adaptation of universal principles to the nature of Hungarians and their economic situation" (Borbándi 1989, 474).

But there were noticeable power shifts apparent in *népi* circles in the revolutionary days as well. Leadership positions were withheld from those perceived as "complicit" in the regime (such as Ferenc Erdei, who had served twice as minister of agriculture, continued to work on peasant-related policy, and would be a deputy prime minister during the revolution) and given to "those with more credibility" (Borbándi 1989, 465).[11] Yet despite their "oppositional" status, "not a single populist writer was imprisoned either under Rákosi or under Kádár" (Deák 1999, 56). And, despite the fact that the Writers Union, headed by Péter Veres, had "launched the country's last appeal to the free world for assistance," most of the *népi* writers signed the manifesto "protesting the UN's condemnation of the suppression of the October Revolution" (ibid., 57) in the aftermath.[12] While the line between "sides" was as blurry as ever, and the image of the revolution and their role in it was fraught with contradiction, *népi* actors retained a kind of legitimacy, not least tied to their oppositional status.

AFTERMATHS: TOWARD LATE SOCIALISM

Beyond this short-lived *népi* participation in the political sphere, and the possibilities to interpret Nagy and *népi* actors as "more Hungarian" and anticommunist, the revolution set off a broader set of transformations that influenced cultural politics and the forms *népi* politics would take. New institutional arrangements in the aftermath of 1956 restructured the field of action, sparking shifts in the economic and cultural spheres in Hungary, as well as changes in Romanian policy toward ethnic Hungarians (Chen 2003, 184).[13]

As the class system extant in Transylvania under Hungarian rule had been particularly harsh to ethnic Romanians, so Romanian rule after 1920 (and again after Hungarian annexation of parts of Transylvania during World War II) involved discrimination against ethnic Hungarians (Kürti 2001). Nevertheless, in the 1950s, seeing "traditional Romanian nationalism as largely detrimental to the Leninist cause," Communist leader Gheorghe Gheorghiu-Dej attempted to weaken the Orthodox Church and introduced new minority policies, establishing the Hungarian Autonomous Region in the central part of the country in 1952 (Chen 2003, 183).[14]

The aftermath of the Hungarian revolution saw a shift toward policies aimed at assimilating the Hungarian minority through "Romanianization of the party, the closing of Hungarian schools, and the merging of the Hungarian Bolyai University with the Romanian Babeş University" (Chen 2003, 184; see also Kürti 2001). By 1960, the boundaries of the autonomous region had been redrawn, decreasing the proportion of ethnic Hungarians from 77 to 62 percent (Chen 2003, 184; Connor 1984, 237). This new round of assimilation was inspired by anticipation that the revolution could "produce undesirable ideological effects on ethnic Hungarians in Transylvania and other parts of the country and therefore threaten the Leninist regime" (Chen 2003, 184).

Starting in 1969, under Gheorghiu-Dej's successor, Nicolai Ceaușescu, minority policy shifted more drastically toward assimilation (Kürti 2001). "Ceaușescu refused to recognize the Hungarians and other minorities as belonging to other nations, claiming that they were all part of the Romanian nation" (Chen 2003, 192; see also Verdery 1995).[15] The 1968 territorial reorganization act eliminating the autonomous region entirely was followed by demographic policies that many saw as designed to dilute the concentration of ethnic minorities through forced dispersion and planned "immigration of large numbers of Romanians, many of them nationalist, into formerly compact areas of minority residence" (Chen 2003, 192). Ceaușescu's reign was characterized by insistence on national unity via denial as overall conditions in the country worsened, perhaps leading to a particularly ethnic kind of resistance (Kürti 2001, 39). History books omitted the role of minorities in Romanian history, and Hungarian-language schools and media broadcasts were practically eliminated (Chen 2003, 183, 192).[16]

Back in Hungary, citizens were experiencing the beginning of a post-1956 thaw related to economic and cultural reforms that would affect cultural production, and the emergence of civil society and the second economy. This liberalization included shifts in the limits to cultural production summed up in János Kádár's famous 1961 announcement: "those who are not against us are with us" (Hanák 1991, 218). By the late 1960s, the three Ts cultural policy, distinguishing "forbidden," "tolerated," and "sponsored" domains, was underway, and the New Economic Mechanism (NEM) had gone into effect, leading to decentralization in production and the support of market mechanisms discussed previously.[17] This marked the beginning of the consumption-based strategy of legitimization (so-called Frigidaire or Goulash Communism) for which Kádár would become famous. The second economy would soon emerge as a defining feature of late socialist Hungary, with economic activities outside state employment playing a key role in transforming economic and social relations (Rona-Tas 1990). As we saw in chapter 4, cultural politics took new forms in this period of liberalization.

While the tendency of socialist systems to overproduce intellectuals provided for a potential class of dissidents (Verdery 1995, 87, 88), the introduction of a market for culture independent from central planning, combined with the maturation of the baby boom generation, led to unexpected changes in cultural production (Kürti 2001, 150).[18] Although self-censorship, a "process of compromise and self-adjustment" was part of the game that cultural producers played (Haraszti 1987, 70), the Hungarian government did crack down on dissident groups "under pressure of the Soviets" in 1973 (Szelényi, Szelényi, and Kovach 1995, 703). In the course of the crackdown, Kádár is said to have "wisely decided to take oppressive measures only against a small group of highly visible philosophers and sociologists" (ibid.), leaving others alone. *Népi* writers who spoke up during this period "restricted their activity to trying to persuade the government and the Party to speak up for the rights of the Hungarian minorities" (Deák 1999, 59). This shift of *népi* emphasis away from the rights of Hungarian citizens to primarily those of Hungarian culture bearers will become more apparent in the first moment of danger I discuss, toward the end of this chapter.

On the Stage, in the Village: Tourism,
Professionalization, Cultivation

In the realm of folk dance, changing circumstances saw an increased focus on developing a tourism industry (Maácz 1981, 74). While at first limited to official ensembles, by the 1970s growing opportunities related to tourism were available to amateur ensembles as well (ibid.). As the state withdrew support, folk dance troupes, much like the houses of culture, were required to produce income to cover expenses (ibid., 75). As ensembles focused more and more on presenting Hungarian dance folklore to foreigners in Hungary and to audiences abroad, disputes developed over the authenticity of productions (Maácz 1981a 76).[19] Amateur groups were better able to adapt to the fluctuating demands of the tourist industry under these changing economic conditions. Their adaptations, among them, the *táncház* idea and form and the pedagogies related to folk dance as mother tongue, were key to the emergence of the *táncház* movement and to the new village visiting: authenticity-based folk dance tourism to Transylvania.

As we have seen, the (re)turn to social dance was understood by participants as a return to the original context and function of folk dance. It was modeled after community participation, the sociable practices of living villagers. Yet as with the Bouquet of Pearls and *regös* Scouts movements, *táncház* practices in villages aimed explicitly at encouraging rural folk to preserve and to revive local dance traditions toward the reproduction of the traditional practices of ethnic Hungarians in rural Transylvania. Simultaneously, in the Hungarian context, new opportunities to professionalize were emerging. Stylistic authenticity would be determined by a slowly growing set of *táncház* experts on the basis of past and present place-based collection. These practices paralleled international trends related to tourism and the heritage regime that began to form in the 1970s and would come to fruition in the postsocialist/neoliberalizing period, discussed in chapter 7 (Taylor 2009).

Long before the *tánchaz* emerged, the socialist administration had already made efforts to reward authentic folk art. The ministerial resolution on the Master of Folk Art (*Népmuvészet Mestere*) award in 1953 established that it would be given "once a year on August 20 by the council of ministers."[20] Nominations for the award would be made by the minister of public education, "based on recommendations from the Institute of Folk Arts and the Association of Hungarian Artists and Craftspeople" (European Folklore Institute 2001, 9). Awards came with a one-time honorarium and the guarantee of a pension (European Folklore Institute 2001).

In 1970, a new title, Young Master of Folk Art (*Népmuveszet Ifjú Mestere*), was introduced, and recipients subsequently founded the Studio of Young Folk Artists (*Fiatal Népmuvészetek Studiója*) in 1973, discussed in chapter 4. While the first award aimed at reinforcing the value of folk art among "traditional practitioners," the Young Master award was aimed at nontraditional creators of new art in a folk art paradigm, specifically, folk artists under the age of thirty-five interested in "renewing folk art on the basis of the traditions of material (*tárgyi*) and spiritual (*szellemi*) culture" (Papers of the Katalin Landgráf collection).

This cohort was at the forefront of the professionalization of folk artists in the 1980s and 1990s. Economic changes requiring leisure time be spent on economically viable activities and associations paralleled the increased emphasis on tourism. The establishment of the annual *Tánchaz* Meeting, held within the confines of the Budapest Spring Festival and featuring amateur and tradition-keeping ensembles, *tánchaz* events, and folk crafts, and the formation of the *Tánchaz* Chamber in 1987 represent connections of this kind in the late socialist period.[21] After 1989, camps supported with private, NGO, and state funds proliferated, and the number of *tánchazes* has grown, many outside the culture houses.[22] While this does not mean that there is a simple calculus of value, growing numbers are dependent on folk art, folk music, and folk dance production as a source of income. As *tánchazes* themselves did and do not bring much money for such cultural workers; it is rather the production of staged events (at home or on tour) and of purchasable recordings (cassettes, CDs) or folk art objects, research, and teaching that provide income.[23] While Sándor Striker suggests that *tánchaz* was an exception to the tendency of amateur activities to be focused on economic or political activity in this period, it might have uniquely combined both.

Awards similar to the Master of Folk Art had also been instituted in Romania and other socialist countries: Japan in the 1950s, South Korea in the 1960s, the Philippines in the 1970s, Thailand in the 1980s, and France in the 1990s (Gömbös 2001). In 1989, the Hungarian Master of Folk Art award would be unified by UNESCO with similar ones under the term "Living Human Treasures" (ibid.).[24]

The increased significance of tourism from the 1970s onward was not limited to Hungary (Bendix 1989, 144).[25] Tourism policy anticipated positive economic impacts on local, regional, and national economies (Mathieson and Wall 1982). It was in this decade that UNESCO adopted the World Heritage Convention, seeking to protect cultural heritage and encourage tourism by supporting the establishment of protected heritage sites.[26] By the 1980s, UNESCO's vision of heritage as an opportunity for tourism-led economic development was broadened to include folklore and cultural practices, defined now as intangible heritage. Protection of intangible heritage was articulated around the cosmopolitan values of human cultural diversity and human rights, conceived as cultural rights (see Cowan, Dembour, and Wilson 2001), a language used by *tánchaz* goers and others in the 1980s to address the woes of ethnic minorities in Transylvania.

A MOMENT OF DANGER: THE TRANSYLVANIA PROTESTS OF 1988

While tourism was becoming an economic opportunity for some Hungarian folk artists, village visiting, the unique *tánchaz* tourism that had inspired a turn toward social dance in Budapest in the 1970s was also expanding. For later participants, trips to Transylvania became de rigueur, functioning as a kind of status symbol (Z. Szabó 1998, 175). But *tánchaz* and associated tourism practices began to emerge just as the Ceaușescu regime initiated stricter measures against expressions of Hungarian national identity, making it more difficult for Hungarians to visit Transylvania or conduct research on ethnic Hungarian themes. In 1969, researchers had been "able to record the complete set of contemporary dances of Szék on film, with soundtrack included, with the cooperation of researchers from the Romanian Academy of Sciences" (Martin 1982, 76). By the early 1970s, according to numerous participants, it was much harder for Hungarians to do research there. Villagers risked punishment for their hospitality to visiting Hungarians (Z. Szabó 1998, 175; Kürti 2001); the law forbade ethnic Hungarians to host Hungarian guests overnight. Many feared consequences for speaking Hungarian in public. Although rarely subject to it themselves, Hungarians visiting ethnic Hungarian villages in 1970s Transylvania were privy to stories about repression, such as those recounted by musicians in the 1991 film *Beyond the Forest* about their experiences with the security apparatus due to having hosted Hungarians (Ronay 1992). *Tánchaz* participants came to see this in a national light. To them, ethnic Hungarians were being repressed for helping Hungarians preserve their culture.

Revivalists came to see this as the fault of not only "the Romanians" but also the Communist governments of both countries: the Romanian government, known as the most nationalist in the bloc, and the Hungarian government playing an internationalist role and suppressing (certain kinds of) nationalist sentiment. Both governments had pursued modernization projects resulting in the uprooting of rural lifestyles and traditions and the exploitation of rural labor. Further, as one *tánchaz*-goer recounted to me, it was evident to all that the security apparatuses of the two countries were in collusion. Discussion of Transylvania and its significant minority was virtually absent from school curricula in socialist Hungary (Gal 1991, 448).[27] Yet through *tánchaz* practices, participants entered into a visceral relationship with the geography and people and folk arts of Transylvania. For them, *tánchaz* became a history lesson of sorts, although just what they understood the lesson to be varied.

In June 1988, nearly sixty thousand Hungarians took to the streets of Budapest in the largest street actions since 1956 to pressure the government into opposing the village destruction, or "systematization," program announced by president Ceaușescu in March of that year. There was widespread belief that this plan targeted ethnically Hungarian villages (*New York Times* 1988a; see also Kürti 2001, 130–35).[28] The text of a letter sent by members of the East European Anthropology group of the American Anthropological Association to Ceaușescu, inspired by a letter written by concerned Romanian intellectuals and the 1986 issue of the *Radio Free Europe Research Report* on the continuing destruction of Romania's cities, demonstrates how the plight of ethnic Hungarians in Romania was seen abroad. Noting "the plans for 'remodeling' Romania's historic Transylvanian cities represents yet another incursion on the unique history and lifeways of Transylvania's German and Magyar-populations," the letter states: "The wholesale transformations in Romanian urban and now rural communities represent an unprecedented assault on culture and history, let alone daily life" (Kideckel 1986).

The protesters employed the language of human rights, calling on Romanians to "fulfill human rights obligations to minority groups that are guaranteed in various international forums" (*New York Times* 1988a, A8). Hungary officially issued a complaint against Romania, claiming the plan

Fig. 6.1 Budapest protests against village destruction in Transylvania, June 27, 1988. Photo by Piroska Nagy.

was "aimed at the weakening of the identity of national minorities" (ibid.). The resettlement, or systematization, policy introduced in 1988, had it proceeded as planned, "would very likely have resulted in the destruction of historic majority-Hungarian villages and the forcible resettlement of their populations" (Chen 2003, 192).

By 1989, Human Rights Watch had published a report entitled *Destroying Ethnic Identity: The Hungarians of Romania* and the American Anthropological Association had issued a resolution against the village destruction programs in Romania (Beck and Kideckel 1989). In 1990, the *táncház* band Muzsikás would release the album *Blues for Transylvania* on Hannibal records. The cover, which circulated widely on the world music circuit, included an essay by well-known world music producer (and owner of Hannibal records) Joe Boyd. In it, he named ethnic Hungarians in Transylvania as the initiators of the revolution that had toppled Ceaușescu in 1989 and Transylvania as the place where the soul of Hungarian music lives. He also identified Muzsikás as bringing "material and cultural aid" to the people of Transylvania (Boyd 1991).

While *táncház* was not organizationally responsible for the June protests around Transylvania, it had contributed to the public's knowledge about the existence, plight, and lives of ethnic Hungarians in Romania

Socialist State Formation 195

Fig. 6.2 Budapest protests against village destruction in Transylvania, June 27, 1988. Photo by Piroska Nagy.

and to the notion that their own government was "un-Hungarian" in its suppression of the relevant information. Articulating the nation and the people in such a way, *táncház* was seen and felt as oppositional to many, perhaps even contributing to its popularity. Some connections between *táncház* and more overtly political manifestations were transparent. The well-known public figure Sándor Csoóri, "neopopulist" writer, president of the Young Folk Artists' Studio, and soon to be politician, was among the initiators of a 1988 "Hungarian Declaration of Solidarity with the Rumanian People," which voiced concern not only for Hungarian minorities but for all Romanians (Hungarian Press of Transylvania 1988).[29] His son, Sándor Csoóri Jr., was a founding member of the Muzsikás ensemble.[30] Other activists and dissidents were also known to frequent *táncház* events.

The government not only tolerated the protests but also granted asylum to refugees from Transylvania. The influx of ethnic Hungarian Romanians had already been visible in Budapest, where women from Transylvanian villages gathered in public squares selling handmade embroidery (often prepared as part of the extensive dowries traditionally brought into the new household formed by marriage). By the middle of 1991 "more than 50,000 refugees from Romania had entered Hungary" (Fullerton 1996; see also

Kürti 2002, 219–21, and 2001, 110–11). *Táncház* events organized around the dance culture of the Csángó, the only Hungarian-speaking minority group with a presence in Romania outside of Transylvania, became very popular after large numbers of Csángó youth arrived as refugees after the Romanian revolution in the spring of 1990 (Sándor 2002, 83–84).[31] *Táncház* had opened up a space of association and popular practices seen as outside the realm of the Communist state that provided for a kind of political cultivation that manifested in this protest. In terms of culture talk, or cultural fundamentalism, however, the Transylvanian protests of June 1988 offer a lens into how national impulses in *táncház* linked with the political sphere and articulated with global discourses on cultural rights as human rights. As a moment of danger, the 1988 protests revealed a framework of sense and shaped it as Hungary, along with other socialist countries forged its path of "transition."

REGIME CHANGE AND THE NATION

The "end of socialism" in Hungary came through what Hungarians refer to as the "regime change" (*rendszerváltás*), a process that János Kis (1995) argues was neither reform nor revolution, as it interrupted the continuity of legitimacy but did not affect the continuity of legality. While parliament passed laws necessary for free elections to take place, it did so within a vacuum of legitimacy. The terms of the elections were the results of bargains between parliament (or the party apparatus controlling it) and various opposition parties differentially influential with the party and virtually unknown to the general populace.

The nature of the transition was also greatly determined by the "liberal approach toward party membership" during the late socialist period, which had allowed experts without Communist Party membership to hold prominent positions in management (Szelényi, Szelényi, and Kovach 1995). By the early 1980s, this new technocracy, led by managers of large enterprises, had successfully placed the idea of property reform on the party agenda, leading to a renegotiation of property rights (703). By 1989, the new technocracy was able to "complete the transformation of property relations," from which many members benefited personally (703–4). While elites did have staying power across the change of regimes, especially in the economic sphere, the circulation of elites was most notable in the political sphere, where, in the first years of transition, legitimacy was based in part on anticommunist credentials, or "moral capital" (Verdery 1996, 104; Szelényi, Szelényi, and Kovach 1995, 705).

In the literary sphere, the *népi-urbánus* opposition is said to have reemerged with new vigor in this period. In 1987, György Spiró, a prominent literary figure (of Jewish heritage), published a poem entitled "The Deep Hungarians Are Coming" in the journal *Mozgó Világ* (World in motion) (Brody 1995, 3).[32] In it, he warns of a return of "deep Hungarian" violent desires and shames others for remaining quiet, asserting that it is not only "trash" who "know Hungarian" (4). In 1990, Sándor Csoóri, famous for his critiques of Communist injustices against the rural population and who, as a human rights advocate for minorities, had been considered sympathetic to Jews (and Roma), declared in the MDF's biweekly *Hitel* (Trust— the party's biweekly) that the "possibility of spiritual and intellectual link between Jews and Hungarians" had ended at the time of the 1919 Hungarian Soviet Republic (10).

Reflecting the circulation of elites in the political sphere, the center right, or "national populist" Hungarian Democratic Forum (MDF) had won the first parliamentary elections, in 1990, on an explicitly *Hungarian* platform.[33] Setting a famous precedent, the first prime minister of the postsocialist era, József Antall, included the five million ethnic Hungarians in neighboring countries along with the 10 million Hungarian citizens in his sphere of responsibility, stating, "I am in spirit the Prime Minister of 15 million Hungarians" (Fox 2003, 455). Csoóri and another "neopopulist" writer, István Csurka, had been founding members of MDF, and it was in *Hitel* that Csoóri made these statements, asserting that contemporary Hungary is faced with a "reverse assimilationist trend" in whose aid the Jewry employs "a more powerful weapon than it has ever possessed" in the form of the parliamentary system (Shafir 2001).[34] Not only did he connect Jews with liberalism, but he also subtly connected liberalism with communism. Both the phrase "deep Hungarian" and the idea of reverse assimilation echo the influential *népi* writer Lászlo Németh's language in the interwar period.

In 1993, MDF expelled its far-right faction, Csurka and Csoóri among them, compelling Csurka and his supporters to found the Hungarian Life and Justice Party (MIÉP).[35] That same year Csoóri would state, "The ghost of an irresponsible and exhausted liberalism roams the world instead of the ghost of the former communism" (Brody 1995, 11). This, along with other accusations made by rightist MDF members, such as that Hungarian-born philanthropist (of Jewish heritage) George Soros was helping communist cosmopolitans turn over power to cosmopolitan dissidents (Shafir 2001), refueled what appears as a self-evident *népi-urbánus* divide.[36] It also added credence to the ethnonationalist elements of the stolen regime change discourse (discussed later) that asserts that there was in fact no change

Fig. 6.3 Viktor Orbán speaks at the burial of Imre Nagy and other "martyrs of 1956," June 16, 1989. Photo by Piroska Nagy.

of regime and that former Communists still control political life. In 1998, MIÉP won fourteen seats in parliament. While MIÉP did not become part of the ruling coalition (Fidesz, FKGP, and MDF), the claim that the party attained influence on media supervisory boards far greater than its proportion in Parliament (BBC News Online 2000) was widespread.[37]

The rhetoric of the nation would continue to be central to parties on the right, including the leading government party from 1998 to 2002 (and later, from 2010 to 2014, 2014 to 2018, and since 2018 as I write in 2020) the Hungarian Civic Union (Fidesz, originally the Young Democrats). Fidesz came to power by tapping into public support of MIÉP and the Independent Smallholders Party (FKGP), and nationalist appeals have been an important strategy for this party ever since.[38] As far back as 1989, a young Viktor Orbán had been one of the featured speakers at Imre Nagy's public burial, attended by hundreds of thousands, which came on the heels of informal protest events celebrating Imre Nagy and the other "martyrs" (*New York Times* 1988c, A6). While Fidesz did not fully adopt MIÉP's overtly antisemitic language, its representatives avoided its outright denunciation and continued to emphasize the nation and Hungarianness, to which MIÉP's more explicit language was supplementary.

A good proportion of the richest individuals in Hungary at this time had managed to achieve such status through administrative closeness to the privatization process, enacting "political capitalism" and "financial clientelism," facilitated through social networks (King 2001). But many people were feeling the negative effects of the transition with unemployment a growing problem, for example, due to the dismantling of state socialist enterprises. Although legitimacy accrued to those who could claim to have been oppositional under the socialist regime, revamped socialist parties were enjoying electoral success across the formerly socialist region by 1995 (Creed 1995).

The charge of un-Hungarian would be employed against the Hungarian Socialist Party (MSZP), which had led the government from 1994 to 1998 (and would be reelected in 2002 and 2006), and its coalition partner, the Alliance of Free Democrats (SZDSZ), commonly referred to as "the liberals." With ethnonational connotations, this charge extends beyond the bounds of the nation-state and casts its shadow within. Combined with the accusation that socialists and liberals are not really (read ethnically) Hungarian, this rhetoric seems to say that it is because of this that they can ignore ethnic brethren over the borders.

A Moment of Danger: Political Polarization and "the Stolen Regime Change"

By the time of my 2004/2005 fieldwork, a division was apparent among Hungarians between nominally "left" and "right" factions.[39] Many people traced this polarization to the campaign period before the 2002 elections, when Fidesz lost its incumbency to the socialist-liberal (MSZP-SZDSZ) coalition. When I encountered the stolen regime change rhetoric for the first time in a speech given by István Csurka at a MIÉP rally in Budapest in 2004, I was struck by the way in which its logic structured the polarization.[40] The phrase *stolen regime change* highlighted the fact that members of the Communist elite continued to hold power in the postsocialist period of so-called democracy through participation in privatization schemes and closed-door agreements.[41] I use it here to describe a cluster of elements that recur in reference to the reproduction of state socialist–era elites combined with the failure of democracy that appeared self-evident to many Hungarians, *táncház*-goers included. While stolen regime change language entered the everyday consciousness of Hungarians through its use by figures in MIÉP, whose version employs an anticosmopolitan rhetoric conflating Jews, liberals, communists, and socialists and the globalization of capital, its elements appeared to have diffused beyond MIÉP circles.[42]

I frequently encountered this cluster in conversation at *tánchaz* events, even though I did not encounter people I knew from *tánchaz* at MIÉP rallies.

While SZDSZ, the liberals, a party of intellectuals referred to frequently by MIÉP members and *tánchaz*-goers alike as a "Jewish party," never achieved a parliamentary majority, it entered coalition with the socialists (MSZP) each time it was in majority and held power in Budapest (and some other cities) until the mid-2000s. Having defined itself in opposition to the Communists in the late 1980s, SZDSZ lost much of its support upon coalition with MSZP in 1994. Csurka, openly antisemitic and irredentist, insisted that "the liberals" were "running the country" on the basis of their disproportionate influence on the media and government policy (BBC News Online 2000).[43]

Insisting that secret pacts have been made between political and economic elites, the language of the stolen regime change points to corruption.[44] But beyond that, it speaks to worries Hungarians had about the "success," or legitimacy, of the regime change. The redistribution of wealth shown in the privatization process and the rise of the costs of health care, housing, and education challenged values taken for granted during the state socialist period and did not align with hopes of what this transition would bring.[45] Fidesz managed to capitalize on these quite legitimate concerns to thicken oppositions in the campaign period to which my interlocutors traced the polarization. The party's loss of the incumbency in the 2002 elections was followed by street protests asserting election fraud (based on alleged socialist control of important institutions, including the media) and demanding a recount. *Népi* architect Imre Makovecz was a visible spokesman for this movement, and folk singer Márta Sebestyén (the Muzsikás ensemble's singer for many years) performed at demonstrations in front of the parliament.[46]

The appearance of this polarizing rift can be seen as a moment of danger. It was reflected both within *tánchaz* and in perceptions of *tánchaz* by outsiders, and it was being actively produced. According to many I spoke with, around that election year and as the Hungarian public was becoming polarized, hostility toward Jews and liberals was voiced openly among *tánchaz* participants, and a number of "liberal" *tánchaz*-goers stopped attending.[47] One individual, who had begun participating in *tánchaz* along with other underground events in the 1980s as a youth, and had returned to Hungary after living in Belgium, put it this way:

> It was exactly 2000 when I returned home. It was when the elections were, and there was critical misery. I discovered after ten years of living far away that these things do not work as they did back when I left this place. There was

Socialist State Formation 201

a really strong division between the people that the media had instigated, I imagine very masterfully, for its political gain. And the people were two types, right or left, or *népiesek* or *urbánusok*, or socialists or MIÉP followers.... It was a strange situation.... For example, I was called a stinky Communist by my own family—I who lived for ten years in Belgium, in a big monarchy. But whatever, the lack of consciousness of the people was used in such depth by the media, and they put little labels on everything, every activity, any way of being. For example, *népies* things, folk music, folk dance, became appropriated. The Right made this culture, tradition, and the rest its own property, and it stuck in there its own ideology. But in return, a little brainwashing happened in the minds of the people, and those people who had been disposed to a kind of openness closed themselves up in their so-called proper way and politically false existence. And it was difficult for me to accept that people had become totally intolerant toward other cultures, other ways of being, conceptions ... the whole thing was a bit foreign from me. I went to *táncház* a few times, but I constantly saw that they *politizál* really explicitly. It's possible that this was just because of the elections, but it was really rough and negative. Irredentist words were flying, and after that, I didn't go any more.

The words of another *táncház*-goer who began participating in the 1970s (and is of Jewish heritage) points to the process contributing to the rift:[48]

After 1990 anything else is open for the people. Before that, *táncház* was a very good situation for meeting and for speaking, for thinking together.... After 1990, it changed and . . . friends/brothers started a different way of life because, those [were the ones] who were thinking together. After 1990, their thinking separated.... It los[t] its magic because before 1990, that was the only place where similar thinking could be. Now they can go here or there.... The thinking—we were, before that, liberal—thought, went in different directions. We didn't know [about] it then, and afterwards, we faced it, and the way of friends separated. This is why you can say that *táncház* has a kind of right-leaning character. Now, of course, but before also. But it was stronger because it was in opposition to force, now it is pinned to the right side of the flag, part of the national right. It is the right side [for] who[m] folk traditions are important.[49]

In 2004 and 2005, all *táncház*-goers that I asked told me that they believed that the majority of participants were Fidesz voters, with MIÉP voters comprising a loud minority. The opinions of outsiders were also telling.[50] When many of the latter learned that I was studying *táncház*, they asked why in the world I would want to study "those people." A student at the Central European University told me that *táncház*-goers were "mostly rural immigrants from neighboring countries."[51] She insisted that people who go to *táncház* have "no" or "different" social skills, that they "go there because they have nowhere else to go," and that "women there are passive and quiet and do not argue." She and her two friends agreed that *táncház*-goers were conservative and nationalist. Another student told me "they are probably not intellectuals."[52] A British ethnic Hungarian who attends *táncház* reported similar perceptions among nonparticipants. She described her experience at a "well-heeled and elegant expat event," where outsiders were quick to assume that *táncház*-goers were nationalists and vote for Fidesz.[53]

It is perhaps not surprising that among the hundreds of *táncház* participants I spoke with in 2004–5, only two openly volunteered to me that they would vote for MSZP or SZDSZ, while disparaging comments about liberals and Jews were commonplace. *Táncház*-goers often suggested that the liberals sought to suppress national expression, that they mismanaged the city of Budapest, and that Jews were in control of the economy. The liberals had shown their true colors, some said, simply by entering into alliance with the socialists in the first place. A frequent point was that the socialist-liberal (MSZP-SZDSZ) coalition had encouraged the public to vote no in the 2004 referendum question addressing dual citizenship (discussed in chapter 7).

Anthropologist Gergő Pulay accounted his own experience of this polarization to me with two stories. In one, he described joining former schoolmates from his conservative Calvinist (Református) high school just after having attended an event held by the liberal magazine *Magyar Narancs* (The Hungarian orange) on the evening before the last major preelection Fidesz rally, at Kossuth square, in 2002.[54] When they saw the copy of the *Magyar Narancs* in his pocket, they began to throw insults at liberals.[55] While they knew that Pulay had relationships with liberals, he had never experienced anything like this with these old friends, who had recently become involved with Fidesz's youth association and had been attending leadership trainings. Another day, at a weekly *táncház* that he had been regularly frequenting in this same period, he witnessed participants singing old folk songs fitted with new words praising Orbán. This event contributed to his decision not to attend anymore, and he subsequently became involved in the more inclusive Roma *táncház* scene.[56]

This kind of talk emerged against the backdrop of a "Jewish renaissance" in Budapest, part of the broader phenomenon of ethnic revival in Eastern Europe after 1989 (Gitelman 1999; E. Kovács and Vajda 1996; Mars 1999; Vincze 2011). Jewish organizations, national and international, supported outreach activities in Budapest to "revive Jewish communal life" and "reinvigorate and reconstruct Jewish identity" in the face of assimilation and the legacy of the Holocaust (Vincze 2011). Synagogues; Jewish schools; museums; magazines; research groups; theaters; cultural centers; Zionist organizations; Hasidic, Orthodox, conservative, reform, and secular study groups; and the Rabbinical college (upgraded to a university in 1990) were all involved in these efforts at "fostering an ethnic revival" (Vincze 2011). A 1999 survey showed that slightly upward of 20 percent of Hungarian Jews between eighteen and thirty-five had more interest in Jewish culture, history, and tradition; were more observant; and had closer ties to Israel than their parents (ibid.).

This post-1989 flurry had been followed by a second wave after 2000, focused on "coming out of the closet" and "facing the past" through reconstructing history, family stories, and Holocaust memories; discovering and learning religious traditions; and "decoding existing anti-Semitism" (Vincze 2011). This second wave "based on a new trend of expressive ethnicity and the cult of being different," was characterized by the emergence of secular cultural institutions and outreach centers offering a "variety of opportunities for experiencing and expressing a non-religious 'cool' Jewish identity" (Vincze 2011).

Kata Zsófia Vincze (2011) notes that as ethnic diversity has enjoyed increasing popularity, and Jewish revival (as well as of other ethnicities, such as the Roma) has had increasing visibility, the "anti-Semitic response," has been equally loud, with the "politically incorrect" language accepted by some young people paralleling the multicultural openness of others (see also Kürti 2011; Tötösy de Zepetnek 2011). This tension has played out in public space. Some *tánchaz*-goers mentioned to me their dismay at the appearance of a large menorah on a public square in Budapest during the winter holiday season. Seeing it as an unwarranted affront, they found it quite appropriate that a large cross be placed next to it (they did not mention and I do not know if they knew that the Jobbik Party had done this). As Vincze (2011) notes: "Putting a huge wooden crucifix next to the Hanukkiot is a response to the symbolic takeover of the public space."[57]

By the time of my fieldwork, there was a very active Roma dancehouse scene in Budapest in which many people who, like Pulay, love folk music and dance but could not abide the politics coming to be expressed openly in *tánchaz* circles were taking part, along with others who had never taken interest in *tánchaz* more generally.[58] Pulay (2014, 21) writes about the encounters in Roma *tánchaz* settings as a kind of experiment in social integration in its "lived and cultural context."

The political polarization, and the cultural polarization with which it interweaves, reflected also in a kind of "cleansing" of *tánchaz* in which those who felt uncomfortable with these politics stopped frequenting it, has important implications for the ways in which people perceive politics in terms of *nép, nemzet,* and Hungarianness and how feelings such as empathy or sympathy are being constructed along ethnonational lines. What work is done by *táncház,* and how, in this context?

CONCLUSION: CITIZENSHIP AND THE CULTURAL TURN

Shifts in the foci of *népi* movements relate directly to the questions of citizenship and state formation, as they are shaped by and shape the role of the cultural sphere and the ethnicization of culture. The *urbánus-népi* opposition arose when both groups placed themselves in opposition to the Christian National government. In contrast to the internationalist, urban, bourgeois approaches of urbanists (against the historical backdrop of 1919), *népi* activists focused on people's national cultivation. They embarked on projects encouraging the use of agrarian cultural practices as the basis of a uniquely Hungarian cultivation; championing the agrarian *Volk* as the source of Hungarianness. These efforts were pursued alongside those aiming at land reform and a broadening of the franchise meant to benefit the agrarian majority: the people, in a classed but also an ethnic sense. During socialism, there was a brief revival of *népi* politics around the revolution of 1956, during which attempts were made to carve out a legitimate oppositional group from the "collaborators." In the late socialist period, when social citizenship was guaranteed (albeit differentially), the popular associative form *táncház* arose from the hearth of the civic cultivation apparatus. But this organizational descendant of earlier populist efforts, ended up focusing on the plight of Hungarians in Transylvania who faced discrimination by the Romanian state both as peasants and as ethnic Hungarians (Kligman 1988). The legacies of populist practices and Christian National irredentism had combined to make Transylvania the hotbed of authenticity, while advocacy for Hungarians in Romania, as opposed to a number of issues in Hungary itself, was tolerated by the Hungarian state by the late 1980s. Indeed, "Hungarians acknowledged pointedly that some similar demands were appropriate in their own country, but could not be so publicly expressed" (*New York Times* 1988b).

Exercising civil citizenship, interwar populists as well as late socialist *táncház*-goers pressured what they conceived as an un-Hungarian government to act more Hungarian. In the earlier period they did so to advocate cultural, social, and political citizenship for the peasantry (implicitly Hungarian). In the later period, they did so to pursue the practice of living folk culture, enacting the *népi-nemzeti művelődés,* or folk cultivation, sought by the earlier generation. In efforts to preserve this living folk culture, it was seen as explicitly agrarian, and in efforts to curb Romanian discrimination toward ethnic Hungarians, it was often implicitly agrarian. In both cases, they pressured the government of Hungary to be more Hungarian. In both cases these *népi* movements occupied a space of "opposition" from which they championed the *nép*. They employed a folk critique, whose content changed across their shifting contexts.

Because *táncház* practices are oriented toward the cultural practices of Hungarianness, culture talk may be particularly salient and meaningful to its public of participants, while *táncház* may also contribute to the salience of culture talk. In *táncház*, as in earlier *népi* movements, culture (the inner spiritual sphere) is emphasized as the primary domain of action, in contrast to the political and material spheres. Yet *táncház* still appears to differ from the interwar *népi* movement in its disengagement from issues of class-oriented social justice or redistribution as related to peasants and agricultural workers. This may be partly attributed to late socialist-era state formation that allowed for an entrepreneurial peasant bourgeoisie to arise (I. Szelényi 1988) and allowed for openings for particular kinds of civic association and expression while the political remained highly circumscribed. It might also be related to the "place of recognition" provided by human rights language, articulated in the international sphere as cultural rights, at a conjuncture when the property regime was in flux and the language of social rights under threat.[59]

Theorists of the cultural turn point to the rollback of the welfare state and a concomitant recourse to culture to solve problems traditionally considered the responsibility of the state. They reveal a "'postsocialist' condition" associated with neoliberalism, in which the rollback of the social state has been naturalized as the answer to the economic problems and a simultaneous emphasis on *culture* as a solution. The situation of formerly state socialist countries of East Central Europe following the demise of state socialism fits into this condition, but its transformation since 1989, even if we take the late socialist reforms into account, has been deeper and more rapid. This is an important key for understanding the rise of ethnonationalism here.

The origins of the *táncház* can be found in part in the liberalization of the economy in the late socialist period. This was liberalizing Hungary, or a (neo)liberalizing Hungarian socialism (Taylor and Kalocsai 2011; Dale and Fábry 2018), and the related acceleration of tourism and professionalization of folk artists. Further, the circumscription of political expression and the "thaw" in cultural expression encouraged protest to take the form of cultural arguments like those articulated around the plight of ethnic minorities in Transylvania. Just as something called "national folk dance" had fit into an internationalist place of recognition, so arguments formulated in the language of human rights fit into a place of recognition encouraged by supranational NGOs.[60] While in the liberal cosmopolitan viewpoint of such organizations, human rights protect basic freedoms including those of cultural expression (conceived as recognition of cultural diversity), the application of the human rights argument also had the potential to combine with the construction of *Gemeinschaft*—the ethnonation—in opposition to socialism, or, as we will see, any cosmopolitanism. Each of these processes can be seen as a reflection of the increased importance of "culture talk" and "cultural fundamentalism."

As global citizenship, measured by numbers and types of NGOs and the spread of cosmopolitan values worldwide (Kaldor, Anheier and Glasius 2003; Ivancheva 2011; Mikuš 2018) is touted as the answer to problems of all kinds, we need to understand better how it may also nurture cultural fundamentalism or an "archipelago approach to cultures" (Hylland-Eriksen 2001). As a moment of danger, the Transylvania protests packaged *népi* politics as being about ethnic brethren threatened by the other, rather than about Hungarians oppressed by other Hungarians. The second moment of danger, a political polarization, also took the shape of a cultural/ethnicized polarization that was (re)produced in *táncház* and effected its membership in 2004–5.

Notes

1. He continues: "the same threat hangs over both: that of becoming a tool of the ruling classes. In every era the attempt must be made anew to wrest tradition away from a conformism that is about to overpower it" (1969, 255).

2. See Ishchenko (2104) for alternative views to mainstream ethnonational interpretations of the war in Ukraine.

3. The best-seller *Balkan Ghosts* is an example of this.

4. One *táncház*-goer told me that the liberals had fought against having the national symbol on identification cards and that under the MDF tenure, SZDSZ had opposed the version of the Hungarian coat of arms with St. Steven's crown, favoring the "republican version" adopted during the 1848 revolution that features a laurel wreath in its place. It should be noted that in the same period, a wordplay became popular on the right in which ZSDSZ, which sounds like the word for Jew (zsídó), was substituted for SZDSZ.

5. Renwick (2006) points out that one feature of the "ethical civil society" characterizing late socialism was its relationship to consensus. "It viewed 'internal differences' pejoratively" and sought to suppress them, "whereas political society sees them as normal" (303). Staniszkis 1984; Cohen, and Arato (1994, 59, 66) also recognize this tendency, which they see as the result of the polarization of state and society in these systems and as having a continued effect (in populism, for example). Some *táncház*-goers expressed judgment of Jews for wanting to be different rather than "being Hungarian." See András Kovács (1994) on Jewish revival.

6. Local scholars often used terms such as *national populist* (Kis 1995) or *nationalist populist* (Žižek 1993) to describe what popular Western journalists tended at the time to refer to as "the Right." As we have already seen, the plural meanings of words such as *nép* and its Slavic equivalent *narod*, referring to people or *Volk*, elude English speakers, as do regional histories of agrarian populism, often collapsed into a narrative emphasizing the recent socialist past or conflated with fascism. In this book, I employ the terms *right* and *left* as they have been used conventionally in Europe. I have argued elsewhere (Taylor 2006), there is good reason to interrogate such usages. See, for example, the literature discussing integralism, such as Holmes (2000), Murer (2005), Gingrich (2006), and more recently Mahmud (2020). Further, some Hungarian intellectuals pointed out to me that they preferred the term *conservative* for those parties on the right, pointing out that these parties emphasize conservation of the social state.

7. Prevailing definitions of *populism* define it as logic or style that does the same, more or less relying on LaClau (2005). Current uses of the term point to politicians who discursively construct a contrast between a virtuous people and a corrupt elite and most often associate this with ethnonationalist framing. On my positions on this debate, see Taylor (2018; 2018b) and Creed and Taylor (2020).

8. In Hungarian the Latin-derived term *populizmus* is used to refer to Orbán's politics, whereas *népi* is more likely to be used to refer to *táncház*. Both, however, are likely to be seen on the *nép* side of the *népi-urbánus* binary. Most authors, when referring to neopopulism in Hungary in English have not explicitly referred to *táncház*. László Kürti (2001) does refer to *táncház* specifically as neopopulist and populist. Since the time when I conducted my research, the term *populism* has come much more into vogue to refer to a whole array of political parties and approaches, most of which would not translate back to *népi* as *táncház* or as *népi* writers would. Bozoki (2012) draws an explicit throughline across time in his discussion of populism in Hungary.

9. This claim about an urbanist position can sometimes simply mean Jewish. It can also refer to the policies of the 1919 Soviet- and the USSR-influenced policies after World War II that imposed collectivization on the agrarian classes, an ostensibly urbanist position. Using them interchangeably, of course, reinforces their equivalence.

10. NÉKOSZ collegers were well represented on the board of the Petőfi Circle, the debate club of the Association of Democratic Youths (DISZ), authorized in 1956. Supported by the Writers Union, whose president was *népi* writer and former Peasant Party politician Péter Veres, the circle became increasingly open in its criticism of the regime after Nagy was dismissed. When students from the Technical University read aloud their demands, representatives of the Writers Union added their own, demanding that NÉKOSZ be reestablished and that democratic practices be restored (Ötvös 1989, 71).

11. While Ferenc Erdei put out the call to reestablish the Peasant Party and played a role in the administration of Nagy's council of ministers (Borbándi 1989, 467), many in *népi* circles also accused him (minister of agriculture during the coalition), József Darvas (minister of public works during the coalition), and Péter Veres, (minister of public works and of defense during the coalition), of "selling out the party and the *népi* idea and joining the Communists" (ibid., 468). Yet Borbándi points out that "the only *népi* writer that we find" among the chief players when the actions broke out on October 23 was Veres (465).

12. Deák (1999, 56) points out that in recognition of *népi* support of communism, János Kádár's postrevoutionary regime "hastened to honor László Németh" with the prestigious Kossuth award despite the fact that "before 1945, Németh was a militant anti-Bolshevik and, in his own peculiar way, a strong anti-Semite."

13. Romania supported Soviet military intervention to quell the revolution in Hungary (Chen 2003).

14. While this showed "a certain amount of tolerance" for the needs and wishes of ethnic minorities, it did not represent a consistent commitment to the regional autonomy of minority

ethnic groups, for other "concentrations of minorities were not given administrative autonomy" (Chen 2003, 183). Bottoni (2003) has argued that Gheorghiu-Dej had no such intentions and that the plan for the autonomous region was authored in the USSR, under Stalin's direct supervision.

15. Sizeable minorities included ethnic Germans, Roma, and Hungarians.

16. See Verdery (1995) for a discussion of Romanian intellectual battle over Romanian ethnicity and territoriality.

17. The three Ts: *tíltott, tűrt, támogatott.*

18. See also Kürti (2001, 154) on the increasing proportion of intellectuals of peasant origin in this period.

19. Maácz writes (1980, 87): "'National consciousness' and 'internationalism' are paired in *tánchaz*es, where the dances of the neighboring peoples are integrated into the repertoire."

20. August 20 is St. Stephen's day, mentioned in chapter 2 as the newly minted holiday on which Bouquet of Pearls groups performed in Budapest.

21. During my fieldwork, the Budapest Spring Festival, and the Dancehouse Meeting within it, was sponsored both by the Ministries of Education and Culture and Local and Regional Development.

22. While the law at the time of my research required the local council to provide a determined sum to the houses of culture, they would be unable to function without proceeds from entrepreneurial activities. Older *tánchaz*-goers complained about the expense of the entrance fees and cost of refreshments, but in comparison to those of private venues, they are low. Younger people tended to complain about the aesthetic (or lack thereof) of the houses of culture, preferring private venues. As one *tánchaz*-goer observed about his experience in 2006: "the Aranytíz *tánchaz* was expensive and empty while the one at Almássy tér (featuring mostly Moldvai dances) was free with expensive refreshments and totally packed." The fact that Moldvai dances are easier to pick up probably helped pack this space as well. I was also told that the bartenders were behind the organization of the Almássy tér one, the implication being that that was how they ensured their income."

23. In recent years, opportunities have arisen for positions of management for the revival, at Heritage House, as well as points of liaison with the NGO networks clustered around heritage, for example, CIOFF, the International Council of Organizations for Folklore Festivals and Folk Art.

24. In later years, it has been institutionalized in UNESCO requirements for the safeguarding of (intangible) cultural heritage: "Proposed cultural expressions and spaces should be a living cultural tradition, demonstrate human creative genius, be a means of affirming the cultural identity of the communities concerned or be at risk of destruction or of disappearing. The candidature files must also include a sound action plan for revitalisation, safeguarding and promotion as awarding recognition of cultural spaces and expressions as Masterpieces does not constitute protection as such" (UNESCO 2006a).

25. International social scientific interest in tourism was also increasing, marked by the publication of the first journal devoted to studying tourism, Annals of Tourism Research, in 1973 (Bendix 1989, 144).

26. Hungary ratified the convention in 1987 and put two sites on the list in 1987.

27. A three-volume history of Hungary (Erdély Története) was published by Akadémiai Kiadó in 1986. Kürti (2001, 40–44) accounts the politics and intellectual debates in which the book can be placed related to heightened awareness about Transylvania and the conflict over how "Hungarian" or "Romanian" it was at that time.

28. June 28, 1988. Kürti (2001) notes that there were protests that day in "major European cities and in Washington, DC, as well. He also writes of a "successful demonstration" at the Romanian consulates in Budapest, Prague, and "a few Western capitals" in February 1988 (129). Others became involved in bringing supplies to ethnic Hungarians in Romania, organized by churches, and in publicizing the attack on minister László Tőkés. This period was marked by

other protests, including a large protest organized around environmental concerns in September 1988 (Harper 2005, 223), and a manifestation on November 15 with a crowd of three hundred supporting the workers' uprising in Brasov, Romania. See Nagy (2011) for a photo-documentary account of the many manifestations of this period.

29. Most specifically, the forword to a 1983 book (*Kutyaszorító*) by (Czecho) Slovakian ethnic Hungarian (later to be politician) Miklós Duray about the fate of ethnic Hungarians in Slovakia.

30. Here I use Ervin Brody's (1995) convention to speak of a generation of younger writers who some have called *népi* as "neopopulist" to distinguish them from interwar *népi* writers and activists. Some of these writers have linked themselves with the earlier generation of populist writers and have occasionally received their mentorship (6). Using Brody's term allows me to refer to this group without determining who belongs to it and to preserve the term *népi* to refer to *táncház* in the postsocialist period. The term *populist* has come to be used in such a different way at this point in history that I prefer not to use it as a descriptor for *táncház* and its participants.

31. The annual "Csángó ball" began in 1997, "to call the attention of the general public to the traditional culture and life of this ethnic minority in Moldavia" (Sándor 2002, 84). Sándor claims that it has resulted in more attention being afforded to the issue in the media, a government office dealing with the Csángó being established, and the Council of Europe adopting a recommendation on language rights for Csángó in Romania (84; see also Council of Europe 2002 [2001]).

32. Spiró has made a point that he is Hungarian, not an assimilated Jew (Spiró (2016). He has no connection to Judaism, even if Hitler's racial laws would make him the latter. I mention his family's heritage only to illustrate the dynamics at work.

33. Antall was the son of a deputy minister of the interior during the Horthy regime, and his economic advisor was the nephew of Count István Bethlen, a prime minister during the Horthy era (Szelényi, Szelényi, and Kovach 1995). Kis (1995, 411) notes that the party attempted to negotiate with MDF at the expense of Fidesz and SZDSZ. This may have to do with the legitimacy the MDF had built up even before it became a political party, especially around the rights and conditions of ethnic Hungarians in Translyvania and ethnic Hungarian refugees in Hungary (Kürti 2001).

34. Both Csoóri and Csurka faced sanctions by the socialist state for their activism.

35. Csoóri became disenchanted with the political sphere, subsequently serving as president of the Federation of World Hungarians (MVSZ), an international NGO dedicated to perpetuating Hungarian identity in the Hungarian diaspora. Interestingly, it was after Csoóri was replaced by Miklós Patrubány as president of the MVSZ that it is said to have veered to the right (M. Kovács 2005; see also Kürti 2001).

36. See Nagengast (1991, 23–29) for a similar set of oppositions that developed in the early days of Polish electoral politics. Regarding Soros, it is important to note that some *táncház* activities received Soros funding, a camp I attended among them.

37. An Antidefamation League (1999) report states: "in exchange for MIÉP's obstructing the nomination process, some extreme-right journalists [have] obtained key positions in Hungarian Television." It is only fair to note that there are allegations from the right that socialists and especially liberals control the media and, therefore, that such influence was designed to counteract this. Csurka himself often claimed that Jews were disproportionally represented in the media.

38. By which time a 5 percent rule had been established that made it impossible for either MIÉP or the Smallholders to create factions in parliament.

39. See Rácz (2003, 750 754), Kósa (2007), and Dale and Fabry (2018) on this rift and the reinforcement of separate publics.

40. It is the title of a 2002 book (*Az Ellópott Rendszerváltozás*) by (radical right) journalist Pál Lakatos. The term for regime change employed here is *rendszerváltozás*, whereas Kis and most others use *rendszerváltás*. The first employs a continuous form of the verb, making it in the act of changing, while the second implies a one-time change, a finished deed.

41. Lakatos argues (in his 2003 work) that the leading elite and bureaucracy of the Communist Party brought about the regime change to its own advantage and that of approximately 2 million bureaucrats, the upper strata remained in leading positions. See Csurka (2002), for his account of the so-called Roszadomb Pact, resulting from a supposed meeting of the leading opposition figures with representatives of the CIA, MOSSAD, and KGB to manufacture the regime change and divvy up the goods. Lakatos does not spare Csurka or MIÉP in his criticisms. Nevertheless, their critiques overlap to the point that they are often indistinguishable.

42. The phrase "unfinished regime change" has been used more recently by Fidesz/Orbán and by Jobbik, whose website states: "The end of the regime change will come when the country truly becomes an independent state." It goes on to say that political power is still in the hands of those who controlled it before 1990 (Jobbik Party n.d.).

43. The fight over control of the media was so intense as to be commonly referred to as the "media wars." See Hankiss (1995) for one account. Csurka was a savvy user of coded language, sometimes using *Jew* and sometimes using *liberal* or *cosmopolitan* to make them interchangeable in meaning. The nearly ninety articles "dealing with Jewish topics" published in MIÉP's Magyar Fórum paralleled the antisemitic line of its editor, Csurka, in 2001 (Gerő, Vargas, and Vincze 2002).

44. Despite his persistent reelection, I often heard complaints among *táncház*-goers about Budapest mayor Gábor Demszky's "mismanagement" of the funds for the repair of roads, his plans for the privatization of city services, and his supposedly shady real estate deals.

45. Many, not only revivalists, articulated growing differentiation not as a function of the political economic system but as the result of a stolen regime change.

These two lenses need not be not mutually exclusive, for the "main substantive achievement of neoliberalism" as a class project "has been to redistribute, rather than generate wealth and income" (Harvey 2005, 159). At the same time that postsocialist states saw their positions in the world system slide into peripherality, the transition provided the conditions for an unprecedented influx of foreign ownership and investment that would distribute the wealth produced by society in new ways (Böröcz 2016).

Yet with class-oriented analysis and critique of capitalism discredited, the stolen regime change rhetoric, laden with antisemitic references with historically familiar tones, appeared to be a widely salient critique of this class project. Coming from the right, stolen regime change rhetoric critiques liberals, communists, and socialists by mobilizing an opposition between Hungarian and foreigner and assigns legitimacy to those who appear to speak on behalf of the *nép* and *nemzet*. While the class connotations of *nép* are nearly silenced by the ethnonational meaning of *nemzet*, this rhetoric nevertheless resonates with very real experiences of dispossession as citizenship was transformed.

46. In the protests against the government coalition (MSZP and SZDSZ) in the fall of 2006, supported openly by Fidesz, antisemitic symbols associated with Hungarian fascism (for example, the so-called flag of Árpád [the tribal leader who conquered the Carpathian basin] used by the World War II–era Arrow Cross) were abundant. Some have accused Fidesz of mobilizing these far-right elements, while others claimed far-right protesters hijacked Fidesz protests.

47. Conversations with self-ascribed "liberal" Hungarians at that time revealed that they saw themselves in opposition to the right in terms of attitudes toward minorities and homosexuality, nontraditional cultural activities, and progressive forms of culture. Generally, they used the term to address cultural issues, not economic policies.

48. While people pointed to the election period, elements contributing to the rift, as I have shown, were present already with the return of the *népi-urbánus* debate and with the rise of party politics. In fact, the addition of MPP to the end of Fidesz's title in 1995, making it Fidesz: The Hungarian Citizens' Party, might be seen (as one Hungarian academic suggested to me) as an attempt to overcome the *népi-urbánus* divide. Rather than *middle class*, they used the term

bourgeois (*polgár*) that had been associated with Jews before the war. Fidesz, whose leaders claim that they were too young to have been implicated as Communists, campaigned as a party of the middle class, *kispolgár* (petite bourgeoisie) attempting a "grassroots politics" involving the spread of "civic circles" after losing 2002 elections (see Halmai 2011). Indeed, without defining the citizen substantively, Fidesz mobilized the language of the citizen "as an integrating stimulus among heterogeneous views" (Rácz 2003, 750). In this way, *citizen* functioned much like the term *nép* has in the past while also overlapping with its connotation in the present, contributing to a set of interweaving oppositions. Fidesz's behavior in office has been, nevertheless, as clientelistic as that of the socialists, if not better organized, targeting a different group. Ultimately, it seems, Fidesz contributed to the possibility of equating the middle class with the *nép*, and this was not the first time this happened (see Frigyesi 1994). Orbán also used the term *az ember* (a person) to speak of "regular people."

49. This person chose to conduct the interview in English. I have made minor changes to aid meaning, but any awkwardness that remains is due to my respect for their manner of expression.

50. Jobbik was virtually unheard of then, and no one mentioned it to me.

51. The CEU is a private university founded by George Soros in 1991 (with origins as a business school founded in the late 1980s). The faculty employs a good number of foreigners and attracts many foreign students. As far back as 2000, I have heard Hungarians, not only *táncház*-goers, comment that one cannot get into the CEU unless he or she has Jewish connections. Since gaining control of the government in 2010, Fidesz has used Soros as a scapegoat, accusing him of being the architect of what has been called the "migrant crisis" that peaked in 2015. The government's attack on the CEU forced the CEU to move its campuses to Vienna in 2019. On the bigger picture of global political advertising in which Jewish consultants have plaid a key role in the anti-Soros campaign, see Grasseger (2019).

52. While by no means a representative sample, these comments illustrate the kinds of reactions I received from many people who did not attend *táncház*. None of these students I spoke with planned to vote yes for dual citizenship either.

53. This person pointed out that there are more and less nationalistic-leaning circles within *táncház*. Identifying the most nationalistic spots, she said that she prefers not to frequent them. She singled out Magyarok Háza (Hungarian House), run by the Federation of World Hungarians (MVSZ), which hosted a weekly *táncház*. In 2004–5, the building hosted a bookstore with far-right literature, with some leftist antiglobalization literature mixed in, and a shop selling Transylvanian folk art and functioned as a kind of culture house. In 2004, I attended "the VI Hungarian World Congress" there. Papers in the "Hungarians and the Orient Prehistoric Conference" subsection made up the largest contingent. Presenters connected Hungarian folk culture to those of Native Americans and Sumerians, to name two examples. Another *táncház*-goer told me that when he had attended archery lessons sponsored by Magyarok Háza, some of the other students showed up in Arrow Cross uniforms.

54. Magyar Narancs is a reference to the 1969 film *The Witness*, directed by Péter Bacsó, which parodied the Communist government's attempt to grow oranges. The term came to signify the gap between party propaganda and the lived experience of state socialism. The magazine was associated with Fidesz back when Fidesz stood for the Alliance of Young Democrats (*Fiatal Demokraták Szövetsége*).

55. He doesn't remember exactly but thinks it was a common slur at the time, *geci SZDSZesek*, (literally: sperm SZDSZ supporters), or possibly *piskos liberalisok* (filthy liberals).

56. Pulay noted another source of his discomfort: despite expressing solidarity with over-the-border migrants, *táncház*-goers rarely showed concern regarding the severe labor conditions these same people faced in Hungary. It was this that inspired his anthropological research on migrant workers from Szék in Transylvania. I met a number of people in *táncház* who employed Transylvanian migrants, who stressed that Transylvanian Hungarians were hard workers in comparison to Hungarians, making me wonder about labor exploitation.

57. Around the seventieth anniversary of World War II, new public memorials appeared throughout Budapest. Kata Ámon (2015) chronicles cultural and political battles over public space in more recent years in the context of illiberalism and revanchism. Táncház-goers contextualized expectations that postsocialist countries face their Holocaust pasts, including the discussion and enactment of reparations, and the apparent enrichment of Jews, in the context of a regime change period redistribution of resources they felt as dispossession. The return of Jewish properties seized in the years of the Holocaust unfolded in the context of the land reforms and restitutions of the 1990s. One *táncház*-goer told me that the Hollywood Jews always point to Hungary as the place where the Holocaust happened. This is hurtful toward Hungarians, he told me, because the reason so many survived was because the Hungarians "delayed deportation for so long." Yet the ubiquity of stereotypes that contrasted Jews and liberals to Hungarians in *táncház* environments suggests a shared *népi* ethic, supported by shared sources of news and affect and reinforced by a relative isolation of publics (Rajagopal 2001), both of which seem to be functions of and contributors to the polarization (J. Kósa 2007). We can imagine an alternative framework of sense stretching far beyond the literary world, into political journalism and daily conversation at sociable events of circumscribed publics. On the question of the Hungarian government's protection of Jews, see László Karsai (2005).

58. These events are also frequently called "Gypsy dancehouses."

59. A number of anthropologists have concerned themselves with the "introduc[tion] of 'culture' into rights talk" (Cowan, Dembour, and Wilson 2001, 3), pointing to a historical shift from a discourse in which rights stood in opposition to culture to one about "the right to culture" or to cultural heritage, paralleling the increase of attention to minority rights by supranational organizations since the 1980s (9). The shift toward claims based on group difference, Nancy Fraser (1997, 2) argues, is a defining feature of the "'postsocialist' condition."

60. Sylvain (2003) draws on Li (2001) to propose how places of recognition determine, at least to some degree, the codes in which identity claims are presented in order to access resources. "Projects pursuing international norms therefore incorporate actors on a number of levels who come together provisionally to activate relationships with funders (and other resources) by slotting into 'places of recognition'" (Taylor 2009).

Chapter Seven

The Place of Heritagization
Culture Talk amid Shifting Property and Citizenship Regimes

JUST AFTER THE 2006 ELECTIONS, in which MSZP won the first incumbency of Hungary's postsocialist period, massive protests filled the streets, prompted by the circulation of a secret recording of Prime Minister Ferenc Gyurcsány admitting to lying about the state of the economy to get elected. Moving to meet the standards of the EU's Maastrict criteria, MSZP quickly began to violate its promise of "reform without austerity" (Fabry 2015). Fidesz's popularity began to soar, while the far-right Jobbik Party gained traction with its rhetorical (re)production of, and physical attack on so-called Gypsy crime (via its paramilitary arm the Magyar Gárda). The liberal left, on the other hand, was beginning to crumble. This would mark a clear shift toward Fidesz's unprecedented control of parliament for three successive terms (as I write).

As Fidesz took the helm with a supermajority in 2010, among its first legislative acts was to grant citizenship to over-the-border Hungarians.[1] The following year, UNESCO inscribed the "Táncház Method: A Hungarian Model for the Transmission of Intangible Cultural Heritage" into the Register of Good Safeguarding Practices as a method that reflects the principles and objectives of the organization's Convention for the Safeguarding of Intangible Cultural Heritage (Taylor 2016). The ethnonational work of *táncház* can clearly be useful to the pursuits for which Viktor Orbán and Fidesz have now become world famous. I aim in this chapter, however, to illuminate the ways in which the ethnonationalism essential to this "illiberalism" and "populism" converges with predominant (neo) liberal approaches to culture and heritage (which used to be called folklore). The impulses and effects of *táncház* thus cannot be viewed solely in terms of political formations at the local level. Like the illiberalism and populism that rely on ethnonational rhetoric, I argue that heritagization is both a sign of and a cultivator of the centrality of culture talk and its political and economic functions today.

The shifting borders of the Hungarian state and the definition of the Hungarian "nation" and its territorial boundaries have been an important background throughout this book. Continuing to explore the conditions that support the centrality of "culture talk" in the context of shifts in property and citizenship regimes, this chapter zooms out and shifts scales to examine how the self-cultivation of a participatory *táncház* public of mostly Hungarian-born nationals is implicated in the production of place in Romania and of the scale of Hungarian "nationhood" and citizenship. I draw on Neil Smith's thoughts on the production of spatial scale as a social process resulting from struggles that establish boundaries that "partition and repartition" the world. "Jumping scales" allows us to reveal the "active social connectedness" of these "apparently different scales" (Smith 1996, 66). In what ways does *táncház* take part in (re)producing local places of ethnic Hungarianness, a national scale, and the space of the world capitalist system?

In contrast to production, services, spectacles, place, and culture have become central sites of capital accumulation in late capitalism, and tourism has become one of the world's biggest industries. By 2002, it was already "the world's number one employer, accounting for approximately 200 million jobs, 11% of global jobs" (Honey and Stewart 2002, 9) and was enjoying rapid growth in developing countries during my fieldwork period (Sylvain 2003, 367n18). UNESCO's World Heritage programs are organized (at least in part) around the potential for tourism, the IMF considers tourism a "viable export strategy for debt-ridden countries," and industry members "support it as a means for achieving sustainable development" (Sylvain 2003, 364). The rise of tourism to this station has coincided temporally with neoliberalization, the end of state socialism, and the so-called second world's loss of economic standing in the global economy. As the productive capacity of the region plummeted, the value created by workers was reaped by private actors, often foreign investors, while social rights were diminished, fitting into broader patterns of enclosure. Hungary, Romania, and Transylvania are situated in a semiperipheral position in a transforming global system of capitalism. While many ethnic Hungarians from Romania have relied on labor migration to the neighboring, and more prosperous, "kin state" of Hungary, labor migration from both countries to the core of the EU is also a key strategy for many.

In a context in which the terms and benefits of citizenship have been rearranged, *táncház* tourism and related processes of heritagization, seeking to reproduce "traditional" cultural practices, can have effects on social organization on the local level as they shape and channel access to resources. The extension of citizenship to over-the-border Hungarians in 2010 adds new dimensions to the flux in the scales of the national and of the state.

The Expediency of Culture: Monopoly Rent, Neoliberal Governance, and the (Re)Production of Cultural Difference

The ways in which culture is framed and acted on have cultivating effects, shaping the ways in which we think about culture and seek its benefits (Taylor 2009, 2016 Coombe 2012). The particular manners in which culture is instrumentalized today are related to the contemporary conditions of capitalism. The rollback of functions of the social state has been met with the "expanded role of culture," while nongovernmental organizations and local actors are expected to solve problems traditionally considered the domain of the state (Yudice 2003, 95). This "new legitimation strategy" has emerged at the same time that new approaches are making culture a useful resource for the accumulation of capital.

These various "expediencies" (Yudice 2003) of culture bring together what might seem otherwise to be unlikely bedpartners. As George Yudice (2003, 11) notes, statements recruiting "instrumentalized" culture include goals such as "multicultural tolerance and civic participation," spurring economic growth, and accumulation. While it is nothing new that struggles around cultural identity are connected to resources (Wolf 2001), the "idea of culture" has had a central role in "attempts to reassert . . . monopoly powers" under conditions presented by neoliberal globalization. This is "because claims to uniqueness and authenticity can best be articulated as distinctive and unreplicable cultural claims" (Harvey 2001a, 399).[2] As production has become less lucrative, and traditional place-based monopolies have been diminished, culture offers new opportunities to assemble monopoly privileges by providing "an enhanced income stream over an extended time due to an exclusive control over a tradable item" (in other words: monopoly rent) (Harvey 2002, 94).

To be expedient for these various purposes, culture must be transformed from processes into "objects." This reification (or, as Marx would have said, "fetishization") allows different practices and objects to take on a kind of equivalence (universalization, homogenization) while also working to delineate "owners," or beneficiaries, of related resources (Taylor 2009, 2016). The standardization of cultural events, experiences, and products that comes about through this, and the resulting greater marketability, however, often compromises their uniqueness (Harvey 2001a, 397). Therefore, in their attempts to "co-opt, subsume, commoditize and monetize" culture, "capitalists of any sort" may be found supporting the very kinds of differentiation and local formations that are "antagonistic" to the smooth functioning of capitalist enterprise (Harvey 2001a, 409–10). They invest in culture at the risk of generating "conservative, reactionary or exclusionist movements" (ibid.) or producing "a political climate 'antagonistic' to the globalization which they take part" (Harvey 2001a, 402).

Since the 1970s, the language of heritage has become dominant in referring to cultural artifacts, environments, and practices, with the term *intangible heritage* replacing *folklore* to refer to cultural practices (Taylor 2009). Scholars have noted how heritage discourse, illustrated in the texts, approaches, institutions, and relationships of UNESCO's heritage arm, can be expedient to both commodification and nationalist pursuits (Taylor 2009, 2016; see also Kaneff and King 2004).

Pointing to the tension between UNESCO's liberal and humanistic intentions and the "archipelago" image of cultures presented in the *Our Creative Diversity* report, Thomas Hylland Eriksen (2001, 134) argues that "the political conclusions to be drawn from the description of the world" inherent in the report "are not necessarily the liberal, tolerant and universalistic ones suggested by the authors." Presenting "cultures" as absolute others to one another, UNESCO's approach provides a "sound basis" for the "isolationism and political particularism" of an array of actors, from "separatists, to "difference multiculturalists," "nationalists seeking stricter border controls and restrictions on the flows of meanings across boundaries," and "inquisitors chasing the Salman Rushdies of the world into hiding" (ibid.).

Carving these boundaries, heritagization often helps to make such mutual exclusion "real." What I call the heritage regime is a form of governance that operates through a process of heritagization that involves defining cultural practices as a kind of cultural property by delineating their discrete boundaries and attaching them to particular owners. Heritagization is thus implicated not simply in the production of cultural "objects" but also in the production and reproduction of discrete groups and boundaries between them that determine access to resources (Taylor 2009, 2016). Heritagization is increasingly promoted as a path toward sustainable economic growth and "socio-economic development, particularly in countries with scarce resources" (DeCesari 2012, 410). With the increasing dominance of "market ideologies in heritage management . . . its means of 'valuation' are closely tied to economic returns whether via tourism or foreign direct investment" (Coombe 2012, 378). Under guise of promoting respect for diversity, and preserving cultural practices, heritagization processes work to cultivate and revalue in ways that constitute a kind of (neo) liberal governance.

Although much of the critical work on heritagization and heritage regimes has focused on UNESCO projects (Foster and Gilman 2015; Meskell and Brumann 2015), processes of heritagization and heritage governance are more widespread than those cases with formal links with UNESCO. This process of fetishization involves the cultivation of understandings of, and relationships with, culture and cultural property and what ownership entails (Brown 2004; Kaneff and King 2004; Taylor 2009, 2016). It is shaped in part by the "places of recognition" determined by preferences of funders, tourists, and other pathways to resources (Li 2001; Sylvain 2003).

These same processes are also implicated in the production of space, (re)producing difference at various scales, and operating according to universalizations that promote certain kinds of homogeneity (Taylor 2016). Various interests come together to (re)produce a particular place associated with Hungarian culture such as a Transylvanian village, but also the scales of the Hungarian culture area, the Hungarian nation, and scope of the Hungarian state. To see how this broader context of heritagization interweaves with politics and everyday life, in the next sections I turn to processes of (re)valuation underway in the contexts of shifting citizenship and property regimes.

The Referendum of 2004: Citizenship and the Nation

In 2001, the last year of Fidesz's first mandate, parliament passed the Status Law in order to afford citizenship-like rights of residence, work, and property ownership to ethnic Hungarians from neighboring countries—or, over-the-border Hungarians. In response to controversy sparked with governments of neighboring countries that regarded it as a violation of sovereignty, parliament introduced minor changes to the law (M. Kovács 2005; Laihonen and Nyyssonen 2002). In 2004, with the socialist-liberal (MSZP-SZDSZ) coalition heading parliament, a referendum was held on the issue of granting preferential citizenship to status card holders. In this moment of danger, we can see *tánchaz*-goers acting collectively in the formal political sphere, in electoral politics.

On December 5, 2004, six months after Hungary entered the European Union along with nine other countries, the question of "whether

Parliament should be obligated to pass a law allowing Hungarian citizenship with preferential naturalization to be granted to those who do not live in Hungary but claiming to have Hungarian nationality" (Election Guide n.d.) was posed to the voting public.[3] A separate question asked whether parliament should repeal the law inconsistent with public health service providers and hospitals remaining in state and local government ownership. The results of the referendum were not binding because of low turnout (37.35 percent of eligible voters participated).[4]

At their core, both questions addressed citizenship, revealing a complex of concerns the Hungarian public faced in 2004. While the first question asks whether citizenship should be defined in ethnic terms, addressing the definition of the nation and its relationship to the state, the second, asking what role the state will play in protecting citizens from the market and ensuring social equality, addresses the substance of citizenship.[5]

Despite the low turnout, heated debates continued in the press, and the referendum remained a central topic of conversation in *táncház* circles in the following months. While many took more nuanced positions, the general sense was that there were two opposing sides: one stressing nationalist positions and the other stressing rationalism and economic costs in the face of emotions (Feischmidt 2004). The procitizenship, nationalist, camp argued that the governing coalition (MSZP and SZDSZ) had frightened citizens from the polls with manipulative predictions of the economic crisis that would follow in the wake of mass immigration. As the government coalition emphasized the well-being of the citizens of the nation-state, rather than of the "nation," it was labeled un-Hungarian by the procitizenship faction.

Insisting that social spending would need to be cut for Hungary to increase its competitiveness (*Magyar Távirati Iroda* 2004), the government warned that the country would be unable to adopt the euro by the target date of 2010 due to budget deficits (Associated Press 2004). Official estimates associated with MSZP suggested that "the resettlement of 800,000 ethnic Hungarians" would push expenditures on education, health, and welfare up 573 billion forint (2.2 billion euro) a year, amounting to more than 5 percent of the annual budget (*Magyar Távirati Iroda* 2004).

The differing positions on the referendum might be approached as "a question of empathy," as one Transylvanian blogger phrased it (H. 2005). Most Hungarian citizens have little to do with Transylvanian Hungarians and have never set foot in Transylvania. Transylvanians in Hungary who are "'co-ethnics' and 'alien labour migrants' at the same time" (Pulay 2007, 2) have been subject to the kinds of discrimination faced by most migrant workers and are viewed "with a combination of suspicion and disdain" (Fox 2003, 456). In a 2003 article, Jon Fox notes that "the nationality of the migrant workers garnered them little more than scorn from their Hungarian hosts" (ibid.). Given the tightness of the labor market, "the abstract notion of shared nationality rhetorically privileged by the Hungarian state was of little consequence in assuaging [these more pressing] economic anxieties" (ibid.). The rhetoric of shared nationality appears to function well only as long as "over the border" Hungarians remain over the border (Paládi Kovács 1996; Fox 2003).

Lack of empathy may have been an element in why many citizens, feeling the squeeze on social citizenship in an already tense economic environment, chose to reject voting yes to citizenship. Yet many people expressed discomfort with voting no. Public intellectuals on the left, such as philosopher and one-time (SZDSZ) politician Gáspár Miklós Tamás (who was raised in Transylvania but has lived in Hungary for decades) advocated abstention. Tamás (2004) argued that while it would be wrong to vote no, a yes vote would do nothing to help Transylvanian Hungarians and, at most, result in Orbán becoming prime minister again. A number of self-ascribed liberal Hungarians told me that they had chosen not to vote in the referendum, hoping that enough people would abstain to make it null and void. They counted their abstention as a kind of a vote. They abstained from answering this politicized question preceding an election year, voting that such an issue should not be taken advantage of for political gain.[6]

Táncház-goers, in contrast, expressed the responsibility not simply to vote but to vote yes. Some phrased it as a matter of respect. After all, they reminded me, *táncház* had been relying on the good will and patriotism of the Transylvanian villagers for over thirty years. In the weeks before the referendum, a statement signed by prominent *táncház* figures was circulated throughout *táncház* events beseeching participants to vote yes for this very reason. While some *táncház*-goers also expressed apprehension about politicization of the issue of the nation, they rejected its discussion in economic terms. They saw the low turnout not as critique of the politicization of a sensitive issue in poor taste but as the betrayal of the nation by a populace duped by misleading predictions. The following conversation came after I asked one *táncház*-goer about why the referendum was so important if both countries would soon be part of the EU.[7]

> It should not have been permissible to make a political target out of the Hungarians across the borders. On either side. Somebody started it—it is not essential who— ... and the other side played along [*kontrázott*], and it should not have been allowed on either side. This is beyond politics, above

politics, outside politics, whatever you like. This has no connection to politics or economics; ... they are playing with people's lives.[8]

MT: So that is why it should have been now? Only because it came to referendum now?

No, as to why it had to happen, I don't know either. But as a voter the reason why it should have been now is [because it is] now that one had to vote. This should have been done back in 1990, when the regime change happened. It should have been done without a question, without a referendum. It was not necessary to do this circus. It shouldn't have been permissible to humiliate a nation in this way ... to ask a question to which I know there is not the very best [*legessleg*] answer. Now we can make it beautiful in vain, but [those] who didn't go out voted no. Let's not beautify it.

Transylvanian *táncház*-goers in Budapest echoed this view. Some stressed that while it would have been purely symbolic, a yes vote would have been extremely important for ethnic Hungarian Transylvanians.

In 2004, participation in *táncház* correlated with a certain level of responsibility, even an empathy, felt toward ethnic Hungarian Transylvanians that was substantiated in the referendum.[9] *Táncház*-goers, who have been to Transylvania and/or have spent time with ethnic Hungarian Transylvanians and work to reproduce and valorize their cultural practices, agreed that it was immoral to vote no and that what equaled a largely symbolic gesture was important for the morale of Transylvanians. Although (according to their own accounts), *táncház*-goers went to the polls in large numbers, this overtly political act nevertheless seemed to further enforce the polarization of two apparent sides: inner/spiritual/Hungarian versus outer/material/un-Hungarian. Although abstainers might not have been comfortable in voting no, *táncház*-goers saw both those who voted no and those who abstained as taking the other side.

The alternative framework of sense that *táncház* participants cultivated in themselves surfaced as collective action in the political sphere when participants went to the polls as yes voters. While in 2004, this did not achieve the narrow political goal of granting citizenship to over-the-border Hungarians, this moment of danger allowed me to spy the presence of a submerged framework of sense and its potential to erupt into the political sphere. *Táncház*-goers further exercise some common sensibilities at home, at work, and in the public sphere, where their opponents must formulate arguments that respond to their critique.[10]

As we have seen, participants emphasized that *táncház* is not a movement and that it is not political. It works, rather, in the inner/spiritual sphere, the cultural sphere, while shaping it as well. It lies outside the sphere of politics, they say, precisely because it refuses to engage "political power" on its terms. One *táncház* musician and cultural worker told me: "That is exactly the point, [*táncház*] doesn't fight . . . and the most dangerous enemy is the one who doesn't put on the glove . . . I would compare it a bit to when the Roman Empire ended . . . a really similar situation to the contemporary global society. And then one day there came a person who said 'not money, love' . . . and said even death is OK. And it was such a manifesto that it reached the whole world . . . and now again we have this kind of society."

Another *táncház* musician explained the tension he saw between political and cultural sides of *táncház*. He saw two "conscious undertakings" in *táncház*: one occupied with Hungarianness and the other a political position. He added: "But it should not be permissible to make a political movement out of the *táncház* movement. That was in it too, enough political too. But that was just a small part, and it was not its basic presumption [*alapsejte*] to be a big *népi* opposition [*nagy népi ellenállás*]. Rather, the *táncház* . . . fulfilled this goal [*kivívta ezt a szerepet*]. But it wasn't that." He explained how he saw *táncház*'s connection to opposition in the 1980s, by contrasting conditions in Transylvania (in socialist Romania) and in socialist Hungary, continuing:

> Well, from this view I had some kind of protection. No kind of power reached me. I absolutely openly and unsuspectingly realized it [*jutottam ki*]. And when I realized for the first time what existing socialism means I was horrified and there was a moment when I felt: "This, no." And starting then, there was an opposition [*ellenállás*] in me. Not like I was making *szamizdat* or those things, that is a different genre again. My opposition was that, from that moment on, I stuck to Hungarian culture.[11]
>
> MT: So it was a different atmosphere that didn't connect with the opposition? An internal resistance? A different level?
>
> Yes, from then on I felt my most important task was that I should familiarize myself with it as much as I am able and that I must make as many other people as possible familiar with it. Not forcefully. I did not want to teach. Only that this material should not just be my own, but that I would be happy to share it.

Although *táncház*-goers used the term *urbánus* with me far less frequently than *népi*, the vilification of liberals, socialists, communists, and Jews in *táncház* environments illustrates these binaries at work and the work behind the polarization. Rather than debates involving many positions in a "public sphere," here we encounter an isolation of publics that precludes them. When I asked *táncház*-goers about antisemitism, they argued (much like Sándor Csoóri and László Németh before him) that rather than being antisemitic, they were simply responding to Jewish, liberal, and Western accusations of antisemitism. *Táncház*-goers participate in reifying a territorialized ethnonation and practices of Hungarianness, and cultivate in themselves a form of empathy on which they act in the political sphere. Just as this sense of empathy must be cultivated, so must the polarization and the binaries within which it operates.

The questions posed in the referendum of 2004 can be seen as asking who should be considered citizens and what kind of citizenship they should enjoy. Read through the stolen regime change lens by a polarizing public, critiques appeared to suggest that the un-Hungarian MSZP/SZDSZ government served foreign interests while ignoring those of "real Hungarians." This story about an elite retaining power, what might be understood as a class project, is combined with a familiar story found among the European radical right that the current state of affairs is engineered by Jewish and international/cosmopolitan/interests in the form of globalization.[1] It indexes rhetoric salient in the interwar period among the ruling elite as well as among some of the populists who stood in opposition to it. Much like the interwar period, the transition was a period in which the terms of citizenship were battled over as the region's place was being remade in a crisis moment of global capitalism.

Táncház-goers took political action in Hungary in the referendum of 2004 to support over-the-border Hungarians. They did so in the context of, and contributing to, a polarization process that would include the use of a Hungarian/un-Hungarian binary, stretching beyond the territorial borders of Hungary. The same practices that cultivated empathy for over-the-border Hungarians among *táncház* participants are implicated in the production of place in Transylvania and of the scale of the national itself.

Shifting Regimes of Citizenship and Property and Struggles over Hungarian Communal Property in Romania

The shifts in citizenship and property regimes that have been underway as part of the transition are not independent of the global shifts that inform the current trends of heritagization. In 2004, *táncház*-goers went to the polls exercising the rights of electoral democracy that signified, along with other liberal norms after 1989, the end of Communist rule. Great emphasis has also been put on developing civil society in the region (Verdery 1996, 104; Mikuš 2018). The achievement of civil society became the focus of oppositional movements (Ivancheva 2011), in part because the state socialist regimes offered social citizenship while denying civil and political citizenship (Seligman 1992, 113; see also Verdery 1996).[12] We might say that new postsocialist subjects took social citizenship, "the right to a modicum of economic welfare and security [and the] right to share to the full in the social heritage and to live the life of a civilized being according to the standards prevailing in society" (Seligman 1992, 113), for granted. When embracing ideas of political and civil citizenship as democracy, they did not expect to trade them for their social citizenship, eclipsed by economic policies purported to promote democracy.

The degrading of socialist personhood concomitant with democratization included attacks on what was seen as inappropriate dependence on state resources, relying on Orientalist tropes about the population, associating it with backwardness. The transition meant new rules of the game at the same time as leftist policies and politics were being weakened on a (near) global scale, dragged rightward toward a new center (Hall 2018; Mouffe 2009).[13] Across Europe leftist parties were adopting neoliberal logics via third-way socialism, making way for our "post-political" moment (Mouffe 2009). Conditions brought about by the policy of shock therapy corresponded with the decrease of social amenities and growing social differentiation, even under the slew of socialist parties elected across the region (Creed 1995). This situation was a far cry from the democracy that dissidents and ordinary citizens in the former socialist bloc had imagined (Krastev 2006; Gagyi 2016). "A human disaster on a previously unimaginable scale" (King 2001, 494) took the form of an increase in "social inequalities and poverty ... in virtually all regions and economic sectors of the postsocialist countries" (Hann, Humphrey, and Verdery 2002, 4). Inequality has continued to climb (Kopasz et al. 2013), even while East Europeans have approved extensive state control in providing social welfare (Rose and Haerpfer 1996) and consider equality important at higher levels than Western Europeans (Perugini and Pompei 2015). Membership in the EU added to the hierarchy of "overseers" demanding that the formerly socialist states limit deficit spending, affecting their ability to redistribute (Creed and Taylor 2020; Szombati 2018).[14]

The "bundle of entitlements" assumed by postsocialist subjects was (at least in part) incongruent with "the construction of capitalist individualism ... and the notion of private property associated with it" (Verdery 1999, 72). The redefinition of citizenship and associated "civil society building" required delinking it from such rights as employment, housing, and health care and emphasizing the sanctity of private property and electoral democracy. As collective property was "dismantled under the pressure of global forces," the question of citizenship "became entangled with questions of national and cultural identity" (ibid., 292). This was due in part to the legacy of state socialism and, in part, to new political and economic conditions.

In this context, civil society was coming to mean something imported from the West and was, therefore, associated with Western aid programs, funding, and NGO activities benefiting a small class of local actors with specific skill sets and well paid jobs (Creed and Wedel 1997; Mandel 1993; Sampson 1996; Hemment 2007; Gagyi and Ivancheva 2019). Critics of this civil society note the elitist, neoimperialist qualities of this process, its role in supporting neoliberal economic values, and the dismissal of local values. To many, civil society–promoting practices of international NGOs, associated with liberalism, came to appear opposed to social citizenship. Many *táncház*-goers saw the focus on minority rights and pluralism by civil society–promoting NGOs as a redistribution of privileges for particular groups, such as Jews or Roma, in which "real Hungarians" are the losers.[15]

Attacks on the expectations and affect of socialist citizenship coincided temporally with the establishment of what Robert Hayden (1992, 655) calls "constitutional nationalism," which "privileges the members of one ethnically defined nation over other residents in a particular state" and is seen throughout the region (Verdery 1996, 295).[16] Claims to national sovereignty were key in the establishment of the many states of the former Yugoslavia (the site of Hayden's observations), the Czech and Slovak Republics, and Moldova (to name some examples) in the flux of changing borders following the end of socialism. This has happened as a "re-ethnicization of citizenship," the extension of citizenship to coethnics outside the nation-state, has been underway in much of Europe, related in part to the emigration of large numbers of people (Joppke 2003; M. Kovács 2005, 53). Permanent and temporary migration from the formerly state socialist polities has been a necessary strategy for many (Vračić 2018; Stratfor 2012), and citizens living abroad have been influential in some national elections (Vertovec 2005; Bayer 2017; Streda 2018).[17]

Ethnonational claims to the right to self-determination were being made in a context of enclosure of formerly common space, as collective goods were being converted into private property; a redistribution of wealth paralleling the "Great Transformation," the introduction of the modern market economy in Europe (Bodnár 2001, 10, Polányi 1957 [1944], 957). In this context of intense meaningfulness of ethnic identities, the restitution of property to former owners could entwine with a sense of land as (ethno)national territory (Kaneff 1998; Verdery 1996, 300).

The proper way to mark the end of state socialism was to treat it as an aberration and to reverse the "conscious efforts to create different property

The Place of Heritagization 225

Fig. 7.1 A map reflecting current nation-state borders in the region. Map by D-maps: https://d-maps.com/carte.php?num_car=29970&lang=en.

and citizen-state relations than those of liberal capitalism" that had marked state socialism (Verdery 1996, 291). Restitution of nationalized property was understood as evidence of the postsocialist state's willingness to respect the rule of law by liberal capitalist standards and hold the sanctity of private property as a fundamental value of democracy (Verdery 2004, 142). The post-1989 processes of restitution have constituted ongoing processes of revaluation, tied to transformations in the rights and obligations of citizenship.

The first years of transition entailed the restoration of private property rights, and the concomitant privatization of state-held assets, including factories and agricultural enterprises that had been the source of employment for many citizens (Alexander 2004, 253; Damşa 2016), as well as housing, public space, and the public goods connected to citizenship. In addition to the sale of various assets to investors, the process of privatization entailed the return of nationalized property to former owners or their descendants. Redistribution of property, in the name of restitution, and its entailments has been central to the transformation of property relations, transfers of wealth, and reshaping of citizenship that have characterized the transition. Involving property transfers through compensation or restitution of private and communal properties nationalized by the Communist regime, these processes have played out under different legislation and across varied timelines in different countries.

In Romania, the processes of restitution have taken many twists and turns (Stan 2006) and are ongoing, with many formal requests remaining unresolved and new claimants appearing (Academic Society of Romania 2008). In the countryside, property has proven to be "elastic" (Verdery 1996) and "fuzzy" (ibid. 1999), informing struggles over what property exists and to whom it belongs. In addition, owning property has not always turned out to be beneficial to new owners, who have faced new debts, obligations, liabilities, and risks (Verdery 2004). Longer-term processes have led to the dispossession of new owners of agricultural land and its concentration, with the language of land-grabbing used to draw parallels with other peripheral regions (Taylor 2018; Borras, Franco, and van der Ploe 2013; Stockmans 2018). Urban tenants also face eviction as property values are transformed into investment opportunities despite what had seemed like tenant-friendly policies (Chelcea 2006; Florea and Dumitriu 2018; Stan 2006).

It is in this context that struggles have unfolded around the restitution of Hungarian communal property as part of a broader politics of autonomy. This notion of autonomy as the "internal self-organization of the Hungarian community" (Csergő 2002) and as a "means of maintaining a separate language, culture, and national identity" (Béla Marko quoted in ibid., 10) is not limited to but also undergirds claims to territorial autonomy in the Szekler region, which is more or less the equivalent of the former Hungarian Autonomous Region.

In most of Transylvania this struggle has centered on church properties and educational institutions but has also involved control over local government and administration (Csergő 2002, 9–10). From the early 1990s on, throughout Transylvania ethnic Hungarians attempted to gain properties once belonging to the four traditional ethnic Hungarian churches in Romania and the schools run by them with the aim to use these resources to promote Hungarian language and cultural education.[18] Despite laws that appear to make the return of such properties possible, a large proportion remains in the hands of the state (Hungarian Human Rights Foundation 2019). Ethnic Hungarians have also sought to expand the possibilities of studying in the Hungarian language, with limited success and quite a bit of controversy, at the Babeș-Bolyai University in Cluj, founded in 1959 by merging a Hungarian university with a Romanian one (Koszorus 2009; Stroschein 2012).[19]

In Szeklerland, where ethnic Hungarians make up the majority, and autonomy is articulated around the pursuit of various versions of regional autonomy (Koszorus 2009, 8), there has been fierce rejection of plans in Bucharest for administrative remapping of the country. Opponents argue that control over local decision-making, including over budgetary decisions, is necessary for ethnic Hungarians to have control over their own lives. As opposed to other parts of Romania with ethnic Hungarian presence, Szeklerland has a Hungarian-speaking majority and far less of the ethnic mixing characterizing the historically Hungarian city of Cluj (Kolozsvár in Hungarian) (Brubaker, Feischmidt, Fox, and Grancea 2006).

Despite this mixing, preventing further assimilation is of deep concern to many ethnic Hungarians, and ethnic Hungarian political parties in Romania. Control over the resources discussed and the maintenance of communal institutions is seen as necessary to reproduce this group as a meaningful community and maintain ethnic (or national) identity (Kiss 2018). Control over said communal property is thus tied up with the (re)production of forms of cultural heritage, including language and religious and folk practices. Communal property and heritage are thus seen as directly tied to the ability to reproduce this group as a self-conscious community Proficiency in the Hungarian language is also necessary to take advantage of the resources offered by the Hungarian state via dual citizenship, while the efforts of the Hungarian government can be interpreted as attempts to prevent assimilation.

Communal property is often referred to as heritage, and common justifications for protecting heritage share at least some premises with these demands for control over communal property (Taylor 2009, 2016). Both are entwined in processes of revaluation under fluxing conditions of citizenship that mark the postsocialist/neoliberalizing moment in the region. Territory, infrastructure, and practices in Transylvania are regarded as cultural property essential for reproducing ethnic Hungarians and to the (re)production of boundaries among discrete ethnonational groups (Taylor 2009, 2016) and their designated collective cultural property.

The same resources for reproducing meaningful communities can also be instrumentalized in the realm of tourism, where they may be revalued in the process. Much like music and dance revivals (Livingston 1999), in the name of preserving cultural practices and products, heritage projects actually reframe and revalue them (and the relationships in which they take part) to meet new needs and demands (Kirshenblatt-Gimblett 1998; Taylor 2009, 2016). *Tánchaz* takes part in struggles around what is increasingly being called heritage, tangible or intangible, against this backdrop of larger shifts in ownership, access, use, and obligations. The growing emphasis on heritage and cultural property squares well with global political economic shifts that have made tourism one of the fastest-growing industries.

Logics of Heritage: The (Re)Production of Difference at Various Scales

As it revalues culture, *táncház* takes part in the production of place and scale. *Táncház* practices cultivate more than the sense of empathy, respect, and shared Hungarianness with Transylvanians that participants expressed in discussions and actions around the referendum. We have seen saw how the practice of folk dance as mother tongue combines with tourism to Transylvanian villages to reinforce a geographical, or territorial, sense of Hungarianness while also fitting local practices into a national repertoire. Beyond "the conduct of conduct" (Foucault, 1994, 237) with regard to the performance of folk traditions, and behavior in moments of danger, *táncház*'s effects can be seen in everyday life and social reproduction in the agricultural areas in which it takes, and makes, place in the context of tourism.[20]

While processes of heritagization, and thus heritage governance, are not limited to cases with links with UNESCO's heritage arm, the organization has been an important force in defining and legitimating heritage, its supposed goods, and its owners in the neoliberal era. I discuss such dynamics with regard to some UNESCO nomination processes in the region before honing in on more specific processes related to *táncház*.

The same year the "táncház method" was inscribed onto UNESCO's Register of Good Safeguarding Practices, as a model for safeguarding cultural practices, the first steps were taken toward nominating the Whitsun Pilgrimage of Csíksomlyó (Romanian: Şumuleu Ciuc) to UNESCO's Representative List of Intangible Heritage.[21] The pilgrimage encompasses a set of rituals related to the Catholic Church in Szeklerland, increasingly attended by secular actors.[22] When the nomination process began in 2011, the political party Democratic Alliance of Hungarians in Romania (Romániai Magyar Demokrata Szövetség, RMDSZ) was part of the governing coalition.[23] RMDSZ's president, serving as Romania's minister of culture and heritage protection at the time, gained approval from the National Intangible Heritage Committee to begin the process (Tánczos 2018). By 2016, although most criteria had been met, and it would have been easy to meet the rest, the process had come to a halt after a series of changes in the government and ministry. Ethnic Hungarian commentators suggest that the failure of the (ethnic) Romanian team to present the remaining materials was due to a desire to keep the nomination of an ethnic Hungarian heritage practice from going through rather than lack of said materials

(Tánczos 2018; Sipos 2016). The idea that Romanian authorities were not willing to respect the integrity of Hungarian culture in Romania was reinforced in part by the representation of "Lads' Dances of Romania," inscribed in 2015 (Szilvay 2017).[24] In this case, one variation of lads' dances shown in the video representing this category on the UNESCO website shows an ethnic Hungarian in the village Méra (Romanian: Mera). The caption states that the dance is "also performed by the Hungarians and Rroma [Roma] of Romania, but on Romanian melodies." Hungarian commentators disagree that these melodies are Romanian alone and see this as an effort to deny the value and presence of Hungarian culture in Romania.

Vilmos Tánczos discusses the various interests converging and competing around the pilgrimage. Although it has historically been a practice of Szeklers (the Hungarian-speaking group that makes up the majority in Szeklerland) reaffirming both their Catholic identity and their relationship to territory, he notes the importance of the pilgrimage (in which decreasing numbers of members of traditionally organized pilgrim groups take part) as a "Hungarian national symbol" (2018, 170).[25] The case demonstrates the ways in which the seemingly countervailing forces of nationalism and universal values may be activated together in heritagization efforts, even as these processes lead to revaluations of various kinds.

Organized through the participation of states parties to the Convention for the Safeguarding of Intangible Cultural Heritage, UNESCO heritage programs have a contradictory relationship to the category of "national." The bureaucratic practices central to the implementation of heritage policy require that distinct groups be defined, and connects them with particular forms of cultural property or heritage. This arguably reflects the nature of any categorization or production of "places of recognition" (Li 2001; Sylvain 2003; see also Taylor 2009, 2016), yet we see here how UNESCO's programs are in tune with the ethnonation-making processes of member (nation-)states. While Tánczos claims that "the national ideologies," or "national myths," developed across Europe throughout the nineteenth century and still alive today qualify as the kinds of religious forms of faith that UNESCO shies away from supporting because of their exclusive character, formal aspects of the process tie it precisely to these national ideologies or myths. States' parties, representing nation-states legitimated through these very same processes, play the essential role of interfacing with UNESCO (Tánczos 2018; Nikočević 2004), reproducing the image of discrete nations and their states.

Discussing Croatia's application to have the Istrian Musical Microcosm named a Masterpiece of Oral and Intangible Heritage of Humanity,

Lidija Nikočević (2004) illustrates limitations imposed by the allocation of UNESCO support via nation-states and related ideas about the ethnonation. Writing as the territorial boundaries of new nation-states were being drawn after the violent breakup of the former Yugoslavia, she shows how UNESCO's "archipelago approach to cultures" (Hylland-Eriksen 2001) was unable to recognize the kinds of cultural exchanges among groups and coproduction of cultural forms alive in this "microcosm." As this approach categorized cultural activities either at the level of national culture or of specific minority groups, Nikočević (2004) found it unable to address the historically active and fluid mixes produced through cultural processes. Since the applicants claimed that the microcosm included practices of ethnic Croats, Montenegrans, Slovenes, and Italians, they were told that each of these groups' nation-states would have to enter into the agreement. This was despite the fact that most of the practitioners representing these diverse ethnicities have never lived in, or been citizens of, said nation-states.

The Csíksomlyó pilgrimage was presented to UNESCO as a local practice, while its status as an ethnic Hungarian practice within Romania was played down in the application (Tánczos 2018). At the same time, RMDSZ represented the gains and failures of the nomination process to its constituency as an affair of "the Hungarian nation, torn apart by the treaty of Trianon" (ibid., 170). While Romanian state actors might have stymied the process simply by virtue of its ethnic Hungarian character, they were likely emboldened by the ways in which RMDSZ addressed its constituency and the passion with which representatives of Hungary stood up in favor of the nomination at the UNESCO congress (ibid., 171).

Beyond the specific historical animosities between Hungarians and Romanians on different scales, the examples of the Csíksomlyó Pilgrimage, the lads' dances of Romania, and the Istrian Musicological Microcosm show how difficult it is to present a practice as shared and multivalent across groups or to present a multiethnic nation within the prevailing notion of the nation-state. The (re)production of discrete groups is in part due to the central role of the nation-state in UNESCO's recognition processes and to the national valence of such practices and can happen at other scales as well.

Carol Silverman describes the application for the wedding ceremony of the village of Galičnik in Macedonia (part of the former republic of Yugoslavia and as of June 2018, part of North Macedonia) to be recognized by UNESCO as a Masterpiece of Oral and Intangible Heritage of Humanity, which is meant to favor practices in danger of disappearing and to support plans for revitalization. The application (by the Union of Macedonian

Folklore Ensembles) legitimized ethnic Macedonian revivalists as the owners of these threatened cultural practices, while (Muslim) Roma who have historically played a central role in Galičnik weddings as musicians went unmentioned (Silverman 2012, 2014). The ethnonational delineation of "Macedonian" here does not include Roma, who are contrasted with (ethnic) Macedonians in the local context, regardless of their Macedonian citizenship or language use.

The application for the táncház method to be listed as a good practice was prepared by Heritage House, supported by a long list of *táncház*-related organizations, and submitted by the secretary general of the Hungarian National Committee for UNESCO (UNESCO 2011). While the text does mention that these practices are taken from the "eastern part of the Hungarian language territory" (ibid.), it stresses the openness of the method (its "multi-cultural nature—enabling transposition of the system to any nationality, ethnic or religious group") and its geographical breadth (global, as both ethnic Hungarian and non-ethnic Hungarian groups have formed dancehouses in the United States, Japan, and Western Europe). It also claims several minority groups outside of Hungary as active participants. Applying for the status of a best practice of safeguarding—as a successful method that can be borrowed by those wishing to preserve heritage anywhere—the application appears to avoid the situation that Nikočević decried. The following quotation represents the sense conveyed in the application that anyone may partake in it and that each individual *táncház* has the freedom to choose the elements it will. "The common content is Hungarian dance and music culture, and the traditional cultures of peoples cohabiting the East Central Europe and part of the Balkans (Romanians, Slovakians, Gypsies, Germans, Southern Slavs, Bulgarians, Macedonians and Greeks) which within the táncház framework manifests as common collective knowledge. This is then augmented by the uniquely created new cultural heritage stemming from local and regional traditions incorporated at the various individual táncház-es, which in turn serve to strengthen and preserve the local specificities of cultural diversity" (ibid., 9).

Through its narrative techniques, the application manages to skirt the question of the revival's part in the (re)production of the (ethnonational) boundaries of cultural property and its owners and mask the importance of the particularly ethnonational content important to many, if not most, participants. This does not mean, however, that this kind of content is not present in the broader processes of heritagization or in *táncház*.

In the 2000s, the chief performing folk ensembles were revivalist bands made up mostly of ethnic Hungarians, a stark contrast with the rural bands made up of Roma from whom revivalists learned to play in the 1970s and 1980s. Whereas some elderly Roma musicians continue to be central providers of authenticity as masters or first fiddlers (their names enthusiastically billed along with those of the ensembles when on tour), younger Roma musicians are often considered to play an adulterated style less authentic than that of the revivalist bands (Hooker 2005, 2007). Those younger Roma who are accepted are often accompanied by revivalists rather than other Roma.

This process instates ethnic Hungarians as the owners of folk music practices by replacing Roma musicians. While not necessarily an explicit goal on the behalf of most revivalists, this return of folk musicianship to ethnic Hungarians offers the ethnicized answer to the wishes of Béla Bartók (1947) and others that Hungarian peasants take back these practices that had been taken over by a professional class of musicians, most of them Roma (Taylor 2009; Haigh n.d.; see also Frigyesi 2000 and Hooker 2013).[26] At the same time that Roma experience this dispossession of their role as essential bearers of Hungarian national culture (Frigyesi 1996), reinforcing their identity as "not Hungarian," the "Gypsy" dance *csingerálás* is increasingly incorporated into the dance cycle at many *táncház* events and thus danced by increasing numbers of ethnic Hungarian *táncház*-goers (Hooker 2005).[27]

The redistribution of such resources into the hands of ethnic Hungarians, a dispossession of Roma from an important cultural and economic role in the case of musicians, is perhaps the most glaring example of this contradictory process.[28] We can see a similar logic, however, in concerns expressed by some *táncház* participants about *táncház*-going Jews. While some considered those who strongly identify with their Jewishness (and therefore probably don't frequent *táncház*) to have "adopted Jewishness and denied their Hungarianness," they also complained that Jews who participate in *táncház* "think they are more Hungarian than the Hungarians" precisely because of their embracing of Hungarian folk culture.[29] But more subtle dynamics are also at work in the production of boundaries around discrete practices and groups. These I discuss as the production of place and scale.

Táncház and the Transylvanian Village(r): Producing Place and Scale

Táncház-going Hungarians depend on Transylvania's ethnic Hungarians as a source of authenticity, even as revivalists police their dance and musical conduct (Hooker 2005; S. Varga 2016; Taylor 2009). While, like most of the movement's pure sources, these "Gypsy" musicians are also from Transylvania, the process described reflects an ethnic Hungarian/Roma distinction. Despite the ethnonational logic dominant in *tánchaz* tourism in Transylvania, there are uneven power relationships between Hungary and Transylvania, between *tánchaz*-goers from Hungary and ethnic Hungarian Transylvanian villagers, between urban and rural populations, and among host nations and their Roma compatriots.[30] Many Transylvanian villagers I spoke with in camp-hosting villages had a hard time connecting *tánchaz* tourism with a betterment of the quality of their lives. Few saw ethnic Hungarian tourists as particularly empathetic or to be expressing solidarity, while they articulated concern about the disruptions introduced by the influx of outsiders and resentment about the differentiation between themselves and neighbors who benefited from this kind of tourism.[31]

Struggles over intangible heritage practices (including language rights), public monuments, and the restitution of communal property make place under conditions Attila Melegh (2000) argues is a new form of colonialism (or "Eastern Expansion") designed to ensure and control access to cheap labor, enacted in part through legislation around dual citizenship.[32] This is enacted via the developing politics of the Hungarian state vis-a-vis Transylvania and ethnic Hungarian citizens of Romania (see Kiss 2018) as well as through the relative wealth and access to resources of the Hungarian citizens who come to Transylvania as tourists of various kinds.[33] *Tánchaz*-goers generally do not see themselves as tourists, and it is not uncommon to see them wearing T-shirts that read, "Magyar vagyok, nem turista" (I'm Hungarian, not a tourist). In the aftermath of the failed referendum, some *tánchaz*-goers anticipated what it would be like to visit Transylvania next time, given the anger expressed toward Hungarians.[34] But just what kind of impact does *tánchaz* tourism have, and how is it related to the (re)production of Hungarian villages and the scale of the nation?

Sándor Varga (2016) discusses the "significant impact" of *tánchaz* tourism on the dances and social organization in the Transylvanian village of Visa (Romanian: Visea). He offers interesting insights into differential access to resources via relationships with revivalists as well as the impact of *tánchaz* on the way local cultural practices are (re)produced as "heritage."[35] For a number of reasons (closeness to Cluj, migration patterns of villagers to Cluj, and the location of the village in the area in which Zoltán Kallos collected and had family ties), Visa has had regular relations with *tánchaz* participants for several decades.[36]

Varga discusses impacts of this relationship, ranging from effects on the dance suite and motifs used within dances, on the processes of organizing dance events, and on the social relations among villagers. He describes important effects of *tánchaz* tourism on the social relations (re)produced in the annual event organized around the measuring of sheep milk, *juhmérés*. While the equivalent of a *tánchaz* in Visa had ceased to exist in the 1960s, the *juhmérés* remained a valued opportunity for dancing, even in the absence of a live band. As this event had lost the traditional element of live music that they favor, Hungarian revivalists took on organizing roles for the music/dance event, rendering it more traditional in their eyes. This, however, put the solidarity-producing capacities of the event, in which rights to the milk of the collectively pastured herd are determined, and social cohesion is "affirmed and maintained," under new strains (S. Varga 2016, 9–10). The timing of the event itself was shifted away from Orthodox Easter, when villagers are guaranteed a good price (from ethnic Romanians preparing feasts) for the separated lambs, to accommodate *tánchaz*-goers. Rivalries emerged in this changing economic landscape in which the resources this cultural property provided access to were affected by outsiders or in which local actors had to choose between resources provided by *tánchaz* tourists and those from other sources.

My own experience visiting dance camps between 2000 and 2005 adds to these insights. Their multiplication since 1990 attests to the large numbers *tánchaz*-goers visiting Transylvanian villages through this modality. In the summer of 2004 alone, the *Tánchaz* Association's website listed upward of fifty dance camps in Transylvania.[37] Others interested in experiences of ethnotourism and ecotourism also stay at *tánchaz* camps, while *tánchaz*-goers also visit other places in Transylvania associated with Hungarians, including Csíksomlyó, during the pilgrimage.

Managed by different coalitions in each location; camps manifest the cooperation of an array of actors including local entrepreneurs; ethnic Hungarian political parties; local, national and international NGOs; and local or national governments, with some camps receiving support from both the Hungarian and Romanian governments.[38] Camps usually feature professional dance instructors from Hungary, well-known Roma fiddlers from the region, and local tradition-keepers, also referred to as informants. At some I attended, Hungarian government funding was used to subsidize admission for Transylvanians and Hungarian citizens, while foreigners were asked to pay the full price.[39] As Lynn Hooker (2007) notes, although foreigners are welcome, these camps are intended for Hungarians, and few ethnic Romanians attend.[40]

While some visitors prefer to camp at the official campgrounds, or stay at dorms made available to camp-goers, others pitch tents in villagers' yards or stay in their homes, usually for a fee. In many cases, the camp fee includes meals. In some cases, agencies may connect tourists with lodging in the homes of local villagers or guesthouses decorated with folk art. Villagers may show up at the camp on the first day to offer rooms. To secure guests with greater ease and for higher fees, hosts must provide certain amenities, including running water and indoor toilets, scarce in more isolated villages, and sometimes food, as well.

Some camps are located in areas designated as agrotourism zones by the Romanian government.[41] In 2006, the agrotourism section of the Romania Tourism website of the Romanian Ministry of Transportation, Construction, and Tourism appealed to potential guests by suggesting they "turn back in time" and behave as "your fathers did" (Romanian Ministry of Transportation, Construction and Tourism 2007). While it is written there that "multiculturalism ... makes this experience even more interesting" and that one may visit "Romanian, Hungarian, Saxon, or Gypsy villages," there was no mention of these Hungarian folk dance camps.[42] The Hungarian-language Transylvanian Tourism site (Erdélyi Turismus), on the other hand, features a "dance camp" category that includes only this type of camp. By 2006, in at least one camp location tourist hospitality courses were being jointly organized by the "homeland program" of the Hungarian Economic and Trade Ministry and the Hungarian National Village and Agro-tourism Association (Mediatica 2006).[43]

A 2005 article in the *Times* online, entitled "Romania's Last Peasants," sums up the romantic orientation of eco/ethno-tourism. The following quote illustrates the lure of tourism as a visit to the idyllic past while emphasizing that this treasure is disappearing before our very eyes at the hands of globalization. "Agrotourism, putting up with peasants, is the joy of traveling in Romania. This is tourism on a human scale, bespoke. You are a lodger but treated as a friend. Catch it before its innocence has been lost and before Romania enters the EU in 2007. Your hosts who are subsistence farmers provide milk for your coffee fresh from the cow at the end of the garden. How much will be lost when EU health regulations bring all this to an end?" (*Times* 2005).

The village locations of folk dance tourism in Transylvania are thus (re)produced, or selectively transformed, through the place-based efforts of multiple actors, with different interests, aimed at generating revenue and encouraging "development" and the "preservation" of what is increasingly referred to as cultural heritage (Taylor 2009).

As the basis of the locational advantage underlying the assembly of monopoly rent, cultural uniqueness must be reproduced. One aim of these

Fig. 7.2 Dance camp tourists perusing embroidery for sale, Szék (Sic), 2004. Hi8 video still by the author.

camps and related activities is to encourage the continuation of these cultural practices in these locations, the very thing that make them worthy of this particular kind of tourism, but which also ensures Hungarianness. In this, the goals of Hungarian political parties seeking to capitalize on (or cultivate) ethnonationalist sentiment and ethnic Hungarian political parties in Romania seeking to halt assimilation and gain autonomy, converge with those of revivalists, other kinds of tourists, entrepreneurs, funders of various sorts, and Transylvanian villagers seeking to eke out a viable living. As Renée Sylvain (2003) notes succinctly, "market demand joins forces with identity politics" in ethno- and eco-tourism.

To date, most camp locations lie beyond the convenience of railroad service and can be reached only by bus, private shuttles run by locals, or car. Their locations, remote agricultural villages surrounded by verdant forest and fields add to the aura of authenticity, allowing the visitor to feel that s/he is at the edges of globalization. But the balance between unique and convenient is delicate. Take the example of one *táncház*-goer, a student of ethnography, who told me that she would never visit certain camps because they are "too established" and "touristy," and she doesn't like to see herself as a tourist. She explained her preference to be among the villagers themselves, unmediated by the tourist apparatus. Her vision recalls the visits of *táncház*-goers to Transylvanian villages in the 1970s and 1980s.

Despite their oft-expressed solidarity with villagers, a significant number of *táncház* tourists I met at camps expressed disappointment with what they deemed the absence of "tradition." One woman was disappointed about what she encountered during her stay in a local villager's home, noting that family members did not dress in folk costume daily. Her notion of tradition seemed only to refer to the realm of expressive culture. She failed to recognize as tradition, for example, the workhorse in the barn and the adolescent son's adept relation with it, a menu determined by local food production, the ubiquity of the outhouse, wood stove heating, or the (gendered) social use of brandy. Nor did she note the greeting "may God grant you a good day" offered to villagers and strangers alike when walking down the lane. While bemoaning the lack of tradition, many camp-goers expected access to hot running water, indoor toilets, and, for some, even vegetarian meals.

In some cases, villagers told me of their plans to adapt to (perceived) tourist preferences, but there is no guarantee that this will serve them well. The limits of tourism as a successful economic strategy are well documented in rural Romania, as are related processes of differentiation. Studies of nearby regions confirm a high correlation between "cultural capital" and high levels of infrastructure with the ability to capture high earnings from tourism. In most cases, income from tourism was too low to support families (Dezsi and Benedek 2011; Klimaszewski, Bader, Nyce, and Beasley 2010; Szabó 2012).[44] My research in villages hosting *táncház* camps also suggested that households that reaped larger amounts of income from tourism were those able to supply superior amenities (indoor toilets, running water) and recognizable heritage (architecture, embroidery, furniture, foods), with others at a comparative disadvantage.

Elsewhere (Taylor 2009), I have described how residents of one village told me of their plans to replace their kitchen gardens with flower gardens at the prompting of organizations promoting tourism. This is not an insignificant choice, given the vital role household food production has played in social reproduction on the household level and the strengthening of kinship networks across rural and urban space in times of economic difficulty in Romania and the region more broadly (Swain 1999; Smith 2007; Stan 2000; Burawoy, Krotov, and Lytkina 2000; Taylor 2016.).

Much of what I have discussed here illustrates the production of a local place, yet it also produces, as we have seen it framed in *tánchàz*, a "national" scale of culture. The production of national scale as it relates to the politics of citizenship is illustrated in events in the village of Szék, the village from which the movement borrowed the term and form of *tánchàz* and which was among the first to have held annual dance camps.[45] In these events, we can see a very clear connection to the Hungarian state and territory as a "kin state," as an actor, and as a scale in the making, and its deep relationship to everyday life and social reproduction. In 2002, an election year in Hungary, I was attending a dance camp in Szék (Romanian: Sic) when Viktor Orbán gave an address on the town square on the village's local holiday commemorating the survival of villagers after a Tatar attack (1717). It might have seemed an odd place for Orbán to visit on his campaign trail. This was, after all, years before his government would grant dual citizenship and these villagers would be eligible to vote in Hungarian elections. I did, however, hear villagers refer to Orbán as "our prime minister" when he visited the dance camp that day.

Gergő Pulay (2007) writes of this same event in the context of his research on the dynamics of labor migration of men from Szék to Hungary to work in the highly exploitative construction industry. Despite their treatment by day, these men were celebrated at night as culture bearers at *tánchàz* events in Hungary. In an interview, Pulay highlighted the glaring contradictions on that St. Bertalan's Day. Orbán arrived several hours late in the company of Bishop László Tőkés, and security arrangements blocked the minivans that would carry these villagers back to Budapest from entering town via its one street leading from the highway, requiring a long walk to the reach them.[46] Those same workers, dressed in the traditional straw hats and blue vests that signify Szék disappeared one by one, and then more conspicuously in larger numbers, from the ceremonies, walking to the end of the village to catch the buses in order to arrive back in Budapest in time for Monday morning work.

While as migrant laborers, these villagers faced epithets (they are often labeled "Romanian") and exploitation, at this ritual event and at *tánchàz* events in Hungary, Pulay argues, their role was reversed. In these cases, they stood as symbols of perseverance, as models for the preservation of cultural values, from whom "the Hungarians should learn" (unnamed Fidesz politician cited in Pulay 2007, 5). Nationalism—that is, becoming "supporters of the Hungarian right wing"—Pulay argues, was "the only way to express their lack of dignity in the labor market."

Pulay told me that migrant workers from Szék organized pro-Fidesz "civic circles" in the period following. Years later, after the Fidesz

Fig. 7.3 A crowd waits for Orbán's address, Szék (Sic), 2004. Hi8 video still by the author.

government legislated dual citizenship, over-the-border Hungarians would be a significant source of votes for the party in the 2014 and 2018 elections (Szymanowska 2011; Streda, 2018). Although some effects of dual citizenship and related politics beyond Orbán and Fidesz's electoral success have been documented, particularly a deepened relationship with Hungarian state apparatus (Kiss 2018), how the situation of these new citizens has changed regarding labor exploitation in Hungary is unclear.[47]

Jumping scale, we see how *táncház* activities in Hungary and in Transylvania fit into the dynamics of the production not simply of Hungarian bodies/sensibilities, of individual Transylvanian villages, or of the scale of an "imagined nation." They are also entwined with the production of the scale of Hungarian citizenship, or, said otherwise, the Hungarian state itself. This production of scale gives deeper meaning to the binary logic of the antimigrant politics Orbán has become famous for since 2015. As migrants to (and mostly moving through) Hungary, who are not ethnic Hungarians, are disencouraged through fences, legislation, and struggles with the EU over migrant relocation quotas, their supporters are constructed by Orbán and Fidesz as un-Hungarian.[48] At the same time, over-the-border Hungarians, whom Orbán has taken to calling "Hungarians living in external homeland" (*külhoni magyarok*) (Kiss 2018) and who are constructed as more Hungarian than these Hungarian citizens, are now able to participate in processes of Hungarian state formation as dual citizens.

CONCLUSION

Bringing the referendum on dual citizenship, the making of Hungarian place in Transylvania, and the making of the scale of the Hungarian state together, this chapter has aimed to make clear some of the processes at work in the polyvalent production of ethnonationalism in the neoliberal and postsocialist moment. In the "postsocialist" moment (on a global scale, that is), the dominance of culture talk is related to transformations of citizenship regimes connected to shifts in global capitalism that drive innovations in the use of culture. Within these dynamics, heritagization appears as a form of (neo)liberal governance which revalues cultural practices and supports the cultivation of particularly ethnonational selfhood, an affect, in an era characterized by the association of culture with property. Despite the stated intent to protect diversity and cultivate respect for it while also recognizing the "universal values of mankind," efforts to safeguard heritage share common logics with their seeming opposite: the attacks on diversity associated with ethnonationalism and "populism."

On the global scale, cultural practices, defined increasingly as intangible heritage, are coming to be defined as a kind of collective property, often of an ethnonational kind. On the local scale, as collective property associated with socialism was dismantled, new opportunities emerged around this concept at the same time that languages of *nép/narod/the people* and nation took on a central role in explaining patterns of elite reproduction and corruption in the transition. The demise of social citizenship associated with (neo)liberalization has been felt as a dispossession, while "culture" has become expedient in ways that bring local ethnonationalist and (what today is being called) "populist" logics close to global approaches to cultural rights and cultural management that claim liberal (and sometimes leftist or anticolonial) genealogies.

Táncház's roles today, simultaneously as a critique of civil society encroachment along with neoliberal state formation, an associative practice constituting a form of civil society, a site of modern power, and a representation of a supranational heritage regime claiming to cultivate respect for diversity by promoting the preservation of cultural practices associated with the ethnonation, are not easy to separate.[49]

Struggles over cultivation of civil society can be seen as part of a struggle over the production of capitalist space itself. Attention to the production of scale tunes us in to the processes that produce national scale in a dialectic of making places of ethnonational tradition, or heritage, and the making of nation-states. These are messy processes. As William Roseberry (1994) writes, the need to speak in a language in which one can be heard may force actors to articulate themselves in a dominant code, a common discursive framework. This does not necessarily indicate consent, however, as hegemony is never complete (Roseberry 1994; see also Hall 1988).[50]

The logic of heritagization has polyvalent outcomes in part because of the way that its different functions are pursued by different sets of actors under different circumstances. Yet the current salience of ethnonational thinking (culture talk, if you will) in the region cannot be explained without attention the cultivating work, *Bildung*, of heritagization under the shifting conditions of citizenship and property that have constituted postsocialism, reorganizing the everyday lives of both *tánchaz*-goers from Hungary and Transylvanian villagers.

Although I have pointed to certain trends, these dynamics do not have only one result. For example, the production of Hungarian identity as primary has not rolled out smoothly in Transylvania. While of the 45 percent of Transylvanian Hungarians who had taken on Hungarian citizenship by 2018, many felt obliged (perhaps even impassioned) to vote for Fidesz, the majority of them also continue assert a "regional" identity over a "Hungarian" one (Kiss 2018). And, in the context of *tánchaz*, the production of a national repertoire of dance/music remains in tension with its need for particular places and their associated traditions. The expansion of the Hungarian state into Romania via ethnic Hungarian dual citizens also reveals this contradiction, gesturing toward, as it does, the liberal ideal of ethnational self-determination via the nation-state.

NOTES

1. This has been the common term used to refer to Hungarians in the countries contiguous with Hungary who are not a typical but rather an accidental diaspora, having ended up in other countries due to changing borders (Kiss 2018). Fidesz favors the term "Hungarians living in external homeland" (Kiss 2018).

2. The monopoly power of private property (whether finance or land) is "both the beginning and the endpoint of all capitalist activity" (Harvey 2001a, 397).

3. Cyprus, the Czech Republic, Estonia, Latvia, Lithuania, Malta, Poland, Slovakia, and Slovenia also joined the EU on May 1, 2004.

4. In the referendum, 37.35 percent of eligible voters participated; 25 percent of the voting population was needed on either side for either result to be valid. The question of the privatization of hospitals and health care was initiated by the tiny Hungarian Workers' Party. The question on citizenship for over-the-border Hungarians was initiated by the World Federation of Hungarians (MVSZ), an NGO dedicated to Hungarians in the diaspora, once headed by Csoóri (M. Kovács 2005, 55; see also Waterbury 2010; Kürti 2001).

5. Of those voting, 51.5 percent were in favor of granting citizenship rights, and 48.4 percent opposed it; 65 percent of those who partook voted to keep health services in state hands, with 34.9 percent against.

6. This kind of abstention strategy is still being used: in 2016 in the referendum regarding the rejection EU migrant quotas, and in a 2017 "national consultation" (a survey sent our by the government) that asked questions about "stopping Brussels." Orbán claimed a mandate regarding the former, despite the lack of turnout, leading many to conclude that the Hungarian public supported him on this.

7. This was a counterargument frequently employed by opponents of a yes vote to those claiming the referendum was really just a way to protect Transylvanians entering "the motherland," Hungary, from the financial requirements of crossing into the EU, which most could not afford. Romania was slated to, and did indeed, enter the EU in 2007.

8. For "playing along," the speaker uses a term very familiar to *táncház*-goers. The verb describes the role of the *kontrás*, the chordal viola player who plays a rhythm part (as opposed to the melody) in a traditional folk band.

9. In her book *Jótékony nemzet: Szolidaritás és hatalom a kisebbségi magyarok segítésében* (The charitable nation: Solidarity and power in the support of Hungarian minorities) Zakariás (2018) explores the vicissitudes of this "empathy."

10. This is the case while *táncház* social activities remain popular and the numbers of people versed in folk dance as mother tongue continue to grow with the help of professionalization, the institutionalization of an educational framework, and a strong focus on youth (Javorszky 2013). The emphasis on exposing children to folk tradition and the proliferation of youth-focused *táncház* activities calls into focus the question of the political potential of future *táncház*-goers.

11. *Szamizdat* is the term used to refer to underground or illegal publications produced during the socialist period, usually with political content or intent.

12. Adam Seligman draws on T. H. Marshall's distinctions among political, civil, and social citizenship. Marshall defines political rights as the "right to participate in the exercise of political power as a member of a body invested with political authority or as an elector of the members of such a body" and civil rights as those "necessary for individual freedom—liberty of person, freedom of speech, thought and faith, the right to own property and to conclude valid contracts, and the right to justice . . .;" (T. H. Marshall, quoted in Seligman 1992, 113).

13. The "Pink Tide" (wave of leftist governments in several countries) in Latin America that would gain strength in the following is a notable exception. Far more common was the adoption of neoliberal policies by the left, a condition related to what Chantal Mouffe (2009) refers to as the "post-political," a "consensus at the middle that suggests that with the disappearance of the adversarial model of politics, democracy has become more mature and that antagonisms have been overcome."

14. See Zsuzsa Gille (2016) for how conflicts between supranational organizations like the EU and local economic interests and their expression in "nationalist" terms.

15. An interesting adaptation to this perceived condition during my fieldwork period was the Hun movement, in which individuals tried on the basis of genetic material to establish their identity as a Hun minority, eligible for minority status. The implication was that they are the "real Hungarians," a minority among other citizens of Hungary. See also Szombati (2019) and Szalai (2013) on the production of racial conflict related to welfare-state provisions that brought Jobbik and Fidesz to their current positions of power.

16. Particularly relevant to us is the Hungarian state's commitment to "Hungarians living over the borders" and the formulation in Romania's constitution: "national sovereignty belongs to the (ethnic) Romanian people" (Verdery 1996, 295).

17. The "diasporic" vote was influential, for example, in the 2007 elections in Croatia and in 2014 and 2018 in Hungary. I use the word *diaspora* here also for "over the border" populations.

18. In the region, religious denomination is tied closely to ethnicity (historically referred to in terms of nations and nationalities). For historical reasons, ethnic Hungarians tended to be Roman Catholic, Lutheran, Unitarian, or Calvinist, while Romanians tended to belong to Eastern Orthodox or Unionate (Greek Catholic) churches. Protestantism spread widely in part because of perceptions under Habsburg rule of Catholicism as the religion of the Habsburg oppressor. The Habsburgs colonized areas that had been depopulated due to ongoing war with the Ottoman Empire. It also increased the Roman Catholic fold through establishment of the Unionate church (in which union was made with the Roman Catholic Church, while the Eastern rite was retained). On the relationship of ethnicity or nationalities and nations to religion in the region, see Verdery (1983) and Sugár (1969).

19. These higher education institutions in Cluj predated the names being used here.

20. "The conduct of conduct" is among Foucault's (1994, 237) most useful formulations of governmentality.

21. On the process, see UNESCO (2011) and Taylor (2016).

22. Whitsun is the Christian festival of Pentecost, the seventh Sunday after Easter. It commemorates the descent of the Holy Spirit on Christ's disciples (Acts 2).

23. In Romanian, Uniunea Democrată Maghiară din România (UDMR). This party has dominated ethnic Hungarian political representation in Romania and has pushed for decentralization "in the spheres of education, culture, health care, and economy," hoping to lead to administrative autonomy for Hungarians (Radio Free Europe 2004b). Founded in 1989, the party has been part of government coalitions several times since 1996. Competing organizations critique RMDSZ's approach, which has relied on the idea that democratization in general can lead to equality for Hungarians and requires the party to cooperate with leading Romanian parties. See Kiss (2018) on Fidesz's attempt to create an alternative power block after the legislation of dual citizenship, and the eventual cooperation with RMDSZ.

24. Szilvay (2017) points to a long tradition dating to Bartok of struggles over the provenance of shared tunes.

25. See Szedlacsek (2015) for an analysis on the construction of Szeklerness in contrast with both Hungarian and Romanian and the politics of memory after 1989. See Verdery (1983, 83–86) for a historical sketch of the position of Szeklers, autonomy and territory vis-à-vis Hungarian and Habsburg rulers.

26. Although not traditionally seen as a nationality (as there is no Roma nation-state or aspiring nation-state), Roma are rarely included the Hungarian or Romanian people in the ethnic sense. While Roma were enslaved in parts of what is now Romania until the mid-nineteenth century, the Habsburg, Austro-Hungarian, and Hungarian states pursued a variety of assimilation policies, including forcibly taking children from their families, and structural discrimination remains the norm. The inability to incorporate Roma into the *nép* illustrates the ethnonational pull on the language of the people. Attempts to assimilate Roma in socialist Hungary were accompanied by denial of the existence of said group. For more, see Dupcsik (2009), Fosztó (2018), Beck (1989), and Stewart (1997).

27. Hooker (2005, 2008) discusses the disdain and fascination toward Roma music/dance forms in *táncház* settings, and sees the embrace of the *csingerálás* as a kind of carnivalesque masquerade of the other, in this case, aiding women to step outside gendered aspects of most Hungarian dances. See Pulay (2014) for discussion of the potentialities offered by Roma dancehouses for overcoming othering. In Budapest in 2018 and 2019, I attended some folk clubs that did not utilize *táncház* pedagogy. According to some of musicians I spoke with there, one purpose of the event was to employ "Gypsy" musicians who have lost clientele in the countryside due to the loss of tradition and also find themselves less essential to *táncház* events.

28. See Hooker (2013) on the history of this dispossession going back to the mid-nineteenth century.

29. See M. Kovács (1992) on such contradictions regarding the perceptions of Hungarians about Jews.

30. As mentioned elsewhere, Transylvania has its own revival movement, which intertwines with the one I am discussing. Varga (2016) observes the effects of Transylvanian revivalists as well.

31. Interviews often revealed complicated and uncomfortable battles among stakeholders in these events. In addition, village women I spoke to resented the late-night activities and increased alcohol drinking of their husbands, behavior that codes as authentic and desirable to many *táncház*-goers.

32. See Böröcz and Kovács (2001) for a discussion of the Eastern Enlargement of the EU. See Stroe (2014) on the Hungarian government's alleged plans to purchase farmland in Szeklerland.

33. I did meet several Hungarian *táncház*-goers who employed Transylvanian Hungarians, many of whom commented that Transylvanian Hungarians were honest and worked harder than Hungarians.

34. Examples include a café in one Transylvanian town displaying a sign that read, "Entrance to Hungarian citizens prohibited," on December 7 in the window to protest the outcome of the referendum. An ethnic Hungarian professor at the Public Administration College in Santo-Gheorghe announced his plan to cease teaching in the Hungarian language and return his status card to the Hungarian government in protest (Radio Free Europe 2004a). The Speaker of the Hungarian Parliament Katalin Szili (of MSZP) was booed when taking part in the celebration of a Hungarian writer born in Kosice (Kassa), Slovakia. "Several demonstrators held banners criticizing the negative attitude of the socialists in the recent referendum about the dual citizenship of Hungarians beyond the borders" (*Magyar Nemzet* 2004).

35. Located forty kilometers northeast of Cluj/Kolozsvár, in the "Transylvanian heath."

36. In the 1970s, laborers who moved or commuted to Cluj from here took part in events connected to Transylvanian *táncház* movement.

37. Beyond that, there are others in Hungary, many expressly for children.

38. In 2004, I asked about the availability of EU funds. Most organizers I spoke with anticipated that this would be an important source in the future but were concerned that they lacked the skills to write the necessary proposals. They relied much more on networks connecting them to funding sources.

39. In 2006, one camp listed prices as the following: 125 euro (approximately $154) (for those without sponsorship); 17,000 Hungarian forint (approximately $68) for those arriving from Hungary (subsidized with sponsorship from the Hungarian government); 1,650 lei (approximately $51) for Transylvanian participants (subsidized with sponsorship of the Romanian government and RMDSZ).

40. Although very few (if any) ethnic Romanians enroll in the camps (which can also include weeklong lodging and board and access to lessons), they do provide room and board to camp-goers in some villages. Local villagers, including some few Romanians, do often attend events in the evening, or the gala some camps have toward the end, to which they are, in most cases, admitted without a fee.

41. I learned they were designated as such by signs posted on the roadside.

42. Authority over tourism institutions was shifted to the Ministry for Small and Medium Enterprises, Commerce, Tourism and Liberal Professions in 2007 (Daniela-Luminitja, Mitrut, and Gruiescu 2009). This may explain why the website mentioned previously ceased to function.

43. In 2004, I ran into RMDSZ's vice-president for cultural (*művelődési*) and religious affairs at a camp. A folk musician himself, he articulated RMDSZ's concern with making Hungarian folk culture and its community-related values relevant to today's youth.

44. Szabó (2012) explores disparities among villages and regions regarding the benefits of tourism in Szeklerland.

45. People from Szék call it a town (Székváros), a tradition that dates to Szék's status as a free town in feudal days, due to its location near a salt mine. The town is called Sic (salt) in Romanian.

46. Tőkés, a pastor of the Reformed Church, is known as a hero of the ethnic Hungarian cause in Transylvania, and an instigator of the revolution that overthrew Ceauşescu. For more on his changing relationship with RMDSZ and Fidesz, see Kürti (2001), Brubaker et al. (2006), and Kiss (2008).

47. Kiss (2018) suggests that this relationship works in similar ways as it does in Hungary to reinforce Fidesz power. See Martin (2017, 276) on the "state capture" intertwined with "cronyism" through which state funds (many from the EU) have been funneled to loyalist oligarchs through multiple paths in Hungary.

48. See Novak (2018) on the attack on scholar Attila Melegh, for one example.

49. While the civic cultivation enacted through "safeguarding intangible heritage" is a product of a universal value package of homogeneity (and differences on certain scales), it cultivates understanding of heritage and diversity in a framework of *equivalency of differences* (Taylor 2016; Meiksins Wood 1990). Capitalism has always worked through differentiation, or "racialization" (Robinson 2000). As Stuart Hall (2018) points out, we must seek to understand how neoliberalization, with its dominant tendency to homogenize, works as a hegemonic "system of *con-forming difference*" if we want to discover where and how "resistances and counterstrategies are likely successfully to develop."

50. But we have spied precisely the revaluing processes UNESCO hopes to encourage—not to preserve traditional practices as such, but to adapt them to a "postsocialist" and neoliberal environment and "solve" economic and social problems wrought by it (Taylor 2009, 2016). See Coombe (2012, 378) for a take on heritage regimes and "neoliberal governmentality" that "focuses less on the rollback of the state associated with neoliberalism and more on a new decentralization and distribution of governmental powers."

Conclusion

I arrived at dawn to Móricz Zsigmond square in Buda, in a little
minibus that had brought me from the verdant hills of Transylvania
after weeks of folk dance camps. There it was: the lowest six feet of the
entire wall of a large apartment building completely plastered with
posters featuring the map of Greater Hungary, with the words
"Justice for Hungary" and "Hungary Deserves More."[1] That was
the summer of 2004. It was when I first learned of Jobbik.
 —*from my field notes, July 2004*

I HAVE PRESENTED TÁNCHÁZ NOT simply as a revival of folk dance and music but as a folk movement and an associational form that, like *népi* movements before it, cultivates an alternative framework of sense and collective action and embodies a form of folk critique. All of these are related to political personhood. I have illuminated how under today's specific political and economic conditions, *táncház* is implicated in the cultivation of ethnonational sensibilities, in a postsocialist/neoliberalizing context in which culture talk is ubiquitous. The political implications of the emergence of such a community of sense are not necessarily what revivalists, investors in development tourism, cultural rights activists, or promoters of heritage protection on different scales intend. This community of sense is the result of the dialectic of form/material practice and historically contingent meaning, under changing, yet specific, material circumstances. Implicated in the current convergence is the threatened condition of social citizenship, a symptom of the "postsocialist" condition, changes in Hungary's position in the world system, and transformations in the contours of

Fig. 8.1 Posters showing borders of Greater Hungary with "Justice for Hungary" and "Hungary Deserves More" at bus stop, Moricz Zsigmond Körtér, 2004. Hi8 video still by the author.

the political economy. They also gesture toward the never-ending work of the nation-state project and the reification of the nation.

Neither *táncház* nor the rise of contemporary Hungarian ethnonational politics can be understood if treated simply as local phenomena. They must be approached with careful attention to the significance of a globalizing idea of culture and its relation to supranational organizations, exemplified by the heritage regime, which appears as a form of national *Bildung* organized at the supranational level, operating at a particular conjuncture within the capitalist world system. What struggles are waged in the name of folk, the people, is a question of hegemony, at a moment when nation-states have little power to choose how to distribute the wealth their populations produce. The globally popular story about Hungary and Hungarians today is a linear one of a nation that has been and remains both ethnonationalist and authoritarian to its core. Are we left to agree with this after what has been discussed in this book? If indeed there is no essence to Hungarianness, then Hungarians today cultivate themselves under conditions that

Fig. 8.2 Posters showing borders of Greater Hungary with "Justice for Hungary" and "Hungary Deserves More" at bus stop, Móricz Zsigmond Körtér, 2004. Hi8 video still by the author.

are rarely of their choosing. In short, the story that draws such neat lines from the ethnonationalist postures and policies of the current government and the Hungarian people as a somehow naturally racist and authoritarian nation, fails to inquire how hegemony is forged at specific historical conjunctures. Examining the cultivation of ethnonational political selfhood in relationship to the enduring concept of the people/folk I have hoped to place them in a relational history of nation making and the production of the nation-state that have been so central to capitalism, and to try to understand the experiment with socialism in the light of civic cultivation.

THE CURRENT SITUATION

A decade after my 2004–5 fieldwork, as the so-called refugee crisis unfolded on the Balkan route, Hungary captured the spotlight of international news as the Orbán government erected fences on the Serbian and Croatian borders. It took actions and enacted policies that disrupted the mobility of migrant/refugees seeking refuge in Hungary or, for most of them, simply to travel through en route to countries where they hoped to seek asylum. In 2016, the government claimed that a referendum, formally nullified by low voter turnout, had given it a clear mandate to reject the quota of migrants assigned for resettlement in Hungary in accordance with EU policy. In the past several years, Fidesz, once seen as on the center right, has been noted for its increasing authoritarianism, illustrated in the replacement of the constitution with the Basic Law, placement of people close to the party in positions of power across the spectrum of state institutions (also those in the cultural sphere), attacks on media, and a systematic concentration of economic and political power with a strategic use of EU funds. Despite, or because of, Fidesz's two-thirds majority in the 2010 and 2014 cycles, support grew for the far-right party Jobbik, which has long replaced MIÉP in parliament, and continues to dance with Fidesz across the supposed lines of "conservative" and "far right." Liberal and leftist parties, in flux both organizationally and ideologically, despite their coalitional efforts, have failed to gain or hold significant power, partly due to a vacuum of legitimacy and partly due to the electoral laws passed under Fidesz reign. It is broadly agreed that opposition speech is suppressed, and the government has introduced laws and methods to stop those who help migrants, slow and delegitimate the foreign funding of civil society organizations, control the press, and make both the Central European University, funded by George Soros, and the discipline of gender studies, illegal. Perhaps the low turnout for the 2016 referendum on refugee resettlement (despite the overwhelming support of rejection by those who did vote) tells us something about how this suppression works.[2]

Fidesz came to wield unprecedented political power following protests beginning in 2006 in which the MSZP prime minister Ferenc Gyurcsány was exposed as having lied about the economy in the lead-up to his reelection. The party won an unprecedented two-thirds majority in parliament in 2010 and 2014 (together in alliance with the Christian Democratic People's Party) while MSZP's partner SZDSZ disappeared altogether. One of Fidesz's first acts of legislation after coming to power in 2010 was to pass the dual citizenship law. Fidesz's rewriting of the constitution as the Basic Law in 2011 (and subsequent amendments) was justified as "completing" the regime change.[3] In 2014, Jobbik gained twenty-three seats in parliament, compared to the twenty-eight gained by the Unity coalition desperately formed by MSZP and four liberal parties. Since 2009, when it sent three MEPs to the European Parliament, and after making international news for its militia arm's policing of "Gypsy" crime, the Jobbik party (anchored in youth associations and paramilitary organizations) has been called the only counter-hegemonic bloc to neoliberalism (Fábry 2015a, 2015b; see also Halmai 2011 on Jobbik's rise). The party "sutured" local experiences into a national rhetoric on "Gypsy" crime (Szombati 2018) that builds on and provides a basis for the opposition of Hungarians to others, whether Roma, Jews, or (nonethnic Hungarian) migrants and refugees. Even while working together with Fidesz, Jobbik "presented itself as a genuine 'antisystemic force'" (Fábry 2015b).[4] Fidesz, at least for now, has managed to retain its position, selectively incorporating Jobbik rhetoric and policy regarding a "work based society" while often "eschewing direct references to ethnicity (be it 'Gypsy criminals' or 'Jewish conspirators')." (Szombati 2018, 165).[5] Jobbik tries now to place itself toward the center from Fidesz.

From Heritage to the Decolonial Option? Bad Pupils of Europe on the East-West Slope

Approaching civil society, as we did at the beginning of this book, as a locus of modern/colonial power situated in the dynamic of civilization and *Kultur* and the making of nation-states, we are left with the question of what kind of civic cultivation *táncház* is implicated in, in this age of culture talk. It would be irresponsible of me to claim to know how *táncház*-goers are talking about politics or how they are poised to vote today. Nor can I say how they have related in their everyday lives or at the polls with (non-ethnic Hungarian) migrants and refugees. What I can write about instead is the knowledge being produced by critical Hungarian, East European, and Balkan thinkers on the left at this conjuncture. Their critiques, which gesture toward the decolonial, overlap in some ways with folk critiques that were part of the institutional and methodological legacy from which *táncház* emerged but has a distinct genealogy. This array of thought/practice articulates a counter-language to culture talk and ethnonationalist essentialisms and offers a powerful critique of global capitalism and a nuanced approach to its effects in this region, developing a useful perspective from which to view fellow citizens, neighbors, and migrants from near or far. Among these writers are those seeking to recognize and valorize the knowledges and experiences of people and peoples within the region in a manner that offers an alternative to heritagization or "museification" (Popovici and Pop 2016). While these writers and activists place themselves on the left, among them are ethnographers, practitioners and lovers of folk art, and advocates of a left-wing patriotism that contrasts with the nationalism of the right (Fourth Republic n.d.).

Scholars of and from the region (Wolff 1994; Bakić-Hayden 1995; Todorova 1997) have long identified the workings of an Orientalism in postsocialist Europe that encourages those in each region to view cultures and religions to its South and East as less than at work in the processes of what now seems like an unending transition. Milica Bakić-Hayden

(1995) coined the term *nesting orientalism* to capture how a group which (re)produces the Orientalized other can simultaneously be subject to this othering by another group. In this paradigm, Islam is more Eastern or other than other cultures of the region, Orthodox cultures are more Eastern than Catholic ones, and so on. Writing of how this hierarchization stretches across the Balkans, Maria Todorova (1997) introduced the phrase *nesting balkanisms*, to speak of the dynamic of identity construction in which the Balkans are perceived of as both part of Europe and its "darker side." During my 2004–5 fieldwork, I encountered many arguments made against Turkey joining the EU, in which such Orientalisms were central. We see them also in the rhetoric employed very publicly on billboards and elsewhere by Fidesz in the lead-up to the referendum regarding the call to reject Muslim migrant/refugees to preserve Christian values (see Böröcz and Sarkar 2017). But "double consciousness" (Fanon 1967) associated with these Orientalisms are not isolated in political rhetoric, or in academic discourse, they are present in everyday life. The authors whom I tentatively associate here with decolonial critique not only build on the critical understandings of the way in which Orientalisms work to reduce options to a false binary between Western democratic and local ethnonational options but also take as central the task of "thinking otherwise of and about" the region (Grubačić 2010, 262).

Attila Melegh's (2006) analysis of sociological and symbolic meanings of the East-West binary in Europe after the end of the Cold War uncovers this valuing process in liberal characterizations of East-West, while also highlighting polarizing effects of ethnonationalism. He shows how an image of an "East-West slope," that is, a civilizational slope tilting downward from West to East, has emerged from the hegemonic liberal utopia. A key factor of Melegh's argument, for which he draws on the work of József Böröcz, is "the ongoing narrative of transition" by which teleological modernization operates through the mode of comparison (Melegh 2006, 29). Transition thus has not only been a mechanism by which the region has been reincorporated as a semiperiphery in the capitalist world system (Tichindeleanu 2016) but has also been a central mechanism in perpetuating an image of a "backward Eastern Europe ... perpetually just about to become white *enough*, capitalist *enough*" (Popovici and Pop 2015). In this process it devalues and distracts from quite real experiences and histories lived by people in the region, whether state socialism and its many accompanying experiments and peculiarities (including the houses of culture examined here), the fluidity and mixture of ethnic identity, or projects such as the Balkan Federation. The line drawn between the civilized and its other(s) is quite clearly an effect of operations of power, and conveniently pits so-termed Easterners against each other in this struggle to be, or be seen as, "more civilized."

Countering the effects of modern/colonial power can only be achieved with analysis of how they are made possible. These Eastern European and Balkan authors refer to the region's peripheral position, and the processes by which it is peripheralized, as a starting point for critical analysis (Živković and Medenica 2013; Živković 2013) and action (Peripheralizing Europe 2015; Popovici and Pop 2016, Tichindeleanu 2016). Two prominent analytical reference points for many of these works are the world-system approach and decolonial theory, often in combination. These collective and individual authors perform the tasks of uncovering the unequal geopolitical power relations and conditions of uneven development in which these polities unfold, in which their politicians maneuver, and in which their populations register discontent. They also interrogate how and why people within the region come to adopt the attitudes of inferiority that attract them to liberal promises of progress and democracy made in the name of the West and Europe or the rhetorical strategies of local ethnonational entrepreneurs. They do this toward the end of a decolonial option that promises to open up solidarities beyond those with a Europe that does not fully embrace the region, even its members of the EU.

Using the terms *democratic antipopulism* and *populist antidemocratism* (and in Hungarian, using the Latinate variant *populizmus*, not *népi*), Ágnes Gagyi (2016), a member of Hungary's Helyzet (Position) Working Group, analyzes the strategies of the two blocs of Hungarian elites acting from within Hungary's condition of dual dependency (Gagyi and Gerőcs 2019), explaining how the right has managed its current victory. The first bloc, the socialist-liberal coalition, had the "upper hand in the country's FDI [foreign direct investment] and credit-led development," while the second, making up the "would be national bourgeoisie" (i.e., Fidesz), appealed to the middle classes of the socialist era, dispossessed through the redistributions discussed previously (Gagyi 2016, 354). The first tended to embrace Euro-Atlantic integration and liberal ideals, while the second cultivated a "nationalist critique of Euro-Atlantic power," offering the solution of a strong state capable of resisting international capital and furthering "Hungarian" interests (ibid., 355; see also Gagyi and Gerőcs 2019).

Gagyi stresses that neither bloc of capitalist elites has actually represented the interests of a population "previously fully proletarianized" at the time of the regime change (Gagyi 2016, 355). Pursuing market solutions, and demanding patience regarding democratic results, the first bloc capitalized on its relationship to democracy. Yet it suffered from an intellectual elitism that dismissed critiques of its policies and expressions of economic discontent "not only as irrational, socialist-communist-statist, irresponsible, or childish" but also in terms central to the second bloc's own bridging technique, as proof of "popular nationalism, itself a threat to democratic progress" (ibid., 356). The second bloc, claiming to protect national wealth from ex-Communist nomenklatura as well as foreign capital, "made symbolic gestures of inclusion towards social groups who mostly suffered from its economic project to establish a national bourgeoisie" (Gagyi 2016, 355).

The socialist-liberal coalition built legitimacy by defending a democracy that it equated with the introduction of Western-type institutions and the help of Western hegemonic actors in the face local resistance from national interests they labeled antisemitic, nationalist, and populist. The kind of democracy the first bloc stood for was made clear by its "introduction of the first major austerity package in 1995, followed by two decades of reform talk" which contrasted these reforms with "irresponsibility, nationalism and populism" (Gagyi 2016, 357). Once in power, the second bloc, seemingly representing the national bourgeoisie, made use of the socialist-liberal bloc's denial of "the significance of economic grievances" and its symbolic disparaging of the local population and its values (ibid., 356).

Gagyi links her analysis to decolonial thinkers from Frantz Fanon (1967) to Walter Mignolo and Madina Tlostanova (2008), who take the question of identification and valuing to be of key importance in both the way in which global hierarchies are experienced locally and to the task of escaping this binary of nonalternatives (see Popovici and Pop 2016). Nevertheless, today, what Gagyi calls "populist antidemocratism" (what Orbán would call illiberal democracy and which builds on the "colonial self love" Gagyi opposes to "self colonizing emancipation") is in the driver's seat, even as working people and an increasingly impoverished population, some now employed in Orbán's underpaying and disciplinary workfare programs (among them, those who built the fences to stop migrants from crossing the Croatian and Serbian borders [Day 2015]) remain or find themselves placed outside of the circle of beneficiaries (see also Koltai 2018; J. Martin 2017).

While such analyses tell us much about the cultural politics of what is called populism today, there remains good reason to question the language of populism itself. We need to ask the sober question of what work it does as an accusation (Taylor 2018; Creed and Taylor 2020). Used by the first bloc and Western commentators to delegitimate the credibility of the opinions of regular people, the term tends to conflate demagogic trickery and regular people, leaving few options for seeing people's, or popular, movements in their (albeit often problematic) making (Creed and Taylor 2020, Taylor 2020). In the very last issue of the largest print circular in Hungary, *Népszabadság*, before its sudden and controversial closure on October 8, 2016, Gábor Czene articulates Gáspár Miklós Tamás's critique of the use of the term to describe Fidesz (Czene 2016). Tamás argues that the term *populism*, which describes an antielite position, is the least apt term to describe the strategy pursued by Fidesz, which favors middle-class citizens. Rather than building on popular movements, he argues, Orbán works toward demobilizing society; the strategies taken by his centralizing, étatist party are the very opposite of populism. Tamás points to the fact that the liberal press constantly conflates populism with demagoguery, the latter of which Orbán can certainly be accused of.

But Tamás also argues that Hungary has no real history of populism and makes no mention of *népi* movements. Although arguing that a left populism (in Hungary or anywhere) is not a real answer and that populism cannot be functional as a manner of running a government, he makes the point that populists believe that the *köznép* (commonfolk) is ethically superior to the ruling class and finds it unfortunate that he sees no sign of this attitude in today's Hungary. This problem of inferiority and superiority is one that the writers I focus on here take seriously and present as a very different problematic than liberals (and also quite differently than the most sympathetic approaches to populism on the left) (LaClau 2005; Mouffe 2009). Their approach is one of "giving voice to the diversity of experiences silenced by the Eurocentric narrative" (Gagyi 2016) within a capitalist world system, giving value to them in a way that points to alternatives that cannot be reduced to nationalist narratives and simplified identity.

Recent years have also seen an attempt to revive the politics of the interwar *népi* movement with a critical twist (Kolozsi 2016). This move can in no way be reduced to the populism associated with Fidesz or to the processes we have seen associated with heritagization as it seeks to make visible a broad swath of the population living in the countryside and peripheries of cities as "the people." While enthusiasts of this project may be held as naive when they express hope that "Gypsies" (Kolozsi 2016) can be successfully included in their version of the *nép*, many would conclude that the term, and the *népi* movement itself, may be too entwined with the (ethno)national narrative.[6] Nevertheless, these enthusiasts suggest a revival of folk colleges for poor rural youth, including "poor Gypsies"

(Papp in Kolozsi 2016). It is also important to note that the Roma *táncház* scene (which emerged, at least in part, from the *táncház* movement) has provided (albeit limited) "space where kinds of togetherness could be tried out between Roma and non Roma participants" (Pulay 2014).[7] Roma dancehouses and folk cafés operate in spaces at the edges of the conventional *táncház* movement infrastructure, in spaces often associated with the liberal left, bringing *táncház* practices into a much more ideologically diverse environment. They also intertwine with heritagization and its vicissitudes, involvement of the world music industry, ongoing strategic use of folk culture by the government, and struggle with the closure (or reluctance) of the spaces that have hosted them under the current regime.[8]

Given the struggles faced by both Roma and ethnic Hungarians that have aided Jobbik to pit the latter against the former, particularly in the provinces, where "postpeasants" have been struck particularly hard by the economic changes (Szombati 2019), a critical evaluation of the lessons of interwar populism and its capture in a *népi-urbánus* opposition (and the related culture of antisemitism and the invisibility of Roma) is important. Can we learn something from successes of the agrarian sector and the relative autonomy agrarian workers gained for themselves in the socialist period? What kind of influence did populists, working within the government and policy sphere, such as Ferenc Erdei have on the agrarian sector?

What work is done, finally, by the antipopulism wielded by a threatened liberal elite that is shocked at the reaction to postsocialist (neo)liberalization, given the conjunctural diversity of what gets called populism in the historical dynamics of hegemony (Taylor 2018; Creed and Taylor 2020; Taylor 2020)? We need to be able to use language carefully to distinguish among "neo-liberal nationalists" (Plavšić 2016), "ethnonationalist elites" (Emin Eminagic in Gallo 2015), authoritarian governments and social movements that organize "the people" in movement formations for social justice. Regional examples of the latter in recent years include the interethnic protests against neoliberal redistributions (beginning with factory closures in Tuzla) associated with leaders of all ethnicities, and their signature popular assemblies, or plenums, during the Bosnian Spring of 2015 (Gallo 2015; Kapovic 2014). If we buy the argument that those who protest elites are always and already ethnonationalist populists, we may overlook the signs, such as "a burning government building in Tuzla, the city where it all began, with the graffiti 'death to nationalism' written on it" (Kapovic 2014) or the many organized acts of solidarity with migrants on the "Balkan Route," including in Hungary. In the same way, by remembering a locally salient language for popular movements (*népi, narodni*), and not reducing it to a binary of democratic antipopulism and populist antidemocratism, we open up an analytical space for asking how this language and the groups who mobilize it are related to ongoing processes that construct hegemonic formations.

NEOLIBERAL GOVERNANCE AND MODERN POWER:
PLURALIST CIVIL SOCIETY, CIVILIZATION AND
KULTUR, AND THE ENCLOSURE OF PEOPLE POWER

The world brands Hungary an ethnonationalist hot zone, and Orbán "the bad boy in the class" (Watson 2013), yet Hungary has been collecting kudos regarding its approach to heritage protection. Two years after the *táncház* method was inscribed onto UNESCO's list, in 2013, *Hungarian Heritage: From Roots to Revival* would be displayed and performed as one of the three main curatorial elements of the annual Smithsonian Folkways Festival on the National Mall in Washington, DC. At the festival, it functioned alongside (and interacting with) *One World, Many Voices: Endangered Languages and Cultural Heritage,* and *The Will to Adorn: African American Diversity, Style, and Identity,* which advertised the imminent opening of the National Museum of African American History and Culture. The result of the Smithsonian Museum's partnership with the Balassi Institute, funded by the Hungarian Ministry of Culture, *Hungarian Heritage: From Roots to Revival* involved the hard work and contributions of ethnographers, folklorists, revivalists, and traditional practitioners (a good proportion of the latter being over-the-border Hungarians). It is hardly conceivable that this event would have happened, and certainly in the form it took, without the *táncház* movement. Naturally, in addition to staged curations, dance lessons were underway every day in the dance barn constructed for this purpose.

Having shown that *táncház* participants hone shared sentiments through revivalist practices, and that their collective actions are involved in *transforming* society (i.e., state formation) under particular political economic conditions, I argue that a critical view toward heritage as civic cultivation should guide us as we observe specific "projects of culture" (Soysal 2009) as they entwine with what I have been calling (neo)liberal heritage governance. Specifically, we need to give attention to the tendency of supranational heritage governance to support national *Bildung* and to enforce an archipelago concept of culture expedient both to essentializing ethnonationalist politics and the assembly of monopoly powers, as property and citizenship regimes shift. "Preserving heritage," here, is a kind of cultivation of (political) personhood that interacts with complex historical roots in any place and with political and economic conditions in any particular historical moment. Contrary to UNESCO's claims to protect diversity and intangible heritage, codifying groups and its practices as it does, reinforces boundaries and thus may support ethnonationalist strife (Taylor 2009). Presented as a solution to sluggish development, heritagization is tied to an economic common sense that overlooks the processes of dispossession linked to the very market solutions offered for economic growth and well-being.

The disjunct, or perhaps perfect overlap, between international outcry about Hungarian nationalism and support for ethnonationally arranged practices of heritage protection illustrates how this locus of modern power remains invisible to us when viewed through the dominant lens of culture talk and reveals the contradictions of neoliberal heritage governance and the liberal pluralisms that lend it credibility (Meiksins Wood 1990; Taylor 2016). It also points to the ongoing work done though the tension between civilization and *Kultur* with which this book began. Postsocialist Hungary finds itself a semiperipheral nation-state within a dynamic capitalist system at a particular political economic moment. While it is easy to see Hungarian ethnonationalism as the result of local and regional chauvinisms and rightist party propaganda, even more so now than when I conducted fieldwork with *táncház*-goers in 2004 and 2005, we also know that culture is central to the workings of millennial capitalism, a crisis-prone period of a "racial capitalism" always dependent on the (re)production of hierarchized difference (Robinson 1983; Gilmore 2007). While the liberal left struggles with legitimacy and the right takes the game, new movements, strategies, and experiments have shown their faces, some explicitly espousing the decolonial option. As of now, they do not do it in the name of the *nép*, but it would be a mistake to ignore the long tradition of folk critiques. The cultivation of the nation, of national conduct or affect, of ethnonational identity and sentiment, is not simply a local affair, and how this cluster of meaning connects with the language of the people has a complex history. A decolonial path, one perhaps framed around inter/nationalist (Salaita 2016) solidarity beyond national(ist) essentialisms and nationstates will require a nuanced project of self-critique (Böröcz 2016, 2020). Recognition of the regional experience of "coloniality" and racialization of its population vis a vis Western Europeans and the peripherality of the region has to be tempered with solidarity with those who have experienced more traditional colonial and postcolonial legacies. The ethnonational and racializing impulses and histories, even of local movements that may otherwise offer a legacy within which to work, must be taken into account. I hope this book can contribute to that end.

Notes

1. "Magyarország többet érdemel!" had been an MSZP slogan in the 2002 election period. These same images appeared on billboards in 2002 (Novák 2006). I have not been able to ascertain their source.

2. See Balogh (2016) on boycott of referenda as a strategy in Hungary.

3. I cannot cover the many changes made to the constitution/Basic Law, but they include changes to the capacities of the Constitutional Court (Scheppele 2011), the institution of new electoral laws essential to Fidesz's continuing majority (Fumarola, n.d.), and the illegalization of homelessness (Taylor 2014; Misetics 2013). The preamble also acknowledges "Christianity's nation-preserving role," placing it in the European tradition, and commits "to safeguarding our heritage … the cultures and nationalities of Hungary, all values/assets of the Carpathian Basin, man-made and given by nature" (Magyarorszag Alaptörvénye 2011).

4. Jobbik did not invent the term, but rather took advantage of a longer tradition of associating "Gypsies" with criminality (Helsinki Watch 1993) and the contemporary anxieties of especially postsocialist rural "post peasants" (Szombati 2019).

5. This rhetoric nevertheless builds on the other binaries activated in Jobbik speech, such as that which pits "work shy Gypsies" against "hard working Magyars" (Szombati 2018, 74). See Kóczé (2020) on how Fidesz's seemingly less extreme approach still cultivates a "banality of evil" regarding Roma in Hungary.

6. Recent research shows that left leaning interwar populists took antisemitic postures (Pastor 2018, Tóth, Csaba Tibor 2012), raising important questions about the possibilities to draw on this tradition, and also ethnonationalism on the left. The nuanced historiography of the left in the region has been difficult for leftists to reckon with, but remains an important task. See Csaba Tibor Tóth's (2016) research on the way in which the category of antifascist was mobilized to justify retaining university employees in the socialist period who we might find hard to accept as such is one example of this.

7. It is telling, perhaps, of the tensions such a project faces, that these authors use the term "Cigány," not Roma here.

8. One example is the television competition *Fölszállott a páva* (The peacock has taken flight), shown on state television channels Duna TV and M1, and (co)sponsored by Heritage House. Its name is an explicit reference to the Repulj Páva (*Fly Peacock*) TV competition, while the show also has clear similarities to *The Voice* (the American voice competition show that aired in 2011, based on *The Voice of Holland* that aired first in 2000), and I was told by this book's anonymous reviewer that the title initially proposed was "Folksztár," in the tradition of *Megasztár* (a Hungarian voice competition show aired originally in 2003). Another example is the funding of the renovation of the Budai Vigadó and the award of the entire building to Hagyományok Háza (which involved the renaming of MMI, its relocation, and a reorganization of its roles). A third is the establishment of the Hungarikum register of not "heritage" but national "values" or "virtues" (some might say "assets") if we translate the term *érték* into English (see Hungarikum Gyüjteménye).

BIBLIOGRAPHY

Ablonczy, Balázs. 2006. *Pál Teleki (1874–1941): The Life of a Controversial Hungarian Politician.* Boulder: Social Science Monographs.
Abrams, Philip. 1988. "Notes on the Difficulty of Studying the State." *Journal of Historical Sociology* 1 (1): 58–89.
Academic Society of Romania (SAR). 2008. "Real Estate Speculations Are the Source of Many of the Fortunes in the National Top 300; on the Other Hand, Former Owners Cannot Get Back Their Properties Confiscated by the Communist Regime." SAR Policy Brief #34. http://www.sar.org.ro/files/330_Policy%20memo34EN.pdf.
Aczél, György. 1977. Introduction to *Sej, a mi lobogónkat fényes szelek fujják . . . Népi Kollégiumok 1939–1949*, edited by László Kardos. Budapest: Akadémiai Kiadó.
Akadémiai Kislexikon. 1990. Budapest: Akadémiai Kiadó.
Alexander, Catherine. 2004. "Value, Relations, and Changing Bodies: Privatization and Property Rights in Kazakhstan." In *Property in Question: Value Transformation in the Global Economy*, edited by K. Verdery, and C. Humphrey, 251–74. Oxford: Berg.
Ámon, Kata. 2015. "The Illiberal Democracy and the Revanchist City: The Spatial and Political Transformation of Budapest since 2010." *LeftEast*, February 20, 2015. https://www.criticatac.ro/lefteast/the-illiberal-democracy-in-budapest/.
Anderson, Benedict. 1984. *Imagined Communities: Reflection on the Origin and Spread of Nationalism.* London: Verso.
Arens, Katherine. 1996. "Central Europe and the Nationalist Paradigm." Working paper, Center for Austrian Studies, Minneapolis, MN.
Asad, Talal. 1993. *Genealogies of Religion.* Baltimore: Johns Hopkins University Press.
Associated Press. 2004. "Hungary Could Miss 2010 Euro Target Date." September 11, 2004.
Bakić-Hayden, Milica. 1995. "Nesting Orientalisms: The Case of Former Yugoslavia." *Slavic Review* 54 (4): 917–31.
Bakonyi, Erika. 2001. "The Táncház Guild." *Hungarian Heritage* (1) 1–2: 54–56.
Balogh, Eva. 2016. "The Only Good Answer to Orban's Referendum Is a Boycott." *Hungarian Spectrum* (blog), August 16, 2016. http://hungarianspectrum.org/2016/08/16/the-only-good-answer-to-orbans-referendum-is-a-boycott/.
Balogh, Sándor. 1990. "Population Removal and Population Exchange in Hungary after WWII." In *Ethnicity and Society in Hungary*, edited by Ferenc Glatz, 407–32. Budapest: Comité des Historiens Hongrois.
Bardos, Lajos. 1969. *Harminc Irás.* Budapest: Zeneműkiadó.
Barna, Emília, and Tamás Tofalvy, eds. 2016. *Made in Hungary: Studies in Popular Music.* New York: Taylor and Francis.
Bartha, László. 1973. "Fúvom az Éneket." *Lanyok Évkönyve.*
Bartók, Béla. 1947. "Gypsy Music or Hungarian Music?" *Musical Quarterly* 33 (2).

———. 1976. "The Influence of Peasant Music on Modern Music." In *Béla Bartók: Essays*, edited by Benjamin Suchoff, 340–344. Bartók Archive Studies in Musicology 8. New York: St. Martin's Press.

Basso, Keith. 1996. *Wisdom Sits in Places*. Albuquerque: University of New Mexico Press.

Bayer, Lili. 2017. "Viktor Orbán Courts Voters Beyond 'Fortress Hungary.'" *Politico EU*, August 22, 2017. https://www.politico.eu/article/viktor-orban-courts-voters-in-transylvania-romania-hungarian-election-2018/.

BBC News Online. 2000. "Battle for Hungary's Media." March 26, 2000. http://news.bbc.co.uk/1/hi/world/monitoring/media_reports/690851.stm.

———. 2005. "Hungary Blocks Hun Minority Bid." BBC News Online, April 12, 2005. http://news.bbc.co.uk/2/hi/europe/4435181.stm.

Beck, S., 1989. "The Origins of Gypsy Slavery in Romania." *Dialectical Anthropology*, 14 (1): 53–61.

Beck, Sam, and David Kideckel. 1989. "Resolutions: Half of Romania's Rural Settlements to Disappear." *Anthropology of East Europe Review* 8 (1–2): 38–39.

Behrendt, Andrew. 2014. "Educating Apostles of the Homeland: Tourism and 'Honismeret' in Interwar Hungary." *Hungarian Cultural Studies* 7:159–76.

"Bemutatkozás." Magyar Néprajzi Társaság. Accessed March 9, 2006. http://www.néprajz.hu/mnt/bemutatkozas.html.

Bendix, Regina. 1989. "Tourism and Cultural Displays: Inventing Traditions for Whom?" *Journal of American Folklore* 102 (404): 131–46.

Benjamin, Walter. 1969. "Theses on the Philosophy of History." In *Illuminations: Essays and Reflections*, edited by Hannah Arendt, 253–264. New York: Schocken.

Berdahl, Daphne. 1999. *Where the World Ended: Re-unification and Identity in the German Borderland*. Berkeley: University of California Press.

Bihari János Táncegyüttes. 2006. "Ferenc Novák." http://www.bihari.hu/index.php?menu=47.

Bimbó, Mihály. 2013. "A 'Népi Írók' Mozgalmáról." *Eszmélet* 99 (1): 61–78.

Bitterli, Urs. 1982. *Vadak és civilizáltak*. Budapest: Gondolat.

Blake, Janet. 2000. "On Defining the Cultural Heritage." *International and Comparative Law Quarterly* 49 (1): 61–85.

Bodnár, Judit. 2001. *Fin de Millenaire, Budapest*. Minneapolis: University of Minnesota.

Bodor, Ferenc. 1975. "Parasztzene a Nagyvárosban." *Fiúk Évkönyve 1975*. Budapest: Móra Könyvkiadó.

———. ed. 1981. *Nomád Nemzedék; Népművészet Magyarországon, 1970–1980*. Budapest: Népművelési Intézet.

Bohlman, Philip V. 1988. *The Study of Folk Music in the Modern World*. Bloomington: Indiana University Press.

Bolle-Zemp, Sylvie. 1990. "Institutionalized Folklore and Helvetic Ideology." *Yearbook for Traditional Music* 22:127–40.

———. 1996. "Pilgrimage, Politics, and the Musical Remapping of the New Europe." *Ethnomusicology* 40 (3): 375–412.

Borbándi Gyula. 1981 "A Horthy-Rendszer Anatomiája." *Új Látóhatár Válogatás, 1950–1989*, edited by Pál Szeredi, 17–36. Püski Kiadó.

———. 1989. *A Magyar Népi Mozgalom*. Budapest: Püski Kiadó.

Böröcz, József. 2001. "Introduction: Empire and Coloniality in the 'Eastern Enlargement' of the European Union." In *Empire's New Clothes: Unveiling EU-Enlargement*, edited by József Böröcz and Melinda Kovacs, 4–50. Telford, UK: Central Europe Review.

———. 2016. "An Incapacity to See Ourselves As Part of the Whole World, and the Insistence to See Ourselves As Part of Europe." *LeftEast*, December 14, 2016. https://lefteast.org/jozsef-borocz-interview-2016/.

———. 2018. "Performing Socialist Hungary in China: 'Modern, Magyar, European.'" *Cold War History* 18 (3): 1–18.

———. 2020. "Whiteness: 'Race,' Capitalism, US, Eastern Europe." *LeftEast*, July 27, 2020. https://lefteast.org/whiteness-race-capitalism-us-eastern-europe/.

Böröcz, József, and Melinda Kovács, eds. 2001. *Empire's New Clothes: Unveiling EU Enlargement*. Telford, UK: Central Europe Review.

Böröcz, József, and Mahua Sarkar. 2017. "The Unbearable Whiteness of the Polish Plumber and the Hungarian Peacock Dance around 'Race.'" *Slavic Review* 76 (2): 307–14.

Borras, Saturnino Jr., Jennifer Franco, and Jan Douwe van der Ploe. 2013. "Land Concentration, Land Grabbing and People's Struggles in Europe." In *Land Concentration, Land Grabbing and People's Struggles in Europe*. Amsterdam: Transnational Institute (TNI). https://www.tni.org/files/download/land_in_europe-jun2013.pdf.

Bottoni, Stefano. 2003. "The Creation of the Hungarian Autonomous Region in Romania (1952): Premises and Consequences." *Régio Yearbook*, 71–93.

Bourdieu, Pierre. 1977. *Outline of a Theory of Practice*. Cambridge: Cambridge University Press.

———. 1991. *Language and Symbolic Power*. Edited by John B. Thompson, translated by Gino Raymond and Matthew Adamson. Cambridge: Polity.

———. 1993. *The Field of Cultural Production: Essays on Art and Literature*. New York: Columbia University Press.

Boyd, Joe. 1991. "Blues for Transylvania: Muzsikás." On *Blues for Transylvania* CD cover. Muzsikás. Hannibal/Ryko Records.

Bozoki, András. 2012. "The Illusion of Inclusion: Configurations of Populism in Hungary." Working Paper, European University Institute SPS, 2012/06. https://cadmus.eui.eu/handle/1814/26934.

Braham, Randoph L. 1981. *The Politics of Genocide*. Vol. 1, *The Holocaust in Hungary*. New York: Columbia University Press.

Brody, Ervin C. 1995. "Literature and Politics in Today's Hungary: Sándor Csoóri in the Populist-Urbanite Debate." *Literary Review* 38, no. 3 (Spring): 426.

Brown, Michael A. 2004. Heritage as Property. In *Property in Question: Value Transformation in the Global Economy*, edited by K. Verdery and C. Humphrey, 49–68. Oxford: Berg.

Brubaker, Rogers, Margit Feischmidt, Jon Fox, and Liana Grancea. 2006. *Nationalist Politics and Everyday Ethnicity in a Transylvanian Town*. Princeton, NJ: Princeton University Press.

Buchanon, Donna. 2006. *Performing Democracy: Bulgarian Music and Musicians in Transition*. Chicago: University of Chicago Press.

Buchowski, Michał. 1996. "The Shifting Meanings of Civil and Civic Society in Poland." In *Civil Society: Challenging Western Models*, edited by Elizabeth Dunn and Chris Hann, 79–98. New York: Routledge.

Bukowski, Jeanie, Simona Piattoni, and Marc Smyrl. 2003. *Between Europeanization and Local Societies*. New York: Rowman and Littlefield.

Bunzl, Matti. 2005. "Between Anti-Semitism and Islamophobia: Some Thoughts on the New Europe." *American Ethnologist* 32 (4): 499–508.

Burawoy, Michael, Pavel Krotov, and Tatyana Lytkina. 2000. "Involution and Destitution in Capitalist Russia." *Ethnography* 1 (1): 43–65.

Bureau of European and Eurasian Affairs. 2007. "Property Restitution in Central and Eastern Europe." U.S. Department of State Archive, October 3, 2007. https://2001-2009.state.gov/p/eur/rls/or/93062.htm.

Burger, Hannalore. 2003. "Language Rights and Linguistic Justice in the Education System of the Habsburg Monarchy." Paper presented at the seminar "Official and Scholastic Language in Austria and in Multilingual Areas," Institute for Central European Cultural Encounters, May 2003, Gorizia, Italy.Cardaro, Janice A. 1998. "The Transmission of Hungarian-Transylvanian Dance to the United States: Receptive Influences in the Hungarian-American Dance Community of Los Angeles." PhD diss., University of California, Los Angeles.

Caffentzis, George. 1995. "The Fundamental Implications of the Debt Crisis for Social Reproduction in Africa." In *Paying the Price: Women and the Politics of International Economic Strategy*, edited by Mariarosa Dalla Costa and Giovanna F. Dalla Costa, 15–41. London: Zed.

Casas-Cortes, Maribel, Michal Osterweil, and Dana Powell. 2008. "Blurring Boundaries: Recognizing Knowledge-Practices in the Study of Social Movements." *Anthropological Quarterly* 81 (1): 17–58.

Caton, Steve. 1990. *Peaks of Yemen I Summon: Poetry as Cultural Practice in a North Yemeni Tribe*. Los Angeles: University of California Press.

Cellarius, B. A., and C. Staddon. 2002. "Environmental Nongovernmental Organizations, Civil Society, and Democratization in Bulgaria." *East European Politics and Societies* 16:182–222.

Chakrabarty, Dipesh. 2000. *Provincializing Europe: Postcolonial Thought and Historical Difference*. Princeton, NJ: Princeton University Press.

Chari, Sharad, and Katherine Verdery. 2009. "Thinking between the Posts: Postcolonialism, Postsocialism, and Ethnography after the Cold War." *Comparative Studies in Society and History* 51 (1): 6–34.

Chatterjee, Partha. 1993. *The Nation and Its Fragments: Colonial and Postcolonial Histories*. Princeton, NJ: Princeton University Press.

———. 2008. *The Politics of the Governed*. New York: Columbia University Press.

Chelcea, Liviu. 2006. "Marginal Groups in Central Places: Gentrification, Property Rights and Post-Socialist Primitive Accumulation (Bucharest, Romania)." In *Social Changes and Social Sustainability in Historical Urban Centres: The Case of Central Europe*, edited by György Enyedi and Zoltán Kovács, 127–26. Pecs, Hungary: Centre for Regional Studies of the Hungarian Academy of Sciences.

Chelcea, Liviu, and Oana Druţă. 2016. "Zombie Socialism and the Rise of Neoliberalism in Post-socialist Central and Eastern Europe." *Eurasian Geography and Economics* 57 (4–5): 521–44.

Chen, Cheng. 2003. "The Roots of Illiberal Nationalism in Romania: A Historical Institutionalist Analysis of the Leninist Legacy." *East European Politics and Societies* 17 (2): 166–201.

Chirot, Daniel. 1976. *Social Change in a Peripheral Society: The Creation of a Balkan Colony*. New York: Academic Press.

Choksy, Lois. 1999. *The Kodály Method I: Comprehensive Music Education*. Upper Saddle River, NJ: Prentice-Hall.

Cienciala, Anna M. 2002. "Domestic Problems and Foreign Policies of Interwar East European States." Lecture notes for History 557. http://web.ku.edu/~eceurope/hist557/lect14a.htm.

Cohen, Jean L., and Andrew Arato. 1994. *Civil Society and Political Theory*. Cambridge, MA: MIT Press.
Connor, Walker. 1984. *The National Question in Marxist Leninist Theory and Strategy*. Princeton, NJ: Princeton University Press.
Coombe, R. J. 2012. "Managing Cultural Heritage as Neoliberal Governmentality." In *Heritage Regimes and the State*, edited by R. Bendix, A. Egert, and A. Peselmann, 375–87. Gottingen: University of Gottingen Press.
Corrigan, Philip, and Derek Sayer. 1985. *The Great Arch: English State Formation as Cultural Revolution*. Oxford: Basil Blackwell.
Council of Europe. 2002 (2001). "Recommendation Adopted by the Council of Europe Parliamentary Assembly on the Csángó Minority Culture." *Hungarian Heritage* 3:9–10.
———. 2004. "Compendium." www.cultpoliticies.net/hu/.
Cowan, Jane. 1990. *Dance and the Body Politic in Northern Greece*. Princeton, NJ: Princeton University Press.
Cowan, Jane K., Marie-Bénédicte Dembour, and Richard A. Wilson. 2001. *Culture and Rights: Anthropological Perspectives*. Cambridge: Cambridge University Press.
Crain, Mary. 1992. "Pilgrims, Yuppies, and Media Men: The Transformation of an Andalusian Village." In *Revitalizing European Rituals*, edited by Jeremy Boissevain, 95–112. New York: Routledge.
Creed, Gerald. 1995. "The Politics of Agriculture: Identity and Socialist Sentiment in Bulgaria." *Slavic Review* 54 (4): 843–68.
———. 2006. "Reconsidering Community." In *The Seductions of Community: Emancipations, Oppressions, Quandaries*, edited by Gerald Creed, 1–20. Santa Fe, NM: School of American Research Press.
———. 2011. *Masquerade and Postsocialism: Ritual and Cultural Dispossession in Bulgaria*. Bloomington: Indiana University Press.
Creed, Gerald, and Barbara Ching. 1997. "Recognizing Rusticity: Identity and the Power of Place." In *Knowing Your Place: Rural Identity and Cultural Hierarchy*, edited by Barbara Ching and Gerald Creed, 1–38. New York: Routledge.
Creed, Gerald W., and Mary N. Taylor. 2020: "Postsocialist Populisms?" In *Beyond Populism: Angry Politics and the Twilight of Neoliberalism*, edited by Jeff Maskovsky and Sophie Bjork-James. Morgantown: West Virginia University Press.
Creed, Gerald, and Janine Wedel. 1997. "Second Thoughts from the Second World." *Human Organization* 56 (3): 253–264.
Cruz Banks, O. 2010. "Critical Postcolonial Dance Pedagogy: The Relevance of West African Dance Education in the United States." *Anthropology and Education Quarterly* 41 (1): 8–34.
Csergő, Zsuzsa. 2002. "Beyond Ethnic Division: Majority-Minority Debate about the Postcommunist State in Romania and Slovakia." *East European Politics and Societies* 16 (1): 1–29.
Csurka, István. 2002. "A Felfeslett Bűntény." *Havi Magyar Fórum*, October. Accessed October 3, 2006. http://lazadas.ho8.com/www.tar.hu/lazadas/csurka.htm.
Czene Gábor. 2016. "TGM: A Fidesz kifejezetten etatista képződmény, amit egyetlen személy, Orbán Viktor irányít." *Népszabadság*, October 8, 2016, Hetvege 3. https://issuu.com/daka255/docs/utolso_nepszabi?e=26614888/39705935.
Czigány, Loránt. 1984. *The Oxford History of Hungarian Literature from the Earliest Times to the Present*. Oxford: Clarendon Press.

Dale, Gareth, and Fabry, Adam. 2018. "Neoliberalism in Eastern Europe and the Former Soviet Union." *The SAGE Handbook of Neoliberalism*, edited by Damien Cahill, Melinda Cooper, Martjin Konings, and David Primrose, 234–47. London: Sage.

Damşa, Liviu. 2016. *The Transformation of Property Regimes and Transitional Justice in Central Eastern Europe: In Search of a Theory*. Cham, Switzerland: Springer.

Daniel, Yvonne. 1995. *Rumba: Dance and Social Change in Contemporary Cuba*. Bloomington: Indiana University Press.

Daniela-Luminitja, Constantin Mitrut, and Mihaela Gruiescu. 2009. "Strategies for Romanian Tourism and Regional Development 2007–2013: Institutional Challenges." Paper presented at European Integration: New Challenges for the Romanian Economy Conference, Oradea, Romania, May 29 and 30, 2009.

Day, Matthew. 2015. "Hungary Using Unemployed to Build Anti-immigration Fence." *The Telegraph*, August 3, 2015. http://www.telegraph.co.uk/news/worldnews/europe/hungary/11780468/Hungary-using-unemployed-to-build-anti-immigration-fence.html.

Deák, István. 1990. *Beyond Nationalism: A Social and Political History of the Habsburg Officer Corps 1848–1918*. Oxford: Oxford University Press.

———. 1994 "Anti-Semitism and the Treatment of the Holocaust in Hungary." In *Anti-Semitism and the Treatment of the Holocaust in Postcommunist East Europe*, edited by Randolph L Braham, 99–124. New York: Columbia University Press.

———. 1999. "On the Leash." *Hungarian Quarterly* 40 (156): 54–63.

De Cesari, Chiara. 2012. "Thinking through Heritage Regimes." In *Heritage Regimes and the State*, edited by Regina F. Bendix, Aditya Eggert and Arnika Peselmann, 399–413. Gottingen: University of Gottingen Press.

Dejeu, Zamfir. 2015. "Lad's Dances in Romania—Representative List, Ministry of Culture, Romania, National Committee for the Safeguarding of Cultural Heritage." Institute Folk Archive of the Romanian Academy. Cluj: University of Bucharest, Institute of Ethnography and Folklore Constantin Brailoiu. Accessed March 20, 2019. https://ich.unesco.org/en/RL/lads-dances-in-romania-01092.

DeLue, Steven. 2006. "The Enlightenment, Public Memory, Liberalism, and the Post-Communist World." *East European Politics and Societies* 20 (3): 395–418.

Deren, Maya. 1953. *Divine Horsemen: The Living Gods of Haiti*. Kingston, NY: McPherson.

Dezsi, Stefan, and Joszef Benedek. 2011. "The Role of Rural Tourism in the Socio-Economic Diversification of Rural Space from Lapusului Land (Tara Lapusului Maramures County, Romania)." *International Journal of Systems Applications* 2 (5): 20.

Dobszay, László. 1972. "The Kodály Method and Its Musical Basis." *Studium Musicologica Academiae Scientarum Hungaranicae* 141 (4): 15–33.

Dubisch, Jill. 1990. "Pilgrammage and Popular Religion at a Greek Holy Shrine." In *Religious Orthodoxy and Popular Faith in European Society*, edited by Ellen Badone, 113–39. Princeton, NJ: University of Princeton Press.

Dudek, Carolyn. 2003. "Creation of a Bureaucratic Style: Spanish Regions and EU Structural Funds." In *Between Europeanization and Local Societies*, edited by Jeanie Bukowski, Simona Piattoni, and Marc Smyrl, 111–32. New York: Rowman and Littlefield.

Dupcsik, Csaba. 2009. *A Magyarországi Cigányság Története. Történelem a cigánykutatások tükrében, 1890–2008*. Budapest: Osiris Kiadó.

Durkheim, Emil. 1976 (1912). *Elementary Forms of Religious Life*. London: George Allen and Unwin.

Dutton, D. G., and A. Aron. 1974. "Some Evidence for Heightened Sexual Attraction under Conditions of High Anxiety." *Journal of Personality and Social Psychology* 30 (4): 510–17.

Eagleton, Terry. 1990. *The Ideology of the Aesthetic*. London: Blackwell.
———. 2000. *The Idea of Culture*. London: Blackwell.
Eellend, Johan. 2008. "Agrarianism and Modernization in Inter-War Eastern Europe" In *Societal Change and Ideological Formation among the Rural Population of the Baltic Area, 1880–1939*, edited by Piotr Wawrzeniuk, 35–56. Huddinge: Södertörns högskola.
Egykor. n.d. "Selyemgombolyító és Selyemfonó (Filatórium)." Egykor website. http://egykor.hu/budapest-iii--kerulet/selyemgombolyito-es-selyemfono-filatorium/3274.
Election Guide. n.d. "Election Profile for Hungary." Accessed February 2005. http://www.electionguide.org/election.php?ID=297.
Elias, Norbert. 1978. *The Civilizing Process*. Vol. 1, *The History of Manners*. New York. Urizen.
Erdélyi Turizmus. Erdélyi Turizmus website. https://www.erdelyiturizmus.hu/.
Errington, Joseph. 2001. "Colonial Linguistics." *Annual Review of Anthropology* 30 (1): 19–39.
Escobar, Arturo. 1991. "Anthropology and the Development Encounter: The Making and Marketing of Development." *American Ethnologist* 18 (4): 658–82.
———. 2000. "Place, Economy and Culture in a Post-Development Era." In *Places and Politics in an Age of Globalization*, edited by Roxann Prazniak and Arif Dirlik, 193–217. New York: Rowman and Littlefield.
Essig, David. 2007. "The Impact of Sovietization: A Case Study of the Hungarian Peasantry under Stalinism." Thesis, Department of History, Central European University.
European Folklore Institute. 2001. European Folklore Institute website. Accessed March 17, 2007. http://www.folkline.hu/efi/index_e.html.
Fábry, Adám. 2015a. "The Far-Right as a Counter-Hegemonic Bloc to Neoliberalism? The Case of Jobbik (I)." *LeftEast*, August 10, 2015.
———. 2015b. "The Far-Right as a Counter-Hegemonic Bloc to Neoliberalism? The Case of Jobbik (II)." *LeftEast*, September 25, 2015.
Fábry, Katalin, and Pál Sóos. 1986. "Some Culture-Political and Historical Questions of Voluntary Organizations." In *On Voluntary Organizations in Hungary and the Netherlands*, edited by J. Katus and J. Tóth, 67–73. Budapest: OKK.
Fanon, Frantz. 1967. *Black Skin, White Masks*. New York: Grove Press.
Federici, Silvia. 2004. *Caliban and the Witch: Women, the Body, and Primitive Accumulation*. New York: Autonomedia.
Feischmidt, Margit. 2004. "Answers." In *About Duel Citizenship: Data, Positions, and Explanations*. Hungarian Minority Research Institute. https://kisebbsegkutato.tk.hu/kettosallampolgarsag/anket/ank_24.html.
Fejtő, Francois. 2001. "Assimilation and Identity." *Hungarian Quarterly* 42 (161): 87–93.
Fél, Edit, and Tamás Hófer. 1969. *Proper Peasants: Traditional Life in a Hungarian Village*. Chicago: Aldine.
Feld, Steven. 1990 (1982). *Sound and Sentiment*. Philadelphia: University of Pennsylvania Press.
Felföldi, László, and András Gombos, eds. 2001. *A Népművészeti Táncos Mesterei*. Budapest: Hagyományok Háza.
Ferguson, J. 2006. "The Anti-politics Machine." In *Anthropology of the State: A Reader*, 270–286. London: Blackwell.
Florea Ioanna and Mihail Dumitriu. 2018. "Transformations of Housing Provision in Romania: Organizations of Subtle Violence." *LeftEast*, October 24, 2018. https://lefteast.org/transformations-of-housing-provision-in-romania-organizations-of-subtle-violence/.

Fonyódi, Péter. 2003. *Beat Korszak a Párt Államban, 1963–1973*. Budapest: XX Század Intézet.
Foster, Michael Dylan, and Lisa Gilman. 2015. *Local Perspectives in Intangible Cultural Heritage*. Bloomington: Indiana University Press.
Fosztó, László. 2018. "Hungarian "Roma" in Transylvania." Project Education of Roma Children in Europe, Council of Europe Report. https://www.academia.edu/36007566/_Hungarian_Roma_in_Transylvania.
Foucault, Michel. 1982. "The Subject and the Power." In *Michel Foucault: Beyond Structuralism and Hermeneutics*, edited by Hubert Dreyfus and Paul Rabinow, 208–26. Brighton: Harvester.
———. 1991. "Governmentality." In *The Foucault Effect: Studies in Governmentality*, edited by Burchell, Gordon and Miller, 87–104. Chicago: University of Chicago Press.
———. 1994. *Dits et Écrits 1954–1988*. Vol. 4, *1980–1988*. Paris: Gallimard.
Fourth Republic. n.d. "The Party Program of the 4K! Fourth Republic Movement." Fourth Republic. Accessed November 2016. http://negyedikkoztarsasag.hu/program-english.
Fox, Jon E. 2003. "National Identities on the Move: Transylvanian Hungarian Labour Migrants in Hungary." *Journal of Ethnic and Migration Studies* 29 (3): 449–66.
Fraser, Nancy. 1997. *Justice Interruptus: Critical Reflections on the "Postsocialist" Condition*. New York: Routledge.
Frigyesi, Judit. 1994. "Béla Bartók and the Concept of Nation and 'Volk' in Modern Hungary." *Musical Quarterly* 78 (2): 255–87.
———. 1996. "The Aesthetic of the Hungarian Revival Movement." In *Retuning Culture: Musical Changes in Central and Eastern Europe*, edited by Mark Slobin, 54–75. Durham, NC: Duke University Press.
———. 2000. *Bartók Bela and Turn of the Century Budapest*. Berkeley: University of California Press.
Friss, Gabor. 1966. "The Music Primary School in Musical Education in Hungary." In *Musical Education in Hungary*, edited by Frigyes Sándor, 133–72. New York: Boosey and Hawkes.
Frith, Simon. 1996. "Music and Identity." In *Questions of Cultural Identity*, edited by Stuart Hall and Paul DuGay, 108–28. London: Sage.
Fügedi, Márta. 2000. "The Discovery of Matyó Folk Art." *Hungarian Heritage* 1:9–18.
Fujimovics, Kinga. 2003. "Jewish Naming Customs in Hungary from the Turn of the Twentieth Century until the Holocaust." Paper presented at twenty-third International Conference on Jewish Genealogy.
Fukuyama, F. 2006 (1992). *The End of History and the Last Man*. New York: Simon and Schuster.
Fullerton, Maryellen. 1996. "Hungary, Refugees, and the Law of Return." *International Journal of Refugees Law* 8 (4): 499–531.
Fumarola, Andrea. 2016. "Fidesz and Electoral Reform: How to Safeguard Hungarian Democracy." *LSE European Politics and Policy (EUROPP)* (blog). March 21, 2016. https://blogs.lse.ac.uk/europpblog/2016/03/21/fidesz-and-electoral-reform-how-to-safeguard-hungarian-democracy/.
Gagyi, Ágnes. 2014. "Smartphones and the European Flag: The New Hungarian Demonstrations for Democracy." *LeftEast*, October 31, 2014. http://www.criticatac.ro/lefteast/smartphones-and-eu-flag-hungarian-demos-for-democracy/.
———. 2016. "Coloniality of Power in East Central Europe: External Penetration as Internal Force in Post-Socialist Hungarian Politics." *Journal of World-Systems Research* 22 (2): 349–72.

Gagyi, Ágnes, and Tamás Gerőcs. 2019. "The Political Economy of Hungary's New 'Slave Law.'" *LeftEast*, January 1, 2019.

Gagyi, Ágnes, and Mariya Ivancheva. 2019. "The Reinvention of 'Civil Society': Transnational Conceptions of Development in East-Central Europe." In *Funding, Power and Community Development*, edited by N. McCrea and F. Finnegan, 55–69. Bristol: Policy Press.

Gal, Susan. 1991. "Bartók's Funeral: Representations of Europe in Hungarian Political Rhetoric." *American Ethnologist* 18 (3): 440–58.

———. 1996. "Feminism and Civil Society." Special issue, *Replika: Colonization or Partnership? Eastern Europe and Western Social Sciences*, 75–81. http://www.replika.hu/replika/si96-08.

———. 2007. "Contradictions of Standard Language in Europe: Implications for the study of Practices." *Social Anthropology* 14 (2):163–182.

Gallo, Mattia. 2105. "Reflection on the Bosnian Spring: An Interview with Emin Eminagic." *LeftEast*, February 4, 2015.

Gellner, Ernest. 1983. *Nations and Nationalism*. Ithaca, NY: Cornell University Press.

Gergély, Ferenc. 1989. *A Magyar Cserkészet Története*. Budapest: Goncol Kiadó.

Gerő, András, László Varga, and Mátyás Vincze, eds. 2002. *Anti-Semitic Discourse in Hungary in 2001: Report and Documentation*. Budapest: B'nai B'rith Első Budapesti Közösség.

Gilbert, Joseph, and Daniel Nugent. 1994. "Popular Culture and State Formation in Revolutionary Mexico." In *Everyday Forms of State Formation*, edited by Joseph Gilbert and Daniel Nugent, 1–23. Durham, NC: Duke University Press.

Gille, Zsuzsa. 2016. *Paprika, Foie Gras, and Red Mud: The Politics of Materiality in the European Union*. Bloomington: Indiana University Press.

Gilmore, Ruth Wilson. 2007. *Golden Gulag : Prisons, Surplus, Crisis, and Opposition in Globalizing California*. Berkeley: University of California Press.

Gingrich, Andre. 2006. "Neo-nationalism and the Reconfiguration of Europe." *Social Anthropology* 14 (2): 195–217.

Gitelman, Zvi. 1999. "Reconstructing Jewish Communities and Jewish Identities in Post-Communist East Central Europe." In *Central European University Jewish Studies Yearbook I*, edited by András Kovács, 35–50. Budapest: Central European UP, 1996–1999.

Glick-Schiller, Nina, Ayse Caglar, and Thaddeus Gulbrandsen. 2006. "Beyond the Ethnic Lens: Locality, Globality and Born again Incorporation." *American Anthropologist* 33 (4):612–33.

Gluckman, Max. 1965. *Custom and Conflict in Africa*. Oxford: Blackwell.

Gömbös, András. 2001. "Master of Folk Art Award for Talented Traditional Performers and Craftpeople in Hungary." In *Living Human Treasures in Hungary-Folk Dance*, edited by László Felföldi and András Gombos. Budapest: European Folklore Institute and the Institute for Musicology of the Hungarian Academy of Sciences.

Gracyk, Theodore. 2004 (2002). "My Introduction to the Aesthetics of Hume and Kant." Minnesota State University, Moorhead. Accessed February 3, 2016 http://web.mnstate.edu/gracyk/courses/phil%20of%20art/hume_and_kant.htm

Gramsci, Antonio. 1971. *Selections from the Prison Notebooks of Antonio Gramsci*. New York: International Publishers.

Granville, Johanna. 2001. "To Invade or Not to Invade? A New Look at Gomulka, Nagy, and Soviet Foreign Policy in 1956." *Canadian Slavonic Papers* 3 (4): 437–73

Grasseger, Hannes. 2019. "The Unbelievable Story of the Plot against George Soros." *Buzzfeed*, January 20, 2019. https://www.buzzfeednews.com/article/hnsgrassegger/george-soros-conspiracy-finkelstein-birnbaum-orban-netanyahu.

Grubacic, Andrej. 2010. *Don't Mourn, Balkanize! Essays After Yugoslavia*. Oakland, CA: PM Press.
Gyarmati, Erika. 1993. "A Népművelési Intézet Története 1957–1972-ig." Master's thesis, Zsámbéki Katolikus Tanitóképző Főiskola.
Györffy, György. 2000. "István Györffy, A Pioneer of Hungarian Ethnography." *Hungarian Heritage* 1 (1–2): 19–28.
Györffy, István. 1992. *A Néphagyomány és a Nemzeti Művelődés*. Debrecen: István Néprajzi Egyesület.
György, Eszter. 2019. "An Attempt to Create Minority Heritage: The History of the Rom Som Club (Rom Som cigányklub) 1972–1980." *Romani Studies* 29 (2): 205–32.
H., Andy. 2005. "The View of Hungary from Here." *Csíkszereda Musings* (blog), June 15, 2005. http://szekely.blogspot.com/2005/06/view-of-hungary-from-here.html.
Habermas, Jürgen. 1996 "The European Nation-State: Its Achievements and Its Limits; On the Past and Future of Sovereignty and Citizenship." In *Mapping the Nation*, edited by Gopal Balakrishnan, 281–294. London: Verso.
Hagyományok Háza. n.d. Hagyományok Háza website. Accessed October 3, 2006 http://www.hagyomanyokhaza.hu/.
Haigh, Chris. n.d. "Hungarian and Gypsy Fiddle." Fiddling around the World. http://www.fiddlingaround.co.uk/hungarian/.
Halbwachs Maurice. 1992. *On Collective Memory*. Edited and translated by Lewis A. Coser. Chicago: University of Chicago Press.
Hall, Stuart. 1981. "Notes on Deconstructing 'the Popular.'" In *People's History and Socialist Theory*, edited by R. Samuel and Kegan Paul, 227–40. London: Routledge.
———. 1988. *The Hard Road to Renewal: Thatcherism and the Crisis of the Left*. London: Verso.
———. 1996. "Gramsci's Relevance for the Study of Race and Ethnicity." In *Stuart Hall: Critical Dialogues in Cultural Studies*, edited by D. Morley and K-H. Chen, 411–40. London: Routledge.
———. 2018 (1998). "The Multicultural Question." In *Essential Essays*, Vol. 2, *Identity and Diaspora*, edited by David Morley. Durham, NC: Duke University Press.
Halmai, Gábor. 2011. "Dispossessed by the Spectre of Socialism: Nationalist Mobilization in 'Transitional' Hungary." In *Headlines of Nation, Subtexts of Class: Working-Class Populism and the Return of the Repressed in Neoliberal Europe*, edited by Don Kalb and Gábor Halmai, 194–239. New York: Berghahn.
Halmos, Béla. 1973. "Ifju Népmuvészek Önmagukrol." *Latohatár*, December, 145–147.
———. 1992. "A Táncházmozgalom Jöveje." *Zöldövezet*, NICHE Alapítvány, Budapest, 47–55.
———. 1994. "The History of the Táncház Movement." In *Explorations in Finnish and Hungarian Folk Dance Music and Dance Research*, vol. 1, edited by Luukola Varpu and Hannu Varpu. Kaustinen, Finland: Folk Music Institute.
———. 2000. "The Táncház Movement." *Hungarian Heritage* 1:29–40.
Halpert, Marta S. 1999. "Hungary: A Growing Tolerance for Anti-Semitism," *ADL International Notes*, December.
Hanák, Péter. 1991. *The Corvina History of Hungary from the Earliest Times until the Present Day*. Budapest: Corvina.
Hankiss, Elemér. 1993. "The Hungarian Media's War of Independence." In *Rights of Access to the Media*, edited by András Sajó and Monroe Price, 243–58. The Hague: Kluwer Law International.
Hann, Chris. 1996. Introduction to *Civil Society: Challenging Western Models*, edited by C. M. Hann and Elizabeth Dunn, 1–26. London: Routledge.

———. 2006. *The Horse We Wanted! Postsocialism, Neoliberalism, and Eurasia.* Münster, DEU: Lit.
Hann, Chris, Caroline Humphrey, and Katherine Verdery. 2002. Introduction to *Postsocialism: Ideals, Ideologies and Practices in Eurasia*, edited by C. M. Hann, 1–28. London: Routledge.
Haraszti, Miklós. 1987. *The Velvet Prison.* New York: Basic Books.
Harper, Krista. 2005. "'Wild Capitalism' and 'Ecocolonialism': A Tale of Two Rivers." *American Anthropologist* 107 (2): 221–33.
Harvey, David. 1990. *The Condition of Postmodernity.* Oxford: Blackwell.
———. 2001a. "The Art of Rent." In *Spaces of Capital*, 394–411. New York: Routledge.
———. 2001b. "From Managerialism to Entrepreneurialism: The Transformation in Urban Governance in Late Capitalism." In *Spaces of Capital*, 345–411. New York: Routledge.
———. 2002. "The Art of Rent: Globalization, Monopoly and the Commodification of Culture." *Socialist Register* 38:94–110.
———. 2003. *A Brief History of Neoliberalism.* Oxford: Oxford University Press.
Haselsteiner, Horst. 1990. "Cooperation and Confrontation." In *A History of Hungary*, edited by Péter F. Sugár, 138–64. Bloomington: University of Indiana Press.
Hayden, Robert M. 1992. "Constitutional Nationalism in the Formerly Yugoslav Republics." *Slavic Review* 51 (4): 654–73.
Hegedűs, András B. 1994. "Széll Jenő (1912–1994)." *Beszélő* 4 (6): 5.
Hemment, Julie. 2007. *Empowering Women in Russia: Activism, Aid, and NGOs.* Bloomington: Indiana University Press.
Herder, J. G. 1968. *Reflections on the Philosophy of the History of Mankind.* Chicago: University of Chicago Press.
Hirsch, Eric. 1997. "Voices from the Black Box: Folk Song, Boy Scouts and the Construction of Folk Nationalist Hegemony in Hungary, 1930–1944." *Antipode* 29 (2): 197–215.
Hirschkind, Charles. 2001. "The Ethics of Listening: Cassette Sermon Audition in Contemporary Egypt." *American Ethnologist* 38 (3): 623–649.
Hobsbawm, Eric J. 1962. *The Age of Revolution 1789–1848.* New York: Mentor.
Hobsbawm, Eric, and Terence Ranger. 1984. *The Invention of Tradition.* Cambridge: Cambridge University Press.
Hofer, Tamás. 1980. "The Creation of Ethnic Symbols from the Elements of Peasant Culture." In *Ethnic Diversity and Conflict in Eastern Europe*, edited by P. F. Sugár, 101–45. Santa Barbara, CA: ABC-CLIO.
———. 1989. "Paraszti hagyományokból nemzeti szimbólumok—adalékok a magyar nemzeti műveltég történetéhez az utolsó száz évben." *Janus* VI (1): 59–74.
Hoffman, Tamás. 1977. "A Népművészetről-Jelenidőben." *Kritika* 77 (2): 3–4.
Holmes, Douglas R. 2000. *Integral Europe: Fast-Capitalism, Multiculturalism, Neofascism.* Princeton, NJ: Princeton University Press.
Honey, Martha, and Emma Stewart. 2002. Introduction to *Ecotourism and Certification: Setting Standards in Practice*, edited by Martha Honey, 1–32. Washington, DC: Island Press.
Hooker, Lynn, 2002. "Transylvania and the Politics of Musical Imagination." *European Meetings in Ethnomusicology* 9:45–76.
———. 2005. "Gypsiness and Gender in the Hungarian Folkdance Revival." *Anthropology of East Europe Review* 23 (2): 52–62.
———. 2007. "Controlling the Liminal Power of Performance: Hungarian Scholars and Romani Musicians in the Hungarian Folk Revival." *Twentieth Century Music* 3 (1): 51–72.

———. 2008. "Performing the Old World, Embracing the New: Festivalization, the Carnivalesque, and the Creation and Maintenance of Community in North American Hungarian Folk Music and Dance Camps." *Hungarian Studies* 22 (1–2): 89–101.

———. 2013. *Redefining Hungarian Music from Liszt to Bartók*. New York: Oxford University Press.

Human Rights Watch. 1993. *The Gypsies of Hungary: Struggling for Ethnic Identity* New York: Human Rights Watch. https://www.hrw.org/sites/default/files/reports/HUNGARY937.PDF.

Hungarian Human Rights Foundation. 2019. "Church Property Restitution: The Dark Shadow Obscuring the 'Bright Future' of U.S.-Romanian Bilateral Relations." Hungarian Human Rights Foundation. https://hhrf.org/2019/01/08/church-property-restitution-the-dark-shadow-obscuring-the-bright-future-of-us-romanian-bilateral-relations/.

Hungarian Press of Transylvania. 1988. "Hungarian Declaration of Solidarity with the Rumanian People." Release no. 3, January 19, 1988. Accessed March 2, 2021. https://hhrf.org/dokumentumtar/irott/hpt/1988.003.pdf.

Hungarikum Gyüjteménye. Hungarikum Gyüjteménye website. http://www.hungarikum.hu/.

Huntington, Samuel P. 1993. "The Clash of Civilizations?" *Foreign Affairs* 72 (3): 2–3.

Huseby-Darvas, Éva. 2003. "Pincézés: A Drinking-Related Male Social Institution in Rural Hungary." *Anthropology of East Europe Review* 21 (1): 83–89.

Hylland Eriksen, Thomas. 2001. "A Critique of the UNESCO Concepts of Culture." In *Culture and Rights, Anthropological Perspectives*, edited by Jane Cowan, Marie-Bénédicte Dembour, and Richard Wilson, 127–48. Cambridge: Cambridge University Press.

———. 2003. *Ethnicity and Nationalism, Anthropological Perspectives*. London: Pluto Press.

Interfax Central Europe. 2007. "Hungarian Gov't Says Opposition Action to Remove Cordons 'Unlawful.'" Interfax Central Europe, February 2007.

International Herald Tribune. 2006. "Moldova's Independence-Seeking Transnistria Region Votes, but Effect Is Uncertain: Most Are Expected to Back Moldova Split." September 17, 2006.

Irvine, Judith, and Susan Gal. 2000. "Language Ideology and Linguistic Differentiation." In *Regimes of Language: Ideologies, Politics, and Identities*, edited by Paul V. Kroskrity, 35–84. Santa Fe: School of American Research Press.

Ishchenko, Volodymyr. 2014. "Ukraine's Fractures." *New Left Review* 87 (May/June): 5–33.

Ivancheva, Mariya. 2011. "The Role of Dissident Intellectuals in the Formation of Civil Society in (Post)Socialist East-Central Europe." In *Protest beyond Borders: Contentious Politics in Europe since 1945*, edited by H. Kouki and E. Romanos, 251–263. Oxford: Berghahn.

Jameson, Fredric. 1991. *Postmodernism, or, The Cultural Logic of Late Capitalism*. Durham, NC: Duke University Press.

Janos, Andrew C. 1982. *The Politics of Backwardness in Hungary, 1825–1945*. Princeton, NJ: Princeton University Press.

Jánosi, Sándor. 1979. *Táncos Kronika*. Budapest: Népművelési Propoganda Iroda.

Jászi, Oszkár. 1929. *The Dissolution of the Habsburg Monarchy*. Chicago: University of Chicago Press.

Jávorszky, Béla Szilárd. 2013. *A magyar folk története*. Budapest: Cultura.

Jeffrey, K., and Joyce Robbins. 1998. "Social Memory Studies: From 'Collective Memory' to the Historical Sociology of Mnemonic Practices." *Annual Review of Sociology* 24:105–40.

Jewish Voice for Peace. 2017. *On Antisemitism: Solidarity and the Struggle for Justice in Palestine*. Chicago: Haymarket.

Jobbik Party. n.d. "Mit ert az alatt, hogy célja a rendszerváltás befejezése?" Jobbik party website. Accessed November 10, 2019. https://www.jobbik.hu/kiskate/mit-ert-az-alatt-jobbik-hogy-celja-rendszervaltas-befejezese.
Jobbitt, Steven. 2011. "Playing the Part: Hungarian Boy Scouts and the Performance of Trauma in Interwar Hungary." *AHEA*, no. 4, 1–15.
Joppke, Christian. 2003. "Citizenship between De- and Re-ethnicization." Working paper no. 204, Russel Sage Foundation. Accessed January 2006. http://www.russellsage.org/publications/workingpapers/Citizenship%20.
Juhász, Katalin, and Zoltán Szabó. n.d. "A Táncházmozgalom, mint egy sajátos magyarországi folkorizmusjelenség." Working paper, provided by the Ethnographic Research Institute of the Academy of Sciences, Budapest.
Kalb, Don. 2002. "Globalism and Postsocialist Prospects." In *Postsocialism: Ideals, Ideologies and Practices in Eurasia*, edited by C. M. Hann, 317–34. London: Routledge.
Kalb, Don, and Gábor Halmai, eds. 2011. *Headlines of Nation, Subtexts of Class: Working-Class Populism and the Return of the Repressed in Neoliberal Europe*. New York: Berghahn.
Kaldor, Mary, Helmut Anheier, and Marlies Glasius. 2003. "Global Civil Society in an Era of Regressive Globalisation." In *Global Civil Society*, edited by Mary Kaldor, Helmut K Anheier, and Marlies Glasius, 3–35. Oxford: Oxford University Press.
Kaldor, Mary, and Diego Muro. 2003. "Religious and Nationalist Militant Groups." In *Global Civil Society*, edited by Mary Kaldor, Helmut K Anheier, and Marlies Glasius, 151–184. Oxford: Oxford University Press.
Kallius, Annastiina, Daniel Monterescu, and Prem Kumar Rajaram. 2016. "Immobilizing Mobility: Border Ethnography, Illiberal Democracy, and the Politics of the 'Refugee Crisis' in Hungary." *American Ethnologist* 43 (1): 1–12.
Kaneff, Deema. 1998. "When 'Land' Becomes 'Territory': Land Privatization and Ethnicity in Rural Bulgaria." In *Surviving Post-socialism: Local Strategies and Regional Responses in Eastern Europe and the Former Soviet Union*, edited by Sue Bridger and Frances Pine, 16–32. New York: Routledge.
Kaneff, Deema, and Alexander D. King. 2004. "Introduction: Owning Culture." *Focaal* 44:3–19.
Kann, Robert A. 1945. "Hungarian Jewry during Austria-Hungary's Constitutional Period (1867–1918)." *Jewish Social Studies* 7 (4): 357–86.
Kann, Robert A., and Zdenek V. David. 1984. *The Peoples of the Eastern Habsburg Lands, 1956–1918*. Seattle: University of Washington Press.
Kaposi, Edit. 1991. "A Népi Kultúra Áttételei A Polgárosódó Közműveltségben." In *Népi Kultúra és Nemzettudat*, edited by Tamás Hófer, 105–19. Budapest: Magyarságkutató Intézet (Institute for Hungarian Studies).
Kapovic, Mate. 2014. "Bosnia on Fire: A Rebellion on Europe's Periphery." *ROARmag*, February 12, 2014. https://roarmag.org/essays/bosnia-protests-nationalism-workers/.
Karády Viktor. 2008. "Emáncipácio Után." *Budapesti Negyed* 59:80–108.
Karády, Viktor, and Peter Tibor Nagy, eds. 2012. *The Numerus Clausus in Hungary: Studies on the First Anti-Jewish Law and Academic Anti-Semitism in Modern Central Europe*. Budapest: Pasts Inc., Centre for Historical Research, History Department of the Central European University.
Kardos, László. 1977. *Sej, a mi lobogónkat fényes szelek fujják . . . Népi Kollégiumok 1939–1949*. Budapest: Akadémiai Kiadó.
Karsai, László. 2005. "Could the Jews of Hungary Have Survived the Holocaust? New Answers to an Old Question." In *Jewish Studies Yearbook IV*, 63–78. Budapest: Department of Jewish Studies, Central European University.

Kassam, Ashifa. 2005. "Ethnotourism a Risky Business for Thailand's Lahu People." CBC News Online, March 23, 2005. Accessed June 2007. http://www.cbc.ca/news/viewpoint/vp_kassam/20050323.html.

Keating Michael. 1985. "Europeanism and Regionalism." In *Regions in the European Community*, edited by Barry Jones and Keating Michael, 1–22. Oxford: Clarendon Press.

Kelemen, László. 2000. "The 'Final Hour' Folk Music Project." *Hungarian Heritage* 1 (1–2): 50–52.

———. 2008. "Szubjektív táncház-történelem az erdélyi táncház első évtizedéről." Hagyományok Haza. https://hagyomanyokhaza.hu/hu/szubjektiv-tanchaz-tortenelem.

Kideckel, David. 1986. "Help Romanian Cities." *Anthropology of East Europe Review* 5 (2): 11–13.

———. 1996. "What's in a Name? The Persistence of Eastern Europe as a Conceptual Category." *REPLIKA* 1:27–34.

King, Lawrence P. 2001. "Making Markets: A Comparative Study of Postcommunist Managerial Strategies in Central Europe." *Theory and Society* 30 (4): 493–438.

Kirshenblatt-Gimblett, Barabara. 1998. *Destination Culture: Tourism, Museums, and Heritage*. Berkeley: University of California Press.

Kis, János. 1995. "Between Reform and Revolution: Three Hypotheses about the Nature of the Regime Change." *Constellations* 1 (3): 399–421.

Kiss, Tamás. 2018. "Dimensions and Effects of the Kinstate Policy: The Transylvanian Hungarian Case." Unpublished paper. Provided by author.

Klein, Bernard. 1982. "Anti-Jewish Demonstrations in Hungarian Universities, 1932–1936: István Bethlen vs. Gyula Gömbös." *Jewish Social Studies* 44 (2): 113–24.

Kligman, Gail. 1988. *The Wedding of the Dead Ritual Politics and Popular Culture in Transylvania*. Berkeley: University of California Press.

Klimaszewski, Cheryl, Gayle E. Bader, James M. Nyce, and Brian E. Beasley. 2010. "Who Wins? Who Loses? Representation and 'Restoration' of the Past in a Rural Romanian Community." *Library Journal* 59 (2): 92–106.

Kóczé, Angéla. 2020. "Enduring Racialization of the Roma and the Banality of Evil." *LeftEast*, March 18, 2020. https://lefteast.org/radicalization-roma-hungary.

Kodály, Zoltán. 1974. *The Selected Writings of Zoltán Kodály*. Edited by Ferenc Bónis. London: Boosey and Hawkes.

Kohn, Margaret. 2003. *Radical Space: Building the House of the People*. Ithaca, NY: Cornell University Press.

Kollega Tarsoly István, Bekény István, and Dányi Dezső. 1996. *Magyarország a XX Században*. Szekszard: Babits Kiadó.

Koltai, Mihály. 2018. "The Economics of Orbánism." *LeftEast*, April 2, 2018.

Kontler, László. 2002. *A History of Hungary: Millennium in Central Europe*. New York: Palgrave.

Kopasz, Marianna, Zoltán Fábián, András Gábos, Márton Medgyesi, Péter Szivós, and István György Tóth. 2013. *Growing Inequality and Its Impact in Hungary*. GINI Project. http://gini-research.org/system/uploads/448/original/Hungary.pdf?1370090544.

Kornai, Janos. 1992. *The Socialist System: The Political Economy of Socialism*. Princeton, NJ: Princeton University Press.

Kósa, Judit. 2007. "Madár es Béka (Bird and Frog)." *Népszabadság*, April 6, 2007.

Kósa, László. 1974. "A Népi Kultura Új Hullama." *Tiszatáj* 28 (9): 38–45.

———. 1998. "Ki Népei Vagytok?" *Magyar Néprajz*. Budapest: Planetás.

———. n.d. "Bemutatkozás." Magyar Néprajzi Társasag. http://www.néprajz.hu/mnt/bemutatkozas.html.

Koszorus, F. 2009. Autonomy: The Path to Democracy and Stability in Romania. *Foreign Policy Review*, 6 (1): 3–15.
Kovács, András. 1992. "Changes in Jewish Identity in Modern Hungary." In *Jewish Identities in the New Europe*, edited by Jonathan Webber. London: Littmann Library of Jewish Civilization.
———. 1996. "Zsidó csoportok és identitásstratégiák a mai Magyarországon." In *Zsidók a mai Magyarországon*, edited by András Kovács, 9–40. Budapest: Múlt és Jövő, 2002.
Kovács, Éva, and Júlia Vajda. 1996. "A kettős kommunikáció mint csoportképző tényező. Családtörténetek a zsidó iskolákban: Azonosság és különbözőség." In *Tanulmányok az identitásról és az előítéletekről*, edited by Ferenc Erős, 27–35. Budapest: Sciencia Humana.
Kovács, Mária M. 2005. "The Politics of Non-resident Dual Citizenship in Hungary." *Régio* 8 (1): 50–72.
———. 1992. "Jews and Hungarians: A View after the Transition." Working paper no. 35, Wilson Center, Global Europe Program. Accessed March 12, 2018. https://www.wilsoncenter.org/publication/35-jews-and-hungarians-view-after-the transition.
Kovalcsik, József. 2003. *A Kultura Csarnokai*. Budapest: epl (editio plurilingua).
Krastev, Ivan. 2006. "The New Europe: Respectable Populism, Clockwork Liberalism." *Open Democracy*, March 21, 2006. http://www.opendemocracy.net/democracyeurope_constitution/new_europe_3376.jsp.
Krasniqi, Ekrem. 2006. "EU Prepares for Separate Accession of Sovereign Montenegro." EUobserver.com, May 25, 2006.
Krausz Tamás. 2006. "Az 1956-os munkástanácsokról." *Eszmélet* 18 (72): 32–38.
Kulish, Nicholas. 2008. "Crisis Comes to Hungary in Loans of Francs and Euros." *New York Times*, October 18, 2008. http://www.nytimes.com/2008/10/19/world/europe/19hungary.html.
Kurin, Richard. n.d. "The UNESCO Questionnaire on the Application of the 1989 Recommendation on the Safeguarding of Traditional Culture and Folklore: Preliminary Results." Center for Folklife and Cultural Heritage, Smithsonian Institution, Washington, DC. Accessed February, 2007. http://www.folklife.si.edu/resources/Unesco/kurin.htm.
Kürti, László. 2001. *The Remote Borderland: Transylvania in the Hungarian Imagination*. Albany: State University of New York Press.
———. 2002. *Youth and the State in Hungary: Capitalism, Communism and Class*. London: Pluto.
———. 2011. "Images of Roma in Post-1989 Hungarian Media." In *Comparative Hungarian Cultural Studies*, edited by Steven Tötösy de Zepetnek and Louise O. Vasvári, 296–307. West Lafayette, IN: Purdue University Press.
Kúti, Éva, Miklós Marschall, and György Nyilas. 1986. "Local Autonomy and Local Financing of Voluntary Activities." In *On Voluntary Organizations in Hungary and the Netherlands*, edited by J. Katus and J. Tóth, 179–188. Budapest: OKK.
Kymlicka, Will. 1995. *Multicultural Citizenship: A Liberal Theory of Minority Rights*. New York: Oxford University Press.
Lackó, Miklós. 1998. "A Két Vilagháboru Közott." *Budapesti Negyed* 20–21 (2–3): 173–240.
LaClau, Ernesto. 2005. *On Populist Reason*. New York: Verso Books.
Laihonen, Petteri, and Heino Nyyssonen. 2002. "On the Preferential Treatment of Hungarians Living in Neighboring Countries." *Anthropology of East Europe Review* 20 (1): 127–133.
Lakatos, Pál. 2002. *Az Ellópott Rendszerváltozás*. Budapest: 4L Reklám-Videa Bt.

Lampland, Martha. 1991. "Pigs, Party Secretaries, and Private Lives In Hungary." *American Ethnologist* 18 (3): 459–79.
Lange, Barbara Rose, 1996. "Lakodalmas Rock and the Rejection of Popular Culture in Post-socialist Hungary." In *Retuning Culture Musical Changes in Central and Eastern Europe*, edited by Mark Slobin, 76–91. Durham, NC: Duke University Press.
———. 2018. *Local Fusions: Folk Music Experiments in Central Europe at the Millennium*. Oxford: Oxford University Press.
Langman, Juliet. 2003. "Growing a Bányavirág (Rock Crystal) in Barren Soil: Farming a Hungarian Identity in Eastern Slovakia through Joint (inter)Action." In *Language and Socialization in Bilingual and Multilingual Societies*, edited by Robert Bayley and Sandra R. Schechter, 182–199. Cleveland: Multilingual Matters.
Lányi, Ágoston, Martin György, and Pesovár Jenő. 1983. *A Körverbunk*. Budapest: Zeneműkiadó.
László, Kürti. "Szexualitás és csujogatás Kalotaszegen." *Kriza János Néprajzi Társaság Évkönyv*, no. 11, 216.
Laušević, Mirjana. 1996. "The Ilahiya as a Symbol of Bosnian Muslim National Identity." In *Retuning Culture: Musical Changes in Central and Eastern Europe*, edited by Mark Slobin, 117–135. Durham, NC: Duke University Press.
Lees, Susan. 1997. "The Rise and Fall of 'Peasantry' as a Culturally Constructed National Elite in Israel." In *Knowing Your Place: Rural Identity and Cultural Hierarchy*, edited by Barbara Ching and Gerald Creed, 219–236. New York: Routledge.
Lenin, Vladimir. 1975 (1920). "The Tasks of the Youth Leagues." In *The Lenin Anthology*, edited by Robert C. Tucker, 661–674. New York: Norton.
Li, Tania Murray. 2001. "Masyarakat Adat, Difference, and the Limits of Recognition in Indonesia's Forest Zone." *Modern Asian Studies* 35 (3): 645–76.
Livingston, Tamara E. 1999. "Music Revivals: Towards a General Theory." *Ethnomusicology* 43 (1): 66–85.
Löfgren, Orvar. 1999. *On Holiday: A History of Vacationing*. Berkeley: University of California Press.
Lorman Thomas. 2002. "István Bethlen and the 1922 Elections in Hungary." *Slavonic and East European Review* 80 (4): 624–55.
Luukola, Varpu, and Hannu Saha, eds. 1994. "Folk Music Research and Folk Music Movements." In *Explorations in Finnish and Hungarian Folk Music and Dance Research*, vol. 1, edited by Varpu Luukola and Hannu Saha. Kaustinan, Finland: Folk Music Institute.
Maácz, László. 1978. "Comments, in Transcript of Debate by the Folk Dance Membership of the Hungarian Association of Dance Artists." June 13 1977. In *Táncművészeti Dokumentumok 1978*. Budapest: A Magyar Táncművészek Szövetsége Tudományos Tagozata.
———. 1981a. "A Magyar Néptáncmozgalom a Hetvenes Években." In *Tánctudományi Tanulmányok 1980–1981*, edited by Beres András and Olga Szentpál, 71–105. Budapest: A Magyar Táncművészek Szövetsége Tudományos Tagozata.
———. 1981b. "Találkozások a tánccal I." Táncmővészet Dokumentumok, Magyartáncművészek Szövetségének az időszakos kiadványa, 134–185.
———. 1982. Talalkozások a tánccal I. Táncmuveszeti Dokumenumok, Magyartáncművészek Szövetségének az időszakos kiadványa, 95–162.
MacKenzie, Mark. 2007. "Meet the People: Going Native on Your Travels; Tourism Can Help Indigenous Communities. But Do They Really Want Us There?" *The Indepen-*

dent (online edition), February 18, 2007. https://www.independent.co.uk/travel/news-and-advice/meet-the-people-going-native-on-your-travels-436908.html.
Magyar Kulturális Minisztérium. 2000. "(I.20.) MKM-rendelet a Magyar Művelődési Intézet alapitásáról." In *Szempontok es Segédanyagok 2000*, 225. Budapest: Nemzeti Kulturális Örökség Minisztériuma Közművelődési Főosztály.
Magyar Művelődési Intézet. n.d. Magyar Művelődési Intézet webpage. Accessed August 2007. http://www.mmi.hu/.
Magyar Nemzet (online edition). 2004. "Speaker Katalin Szili Bood and Hissed in Kassa." December 13. Accessed January 3, 2005. http://mno.bfsdemo.hu/index.mno?cikk=256249&rvt=48&norel=1&PHPSESSID=efe36c837d747079842bfd58429f6117&pass=2.
Magyar Népművelési Intézet. 1976. "Kiserleti Tanchazvezetoket kepzo tanfolyam nyitofoglalkozasa. *HÍRADO: A Népművelési Intézet Szakmai Tájékoztatoja* 5–6:24.
Magyarorszag Alaptörvénye. 2011. Hungarian Parliament webpage. http://www.parlament.hu/irom39/02627/02627.pdf.
Magyar Szemle. 2003. "A Magyar Táncnyelv és a Táncszinház: Interjú Novák Ferenccel." *Magyar Szemle* 4 (7–8): 55–57.
Magyar Távirati Iroda. 2004. "Hungary Is One of Europe's Least Competitive Countries, Prime Minister Ferenc Gyurcsány Said on Public Television on Wednesday." November 12, 2004.
———. 2007. "More Hungarians Dissatisfied with Transition." March 19, 2007.
Magyar Televizio. n.d. "Csak Beszélj Gonosz Korondi! Portrait of Lajos Lorincz." Interview by Ferenc Sebő. Budapest: Magyar Televizio.
Mahmud, Lilith. 2020. "Fascism, a Haunting: Spectral Politics and Antifascist Resistance in Twenty-first Century Italy." In *Beyond Populism: Angry Politics and the Twilight of Neoliberalism*, edited by Jeff Maskovsky and Sophie Bjork-James, 141–166. Morgantown: West Virginia University Press.
Mamdani, Mahmood. 2005. *Good Muslim, Bad Muslim: America, the Cold War, and the Roots of Terror*. New York: Doubleday.
Mandel, Ruth. 1993. "Seeding Civil Society." In *Ideals, Ideologies and Practices in Eurasia*, edited by C. M. Hann, 279–296. New York: Routledge.
Mars, Leonard. 1999. "Anthropological Reflections on Jewish Identity in Contemporary Hungary." In *Central European University Jewish Studies Yearbook I*, edited by András Kovács, 157–69. Budapest: Central European University Press.
Martin, György. 1968. Performing Styles in the Dances of the Carpathian Basin. *Journal of the International Folk Music Council* 20:59–64.
———. 1974. "Válaszol: Martin György." Interview by Ilona Budai. *Tiszatáj* 28 (1974/9): 60–64.
———. 1980a. "A Kárpát Medence Népeinek Tánckultúrája." In *Magyar Néptánchagyományok*, 11–14. Budapest: Zeneműkiadó.
———. 1980b. "Körtáncok, Lánctáncok." In *Magyar Néptánchagyományok*, 45–102. Budapest: Zeneműkiadó.
———. 1980c. "Néphagyomány, Néptánc." *Tiszatáj* XXXIV (1): 107–12.
———. 1981. "Szék Felfedése és Tánchagyományai." *Tánctudományi Tanulmányok 1980–1981*, edited by Beres András and Mária Szentpál, 239–77. Budapest: A Magyar Tancmuveszek Szövetsége Tudományos Tágozata.
———. 1982. "A Széki Hagyományok Felfedése és Szerepe a Magyarországi Folklorizmusban." *Ethnographia* 93 (1): 74–83.

———. 1988 (1974). *Hungarian Folk Dances*. Translated by Dienes Gedeon. 2nd rev. ed. Budapest: Kner Printing House.
———. 2001. "Discovering Szék." *Hungarian Heritage* 2:31–53.
Martin, József Péter. 2017. "Continuity of Disruption? Changing Elite and the Emergence of Cronyism after the Great Recession: The Case of Hungary." *Corvinus Journal of Sociology and Social Policy* 8 (20): 255–81.
Marx, Karl. 1991 (1869). *The Eighteenth Brumaire of Louis Bonaparte*. New York: International Publishers.
Mathieson, Alister, and Geoffrey Wall. 1982. *Tourism: Economic, Physical and Social Impacts*. Essex, UK: Longman House.
Mauss, Marcel. 1973 (1934). "Techniques of the Body." In *Sociology and Psychology*, 95–135. Translated by B. Brewster. London: Routledge.
Maynard, David. 1997. "Rurality, Rusticity, and Contested Identity Politics in Brittany." In *Knowing Your Place: Rural Identity and Cultural Hierarchy*, edited by Barbara Ching and Gerald Creed, 195–218. New York: Routledge.
McIntyre, Alistair. 2007. *After Virtue*. Notre Dame, IN: University of Notre Dame Press.
Mediatica. 2006. "Jó gyakorlat a falusi turizmusban—tanfolyamzáró Kalotaszentkirályon." February 9, 2006. http://www.mediatica.ro/hirek/kozelet/10786/jo-gyakorlat-a-falusi-turizmusban-8211-tanfolyamzaro-kalotaszentkiralyon.html.
Meiksins Wood, Ellen. 1990. "The Uses and Abuses of 'Civil Society.'" *Socialist Register* 26:60–84.
———.1999. "Unhappy Families." *Monthly Review* 51 (3): 1–12.
Melegh, Attila. 2000. "Mozgó Kelet. Globális térképek es statustörvény." In *A Zárva Várt Nyugat*, edited by János Kovács, 105–137. Budapest: Sík Kiado.
———. 2006. *On the East/West Slope: Globalization, Nationalism, Racism and Discourses on Central and Eastern Europe*. New York: Central European University Press.
Melucci, Alberto. 1988. "Social Movements and the Democratization of Everyday Life." In *Civil Society and the State*, edited by John Keane, 245–260 London: Verso.
Meskell, Lynn, and Christoph Brumann. 2015. "UNESCO and New World Orders." In *Global Heritage, a Reader*, edited by Lynn Meskell, 22–42. Malden, MA: Wiley-Blackwell.
Mignolo, Walter D., and Madina Tlostanova. 2008. "The Logic of Coloniality." In *The Postcolonial and the Global*, edited by Revathi Krishnaswamy and John Charles Hawley, 109–221. Minneapolis: University of Minnesota Press.
Mikuš, Marek. 2018. *Frontiers of Civil Society: Government and Hegemony in Serbia*. New York: Berghahn.
Mócsy, István I. 1983. *The Effects of World War I: Hungarian Refugees and Their Impact on Hungary's Domestic Politics, 1918–1921*. New York: Columbia University Press.
Monsters and Critics. 2007. "Hungarian Opposition Plans Referendum for Next Spring." Monsters and Critics, June 26, 2007. Accessed July 3, 2017 http://news.monstersandcritics.com/europe/news/article_1322541.php/Hungarian_opposition_plans_referendum_for_next_spring.
Mooney, James. 1991. *The Ghost-Dance Religion and the Sioux Outbreak of 1890*. Lincoln: University of Nebraska Press.
Mouffe, Chantal. 2009. "Democratic Politics in the Age of Post-Fordism." *Open: Cahier on Art and the Public Domain* 16 (2): 32–40.
Muñoz, José Esteban. 2000. "Feeling Brown: Ethnicity and Affect in Ricardo Bracho's 'The Sweetest Hangover (and Other STDs).'" *Theatre Journal* 52 (1): 67–79.
Murer, Jeffrey Stevenson. 2005. "Against the Radical Center: Transcending the Left-Right Political Spectrum." Paper presented at the tenth-annual Convention of the Association for the Study of Nationalities, April 14–16, 2005. Columbia University, New York.

Nadra, Valeria. 1977. "'Semmi Újat Nem Találtunk Ki:' Beszélgetes Sebő Ferenccel." *Kritika* 77 (2): 4–6.
Nagengast, Carol. 1991. *Reluctant Socialists, Rural Entrepreneurs*. Boulder, CO: Westview Press.
Nagy, Piroska. 2011. *Az Eufória Évei/Years of Euphoria 1988–1990*. Budapest: Keiselbach Gallery.
Negyedik Köztársaság. n.d. "A Program Alapja: A Patriotizmus." http://negyedikkoztarsasag.hu/program.
Nemes, Robert. 2001. "The Politics of the Dance Floor: Culture and Civil Society in Nineteenth-Century Hungary." *Slavic Review* 60 (4): 802–823.
Nemzeti Kulturális Örökség Minisztériuma Közművelődési Főosztálya. 2000. *Szempontok és Segédanyagok*. Budapest: Nemzeti Kulturális Örökség Minisztériuma Közművelődési Főosztály.
Népszabadság. 2006. "Az MDF Nem Kér a 'Fidesz halálos öleléséből.'" April 10, 2006. http://nol.hu/cikk/400237.
New York Times. 1988a. "Hungarians March to Protest Rumania Plan." June 29, 1988, A8.
———. 1988b. "Hungary-Rumania Rift Unresolved." September 1, 1988.
———. 1988c. "Protesters March to Remember Nagy." June 17, 1988, A6.
Nikočević, Lidija. 2004. "The Intangibility of Multiculturalism." Paper presented at Museums and Intangible Heritage ICOM general conference, October 2004, Seoul, Korea. Accessed April 25 2006. http://museumsnett.no/icme/icme2004/Nikocevic.html.
Noszkai, Gábor. 2009. "Barátok Közt." *Beszélő* 14 (11): 35–47.
Novak, Benjamin. 2018. "More than 500 Academics Sign Petition Denouncing Gov't for Attacking Professor and Targeting Civil Society." *Budapest Beacon*, March 1, 2018. https://budapestbeacon.com/500-academics-sign-petition-denouncing-govt-attacking-professor-targeting-civil-society/.
Olick, J. K., and Robbins, J., 1998. "Social Memory Studies: From 'Collective Memory' to the Historical Sociology of Mnemonic Practices." *Annual Review of Sociology* 24 (1): 105–40.
Olverholser, Lisa. 2008. "The Hungarian State Folk Ensemble as a Dynamic Institution in Hungarian Ethnography." *Hungarian Studies* 22 (1–2): 31–42.
Ötvös, Ervin. 1989. "Szabad Sajtó Magyarországon: 1956." *Új Látohatár Valogatás 1950–1989*. Budapest: Püski.
Paládi Kovács, Attila. 1996. *Ethnic Traditions and Classes and Communities in Hungary*. Budapest: Institute of Ethnology.
———. 2004. "A Nemzeti Kulturális Örökség fogalma, tárgya." *Honismeret* 32 (2): 61–67.
Pálfi Csaba. 1970. "A Gyöngyösbokréta Története." *Tánctudományi Tanulmányok 1969–1970*, edited by Zoltán Dienes and László Maácz, 115–160 Budapest: A Magyar Táncművészek Szövetsége Tudományos Tágozata.
Pallás Lexikon. 1893. Budapest: Pallás Irodalmi és Nyomda Reszvény Tarsaság.
Paluch, Norbert. 2004. "Aki A Székieket behívta a próbateremebe; Timár Sándor ('Mesti')." *FolkMAGazin* 11 (5): 38–41.
Pap, Gábor. 1999. *Hazatalalás: Művelődéstörténeti Írások*. Budapest: Püski.
Parakilas, J. 1995. "Folk Song as Musical Wet Nurse: The Prehistory of Bartók's 'For Children.'" *Musical Quarterly* 79 (3): 476–99.
Pastor, Peter. 2018. "The Travelogues of Gyula Illyés and Lajos Nagy on Their Visit to the Soviet Union." *Hungarian Cultural Studies* 11:32–47.
Pávai, István. 2001. *Barozda 1976–2001*. Csíkszereda: Alutus.
Peck, Jamie, and Adam Tickell. 2002. "Neoliberalizing Space." *Antipode* 34 (3): 380–404.
Perugini, Cristiano, and Pompei, Fabrizio, eds. 2015. *Inequalities during and after Transition in Central and Eastern Europe*. New York: Palgrave.

Pesovár, Ernő. 1980. "Europai Tánckultura-Nemzeti Tánckulturánk." In *Magyar Néptánchagyományok*, edited by Lajos Lelkes, 8–10. Budapest: Zeneműkiado.
———. 1982. *A Magyar Tánctörténet Évszázadai*. Budapest: Népművelési Propoganda Iroda.
———. 2003. "Hagyomány és Korszerűség." In *Hagyomány és Korszerűség: A Magyar Állami Együttes 50 Éves*. Budapest: Hagyományok Háza.
Pesovár, Ferenc. 1978. *A Magyar Nép Tancélete*. Budapest: Népművelési Propaganda Iroda.
Péteri, Lóránt. 2013. "'A Mi Népünk Az Ön Népe, De Az Enyém Is . . .': Kodály Zoltán, Kádár János és a paternalista gondolkodásmód." *Magyar Zene* 51 (2):121–41.
Pethő, V. 2009. "Az életreform és a zenei mozgalmak." *Iskolakultúra* 19 (1–2): 3–19.
Piattoni, Simona, and Marc Smyrl. 2003. "Building Effective Institutions: Italian Regions and the EU Structural Funds." In *Between Europeanization and Local Societies*, edited by Jeanni Bukowski, Simona Piattoni, and Marc Smyrl. New York: Rowman and Littlefield.
Pizzorno, Alessandro. 1983. "The Rationality of Democratic Choices." *Telos* 18 (63): 41– 69.
Plavsic, Dragan. 2016. "Bosnia, a Serb Referendum and the Left." *LeftEast*, September 27, 2016.
Polányi, Karl. 1957 (1944). *The Great Transformation*. Boston: Beacon Press.
Polgár, Hajnalka. 1994. "Az Országos Közművelődési Központ Művelődéskutató Intézetnek Tevékénysége 1986, Marc. 1–1991, Dec. 31 Amély a Magyar Művelődési Intézet Jogelődje." Master's thesis, Zsámbéki Katholokus Tanitoképző Főiskola.
Polgár, Katalin. 1994. "A Népművészeti Intézet Története/1951–1957. marc.1/A Magyar Művelődési Intézet Jogelődje." Master's thesis, Zsámbéki Katholikus Tanitóképző Főiskola.
Popovici, Veda, and Ovidiu Pop. 2016. "From over Here, in the Periphery: A Decolonial Method for Romanian Cultural and Political Discourses." *LeftEast*, February 11, 2016.
Portes, A., 1998. "Social Capital: Its Origins and Applications in Modern Sociology." *Annual Review of Sociology* 24 (1): 1–24.
Prott, Lyndel V. n.d. "Some Considerations on the Protection of the Intangible Heritage: Claims and Remedies." Chief International Standards Section, Division of Cultural Heritage, UNESCO. Accessed January 2006. http://www.folklife.si.edu/resources/Unesco/prott.htm.
Pulay, Gergő. 2007. "Ethnicity, the Labour Market and Returning Migrants between Hungary and Transylvania." Multicultural Center Prague, June 2007. Migrationonline.cz.
———. 2014. "Staging Ethnicity: Cultural Politics and Musical Practices of Roma Performers in Budapest." *Acta Ethnographica Hungarica* 59 (1): 3–24.
Putnam, R. 1993. "The Prosperous Community: Social Capital and Public Life. *The American Prospect* 4, no. 13 (Spring). http://www.prospect.org/print/vol/13.
Quigley, Colin. 2014. "The Hungarian Dance House Movement and Revival of Transylvanian String Band Music." In *The Oxford Handbook of Music Revival*, edited by Caroline Bithell and Juniper Hill, 182–202. New York: Oxford University Press.
Rácz, Barnabas. 2003. "The Left in Hungary and the 2002 Parliamentary Elections." *Europe-Asia Studies* 55 (5): 749–69.
Radio Free Europe. 2004a. "Ethnic Hungarians in Romania Unhappy with Outcome of Hungarian Referendum." Radio Free Europe, August 18, 2004.
———. 2004b. "UDMR Says Decentralization Must Continue in Romania." Radio Free Europe, December 13, 2004.
———. 2004c. "While Szeklers Push For Referendum on Autonomy." Radio Free Europe, April 26, 2004.

Rainer, János. 2002. "The New Course in Hungary." Working paper no. 38, Woodrow Wilson International Center for Scholars. Accessed June 12, 2003. https://www.wilsoncenter.org/publication/the-new-course-hungary-1953.
———. 2009. *Imre Nagy, A Biography*. London: I. B. Tauris and Co.
Rajagopal, Arvind. 2001. *Politics after Television: Hindu Nationalism and the Reshaping of the Public in India*. Cambridge: Cambridge University Press.
Rajk, András. 1980. "Magyar Kulturális Hetek Salzburgban." *Muzsika* 33 (1): 21–23.
Renwick, Alan. 2006. "Anti-political or Just Anti-Communist? Varieties of Dissidence in East-Central Europe and Their Implications for the Development of Political Society." *East European Politics and Societies* 20 (2): 286–318.
Réthelyi, Mari. 2018. "Good Writers, Bad Jews: The 'Jewish Question' among Hungarian Intellectuals of the Interwar Period." *Journal of Modern Jewish Studies* 17 (2): 222–35.
Robin, Regine. 1990. "Stalinism and Popular Culture." In *The Culture of the Stalin Period*, edited by Hans Gunter, 15–40. London: Macmillan.
Robinson, Cedric. J., 2000. *Black Marxism: The Making of the Black Radical Tradition*. Chapel Hill: University of North Carolina Press.
Romanian Ministry of Transportation, Construction, and Tourism. 2007. "Destination Romania." Agrotourism webpage. Accessed March 2007. http://www.destinationromania.eu/agroturismul.php.
Romsics, Ignác. 2015. "The Great War and the 1918–19 Revolutions as Experienced and Remembered by the Hungarian Peasantry." *Region* 4 (2):173–94.
Romsics, Imre. 2001. "The Folk Art of Kalocsa." *Hungarian Heritage* 2:7–30.
Rona-Tas, A. 1990. "The Second Economy in Hungary: The Social Origins of the End of State Socialism." PhD diss., University of Michigan, Minneapolis.
Ronay, Esther, dir. 1992. *Beyond the Forest: Hungarian Music in Transylvania*. London: Flashback Television and British Arts Council for Channel 4.
Ronström, Owe. 1998. "'Revival in Retrospect': The Folk Music and Dance Revival." *European Centre for Traditional Culture, Bulletin IV*.
Rose, R., and Haerpfer, C. 1996. *Change and Stability in the New Democracies Barometer: A Trend Analysis* (No. 270). Studies in Public Policy No. 262, Centre for the Study of Public Policy, University of Strathclyde, Glasgow.
Roseberry, William. 1989. *Anthropologies and Histories, Essays in Culture, History, and Political Economy*. New Brunswick, NJ: Rutgers University.
———. 1994. "Hegemony and the Language of Contention." In *Everyday Forms of State Formation*, edited by Gilbert M. Joseph and Daniel Nugent, 355–66. Durham, NC: Duke University Press.
Rosenberg, Neil V., ed. 1993. *Transforming Traditions: Folk Music Revivals Examined*. Urbana: University of Illinois Press.
Sági, Mária. 1977. "Táncház a Kassákban." *Kultura és Közösség* 3:105–15.
———. 1978. "A Táncház." *Valóság* 5:68–76.
Sakmeister, Thomas. 2006. "Gyula Gömbös and Hungarian Jews, 1918–1936." *Hungarian Studies Review* 33 (1–2): 157–68.
Salaita, Steven. 2016. *Inter/Nationalism: Decolonizing Native America and Palestine*. Minneapolis: University of Minnesota Press.
Sampson, Steven 1996. "The Social Life of Projects: Importing Civil Society to Albania." In *Civil Society; Challenging Western Models*, edited by C. M. Hann and Elizabth Dunn, 121–42. London: Routledge.
Sándor, Ildikó. 2002. "Csángó Táncház-Minority Culture-Identity." *Hungarian Heritage* 3:80–86.

Sárkány, Mihály. 1997. "Cultural and Social Anthropology in Central and Eastern Europe." In *Three Social Science Disciplines in Central and Eastern Europe, Handbook on Economics, Political Science and Sociology* (1989–2001), edited by M. Kis ax Kaase, Vera Sparschuch, and Agnieszka Wenninger, 558–66. Budapest: Social Science Information Centre (IZ)/Collegium Budapest.

———. 2005. "Hungarian Anthropology in the Socialist Era." In *Studying Peoples in the People's Democracies*, edited by Chris Hann, Mihály Sárkány, and Peter Skalník, 87–108. Münster: LitVerlag.

Sárosi Bálint. 1993. "Hungary and Romania." In *Ethnomusicology, Historical and Regional Studies*, edited by Hellen Myers, 187–96. New York: W. W. Norton/Grove.

Schachter, S., and J. E. Singer. 1962. "Cognitive, Social and Physiological Determinants of Emotional State." *Psychological Review* 69 (5): 379–99.

Scheppele, Kim Lane. 2011. "Hungary's Constitutional Revolution." *Conscience of a Liberal* (blog), December 19, 2011. http://krugman.blogs.nytimes.com/2011/12/19/hungarys-constitutional-revolution.

Schneider, David E. 2006. *Bartok, Hungary, and the Renewal of Tradition: Case Studies in the Intersection of Modernity and Nationality*. Berkeley: University of California Press.

Schneider, Jane. 1998. "Introduction: The Dynamics of Neo-orientalism in Italy (1848–1995)." In *Italy's Southern Question: Orientalism in One Country*, edited by Jane Schneider, 1–23. Oxford: Berg.

Scott, David. 1999. *Refashioning Futures*. Princeton, NJ: Princeton University Press.

Sebő, Ferenc. 1973. "Ifjú Népművészek Önmagukrol." *Latohatár*, December, 145–48.

———. 1976a. "Beszelgetés Sebő Ferenccel." *Kultura es Közösseg*, no. 2–3.

———. 1976b. "Szemtől Szembe Sebő Ferenccel." *Latohatár*, February, 188–95.

———. 1977. "Semmi Újat Nem Találtunk Ki." *Kritika* 77 (2): 4–6.

———. 1981. "Aprók Tánca," *Nyári Vakácio*. Budapest: RTV Minerva.

———. 1983. "A Népzenéről." In *Lányok Könyve*, 74–75. Budapest: Mora Könyvkiadó

———. 1993. "A Revival Mozgalmak és a Táncház Magyarországon." *Az Anyanyelvi Konferencia Tájékoztatója*. Budapest: A Magyar Nyelv és Kultúra Nemzetközi Tarsasága.

———. 1998. "The Revival Movements and the Dancehouse in Hungary." *European Center for Traditional Culture Bulletin* 4: 34–38.

———. 2001. "Pátria: Magyar Népzenei Gramofónfelvételetek." *Hungarian* Heritage 2:111–14.

Seligman, Adam. 1992. *The Idea of Civil Society*. New York: Free Press.

Shafir, Michael. 2001. "Hungary and the Holocaust: The Nationalist Drive to Whitewash the Past (Part 2)." Radio Free Europe/Radio Liberty Reports, October 31, 2001. Accessed August 2007. http://www.rferl.org/reports/eepreport/2001/10/19-311001.asp.

Sharma, Aradhana, and Akhil Gupta. 2006. "Rethinking Theories of the State in an Age of Globalization." In *The Anthropology of the State, a Reader*, edited by Aradhana Sharma and Akhil Gupta, 1–41. Oxford: Blackwell.

Siegelbaum, Lewis H. 1999. "The Shaping of Soviet Workers' Leisure: Workers' Clubs and Palaces of Culture in the 1930s." *International Labor and Working Class History* 56:78–92.

Sieyes, Emmanuel Joseph. 1964. *What Is the Third Estate?* Edited by S. E. Finer. Translated by M. Blondel. New York: Praeger.

Siklos, László. 1977. *Táncház*. Budapest: Zeneműkiadó.

———. 1987. "The Dancehouse: Folklorism in Hungary in the 1970's." *Forum* 1.

Silverman, Carol. 1983. "The Politics of Folklore in Bulgaria." Special issue, *Anthropological Quarterly* 56 (2).

———. 2012. *Romani Routes: Cultural Politics and Balkan Music in Diaspora.* New York: Oxford University Press.
———. 2014. "Balkan Romani Culture, Human Rights, and the State: Whose Heritage?" In *Cultural Heritage in Transit: Intangible Rights as Human Rights,* edited by Deborah Kapchan, 125–47. Philadelphia: University of Pennsylvania Press.
Simmel, Georg. 1971. *On Individuality and Social Forms.* Chicago: University of Chicago Press.
Sipos, Zoltán. 2016. "Csíksomlyó az UNESCO-ban." Átlátszó Erdély, September 12, 2016. https://atlatszo.ro/oroksegvedelem/csiksomlyo-az-unesco-ban-magyarorszag-frontalisan-tamad-romania-ravaszul-kiter/.
Sklar, Deidre. 1991. "On Dance Ethnography." *Dance Research Journal* 23 (1): 6.
Slobin, Mark. 1996. "Introduction." In *Retuning Culture Musical Changes in Central and Eastern Europe,* edited by Mark Slobin, 1–13. Durham: Duke University Press.
Smith, Adrian. 2007. "Articulating Neo-Liberalism: Diverse Economies and Everyday Life in 'Post-Socialist' Cities." In *Contesting Neoliberalism: Urban Frontiers,* edited by Helga Leitner, Jamie Peck, and Eric Sheppard, 204–22. London: Guilford.
Smith, Neil. 1996. "Contours of a Spatialized Politics: Homeless Vehicles and the Production of Geographical Scale." *Social Text* 33:55–81.
Soysal, Levent. 2009. "Introduction: Triumph of Culture, Troubles of Anthropology." *Focaal* 55:3–11.
Spiró, György. 2016. "I Am not an Assimilated, I'm Hungarian." *Mandiner,* April 5, 2016. https://mandiner.hu/cikk/20160405_spiro_gyorgy_nem_asszimilans_vagyok_hanem_magyar.
Springer, Chris. 1997. "Moldova and Romania: the Broken Engagement." Paper prepared for the East West Working Group. Accessed September 2007. http://www.east-west-wg.org/index.html.
Staddon, C., and Cellarius, B. 2002. "Environmental Non-governmental Organizations, Civil Society and Democratisation in Bulgaria." *East European Politics and Societies,* 16 (1): 182–222.
Stagl, Justin. 1998. "Rationalism and Irrationalism in Early German Ethnology: The Controversy between Schlözer and Herder, 1772/73." *Anthropos* 93:521–36.
Stan, Lavinia. 2006. "The Roof over Our Heads: Property Restitution in Romania." *Journal of Communist Studies and Transition Politics* 22 (2):180–205.
Stan, Sabina. 2000. "What's in a Pig? 'State,' 'Market' and Process in Private Pig Production and Consumption in Romania." *Dialectical Anthropology* 25:151–60.
Staniszkis, Jadwiga. 1984. *Poland's Self-Limiting Revolution.* Princeton, NJ: Princeton University Press.
Stewart, Michael. 1997. *The Time of the Gypsies.* Boulder, CO: Westview Press.
Stockmans, Pieter. 2018. "This Is a War for Land, Romania Is the Battlefield.' *Mondial News,* August 13, 2018. https://www.mo.be/en/report/war-land-romania-battlefield.
Stokes, Martin. 1992. *The Arabesque Debate.* Oxford: Oxford University Press
Stolke, Verena. 1995. "Talking Culture: New Boundaries, New Rhetorics of Exclusion in Europe." *Current Anthropology* 36 (1): 1–24.
Stratfor. 2012. "Central and Eastern Europe Face Emigration Challenge." *Stratfor,* April 23, 2021. https://worldview.stratfor.com/article/central-and-eastern-europe-face-emigration-challenge.
Streda, Dunajska. 2018. "Hungary's Orban Courts Diaspora for Election Boost." *France24,* March 28, 2018. https://www.france24.com/en/20180328-hungarys-orban-courts-diaspora-election-boost.

Striker, Sándor. 1984. "The Dancehouse; Folklorism in Hungary in the 1970s." *Forum* 1:100–31.

———. 1987. "Voluntary Education as Public Communication in Hungary." In *On the Role of Voluntary Associations in Social and Cultural Development in Hungary and the Netherlands*, 233–47. Budapest: OKK.

———. 1989a. "Az öntevékenység társadalmi üzenete." *Kultúra és Közösség* 13:79–91.

———. 1989b. "Culture for Sale: Voluntary Education under Pseudo-Market Conditions in Contemporary Hungary." Paper presented at the INTERPHIL Regional Meeting, Budapest, 1989.

Stroe, Daniel. 2014. "Hungary Sets up Program to Buy Land in Romania's Transylvania." Independent Balkan News Agency, August 1, 2014. https://balkaneu.com/hungary-sets-program-buy-land-romanias-transylvania/.

Stroschein, Sherrill. 2012. *Ethnic Struggle, Coexistence, and Democratization in Eastern Europe*. New York: Cambridge University Press.

Suchoff, Benjamin. 1961. "Béla Bartók's Contributions to Music Education." *Journal of Research in Music Education* 9 (1): 3–9.

Sugár, Péter. 1969. "External and Domestic Roots of Eastern European Nationalism." In *Nationalism in Eastern Europe*, edited by Péter Sugár and Ivo Lederer. Seattle: University of Washington Press.

Swain, Nigel. 1999. "Small Scale Farming in the Post-Socialist Rural Transition." *Eastern European Countryside* 5 (35): 27–41.

Sylvain, Renee. 2003. "Disorderly Development: Globalization and the Idea of "Culture" in the Kalahari." *American Ethnologist* 32 (3): 354–70.

Szabó, Árpád Töhötöm. 2012. "Where Are the Tourists? Shifting Production, Changing Localities in a Szekler Village." In *From Production to Consumption: Transformation of Rural Communities*, edited by Hana Horakova and Andrea Boscobolnik, 63–78. Vienna: Lit.

Szabó, Zoltán. 1998. "Indulj El Egy Úton: Adatok a Táncházas Turizmus Kerdéséhez." In *A Turizmus Mint Kulturalis Rendszer*, edited by Zoltán Fejős, 169–81. Budapest: Néprajzi Muzeum.

Szalai, Julia. 2013. "Hungary's Bifurcated Welfare State Splitting Social Rights and the Social Exclusion of Roma." Working Paper 2013:05, University of Glasgow. Accessed September 12, 2017. https://www.gla.ac.uk/media/media_278875_en.pdf.

Szalay, Karoly. 1974. "Örzők ás tékozlok." *Tiszatáj* 28 (9): 52–56.

Szász, János. 1981. "Beszélgetés Martin Györgyyel Az Új Folklorhullam és Néptáncmozgalom Előzményeiről." *Kultura és Közösség* 81 (4): 42–53.

Szedlacsek, Petru. 2015. "Instrumentalizing Szeklerland Autonomy through Szekler Memory Sites and Rites in Post-1989 Romania." *Culture* 9:39–50.

Szelényi, Iván. 1988. *Socialist Entrepreneurs*. Madison: University of Wisconsin Press.

Szelényi, Ivan, Robert Manchin, Pál Juhász, Bálint Magyar, and Bill Martin. 1988. *Socialist Entrepreneurs: Embourgeoisement in Rural Hungary*. Madison: University of Wisconsin Press.

Szelényi, Sonja, Iván Szelényi, and Imre Kovach. 1995. "The Making of the Hungarian Postcomunist Elite: Circulation in Politics, Reproduction in the Economy." *Theory and Society* 24 (5): 697–722.

Széll, Jenő. 1986. *Huzzad, Huzzad, Muzsikásom: A Hangszeres Népzene Feltámadása*. Budapest: Muszaki Közművelődési Kiadó.

Szemere, Anna. 2010. *Up from the Underground: The Culture of Rock Music in Postsocialist Hungary*. University Park: Pennsylvania State University Press.

Szilvay, Gergely. 2017. "Botrány a kultúrdiplomáciában: lerománozzák a magyar néptánc zenéjét?" *Mandiner,* July 6, 2017. https://mandiner.hu/cikk/20170704_kultur diplomacia_botrany_leromanozzak_a_magyar_nepzenet_ 2017.

Szolláth, David. 2008. "The Communist Aesthetic of Asceticism." PhD diss., University of Pécs. https://pea.lib.pte.hu/bitstream/handle/pea/14775/szollath-david-phd-2009.pdf.

Szombati, Kristóf. 2018. *The Revolt of the Provinces: Anti-Gypsyism and Right-Wing Politics in Hungary.* New York: Berghahn.

Szűcs, Jenő. 1990. "The Peoples of Medieval Hungary." In *Ethnicity and Society in Hungary,* edited by Ferenc Glatz, 11–20. Budapest: National Committee of Hungarian Historians.

Szymanowska, Lucie. 2011. "The Implementation of the Hungarian Citizenship Law." Center for Eastern Studies, February 2, 2011. https://www.osw.waw.pl/en/publikacje/analyses/2011-02-02/implementation-hungarian-citizenship-law.

Tamás, Gáspár Miklós. 2004. "Tartózkodunk a szavazástól." *Népszabadság,* November 14, 2004.

Tánczos, Vilmos. 2018. "The New Cultural Economy and the Ideologies of the Csíksomlyó (Şumuleu Ciuc) Pilgrimage Feast." In *Cultural Heritage and Cultural Politics in Minority Conditions,* edited by Árpád Töhötöm Szabó and Mária Szikszai, 145-178. Cluj-Napoca: Aarhus, Kriza János Ethnographic Society—Intervention Press.

Tarrow, Sidney. 1988. "National Politics and Collective Action: Recent Theory and Research in Western Europe and the United States." *Annual Review of Sociology* 14:421–40.

Taylor, Mary N. 2003. "What's Right in Hungary? The Politics of Citizenship and Nation and the Referendum of 2004." Paper presented at the Society for the Anthropology of North America Annual Meetings, April 22, 2006, Baruch College, New York, NY.

———. 2009. "Intangible Heritage Governance, Cultural Diversity, Ethnonationalism." *Focaal* 55:41–58.

———. 2014. "Struggles in and over Public Space: Hungarian Heritage as a Homeless Free Zone." Critical Commentary: A Forum for Research and Commentary on Europe, June 18, 2014. http://councilforeuropeanstudies.org/critcom/struggles-in-and-over-public-space-hungarian-heritage-as-homeless-free-zone/.

———. 2016: "Intangible Heritage Protection and the Cultivation of a Universal Chain of Equivalency." Ed. Clemence Scalbert-Yucel, special issue, *Nationalism and Ethnic Politics,* 22 (1): 27–49.

———. 2018. "Land-grabbing and the Financialization of Agricultural Land." *LeftEast,* May 21, 2018. https://lefteast.org/land-grabbing-and-the-financialization-of-agricultural-land/.

———. 2020. "Hungarian 'Populism' and Antipopulism Today through the Looking Glass of the Interwar 'Populist' Movement. In *Back to the 30s?* edited by Jeremy Rayner, Susan Falls, George Souvlis, and Taylor Nelms, 179–200. New York: Palgrave.

Taylor, Mary N., and Csilla Kalocsai. 2011. "(Neo)liberalization of Socialism and Crises of Capital." Course description, Central European University summer university. https://summeruniversity.ceu.edu/node/161.

Tichindeleanu, Ovidiu. 2016. "NO to Transition 2.0: Social Recomposition, Decolonisation, and Transautonomism." *LeftEast,* February 17, 2016.

Tilly, Charles. 1978. *From Mobilization to Revolution.* Reading, PA: Addison-Wesley.

———. 1983. "Social Movements and National Politics." In *Statemaking and Social Movements,* edited by Charles Bright and Susan Harding, 297–317. Ann Arbor: University of Michigan Press.

Timár Sándor. 1999. *Néptáncnyelven: A Timár-módszer Alkalmazása A Jatékba és Táncra Nevelésben*. Budapest: Püski.

Times (online edition). 2005. "Romania's Last Peasants." October 13, 2005. http://www.timesonline.co.uk/tol/news/world/europe/article578172.ece.

Tlostanova, Madina. 2014. "Why the Socialist Cannot Speak: On Caucasian Blacks, Imperial Difference, and Decolonial Horizons." In *Postcoloniality–Decoloniality–Black Critique: Joints and Fissures*, edited by Sabine Broeck and Carsten Junker, 159–73. Frankfurt: Verlag.

Todorova, Maria. 2009. *Imagining the Balkans*. Oxford: Oxford University Press.

Tóth, Csaba Tibor. 2012. Szekfű és Erdei, mint toposzok: Néhány megjegyzés a 2012-es 'antiszemitizmus-vita' társadalmi-történeti hátteréhez." *Egyenlítő* 10 (10): 30–34.

———. 2016. "Fasiszta nép, demokratikus nemzet? Az oktatás nacionalizálása majdállamosítása 1945 után [Fascist people, democratic nation? The nationalisation and state-grab of the school system in Hungary post-1945]." 1956 és szocializmus: Válság és újragondolás" conference, September 8–10, 2016. Károly Esterházy College, Eger, Hungary.

Tóth, János. 1983. "Folk High School Movement and Voluntary Cultural Activity 1939–1945, a Historical Outline." In *Voluntary Organizations in Hungary and the Netherlands*, edited by József Katus and János Tóth. Budapest: OKK. Tötösy de Zepetnek, Steven. 2011. "The Anti-Other in Post-1989 Austria and Hungary." In *Comparative Hungarian Cultural Studies*, edited by Steven Tötösy de Zepetnek and Louise O. Vasvári, 332–44. West Lafayette, IN: Purdue University Press.

Touraine, Alain. 1977. *The Self-Production of Society*. Chicago: University of Chicago Press.

Trencsényi, Balázs, and Michal Kopeček, eds. 2007. *National Romanticism: The Formation of National Movements; Discourses of Collective Identity in Central and Southeast Europe 1770–1945*. Vol. 2. Budapest: Central European University Press.

Trencsényi, László. 1985. "Kalandozások Multban és Jövőben." In *Mozgalmi: Nevelési Tájékoztatás A Magyar Úttörök Szövetségében*, vol. 3, 6–15. Budapest: Ifjúsági Lap-es Könyvkiadó.

Tucker-Mohl, Jessica. 2005. "Property Rights and Transitional Justice: Restitution in Hungary and East Germany." Unpublished paper. Accessed December 2007. https://ocw.mit.edu/courses/urban-studies-and-planning/11-467j-property-rights-in-transition-spring-2005/projects/jtuckermohlfinal.pdf.

Turner, Victor. 1995. *Liminality and Communitas in the Ritual Process: Structure and Anti-Structure*. New York: Aldine.

Újváry, Ferenc. 1982. "A Gyöngyösbokréta Boldogi Csoportjának Története." In *Táncművészeti Dokumentumok*, 59–94. Budapest: Magyartáncművészek Szovetség.

UNESCO. 1989. Recommandation on the Safeguarding of Traditional Culture and Folklore adopted by the General Conference at its twenty-fifth session. Paris, November 15, 1989. UNESCO.org. Accessed September 2007. http://www.unesco.org/culture/laws/paris/html_eng/page1.shtml.

———. 1993. International Consultation on New Perspectives for UNESCO's Programme: The Intangible Cultural Heritage. Annex to Final Report. UNESCO.org.

———. 1998. "Culture Creativity and Markets." 1998 World Culture Report. UNESCO.org. Accessed April 13, 2007. http://portal.unesco.org/culture/en/ev.php-URL_ID=22452&URL_DO=DO_TOPIC&URL_SECTION=201.html.

———. 2000. "Meeting of the Experts Committee on the Strengthening of UNESCO's Role in Promoting Cultural Diversity in the context of Globalization." UNESCO.org. Accessed July 2007. http://www.unesco.org/culture/industries/html_eng/paris3.shtml.

———. 2001. "UNESCO Universal Declaration on Cultural Diversity." UNESCO.org, November 2, 2011. http://portal.unesco.org/en/ev.php-URL_ID=13179&URL_DO =DO_TOPIC&URL_SECTION=201.html
———. 2006a. "Proclamation Program (for the Safeguarding of Intangible Cultural Heritage)." UNESCO.org. Accessed April 2006. http://portal.unesco.org/culture/en/ev.php-URL_ID=21427&URL_DO=DO_TOPIC&URL_SECTION=201.html#def.
———. 2006b. "Protecting Our Heritage and Fostering Creativity." UNESCO Culture section. UNESCO.org. Accessed March 30 2006. http://portal.unesco.org/culture/en/ev.php-URL_ID=2309&URL_DO=DO_TOPIC&URL_SECTION=201.html.
———. 2007a. "Brief History." World Heritage Centre. UNESCO.org. Accessed March 17, 2007. http://whc.unesco.org/en/169/. UNESCO.org. Accessed April 13, 2007
———. 2007b. "Mission of the Culture Sector 2006–2007." UNESCO.org. Accessed April 13 2007. http://portal.unesco.org/culture/en/ev.php-URL_ID=11498&URL_DO= DO_TOPIC&URL_SECTION=201.html.
———. 2007c. "What Is It? What Does It Do?" About UNESCO. UNESCO.org. http://portal.unesco.org/en/ev.php-URL_ID=3328&URL_DO=DO_TOPIC&URL _SECTION=201.html.
———. 2007d. "World Heritage." World Heritage Convention. UNESCO.org. Accessed April 13, 2007. http://whc.unesco.org/en/about/.
———. 2011. "Convention for the Safeguarding of the Intangible Cultural Heritage." Intergovernmental Committee for the Safeguarding of the Intangible Cultural Heritage, Proposal No. 00515, Programme, Project and Activity Best Reflecting the Principles and Objectives of the Convention in 2011. Bali, Indonesia, Sixth Session, November 2011. http://www.unesco.org/culture/ich/index.php?lg=en&pg=00011&Art18=00515.
———. n.d. "Táncház Method: A Hungarian Model for the Transmission of Intangible Cultural Heritage." Intangible Cultural Heritage. UNESCO.org. Accessed August 2016. http://www.unesco.org/culture/ich/en/BSP/táncház-method-a-hungarian -model-for-the-transmission-of-intangible-cultural-heritage-00515.
Utolsó Óra, n.d. Utolsó Óra website. Accessed March 12, 2019. http://utolsoora.hu/.
Vadási, Tibor. 2001. *Szálljatok, fiókám . . .* Budapest: Hagyományok Háza.
Vardy, Steven B. 1983. "The Impact of Trianon on Hungary and the Hungarian Mind: The Nature of Interwar Irredentism." *Hungarian Studies Review* 1 (10): 21–42.
Varga, Sándor. 2016. "The Influence of Dance-House Tourism on the Social Relationships and Traditions of a Village in Transylvania." *Ethnomusicology Translations* 4. https:// doi.org/10.14434/emt.v0i4.22718.
Varga, Zuzsanna. 2009. "The Agrarian Elite in Hungary before and after the Political Transition." In *European Economic Elites between a New Spirit of Capitalism and the Erosion of State Socialism*, edited by Christoph Boyer and Friderike Sattler, 223–50. Berlin: Duncker and Humblot.
Vargyas, Lajos. 1974. "A Népdal Helye Közművelődésunkben." *Tiszatáj* 9:46–51.
Vasáry Ildikó. 1989. "The 'Sin' of Transdanubia: The One Child System in Rural Hungary." *Continuity and Change* 4 (3) 429–68.
Verdery, Katherine. 1983. *Transylvanian Villagers*. Berkeley: University of California Press.
———. 1993. "Ethnic Relations, Economies of Shortage and the Transition in Eastern Europe." In *Socialism; Ideals, Ideology, and Local Practice*, edited by C. M. Hann, 172–86. London: Routledge.
———. 1995. *National Ideology under Socialism*. Los Angeles: University of California Press.
———. 1996. *What Was Socialism? Why Did It Fall?* Princeton, NJ: Princeton University Press.

———. 1999. "Fuzzy Property: Rights, Power, and Identity in Transylvania's Decollectivization." In *Uncertain Transition Ethnographies of Change in the Postsocialist World*, edited by Michael Burawoy and Katherine Verdery, 53–81. New York: Rowman and Littlefield.

———. 2003. *The Vanishing Hectare: Property and Value in Post Socialist Transylvania*. Ithaca, NY: Cornell University Press.

———. 2004. "The Obligations of Ownership: Restoring Rights to Land in Postsocialist Transylvania." In *Property in Question: Value Transformation in the Global Economy*, edited by Katherine Verdery and Caroline Humphrey, 139–59. Wenner-Glen International Symposium Series. Oxford: Berg.

Vertovec, Steven. 2005. "The Political Importance of Diasporas." Migration Policy Institute. https://www.migrationpolicy.org/article/political-importance-diasporas/.

Vincze, Kata Zsófia. 2011. "About the Jewish Renaissance in Post-1989 Hungary." In *Comparative Hungarian Cultural Studies*, edited by Steven Tötösy de Zepetnek and Louise O. Vasvári, 259–69. West Lafayette, Indiana: Purdue University Press.

Vitányi, Iván. 1964. "A Magyar Néptáncmozgalom Története 1948-ig." In *Tanulmányok a Magyar Táncmozgalom Történetéből I-II*, edited by Edit Kaposi, 7–135. Budapest: Dance Department of Népművelési Intézet.

———. 1971. *Második Prométheuszi Forradalom*. Budapest: Magvető.

———. 1972. "Gondolatok a Táncházban." *Élet és Irodalom* 52:15–17.

———. 1974 "A Népművészet Távlatai." *Kritika* 10:10–11.

———. 1993. *5 meg 5 az 13: Az Áprilisi Front Története*. Budapest: Gondolat.

———. 2003. "A Táncházmozgalom Kezdetei Szociológus Szemmel." Lecture given at Hagyományok Háza, April 16, 2003. Transcript provided by the Martin médiatár, Hagyományok Háza, Budapest.

Volkman, Toby Alice. 1990. "Visions and Revisions: Toraja Culture and the Tourist Gaze." *American Ethnologist* 17 (1): 91–110.

Vörös Károly. 1998. "A Vilagváros Útján: 1873–1918." *Budapesti Negyed* 20–21 (2–3): 112–22.

Vračić, Alida. 2018. "The Way Back: Brain Drain and Prosperity in the Western Balkans." ECFR Policy Brief. https://ecfr.eu/publication/the_way_back_brain_drain_and_prosperity_in_the_western_balkans/.

Wallerstein, Immanuel. 1974. *The Modern World System*. New York: Academic Press.

Waterbury, Myra. 2010. *Between State and Nation: Diaspora Politics and Kin-State Nationalism in Hungary*. New York: Palgrave.

Watson, Graham. 2013. "Orbán 'Enjoys Playing the Bad Boy in the Class.'" Euractiv.com, March 15, 2013. https://www.euractiv.com/section/central-europe/interview/graham-watson-Orbán-enjoys-playing-the-bad-boy-in-the-class/.

Weber, Eugene. 1976. *Peasants into Frenchmen: The Modernization of Rural France, 1870–1914*. Palo Alto: Stanford University Press.

White, Anne. 1990. *De-Stalinization and the House of Culture: Declining State Control over Leisure in the USSR, Poland, and Hungary, 1953–89*. London: Routledge.

Williams, Raymond. 1966. *The Long Revolution*. New York: Harper and Row.

Wolf, Eric R. 1969. *Peasant Wars of the Twentieth Century*. New York: Harper and Row.

———. 1982. *Europe and the People without History*: Berkeley: University of California Press.

———. 2001. "Incorporation and Identity in the Making of the Modern World." In *Pathways of Power: Building an Anthropology of the Modern World*, edited by Aram A. Yengoyan, 353–69. Berkeley: University of California Press.

Wolff, Larry. 1994. *Inventing Eastern Europe: The Map of Civilization on the Mind of the Enlightenment*. Stanford: Stanford University Press.
World Bank. 2004. "Central American Indigenous Communities to Strengthen Ecosystem Management With US$9 Million Grant." WorldBank.org. Accessed August 2007. http://web.worldbank.org/WBSITE/EXTERNAL/NEWS/0,,contentMDK:20296 028~pagePK:6425704.
World Intellectual Property Organization. 2002. "Annex I Russian National House of Folk Arts." In *Intergovernmental Committee on Intellectual Property and Genetic Resources, Traditional Knowledge and Folklore*. Geneva: WIPO.
World Jewish Restitution Organization. n.d. "WJRO Hungary Operations." WJRO.org. Accessed October 2015. http://wjro.org.il/our-work/restitution-by-country/hungary/.
Yudice, George. 2003. *The Expediency of Culture: The Uses of Culture in the Global Era*. Durham, NC: Duke University Press.
Yurchak. Alexei. 2005. *Everything Was Forever until It Was No More*. Princeton, NJ: Princeton University Press.
Zakariás, Ildikó. *Jótékony nemzet: Szolidaritás és hatalom a kisebbségi magyarok segítésében*. Budapest: MTA TK Kisebbségkutató Intézet, Kalligramm.
Zilahi, Lajos. 1981. "*Csujogatás, nóta, banda*." *Magyar Nyelvőr* 105 (1): 162–64.
Živković, Andreja. 2013. "The Future Lasts a Long Time: A Short History of European Integration in the ex-Yugoslavia." *LeftEast*, October 25, 2013.
Živković, Andreja, and Matija Medenica. 2013. "Balkans for the Peoples of the Balkans." *LeftEast*, May 31, 2013.
Žižek, Slavoj. 1993. *Tarrying with the Negative: Kant, Hegel, and the Critique of Ideology*. Durham, NC: Duke University Press.

INDEX

1919 Soviet. *See* Republic of Councils
1956 revolution, 187–90; folk art and, 91, 92; *népi* movement and, 188–89, 205; *táncház* and, 14, 19, 181–82, 186–87

aesthetics: cultivation/education, 8, 12, 51, 52, 79n1, 94; Hungarian nation-state and, 23; *népi* movement and, 75; political personhood and, 4–5, 10; revivalist, 158, 175; *táncház* and, 4, 18, 115, 125–26, 129, 158
affect: national, 4, 6, 241, 258; socialist, 225; social movements and, 150
Agrarian Socialist Union, 53, 59n17
Alliance of Free Democrats. *See* SZDSZ
amateur art: civic/folk cultivation and, 5; voluntarism and, 85, 95; socialism and, 88, 94–98, 104; *táncház* as, 159. *See also* voluntarism
antisemitism: interwar regimes and, 55, 58–59, 64–65; *népi* movement and, 58–59, 61, 62–63, 65, 66–67, 75, 77, 256; *numerus clausus* law, 38, 39, 55, 58; postsocialist right and, 182, 184, 190, 198, 200–201, 204, 223, 225, 250–51; *táncház* and, 170–72, 183, 200–201, 203–4, 222–23, 233. *See also* Holocaust
aristocracy/nobility, 27, 29, 30, 32, 36, 38, 44, 45, 55, 58, 68, 77
Arrow Cross Party, 58, 74, 78
assimilation: in Hungary, 30, 54, 55, 203–4; "reverse," 198; in Romania, 155, 175, 189, 190, 228, 237. *See also* Magyarization
association: in nineteenth century, 8–9, 27, 53–54; interwar, 34, 54, 57, 61, 67–69, 73; in socialism, 13–15, 18, 54, 84–85, 88, 96, 97, 100, 107, 139, 197, 206; social aspects of, 149–50, 152; *táncház* as, 197, 247. *See also* civil society
Association of Népi Colleges. *See* NÉKOSZ
Attila, József, 68, 113, 114n3
Austro-Hungarian Empire. *See* Habsburg Empire

Babeş-Bolyai University, 189, 227
Bakić-Hayden, Milica, 251–52
Balassi Institute, 257
Bartók, Béla, 34, 35, 64, 105, 124, 127, 154, 156, 233
Bartók ensemble, 114, 115, 117, 118, 129, 132
Basic Law, 250. *See also* constitution
Beat movement, 98, 101–4, 107, 113, 114, 120, 123, 124, 139, 141
Benjamin, Walter, 19, 181
Berán, István, 134
Beyond the Forest, 193–94
Bihari ensemble, 111, 117, 129
Bildung, 2, 3, 8, 9, 10, 12, 15, 19–22, 52, 242, 248, 257. *See also* civic cultivation
Blues for Transylvania, 195. *See also* Muzsikás ensemble
Bodnár, Judit, 84
Borbándi, Gyula, 59, 62–63, 68, 78
borders, 23, 25, 34–35, 36, 215, 223, 225, 226f, 248f, 249, 254; "Hungarians across the," 171, 186–87, 200, 220–21
Böröcz, József, 211n45, 245n32, 252, 258
Bouquet of Pearls (Gyöngyös Bokréta), 40–46, 128–29, 154–55, 191
Budapest Spring Festival, 134, 192

camps. *See* dance camps
capitalism: art in, 123–24; civil society and, 15; culture and, 22, 216, 217, 241, 248, 258; nation-state and, 9, 12, 24, 25, 26, 184, 241–42, 249; *népi* movement and, 63, 67, 68, 77; political, 200; postsocialist, 17, 142, 153, 185, 215, 223–26, 252, 253–54; racial, ix, 258; *táncház* and, 19, 186, 215, 251; tourism and, 215
Ceauşescu, Nicolai, 130, 190, 193, 194, 195
Chatterjee, Partha, 11
Christianity: right wing and, 38, 87, 88, 252; *táncház* and, 170, 172–73

291

Christian National regime, 36; antisemitism, 58–59, 64; as feudal, 66; folk schools and, 88; *népi* and, 61, 63, 65, 66, 68, 75–76, 77, 155, 205; Transylvania and, 161, 205

citizenship: civic cultivation and, 8, 12, 51–53, 85–86; class and, 12, 44, 55, 223; culture talk and, 215; dual for Hungarians abroad, 19, 171, 214, 216, 218–20, 228, 234, 239–40, 242, 250; folk and, 2, 12; global, 207; Jews and, 64; nation-state and, 9–10, 23, 26, 27, 30, 215, 219, 225, 239, 240, 241, 257; neoliberalism and, 13, 241; *népi* movement and, 59, 65, 67, 76, 77, 205; postsocialist, 224, 226, 228, 242; social, 13, 183, 186, 224, 225, 241, 247; socialist, 1, 223, 226; *táncház* and, 3, 4, 14–15, 19, 148, 152, 171, 183, 205, 221

civic cultivation (*művelődés*), 2, 7–8, 12, 51–53; amateur art and, 5, 94–96; civil society and, 13; in Habsburg Empire, 53–54, 86; heritage and, 257; Horthy era, 54; *népi* movement and, 12, 51–52, 59, 61, 65–66, 75; socialism and, 18, 54, 85, 87–88, 90–91, 94–96, 103–7, 124, 141, 249; *táncház* and, 12, 105, 205, 251. *See also* folk national cultivation; *művelés/művelődés*

civilization: civic cultivation and, 52; "clash of," 183, 186; colonialism and, 9, 10; culture and, 9–10, 12, 52, 251, 258; "East-West slope" of, 252

civil society, 8–9; amateur art and, 94; civic cultivation and, 8, 12, 13, 94; "ethical," 14, 63–64, 184n5, 186, Fidesz and, 250; nation state and, 8–9, 241–2; power and, 8, 11–12, 15; postsocialist, 13–14, 132, 152–53, 184, 223, 224–25; socialist, 13–14, 140, 152–53, 141, 186, 190; *táncház* as, 241, 251

club movement, 93–94, 98, 101–2, 104, 106. *See also* houses of culture; individual clubs

Cluj, 128, 130, 227, 228, 234

collection: ethnographic, 32, 34, 35, 68, 70, 89, 92, 99; music and dance, 25, 29, 34, 35–36, 114, 121, 135; *regös* scouts and, 70–71; in socialism, 122, 127; *táncház* and, 128, 130, 131, 134, 191. *See also* ethnography; Museum of Ethnography; village visiting

collective memory: historical memory and, 150; "mother tongue" and, 157; production of, 148, 150–51, 153, 157–58, 174; *táncház* and, 3, 6–7, 19, 147, 148, 151, 159, 161, 170, 174

colleges (*népi*/folk/popular): 69, 72–73, 74, 77, 85, 88, 255. *See also* NÉKOSZ

Communist Party: post-1945, 74, 88, 94, 107, 140, 171, 197; *pre*-1945, 57, 64, 72, 74, 87; names, 103n30

Communist Youth League. *See* KISZ

community of sense, 19, 149n3, 181; *táncház* as, 149, 247

Convention for the Safeguarding of Intangible Cultural Heritage, 214, 230. *See also* UNESCO

courtship, *táncház* and, 130, 164, 165

Cowan, Jane, 6, 164–65, 166, 193

Creed, Gerald, 14, 200, 224

Csángós, 166n40, 197, 197n31

csárdás dance, 27, 39, 44, 127

Csergő, Zsuzsa, 227

Csíksomlyó pilgrimage, 229, 231, 235

csingerálás dance, 233

Csoóri, Sándor, 196, 198, 222

Csoóri, Sándor Jr., 127, 196

Csurka, István, 198, 200, 201

cultural centers, 87, 88, 92, 125, 204. *See also* houses of culture

cultural heritage. *See* heritage

cultural turn, 4, 182, 185, 186, 206

culture talk, 186, human rights and, 207, 258; "postsocialist" condition and, 19, 186, 197, 215, 241, 242, 247; *táncház* and, 206, 251

dance, 5–6. *See also* folk dance; *táncház*

dance camps, 1, 15, 18, 131–34, 141, 155, 162–63, 192, 235–39, 247

dancehouses. See *táncház*

dance suites/cycles, 115n5; adaptation and authenticity of, 114–15, 118, 128, 129, 150, 159, 234; ethnic/geographical origins of, 125, 126, 149, 161, 233; in *táncház* events, 120, 160–61, 170

Deák, István, 78, 188

decolonial theory/politics, 22, 251–53, 254, 258

Democratic Alliance of Hungarians in Romania. *See* RMDSZ

double consciousness, 252

dual citizenship: for Hungarians abroad, 19, 171, 203, 228, 234, 239–41, 250. *See also* citizenship

Eagleton, Terry, 4, 8–9, 10, 12, 51

Elias, Norbert, 9, 10, 12

ensembles. *See* folk ensembles

Erdei, Ferenc, 70, 70n42, 74, 188, 256

ethnography: amateur, 116, 139, 171; Bouquet of Pearls and, 42–43, 44; collection and, 32, 35, 68; of dance, 16; folk revival and, 32, 42; institutions, 32, 172; nation-state and, 18, 33–34, 71; *néprajz* term, 32–33; *táncház* and, 113, 130, 161, 171, 173, 257; Transylvania and, 161. *See also* collection; tourism; village visiting

ethnonationalism, 75, 77, 183–84, 185, 206, 214, 241, 252, 258. *See also* nation; nation-state; nationalism.

etiquette and manners: dance and, 5, 164; gender and, 164; in *táncház*, 16, 19, 149–51, 160, 168, 176

Fábry, Katalin, 95
Fanon, Frantz, 252, 254
Federation of World Hungarians (MVSZ), 203n53, 219n4
Féja, Géza, 63, 63n25
Fidesz: antisemitism and, 199; authoritarianism of, 250; class base, 253; dual citizenship and, 218, 250; ethnic Hungarian migrants and, 239–41, 242; Jobbik and, 251; populism and, 184–85, 255; rise of, 199, 201, 214, 250; *táncház* and, 183, 202–3, 214
film, 40, 42, 98, 116, 117, 118, 129, 161
First Hungarian Republic, 23, 36, 38, 54, 58
folk, the, 3–4, 7; ancient/biblical atributions of, 172–73; civic/national cultivation, 52, 249; colonialism and, 11; hegemony and, 248; Jews and, 172, 233; language and, 29; nation-state formation and, 17, 23; *nép* meanings, 3, 18, 19, 66, 255, 258; political potential of, 258; rural/urban, 45 (*see also népi-urbánus*); as spiritual, 12; Transylvania and, 174. *See also* folk revival movement; folk national cultivation; *nép*; people, the

folk art: ancient origins, 169, 173; authenticity of, 153; Christianity and, 173; community-building and, 5–6, 147; economic development and, 31–32, 40–41, 43, 45, 193, 217 (*see also* tourism); fine arts and, 5; human rights and, 193; institutions (*see* Heritage House, Institute for Culture); interwar youth movement, 18, 45–46; professionalization of, 192–93, 206; right-wing politics and, 202; socialism and, 89–92, 99, 101, 124, 131–32, 147, 184, 192; tourism and, 40–42, 43, 193, 236;

Transylvania and, 131, 169, 196. *See also* folk dance; folk music; *táncház*

"folk art movement of the youth," 44, 46, 67, 70, 73, 120

folk costume, 32, 43, 129, 130, 131, 134, 238

folk critique, 16, 22; citizenship and, 12; *népi* movement and, 206; political potentials of, 251, 258; *táncház* and, 14, 247. *See also népi* movement

folk culture: ancient origins of, 173; as agrarian, 206; authenticity and preservation, 45, 161; Christian origins of, 172; civic cultivation and, 46, 138–39, 205–6 (*see also* folk national cultivation); folkdance revival and, 44; heritization, 256; Jews and, 172, 233; literature and, 29, 62; research (*see* ethnography); socialism and, 184; Transylvania and, 126, 174. *See also* folk art, folklore

folk dance, 1–6; abstraction of, 158, 161; authenticity of, 159, 161–62, 191; bourgeois individualism and, 164; decline in village life, 129–30; etiquette in, 164; gender and, 164–68; human rights and, 207; Hungarian nation and, 229; institutions, 18, 25, 42–43, 91–92, 103–4, 117, 134–37, 139; mother tongue, 7, 149, 150, 152, 153, 155–57, 160, 176, 191; *népi* movement and, 51, 71, 73–74, 76; pedagogy of, 156–57, 191; postsocialism and, 15; postwar youth movements, 138; research, 70–71, 91–92, 117, 122, 125–26, 135; revival, 18, 25, 27–28, 39–46, 191; right-wing politics and, 202; Roma and, 204, 256; self cultivation and sensibility, 7, 176; as social dance, 150, 151, 157, 163, 191; socialism and, 88–92, 95, 97, 99–103, 115–16, 122–24, 138–39; *táncház* and, 111, 113, 115–17, 121–22, 129; 140–41; tourism, 191, 193, 236; Transylvania and, 128–30, 161, 168, 191. *See also táncház*

Folk Dance Research Group, 92, 117
folk ensembles: Bouquet of Pearls and, 42, 43; socialist, 90, 111, 113, 115–16, 130, 141; *táncház*, 117–18, 120–21, 122, 124–25, 128–29, 132, 162, 192, 232–33; tourism and, 191. *See also individual ensembles*

folk festivals: community and, 175; folk revival, 41; international heritization, 2, 257; interwar socialist period, 91, 103, 104, 115–16; *táncház* origins, 134, 141, 192; in Transylvania, 130

Index 293

folk high schools (*népfőiskolák*), 65, 87–88, 136, 255
folklore: heritage and, 214, 217; state formation and, 24; tourism and, 40. *See also* ethnography; folk culture
FolkMAGazin, 126, 134, 135
folk music, 134; authenticity of, 162; collection/research, 18, 25, 29, 34, 35–36, 68–71, 114, 121, 125–26, 130; Hungarian appropriation, 232–33; literature and, 29; as "mother tongue," 154; *népi* writers and, 64; pedagogy, 153–54; postwar youth and, 138; right-wing politics and, 203; Roma and, 127, 162, 204, 233; socialism and, 116, 121–23, 138–39; *táncház* and, 114–17, 122, 130, 140–41, 170; tourism and, 40; Transylvania and, 128–29, 130
folk national cultivation (*népi-nemzeti művelődés*), 65–66; civic cultivation and, 51; Hungarian nation and, 46, 154, 206; meanings of, 65–66, 65n29; *népi* movement and, 18, 51, 52, 61, 65–67, 75; socialist period, 90–91; *táncház* and, 76; postsocialist, 205–6; *See also* civic cultivation; *művelés/művelődés*
folk revival movement, 1–4; abstraction and, 158; citizenship and, 148, 247; ethnonationalism and, 183; hegemony and, 16–17; interwar, 18, 39–46, 51, 67, 70–76; musical recodings and, 35; nation-state and, 17; *népi* legacy, 76; political economy and, 181–82; political possibilites for, 251; socialism and, 14–15; *táncház* and, 18, 159–63, 175, 257; Transylvania and, 191
folsky aesthetic. *See népies* (folsky aesthetic)
Fonyódi, Peter, 103–4
foreigners, 38, 55, 67, 173, 187; *táncház* and, 165, 191, 235
frameworks of sense, 7, 148, 149–50, 158; *táncház* and, 3, 15, 16, 19, 149–52, 159, 174, 176, 181, 197, 221. *See also* collective memory
Frigyesi, Judith, 115, 122, 125, 127

Gagyi, Ágnes, 185, 253–54
Gemeinschaft, 3, 152–53, 176n4, 186, 207
Gesellschaft, 3, 149, 152, 176n4
Gheorghiu-Dej, Gheorghe, 189, 190
Gömbös, Gyula, 58, 64, 66, 87, 155
Greater Hungary, 35, 41, 149, 161, 168, 174, 247, 248f, 249f

Gyöngyös Bokréta. *See* Bouquet of Pearls
Györffy, István, 42, 66, 66n31, 69, 70, 73, 154, 155, 157
Györffy Kollégium, 61, 74. *See also* NÉKOSZ
Gypsies. *See* Roma
Gyurcsány, Ferenc, 214, 250

habitus, 175
Habsburg Empire, 8, 10, 12, 25–26, 28, 29–30, 31, 33–34, 36, 37f, 53, 227n18
Halbwachs, Maurice, 7, 150–51, 157, 176
Hall, Stuart, 24
Halmos, Béla, 92, 113–14, 116, 118, 121, 122, 125, 131, 132, 135, 141, 165
Hann, Chris, 13, 14, 38n36, 224,
Harvey, David, 216–17
Hayden, Robert, 225
Helyzet Working Group, 253
Herder, Johann Gottfried, 28–29, 32
heritage: civic cultivation and, 136, 241–42, 257; collective property and, 228, 234, 241; cultural change and, 138; dance as, 5; ethnonationalism and, 182, 214, 217, 230, 232, 234, 241, 242, 247–48, 257–58; Heritage House and, 136, 142, 232; heritagization, 19, 186, 215–16, 217–18, 223, 229, 230, 232, 241–42, 251, 255, 258; human rights and, 193; of Hungarians in Romania, 229–30, 234, 236; intangible, 193, 217, 229, 230–31, 234, 241, 258; Ministry of Cultural Heritage, 131, 135; neoliberalism and, 214, 241, 258; safeguarding of, 1, 2, 193, 228, 232, 241, 257; social, 224; supranational regime, 15, 19, 191, 217–18, 241, 248, 257–58; *táncház* and, 19, 186, 214, 215–16, 228, 229, 232, 234, 238, 241, 247, 256; tourism and, 19, 191, 193, 217–18, 228–29, 234, 236, 238; UNESCO and, 193, 217–18, 229, 230, 257, 258
Heritage House (Hagyományok Háza): author's research and, 16, 135; collection, 135–36; foundation and purpose of, 131, 135–36, 137, 142, 155; *táncház* and, 135, 142, 232
Hofer, Tamás, 25, 27, 32, 166n39
Hirschkind, Charles, 7, 175–76
Holocaust, the, 18, 58–59, 64–65, 75, 172, 203–4, 204n57
Hooker, Lynn, 162, 164n35, 235
Horthy, Miklos, 36, 60f, 72; regime, 54, 57–59, 63, 65, 66, 73, 77, 86. *See also* Christian National regime

houses of culture, 84–87; entrepreneurialism, 97, 101, 106; socialist cultivation and, 18, 84–85, 92–94, 95–96, 102, 252; origins of, 85–87, 90; *táncház* and, 85, 118, 142, 166; youth appropriation of, 106; *See also* club movement
Houses of the People (Western Europe), 85, 86, 152
Hungarian Academy of Sciences, 16, 32, 92, 117
Hungarian Autonomous Region (Romania), 130, 189, 227. *See also* Transylvania
Hungarian Declaration of Solidarity with the Rumanian People, 196
Hungarian Heritage: From Roots to Revival, 257
Hungarian Institute for Culture. *See* Institute for Culture
Hungarian Life and Justice Party. *See* MIÉP
Hungarian National Defense League. *See* MOVE
Hungarian Socialist Party. *See* MSZP
Hungarian Soviet Republic. *See* Republic of Councils
Hungarian State Folk Ensemble, 18, 89, 128
Hungarian Worker's Party. *See* Communist Party
Huntington, Samuel, 183, 186
Hylland Eriksen, Thomas, 217

illiberalism, 19–22, 214–15, 254
Illyés, Gyula, 62, 62n20, 68–69, 69n34, 89
Institute for Culture: club movement and, 102; vs. Heritage House, 135–37; names of, 85n4; *népi* movement and, 78; socialist cultural management and, 85, 89–92, 104–6, 113; *táncház* and, 18, 105, 113, 117, 120, 131, 139. *See also* Heritage House; houses of culture, Hungarian State Folk Ensemble
Institute for People's Culture. *See* Institute for Culture
Institute of Folk Art (Népművészeti Intézet), 89, 92
Institute of Népi Cultivation. *See* Institute for Culture
Istrian Musicological Microcosm, 230–31

Jagamas, János, 130
Jászberény folk ensemble, 132
Jews: class and, 38, 55, 62–63; genocide of (*see* Holocaust); in Habsburg Empire, 30, 55; in interwar, 54, 55, 69;

népi-urbánus dichotomy and, 59, 62, 197–98; postsocialist revival, 203–4; in socialism, 78, 188; *táncház* and, 128, 170–71, 202, 233. *See also* antisemitism.
Jobbik Party, 204, 214, 247, 250–51, 256
Juhász, Katalin, 113, 125
juhmérés, 235

Kádár, János, 100, 187, 189, 190, 191
Kallos, Zoltán, 130–31, 234
Karácsony, Sándor, 70
Kassák Klub, 118, 123, 132. *See also* club movement
Kelemen, László, 135
KIE (Catholic Youth Association), 61, 69
Ki Mit Tud? (*Who Can Do What?*), 98, 99f, 105, 114, 139
Kiss, Támas, 228, 229n23, 234, 240, 241, 242, 242n1
KISZ (Communist Youth League), 93, 102–3, 104
Klebelsberg, Kuno, 86–87
Kodály, Zoltán; collection and research, 34, 35, 68, 92, 124, 127, 128, 135; method, 116, 121, 153–54, 156; *népi* movement and, 64; works, 40–41
Kohn, Margaret, 85, 152
kollégium. *See* colleges
Kolozsvár, *see* Cluj
Kovács, Imre, 71, 72
Kovalcsik, József, 53, 54, 57, 61, 86, 87, 94
közművelődés: vs. *népművelés*, 105–6; in socialist cultural management, 105–7, 124, 142. *See also* civic cultivation; folk national cultivation; *művelés/művelődés*
Krastev, Ivan, 184–85
Kultur, 10, 12, 15, 52, 251, 258. *See also* *Bildung*; *művelés/művelődés*
Kürti, Lászlo, 67, 186n8

lads, 130, 230, 231
Lajtha, László, 35, 128, 137
land of three million beggars, 57, 66, 67, 75, 77
lasses, 130
László Lajtha Folklore Documentation Center, 137
Lenin, V.I., 94, 95
Levente, 67, 73–74
Living Human Treasures, 193. *See also* UNESCO
Livingston, Tamara, 158, 159–60, 175
Lukács, György, 94, 94n25, 105

Index 295

Maácz, László, 115
Magyarization, 30, 54
Magyar nóta, 127, 159
Makovecz, Imre, 201
Mamdani, Mahmood, 185–86
manners. *See* etiquette
March Front, 61, 63, 68, 71–72, 140. *See also népi* movement
Master of Folk Art, 99, 192, 193; Young Master of Folk Art, 192
Masterpiece of Oral and Intangible Heritage of Humanity (UNESCO), 230–32
MDF (Hungarian Democratic Forum), 198–99
Melegh, Attila, 234, 252
Melucci, Alberto, 2–3, 7, 148–49, 150
Méra, 230
middle class, 38, 43, 45, 69, 157, 202n48, 253
MIÉP (Hungarian Life and Justice Party), 198–99, 200–201, 202, 250
migrants: after Habsburg Empire, 34, 38, 54; Muslim, 252; "refugee crisis," 249–50; right wing and, 182, 240–41, 249–51, 252, 254; from Romania, 196–97, 219–20; solidarity with, 256; workers, 219–20
Míklos Bartha Association, 68
Ministry of Cultural Heritage, 131, 135
MMI (Magyar Művelődési Intézet). *See* Institute for Culture
Molnár, István, 117, 117n8
mother tongue: folk dance as, 7, 149, 150, 152, 153, 157, 176; folk music as, 153–54; frameworks of sense and, 157–58, 176; Heritage House and, 135; Hungarian culture as, 155; linguistic nationalism and, 28, 55, 152, 155; *táncház* and, 155–56, 163, 166, 174; Transylvania and, 174, 176
MOVE (Hungarian National Defense League), 69, 87
MSzMP (Hungarian Socialist Worker's Party). *See* Communist Party
MSZP (Hungarian Socialist Party), 200–201, 203, 214, 218, 219, 223, 250
Muharay, Elemér, 73–74, 105, 134, 155; ensemble, 73, 120, 121, 128
Muscovites, 187–88
Museum of Ethnography, 35, 71
művelés/művelődés (cultivation/culture); 7–8, 51, 52–53, 65–66, 65n29, 140; folk art and, 136. *See also Bildung*; civic cultivation; folk national cultivation; *közművelődés*
Muzsikás ensemble, 118, 195, 196, 201

Nagy, Imre, 14, 91, 187–88, 189, 199
Nagykálló, 132–33
narod (folk/people), compared to *nép*, 66, 184n6
narodnyik movement, 63n24; 105n38
nation, the: citizenship and, 23, 24, 26–27, 52, 55; civic cultivation and, 75, 86; culture and, 9–10, 31–32, 65–66; decolonial, 258; ethnic vs. political, 8–9, 26, 65–66; ethnonationalism and, 225, 248–49; folk cultivation and, 154–55; folk dance and, 5, 39, 44, 160; Hungarians abroad and, 219, 220–21; language and, 28–30, 33, 54; *nemzethalál* (death of the nation), 29, 55; *natio* and, 25, 28, 66; nationality (*nemzetiség*) and, 28, 33; *nemzet* and, 65–66, 67, 205; *nép* and, 3, 66–67, 186; postsocialist, 13, 152–53, 184, 186; right wing and, 58, 66, 199; Roma and, 127; Romanian, 184, 190; scales of, 218, 240–42; socialism and, 152–53, 184; state and, 23, 24, 26 (*see also* nation-state); as spiritual, 11–12; *táncház* and, 4, 12, 186, 196, 220–21, 234, 247–48; tradition and, 24, 45. *See also* ethnonationalism; folk, the; nation-state; nationalism; *nép*
national awakening/national romanticism, 8, 18, 25
National Cottage Industry Association, 32
nationalism: anticolonial, 11; Christian, 58, 88; citizenship and, 9; constitutional, 225; ethnic Hungarian migrants and, 239; ethno-nationalism, 75, 77, 183–84, 185, 206, 214, 241, 252, 258; Habsburg Empire and, 26; heritagization and, 230, 258; left-wing patriotism and, 251; linguistic, 18, 33, 54, 152, 155; opposition to, 254, 256; popular culture and, 23; Romanian, 189; *táncház* and, 1, 5, 105, 124, 152, 155. *See also* nation; nation-state
nationality (*nemzetiség/Volksstamm*), in Habsburg Empire, 26n5, 28, 33, 34. *See also* nation
National Regional and Folk Research Center, 69, 69n37, 71
National Theater, 27, 135
nation-state, the: association and, 8; citizenship and, 9; colonialism and, 10–11;

emergence of, 9-12, 24, 26; ethnography and, 33, 34; ethnonationalism and, 55, 249; folk and, 3-4, 17, 31-32; heritage regime and, 230-31; Hungarians abroad and, 242; language and, 30, 33, 54; making in Hungary, 2, 8, 10-12, 18, 23, 24-36, 215; *népi* movement and, 76; postsocialist, 2, 248, 258; right wing and, 66, 200; Romanian, 129; *táncház* and, 247-48, 251; tradition and, 45; Transylvania and, 169. *See also* citizenship; nation
NÉKOSZ, Association of Népi Colleges, 72-75, 78, 88, 105, 128. *See also* colleges
nemzet (nation): meanings of, 65-66, 67
nemzethalál (death of the nation), 29, 55
neoliberalism: citizenship and, 13; civil society and, 225; culture and, 19, 185, 215-16, 228; ethnonationalism and, 183, 241, 250, 258; opposition to, 250, 256; "postsocialist" condition and, 186, 206, 224; *táncház* and, 2, 15, 191-92, 241, 247. *See also* "postsocialist" condition
neopopulist writers, 196, 196n30, 198
nép (folk/people), 3; folk arts and, 45, 152; meanings of, 3, 18, 19, 65n29, 66, 66n32, 184n6, 255, 258; nation and, 12, 161, 186, 205, 206; 255; postsocialism and, 241. *See also*, folk, the; people, the
népies (folksy aesthetic), 29, 62, 77, 118, 202; *népnemzeti* and, 29
népi movement (*népi mozgalom*): antisemitism in, 58-59, 61, 63-65, 68; civic/folk cultivation and, 51-52, 59, 61, 65-67, 76, 90, 91, 107, 140, 154, 157, 205; folk arts and, 44, 46, 70-71, 73, 89-90, 105, 116, 155; literature and, 29, 59, 60-65; political demands of, 59, 61-65, 67-68, 71-72, 75-78; political potentials of, 22, 255-58; "postsocialist" condition and, 182; rural research and, 68-70, 73, 89-90; socialism and, 74, 76-78, 140, 182, 188-89, 191, 205, 206; as spiritual, 18, 59, 63-64, 72, 76; *táncház* and, 105, 107, 113, 116, 152, 161, 186, 206, 247
népi-nemzeti művelődés. *See* folk national cultivation
népi-urbánus (populist-urbanist) opposition, 52, 59, 62-63, 67, 76-78, 124, 188, 197-98, 205, 256
Népszabadság (periodical), 255
New Economic Mechanism, 96, 101, 190
New Living Folk Music, 134

New Spiritual Front, 64, 155. *See also* Gömbös, Gyula
Nikočević, Lidija, 231, 232
nobility. *See* aristocracy/nobility
Novák, Ferenc, 111, 117, 129
numerus clausus law, 38, 39, 55, 58

OKK (National Center for Public Cultivation). *See* Institute for Culture
Orbán, Viktor: antimigrant policies of, 240, 249; dual citizenship and, 240-41; nationalism and, 199, 257; as populist, 185, 254, 255; *táncház* and, 203, 214, 239. *See also* Fidesz
ORI (National Events Office), 103-4
Orientalism, 11, 251-52
Ortutay, Gyula, 35, 36n30
OSZK (National Entertainment Center), 103-4
Ottoman Empire, 10, 31

Pap, Gábor, 172-73
Pátria record company, 35, 128, 135
Paulini, Béla, 40-41, 42, 43, 44, 45
Pávai, István, 116, 128n27
Peasant Party, 71, 72, 74, 78, 188
peasants: as class, 44, 77, 206; folk and, 34, 45; folk revival and, 31-32, 36, 39, 43, 44, 70; movements, 57, 59; national identity and, 25; *népi* movement and, 62, 77-78; romanticism of, 27, 73; social conditions, 57; *táncház* and, 130, 150, 153, 154, 159
people, the: civic/folk cultivation and, 9, 24, 46, 51-52, 53, 86, 88-89, 90-91, 107; class and, 205; folk revival and, 45, 106; hegemony and, 248; heritization and, 255; nation state and, 10-11, 12, 23, 25-26, 29, 33-34, 67, 75, 186, 249, 258; *nép* meanings and, 3, 65n29, 66, 66n32, 184n6; populism and, 185; postsocialism and, 241; Roma and, 233n26; social movements and, 256; *tánchaz* and, 4, 196. *See also*, folk, the; *nép*
periphery, the: folk/popular culture and, 24, 40; nationalism in, 11-12; Orientalism and, 11-12; postsocialism and, 215, 227, 252-53, 258
Petőfi, Sándor, 29, 71, 188
Petőfi Circle, 188
Pioneers (Úttörök), 132
politizálás (politicization), 170, 173, 202
popular culture, 23-24, 123

Index 297

populism: antisemitism and, 62, 75, 77, 223, 255n6; civic/folk national cultivation and, 12; class and, 59, 61, 62, 66, 75, 78, 223, 253–54; definitions of, 185, 185n7, 254–55; democracy and, 253–54; ethnonational, 184, 198, 223, 241; folk revival and, 45; heritization and, 241; interwar, 18, 52, 59, 61–68, 75–77; liberal antipopulism, 185, 253–54, 256; neoliberalism and, 182–83, 214–15, 241; *népi* and, 66; *népi-urbánus* and, 18, 52, 61, 62, 75–78, 256; Orbán regime and, 3, 184–85, 186n8, 254, 255; political potentials of, 255–57; right/left and, 184n6; socialism and, 75, 90–91, 124, 188; *táncház* and, 1–2, 15, 19, 22, 105, 141, 186, 186n8, 196n30, 205. See also *népi* movement

populist (népi) writers, 61–65, 67, 72, 78, 189, 196n30, 198. See also *népi-urbánus* opposition; neopopulist writers

postsocialism: citizenship and, 183, 198, 214, 223–24, 228; civil society and, 8, 13–14, 132, 152–53; culture and, 3–4, 19; ethnonationalism and, 184–85, 198, 241, 242, 258; heritagization and, 242; liberalism and, 184–85, 256; Orientalism and, 251; politics in, 214; vs. "postsocialist" condition, 17; property and, 226, 228; "stolen regime change," 200; *táncház* and, 2, 3, 242, 247–48. See also regime change

"postsocialist" condition, 17; civil society and, 13; culture and, 3–4, 19, 182, 185–86, 206, 241; ethnonationalism and, 185–86; vs. postsocialism, 17; *táncház* and, 2, 186, 191–92, 247–48. See also neoliberalism

privatization, 183, 185, 200, 201, 226. See also property

property: art and, 5; civil society and, 15; communal, 227–29, 234; culture/heritage and, 5, 19, 97, 215, 217–18, 223, 228–29, 230, 232, 235, 241, 257; postsocialist, 17, 206, 218, 224, 225–29; restitution, 225–27; socialism and, 197; state and, 19. See also privatization

Protection Association, 27

Pulay, Gergő, 203–4, 239–40

pure source (*tiszta forrás*), 111, 126, 233–34

Rábai, Miklos, 128

race, 6, 10, 33, 58, 68, 182, 258. See also antisemitism; ethnonationalism

referendums: on dual citizenship, 19, 171, 183, 203, 218–21, 223, 229, 234, 241; on refugees, 249–50, 252

regime change, 19, 197, 253–54; "stolen," 198–200, 201, 223, 250

regös cserkészet (caroling scouts). See scouts: caroling (*regös cserkészet*)

Republic of Councils, 36, 54, 58, 198

Repülj Páva (Fly peacock), 98, 105, 114, 139

RMDSZ (Democratic Alliance of Hungarians in Romania), 229, 231, 229n23, 236

Roma: dance, 125, 203–4, 256; Hungarian nation and, 126–27, 204, 225, 232–34, 250–51, 255–56; musicians, 127, 133, 162, 232–34; right-wing and, 182, 214, 250–51, 255

Romania: ethnic Hungarians in, 14, 18, 19, 189–90, 194–96, 205–6, 227–31, 232, 241–42; migrants from, 215, 239–40; nationalism, 184; restitution in, 223–27; *táncház* and, 1, 19, 125, 126, 127–28, 129, 130–31, 193–94, 197, 215, 222, 234–41. See also Transylvania

Ronström, Owe, 138

Roseberry, William, 45, 242

Sági, Mária, 120–21, 122–23

Saint Stephen, 30–31, 41

Scott, David, 11

scouts: Bouquet of Pearls and, 44; Boy Scouts, 69; caroling (*regös cserkészet*), 68, 69–71, 73, 155, 191; cultivation and, 69; *népi* movement and, 46, 61, 155; Sarló, 68; Wandervogel, 68–9

Sebő, Ferenc, 113–14, 118, 119, 121, 122, 124, 125, 131–32, 135, 155

Sebő Club, 118, 120, 123

Shoah. See Holocaust

Siegelbaum, Lewis H., 140

Silverman, Carol, 231–32

Simmel, Georg, 149–50

Smallholders Party, 74

Smith, Neil, 215

socialist cultural management: amateur art and, 88, 95–101, 104; club movement and, 101–6; houses of culture and, 84–85, 92–95; Institute for Culture and, 88–92, 136–37, 139–40; *művelődés* terms and, 105–7, 124, 140, 141, 142; professionalization of folk art, 192; *táncház* and, 4, 5–6, 18–19, 85, 107, 120, 121–22,

124–25, 131–32, 141–42, 192; "three Ts," 100, 190; *See also* club movement; Houses of Culture; Institute for Culture
social movements, 6–7, 15, 148–49, 158, 175, 256
sociographers, *see* populist (*népi*) writers
Soós, Pal, 95
Soros, George, 198, 250; foundation, 132
Soviet Union. *See* USSR
spirituality: *Kultur* and, 10; *népi* movement and, 18, 59, 63–64, 72, 76; state and, 8–9, 11–12, 52; *táncház* and, 12, 14, 99, 172, 173, 206, 221
Spiró, György, 197–98
Stalin, Joseph, 90, 95; -ism, 75, 100, 187
state, the: Christian National, 38–39, 44; culture/*Bildung* and, 8–10; formation, 2, 8, 23, 24; Habsburg, 25; postsocialist, 219; in "postsocialist" condition, 206, 216; socialist, 13–14, 140–41, 153, 223. *See also* nation-state
Status Law, 218
Stolke, Verena, 182–83
Striker, Sándor, 93, 95–98, 100–101, 104, 106, 111, 113, 116, 192
Szabad Szó (periodical), 188
Szabó, Dezső, 68
Szabó, Zoltán, 40, 69, 113, 125
SZDSZ (Alliance of Free Democrats), 200–201, 203, 218, 219, 220, 223, 250
Szék (Sic), 111, 117, 118, 121, 126, 127, 128–29, 130, 164, 193, 239
Szeklerland, 227–28, 229, 230. *See also* Romania
Széll, Jenő, 91, 92
Szombati, Kristóf, 224, 226n15, 250, 251, 251n5, 251n5, 256,

Tamás, Gáspár Miklós, 220, 255
táncház, 1–4, 6, 18–22, 247–48; aesthetics, 4, 18, 115, 125–26, 129, 158; as apolitical, 12, 148, 170, 173, 206, 221–22; camps, 1, 133–34, 235–38; civic/national cultivation and, 7–8, 76, 136, 139–40, 251; community and, 5–6, 147, 149–53, 156–57, 168, 174–76; culture talk and, 206, 214–15; gender and, 164–68; as "heritage," 228–29, 232, 234, 242, 257; Hungarian nation and, 1, 12, 125, 128, 152–53, 155–57, 161, 168–69, 171–74, 183, 186, 193–207, 214–15, 218–20, 223, 229, 233, 240–42; Jews and, 170–72, 200–204, 222–23, 225, 233; participants, 165, 202–3; populism/*népi* and, 76, 113,

186, 205–6; "postsocialist" condition and, 206, 241–42, 247; as revival, 159–63, 175, 257; right-wing politics and, 170–74, 183, 200–205, 214, 225; Roma and, 127–28, 162, 225, 233, 256; scholarship on, 125–26; socialism and, 5–6, 13–15, 85, 97, 100–107, 111–12, 115–25, 131–32, 138–42, 186, 191–97, 205–6; as social movement, 6–7, 148–49, 158, 196; as spiritual, 12, 14, 99, 172, 173, 206, 221; Transylvania and, 126, 128–31, 161, 168–69, 193–97, 207, 220–21, 223, 229, 233–40
Táncház Chamber, 131, 134, 192
Táncház Foundation, 126, 134
táncház leader course, 118, 120, 124–25, 132
Táncház Meeting, 131, 134
Tánczos, Vilmos, 230
Téka: camp, 132–34; ensemble, 132, 133f, 142
Teleki, Pál, 69, 69n37, 71, 154–55
Timár, Sándor, 117, 125, 129, 132, 155–57
Todorova, Maria, 251, 252
Tőkés, László, 239, 239n46
Tóth, Csaba Tibor, 62n21, 255n6
Tóth, János, 88
tourism: capitalism and, 215, 217–18; heritage and, 228–29; as *honismeret* (knowledge of the homeland), 40; interwar folk revival and, 40–42, 43, 45; objectification and, 158; socialism and, 126, 141, 206; *táncház* and, 18–19, 115, 125, 126, 130, 133, 159, 168–69, 176, 191–92, 193, 215–16, 233–38; Transylvania impacts, 234–38; UNESCO and, 193, 218. *See also* dance camps; ethnography; village visiting
tradition: Bouquet of Pearls and, 44, 45–46, 128–29; civic cultivation and, 136, 142, 157; creativity and change, 138; invention of, 23, 24–25, 27, 31, 39, 45, 55, 151n8; -keeping (*hagyományőrző*), 117, 192; nationalization of, 161, 242; revival and, 158, 159; right wing and, 62, 202; selective, 116, 159; *táncház* and, 115, 127, 129, 150, 151, 159, 161–62, 238; Transylvania and, 126, 139, 238
Transylvania, 2; 1988 protests, 194–97, 205; assimiliation, 189–90; as authentic source, 36, 126, 139, 161, 162, 174–75, 233–34; dual citizenship referendum, 221; Hungarian nation and, 168–69, 228, 239, 24–42; migrants, 219–20; property restitution, 227; *táncház* and (see under *táncház*); tourism to, 133, 169, 234–38. *See also* Romania
Trianon, Treaty of, 34, 35, 36

Index 299

Új Pátria/ Utolsó Óra (recordings), 135–36
Újváry, Ferenc, 43
UNESCO, 1, 2, 193, 214, 215, 217–18, 229–32, 257–58
urbánus (urbanist). See *népi-urbánus* (populist-urbanist) opposition
USSR, 44, 65, 90, 91, 92, 140, 187, 191

Varga, Sándor, 234–35
verbunkos (dance), 39
Verdery, Katherine, 13, 26, 184
Veres, Péter, 70, 74, 189
village destruction, 14, 194, 195
village researchers. See populist writers
village visiting, 76, 111, 116, 129, 139, 140, 169, 191, 193. See also collection; ethnography; tourism
Vincze, Kata Zsófia, 204
Visa, 234–35
Vitányi, Iván, 5–6, 44–45, 66–67, 70–71, 73–74, 76, 88, 95, 98, 105, 120, 121, 123–24, 140, 147, 153, 164
Volk. See folk

Volkman, Toby, 158–59
Volksgeist, 28, 33, 34
Volksstamm. See nationality (*nemzetiség/ Volksstamm*)
voluntarism, 85, 91, 94–97, 100, 105–6. See also amateur art

weddings, 97, 130, 131, 158
White, Anne, 92–93, 94–95, 105–6
world system, 9, 12, 15, 22, 229, 247, 248, 252, 255. See also capitalism; periphery

Young Folk Artists' Studio, 99, 131, 132, 192, 196
youth movements, 44–46, 67, 70, 71–72, 72–73, 103, 120, 139, 148, 165. See also Beat movement; club movement; KIE (Catholic Youth Association); KISZ (Communist Youth League); scouts
Yudice, George, 216
Yurchak, Alexei, 140

Zhdanov, Andrej, 184
Žižek, Slavoj, 3–4, 152–53, 184

MARY N. TAYLOR is Assistant Director at the Center for Place, Culture and Politics at the Graduate Center, City University of New York. She is editor (with Abby Cunnane, Charlotte Huddleston, and Sakiko Sugawa) of *Co-Revolutionary Praxis: Accompaniment as a Strategy for Working Together.*

www.ingramcontent.com/pod-product-compliance
Lightning Source LLC
Chambersburg PA
CBHW021346300426
44114CB00012B/1099